RESEARCH IN ECONOMIC HISTORY

Supplement 5 • 1989 (Part B)

AGRARIAN ORGANIZATION IN
THE CENTURY OF INDUSTRIALIZATION:
EUROPE, RUSSIA, AND NORTH AMERICA

RESEARCH IN ECONOMIC HISTORY

A Research Annual

AGRARIAN ORGANIZATION IN THE CENTURY OF INDUSTRIALIZATION: EUROPE, RUSSIA, AND NORTH AMERICA

Editors: GEORGE GRANTHAM
Department of Economics
McGill University

CAROL S. LEONARD
Department of History
State University of New York
   College at Plattsburgh

Russian Research Cent
Harvard University

SUPPLEMENT 5 • 1989   (Part B)

JAI PRESS INC.

Greenwich, Connecticut   London, England

Copyright © 1989 JAI Press Inc.
55 Old Post Road, No. 2
Greenwich, Connecticut 06836

JAI Press Ltd.
3 Henrietta Street
London WC2E 8LU
England

All rights reserved. No part of this publication may be reproduced, stored on a retrieval system, or transmitted in any form or by any means, electronic, mechanical, photocopying, filming, recording or otherwise without prior permission in writing from the publisher.

ISBN: 0-89232-855-X

Manufactured in the United States of America

CONTENTS

PART B

List of Contributors — xi

Acknowledgments — xiii

PART III. FAMILY FARMING AND THE MARKET IN NORTH AMERICA

INTRODUCTION — 253

FAMILIES, FARMS AND RURAL SOCIETY IN PREINDUSTRIAL AMERICA
  David F. Weiman — 255

LAND AND THE DEVELOPMENT OF MID-NINETEENTH CENTURY AMERICAN AGRICULTURE IN THE NORTHERN STATES
  Jeremy Atack and Fred Bateman — 279

THE SIZE AND STRUCTURE OF FARMING, CANADA WEST, 1861
  Marvin McInnis — 313

FARM SIZE OF TENANT AND OWNER-OCCUPIED FARMS IN YORK COUNTY, ONTARIO, 1871: A CASE STUDY
  William L. Marr — 331

PART IV. ORGANIZATION AND AGRICULTURAL DEVELOPMENT IN RUSSIA

INTRODUCTION   349

THE DISTRIBUTION OF LAND
AND AGRICULTURAL OUTPUT IN
NON-BLACKEARTH RUSSIA ON THE EVE
OF EMANCIPATION (MALOGA UEZD)
   Carol S. Leonard   353

AGRICULTURAL STRUCTURE AND
THE ORIGINS OF MIGRATION IN
CENTRAL RUSSIA, 1810-1850
   Rodney Bohac   369

BRIDEWEALTH, DOWRY, AND
SOCIOECONOMIC DIFFERENTIATION
IN RURAL RUSSIA
   Steven L. Hoch   389

THE RUSSIAN PEASANT MOVEMENT IN
THE EIGHTEENTH AND NINETEENTH CENTURY
   Viktor Ivanovich Buganov   411

WERE RUSSIAN SERFS OVERCHARGED FOR
THEIR LAND BY THE 1861 EMANICIPATION?
THE HISTORY OF ONE HISTORICAL TABLE
   Evsey D. Domar   429

THE GENERAL AND THE SPECIFIC IN
SIBERIAN AGRARIAN DEVELOPMENT
IN THE SECOND HALF OF THE
NINETEENTH AND BEGINNING OF
THE TWENTIETH CENTURY
   Leonid Mikhailovich Goriushkin   441

THE PEASANT ECONOMY IN
CENTRAL RUSSIA IN THE LATE
NINETEENTH AND EARLY
TWENTIETH CENTURY
   I.D. Koval'chenko   455

THE POLARIZATION OF PEASANT
HOUSEHOLDS IN PREREVOLUTIONARY
RUSSIA: ZEMSTVO CENSUSES AND
PROBLEMS OF MEASUREMENT
  Daniel Field 477

POSTSCRIPT
  Carol S. Leonard 507

INDEX 515

CONTENTS

PART A

List of Contributors   xi

Acknowledgments   xiii

AGRARIAN ORGANIZATION IN THE
CENTURY OF INDUSTRIALIZATION:
EUROPE, RUSSIA, AND NORTH AMERICA
   George Grantham   1

PART I.   ENCLOSURE AND AGRICULTURAL PRODUCTIVITY IN EIGHTEENTH- AND NINETEENTH-CENTURY ENGLAND

INTRODUCTION: ENCLOSURE, PRODUCTIVITY, AND
CAPITALIST AGRICULTURE IN ENGLAND   27

AGRICULTURAL PRODUCTIVITY AND
AGRICULTURAL SOCIETY IN
EIGHTEENTH-CENTURY ENGLAND
   Gordon Mingay   31

BENEFITS BUT AT COST: THE DEBATES
ABOUT PARLIAMENTARY ENCLOSURE
   Michael Turner   49

ENCLOSURE, FARMING METHODS, AND
THE GROWTH OF PRODUCTIVITY
IN THE SOUTH MIDLANDS
   Robert C. Allen   69

PARLIAMENTARY ENCLOSURE AND
THE DISAPPEARANCE OF THE
ENGLISH PEASANTRY, REVISITED
   J.M. Neeson   89

PART II. EUROPEAN AGRICULTURE DURING INDUSTRIALIZATION: CRISIS AND ADJUSTMENTS

INTRODUCTION	123
AGRARIAN CHANGE AND LANDLORD-TENANT RELATIONS IN THE FRENCH NIVERNAIS *John W. Shaffer*	125
CAPITAL AND AGRARIAN STRUCTURE IN EARLY NINETEENTH-CENTURY FRANCE *George Grantham*	137
DEBT AND AGRICULTURAL PERFORMANCE IN THE LANGUEDOCIAN VINEYARD, 1870-1914 *Gilles Postel-Vinay*	161
RURAL SOCIETY AND AGRICULTURAL CHANGE IN NINETEENTH-CENTURY BRITAIN *F.M.L. Thompson*	187
THE "MACHINERY QUESTION" IN ENGLISH AGRICULTURE IN THE NINETEENTH CENTURY *E.J.T. Collins*	203
THE SOCIAL DISTRIBUTION OF LANDED WEALTH IN HUNGARY CA. 1910 *Scott M. Eddie*	219

LIST OF CONTRIBUTORS

Robert C. Allen	Department of Economics University of British Columbia
Jeremy Atack	Department of Economics University of Illinois
Fred Bateman	School of Business Indiana University
Rodney Bohac	Department of History Brigham Young University
Viktor Ivanovich Buganov	Institute of History of the USSR
E.J.T. Collins	Institute of Agricultural History and Museum of English Rural Life The University of Reading
Evsey D. Domar	Department of Economics Massachusetts Institute of Technology
Scott M. Eddie	Department of Economics University of Toronto
Daniel Field	Department of History Syracuse University
	Russian Research Center Harvard University
Leonid Mikhailovich Goriushkin	Institute of History, Philosophy and Philology Novosibirsk, Siberia
George Grantham	Department of Economics McGill University
Steven L. Hoch	Department of History Iowa University

LIST OF CONTRIBUTORS

I.D. Koval'chenko — Department of Source Study of the History of the USSR, Moscow University

Carol S. Leonard — Department of History, State University of New York College at Plattsburgh

Russian Research Center, Harvard University

Marvin McInnis — Department of Economics, Queen's University

William L. Marr — Department of Economics, Wilfrid Laurier University

Gordon E. Mingay — Rutherford College, The University, Canterbury

J.M. Neeson — Department of History, York University

Gilles Postel-Vinay — Institut National de la Recherche Agronomique, Paris

John W. Shaffer — 3435 Middleton Avenue, Castro Valley, California

F.M.L. Thompson — Institute of Historical Research, University of London

Michael Turner — Department of Economic and Social Hsitory, The University of Hull

David F. Weiman — Department of Economics, Yale University

ACKNOWLEDGMENTS

The editors wish to thank those who made possible the May 1983 Montreal Conference on Nineteenth-Century Agrarian Structures, which was held under the joint auspices of the Inter-University Centre for European Studies, the State University of New York Central Administration, Office of International Programs, and the ACLS-USSR Academy of Sciences Commission on Quantitative Research in History, an International Research and Exchanges Board Program. We are especially grateful to the co-organizers of the conference, Michel Grenen, Director of the Inter-University Centre for European Studies, and to Ivan Dmitrievich Koval'chenko, Academician and Chair of the Department of Source Study of the History of the USSR at Moscow University. Laura Petrochko, former program director, and Thomas Scott, Associate Vice-Chancellor for International Programs at SUNY, provided invaluable assistance. A strategic grant from the Social Sciences and Humanities Research Council of Canada and funds provided by Vice-Rector Claude Corbeau of the Université du Quebec à Montreal and Vice-Principal Gordon MacLachlan of McGill University were critical in the organization of this conference. We also express appreciation to the Rockefeller Foundation for a conference grant and to the Exxon Foundation, which assisted in the publication of these papers. For their generous support throughout this project, we express appreciation to administrative officials at the College of Plattsburgh of the State University of New York, Jerome Supple, former Vice-President, H.Z. Liu, Dean of Faculty of Arts and Sciences, Richard Beach, Director of the Center for the Study of Canada, and Griff Walling, Director of Conferences. We thank Odile Civetello and Lislene Dind at ICES for local arrangements.

Finally, since the Montreal Conference was the beginning of a Soviet-American exchange in agrarian history, a selection of U.S. papers will also be published in Russian in the Soviet Union by the Academy of Sciences of the USSR as a part of the IREX agreement on joint publication of papers presented at Commission conferences. For their work on the Soviet publication, we would like to thank Ivan Dmitrievich Koval'chenko and Valerii Tishkov.

We express appreciation for the permission granted by VAAP (Moscow) to translate (under the auspices of Carol S. Leonard) and reprint those chapters by V.I. Buganov, L.M. Goriushkin, and I.D. Koval'chenko.

PART III

FAMILY FARMING AND THE MARKET IN NORTH AMERICA

INTRODUCTION

The outstanding difference between farming in North America and Europe was the availability in the United States and Canada of land and credit on terms that were accessible to a broad stratum of the farming population. The papers on Canada and the United States present a series of studies of how an agrarian organization composed of medium-sized family farms was imprinted on the carte blanche of the southern and midwestern wilderness. In the history of the family farm in America, one of the central questions is whether the Jefferson's resurrection of the classical ideal of an independent farming citizenry reflected deep-seated values of American farmers that they were ready to defend at the cost of some foregone income, or whether the persistence of "yeoman" farmers was a result of economic isolation. Weiman's analysis of the social structure in two Georgia counties before the Civil War suggests that market isolation played a role in maintaining communitarian mechanisms for coping with activities that exceeded the resources of isolated farm families.

The papers by Atack and Bateman and McGinnis clearly reveal the effect of the policies of land disposition on the size distribution of midwestern farms. The two papers reveal what is probably a fundamental similarity in size distributions of holdings that reflects common technological and market opportunities exploited by people who belonged to a common stock of Anglo-Saxon settler. Marr's study of sharecropping tenancies in Ontario finds that they were most common in the regions of older settlement, suggesting that this form of tenancy, in addition to providing a step of the agricultural ladder to full ownership, was probably one means by which retired farmers could administer their land.

Agrarian Organization in the Century of Industrialization:
Europe, Russia and North America
Research in Economic History, Suppl. 5, page 253.
Copyright © 1989 by JAI Press Inc.
All rights of reproduction in any form reserved.
ISBN: 0-89232-855-X

FAMILIES, FARMS AND RURAL SOCIETY IN PREINDUSTRIAL AMERICA

David F. Weiman

The logic of the family farm continues to elude the grasp of economic and social historians. Nowhere is this confusion more evident than in the recurrent and seemingly interminable debates over the extent of self-sufficient and market production on farms in preindustrial America (roughly defined as the period before the Civil War).[1] At the heart of this debate are two very different conceptions of the family farm and its relationship to the market system, and relatedly of the process of market formation.

This paper reexamines the structure of rural society in preindustrial America. In contrast to the views found in the literature, the interpretation presented here emphasizes a fundamental tension among rural households between their bourgeois ethic of private accumulation and the kin and communal relations that structured their private economic activities.[2] Together, these two forces produced a distinctive economic dynamic, expressed in the extent of social and economic differentiation and the pattern of wealth holdings among rural households.

The first section of this paper develops this alternative interpretation of rural society and market integration and distinguishes, what I call, petty production in agriculture from commercial production by the social and economic structure of the farm community and corresponding mode of wealth accumulation among farm households. As a test of this interpretation, the remaining sections of the paper compare the economic and social structure of farm communities in two counties of the Georgia Upcountry in 1860—DeKalb and Floyd. Situated on the periphery of the antebellum Georgia Cotton Belt, these communities were comprised mainly of yeoman farm households. Yet, because of differences in ecological conditions and in the timing and extent of internal improvements in each, only those communities in Floyd County were integrated into the cotton economy by 1860.[3] This comparison reveals the marked differences in the system of farming and patterns of wealth accumulation among households in the two counties that reflect their position within the market system.

PETTY PRODUCTION IN AGRICULTURE AND MARKET INTEGRATION: AN INTERPRETATION

Household Production and Wealth Accumulation

The analysis of petty production begins with the individual household, which was the basic unit of production and wealth ownership in rural communities.[4] The annual work routine of the farm household embraced a wide range of productive activities, of which the most important was farming. Farmers planted a diverse mix of food crops, which were fed to draft animals or were consumed by the family, and often grew small crops of fibers that were worked up into clothing within the household. The cultivation of field crops also provided households with barter or cash income. Food surpluses were sold in local markets and more often were used to fatten livestock, especially swine, for shipment to distant markets.

Livestock were allowed to graze on unclaimed or unimproved land and were penned in and fattened before they were sold to drovers. This practice of open-field grazing enabled households to maintain and enlarge their stocks of swine and cattle without having to purchase additional land or to expand the production of feed crops.[5] Finally, produce from small garden plots, orchards, chicken coops, and dairy cows rounded out the annual fare of most households and occasionally brought in extra income.

In addition to farming, households manufactured simple items of consumption and produced or at least repaired many of the tools and implements used on the farm.[6] They also relied on hunting and gathering, or as they euphemistically are called in the literature, informal activities. For this reason, petty producers tended to settle forested areas, near streams and lakes.[7] Forest products provided them with additional sources of food and materials, and many of these items provided households with an additional source of income.

Household production depended primarily on the supply of family labor, which was organized into a sexual division of labor.[8] Following established norms of men's and women's work, tasks were allocated to the members of the household according to their age and gender. Husbands and their older sons worked primarily on the farm; clearing and preparing land for cultivation, tending field crops and livestock, and building and maintaining structures. They provided the family with its basic foodstuffs and most of its income. Men also hunted, fished, and performed those domestic chores that employed the skills used in farming, such as carpentry and metal-working.

Wives and their younger children were responsible for the direct provisioning of the household's consumption needs. Along with work in the home, they tended the garden and orchard, milked cows, and gathered forest products. Also, women and children assisted in the harvest and, if necessary, worked in the fields.

Households preserved the family labor system through the intergenerational transfer of wealth.[9] Children typically worked on their parents' farm until they formed their own households. Even after that point, they continued to assist their parents and were expected to care for them in their old age. In return, children received part of their inheritance (a small plot of land and livestock) at their marriage and the rest upon their parents' death. This practice both cemented the reciprocal obligations between parents and their children and provided the family with a stable mode of wealth accumulation.

The reproduction of the family governed its wealth accumulation over time and determined the allocation of resources within the household between self-sufficient and market production. Younger households, constrained by their limited supplies of capital and family labor, typically did not form independent farms. Instead, male heads provided labor services to their parents or established, older neighbors and accumulated the tangible wealth and skills necessary to set up a farm.[10] By the time they reached their late thirties or early forties, they could afford to purchase, or inherited, enough land to build a farm and provide for their children, and with the assistance of their older sons, they began to improve and cultivate it.

Given their marginal position in the market system, households ensured their reproduction each year by first producing the means to satisfy their essential consumption needs and then devoting their surplus labor time and other resources to farm construction and market production.[11] Over time households cleared larger plots of land, built necessary structures and acquired additional livestock and farm equipment. With the corresponding maturation of their children and decline in dependency ratios, they were able to expand the scale of agricultural production and to devote increasing shares of their labor time and improved acreage to the cultivation of cash crops.

This simple logic, then, implied a tendency toward increasing market production on family farms with the age and wealth of the household head, as well as a familiar life cycle pattern of wealth accumulation.[12] The accumulation of farm capital and greater supplies of family labor over the life cycle enabled farm households to realize larger net incomes. Consequently, they enjoyed a higher standard of living, often substituting manufactured commodities for local or homespun varieties, and accumulated wealth more rapidly, expanding their holdings of land and livestock to provide for their children. This mode of wealth accumulation, while fueled by demographic and territorial expansion, also depended on conditions in the local economy and in the external market that will be explored in the following section.

Economic and Social Structure of Farm Communities

Household production enabled farm families to satisfy their basic consumption and production requirements and at the same time to accumulate wealth gradually. The reproduction of the household and its accumulation of wealth also depended on the social and economic structure of the farm community. The local economy and cooperative forms of organizing labor augmented the productive activities of farm households, whereas common rights protected claims over unimproved and unclaimed land.

The local economy of rural society was organized into what Lewis Gray has called a system of community diversification, a local social division of labor comprised of skilled artisans, small manufacturers, and merchants.[13] Artisans produced household furnishings and utensils, tools, and farm equipment, and local mills processed farm products. These services complemented the productive activities of farm households and further insulated them from direct contact with the external market. Within the local economy farm households bartered their surpluses of foodstuffs, raw materials and when necessary labor time, for goods and services that could not be produced domestically.[14] Moreover, unlike long distance trades, these transactions involved direct, reciprocal relationships among members of the farm community and were often regulated by social norms either formally or informally.

The nonagricultural sector also helped to forge the commercial ties between farmers and the external market. Mills, for example, processed grains into meal, flour, and even liquor so that they could be profitably shipped to distant markets.[15] Smiths and implement makers fashioned improved equipment to enhance the productivity of farm labor and so the production of marketable surpluses.

Local merchants formed the critical link in this chain, as they mediated all aspects of long distance trades. They conducted a small, but thriving retail trade; arranged the sale of or directly marketed farm produce in distant markets; and supplied farm households with credit.[16] Rural merchants, nonetheless, occupied an ambivalent position within the farm community. To expand their own business, merchants sought to deepen the dependence of farm households on the external market and hence diminish the self-sufficiency of the individual household and community.

In addition to their interactions in the local economy, households cooperated in building and maintaining the local infrastructure, and in clearing their land and building their homes and barns.[17] They also assisted each other with those tasks that strained the limited resources of the individual household. They shared draft animals and worked together during periods of peak labor demands, for example, at the harvest.[18]

The ethic of cooperation also governed the informal exchanges of labor among individual households, the most common type being the intergenerational transfer of labor. Unlike a simple wage contract, this exchange of labor was modeled after kin relations within the family.[19] It served as an apprenticeship for young farmers, providing them with the necessary skills and the use of implements and draft animals.

The coexistence of private ownership and common rights is further evidence of the unique blend of private and communal social relations in rural society. Custom limited the exclusive use of property only to improved lands under cultivation and entitled households to graze livestock, hunt, fish, and forage on the rest. The practice of open-field grazing was predicated on such rights and was enforced by the absence of fencing or "stock" laws.[20] While placing the burden of protecting crops from herds of cattle and swine on cultivators, these rights benefited tenants and small owner-operators. Natural sources of water and forest products were also considered to be public goods. Farm communities, in addition, established preemption rights for squatters, long before they were enacted into law, and extended these rights to small land owners so that they could expand their holdings without having to compete with local or outside speculators.[21]

These forms of social and economic organization circumscribed the productive activities of individual households and, in turn, dampened the impact of private wealth as a force in differentiating households socially and economically. Wealthier households were prevented from aggrandizing themselves at the expense of their economically weaker neighbors, while communal arrangements effectively transferred wealth to those at the lower end of the distribution. Wealth holdings in these farm communities were far from equally distributed, but they were significantly less concentrated than in more settled and commercialized regions. More importantly, differences in wealth and economic status among households depended largely on the age of the household head and reflected the transitory effects of the life cycle pattern of wealth accumulation.[22] The absence of sharp economic divisions among households was most clearly evident in the informal system of tenancy in these communities and may help to explain why census agents did not systematically enumerate tenant farms until 1880, when contractual forms of tenancy became the norm.

Market Integration and the Transformation of Rural Society

According to this interpretation, petty production in agriculture did not preclude market production and the private accumulation of wealth. Rather, the complex familial and communal relations among petty producers limited the extent of these economic activities. Viewed from a more dynamic perspective, petty production in agriculture can be best understood as a form of primitive or original accumulation of capital in the sense of Marx. It involved the accumulation of capital based on pre- or noncapitalist social relations and established the conditions necessary for the integration of petty producers into the market and thus for the emergence of capitalist production in agriculture.[23]

Petty production, therefore, was an inherently transitory system of economic and social relations. As petty producers accumulated wealth, they increased their production for the market and their purchases of manufactured commodities. The expanding volume of reciprocal trades between farm communities and nearby cities induced the growth of the local merchant class, investments in processing and storage facilities, and the articulation of the transportation network. Flows of capital from commercially developed areas, in the form of trade credit, direct investments in transportation improvements and land (or mortgages), and the migration of merchants and wealthy farmers, accelerated these trends.[24]

Yet despite the transitory nature of petty production, market integration was not the natural outcome of private accumulation and hence a market process. Market integration also required the replacement of kin and communal bonds with contractual relations based solely on the exchange of private property. This transformation often sparked intense social and political struggles over such critical issues as the rights of tenants and property owners over common lands, the forms and incidence of taxation, the subsidization of commercial improvements by local governments, and even the nature of the obligations between parents and their children.[25]

Market integration, in turn, was an irreversible process, which made all households in the community increasingly dependent on the market for their reproduction. The growing volume of long distance trade fostered greater specialization in merchandising and local manufacturing and so undermined the system of community diversification.[26] Moreover, the erosion of kin and communal relations forced households to rely more heavily on private wealth for their livelihood.[27] Consequently, farm households specialized their production in two distinct, but related ways. They devoted a larger share of their labor time to agricultural production, and allocated increasing shares of their farm labor and improved acreage to production for the market.

In this milieu private wealth exerted a greater force in differentiating farm households economically and socially. In contrast to the pioneering methods of petty producers, farm capital formation involved the direct purchase of land and specialized inputs and so required greater out-of-pocket expenses. These increasing capital requirements for farm construction defined an agricultural ladder, in which the land tenure of the household head depended primarily on the ownership of wealth, not age.[28] Household heads with little initial wealth worked as wage laborers and then tenants until they accumulated sufficient capital to build their own farms, while those with substantial wealth holdings capitalized on their economic advantage by expanding the extent of their commercial production and, over time, their wealth. This more capitalistic mode of wealth accumulation, in turn, implied a stronger tendency toward increasing market production as farm size and household wealth increased.

The Social and Economic Structure of Upcountry Farm Communities

The domain of the empirical analysis are farm communities in two representative counties of the Georgia Upcountry, DeKalb, and Floyd.[29] Systematic samples of households in each county were drawn from the population schedules of the 1860 manuscript census. Household heads in each sample were matched with farm operators and slaveowners enumerated in the agricultural and slave schedules.[30] These data provide a cross section of farm communities in the two counties, which includes those household heads employed outside of agriculture in skilled trades, commerce, professions, and services as well as "farmers without farms." Thus, they delineate more completely the structure of rural society than samples based solely on the agricultural census schedules.

Table 1 presents the distribution of occupations among household heads in each sample. Occupational categories situate each individual with a particular branch of the local social division of labor and indicate the extent of community diversification in each county. Several household heads who worked in agriculture reported a second occupation in addition to farming. Therefore, they could not be classified according to these divisions. The original estimates in Table 1 count these individuals as farmers, while the alternative estimates in parentheses consider only their second occupation. The differences between the two distributions are significant only in the case of Floyd County and will be discussed in more detail.

Table 1. Distribution of Occupations of
White Household Heads DeKalb and Floyd Counties, 1860

	Percentage of Household Heads					
	Farmer	Trade and Transport	Professional and Service	Artisan	Laborer	None
DeKalb County	75.1	1.9	1.9	13.5	2.7	4.9
	(70.5)	(2.1)	(4.1)	(15.1)	(2.7)	(5.4)
Floyd County	73.5	4.4	4.7	11.4	2.2	3.7
	(65.6)	(5.2)	(8.9)	(14.1)	(2.2)	(3.9)

Notes: Household heads reporting no occupations and not enumerated in the agricultural census were primarily single women. They made up 3.8% of the household heads in DeKalb County and 2.7% in Floyd. The figures in parentheses are the revised occupational distributions that count the non-agricultural occupations of those household heads with dual occupations.

Source: Manuscript Census, Georgia, DeKalb, and Floyd Counties, 1860, Schedule I.

The data in Table 1 show that most households in the Upcountry derived all or part of their livelihood from agricultural production. Three-quarters of the household heads reported farming as their main occupation in the population census, or were listed as farm operators in the agricultural schedules. The distribution of occupations in Upcountry Georgia is similar to that in rural communities in the North during this period, where 70 to 80% of the household heads worked in agriculture.[31]

Of the remaining 20% of the household heads who reported occupations in the census, two-thirds in DeKalb County and almost one-half in Floyd County were artisans or operated small processing mills. Local producers possessed a wide range of skills, but most, approximately three-quarters in each county, were employed as carpenters, smiths, mechanics, wheel rights, sawyers, and shoemakers.[32] A smaller fraction of household heads were employed in commerce, as merchants, traders, and clerks, and in professions and services, most often as lawyers, preachers, and doctors. Together, the latter two groups accounted for only 4 to 5% of the household heads in DeKalb County, and between 9 and 13% in Floyd County. Unskilled laborers comprised only 2 to 3% of the household heads in both counties and worked in large shops and mines.[33]

Despite the similarities in their economic and social structure, farm communities in DeKalb and Floyd Counties were located in distinct ecological subregions of the Georgia Upcountry, and occupied different positions within the cotton economy during the late antebellum period.[34] The hilly terrain and cooler climate of DeKalb County, which were characteristic of the eastern half of the Upcountry, made these lands less suited to the cultivation of cotton. Moreover, this territory had been settled by the early 1820s and remained geographically isolated until the late 1840s when the Georgia Railroad was extended to Atlanta. The construction of the railroad and the subsequent growth of Atlanta certainly benefited farm households in the county, but did not fundamentally alter their marginal position in the cotton economy and established way of life.

Floyd County was located in the more recently settled Cherokee territory, which extended from the western half of the Upper Piedmont to the lower tier of the Appalachian Valley. The county contained several rivers, which supported local navigation, and the broad river bottoms had extremely fertile soil and milder climates. This territory was also rich in mineral deposits, most notably gold. The initial advantages of the Cherokee Territory, afforded by its resource endowment, were augmented by the construction of the Western and Atlantic Railroad. The road, which was financed and operated by the state, spanned the entire length of the region, and when completed in 1848, integrated agricultural producers there into the cotton economy via Atlanta.

Differences in the distribution of occupations and extent of specialization within occupational categories reflect the divergent trends of development in each section during the late antebellum period. In DeKalb County economic life was centered around small towns, often no more than a cross-road. Country storeowners and itinerant merchants conducted all aspects of local trade and operated on a small scale.[35] Professionals and artisans performed only the basic services previously enumerated that were necessary for the economic and social reproduction of the community.

Economic opportunities in the western Cherokee territory fostered the growth and geographical concentration of commercial and ancillary activities in small and medium-sized cities. One-third of the household heads in Floyd County were employed outside of agriculture, at least part-time (see the revised estimates of the distribution of occupations in Table 1). Most of them lived in Rome, a medium-sized city that served as a distribution center for farm communities in the Valley region of Georgia and Alabama.[36] Rome's position in the regional economy is evidenced by the larger percentage of individuals employed in trade and transportation and in professions and services. Rome's merchant class was extremely prosperous, owning 14% of the toal wealth in the county, and included a commission agent, several traders, a warehouse owner, in addition to numerous retail merchants and country storeowners. Druggists, tavern and boarding housekeepers, educators, and newspaper publishers served both the urban and rural population, and the city supported more diverse skilled trades, such as construction workers, machinists, and printers.

WEALTH, LAND TENURE, AND COMMERCIAL PRODUCTION IN THE UPCOUNTRY

Until 1880 the census ignored the system of land tenure in agriculture. The vast majority of household heads employed in agriculture simply reported their

Table 2. Land Tenure in the Georgia Upcountry, 1860

	Percentage of Household Heads	Age of Head	Age of Spouse	Real Wealth	Total Wealth	Slaves
DeKalb County						
Owner-Operators	0.59	45.4	37.5	1771.1	5211.1	3.0
Farmers with Real Estate	0.06	42.8	29.0	1641.8	3952.4	2.5
Tenant	0.08	43.3	28.2	6.8	787.3	0.3
Farmers without Real Estate	0.25	35.7	29.8	0.0	71.4	0.0
Overseer	0.01	27.5	25.0	0.0	0.0	0.0
Laborer	0.01	30.5	26.5	0.0	50.0	0.0
Floyd County						
Owner-Operators	0.60	44.1	33.7	5088.3	13452.1	7.6
Farmers with Real Estate	0.01	47.5	41.0	1500.0	1500.0	0.0
Tenant	0.22	38.9	29.4	62.3	677.6	0.9
Farmers without Real Estate	0.07	34.4	29.2	22.6	395.0	0.3
Overseer	0.02	32.0	28.0	46.4	389.3	0.1
Laborer	0.09	33.7	27.0	0.0	75.4	0.2

Notes: Owner-operators are farm operators who own their farms. Farmers with real estate reported owning real wealth in the population schedules, but were not enumerated in the agricultural schedules. Tenants are farm operators who own no real wealth, improved acreage and farm value. Farmers without real estate reported their occupation as farmer, but owned no wealth and were not enumerated in the agricultural schedules.

Sources: Manuscript Census, Georgia, DeKalb, and Floyd Counties, 1860. Schedules I & II

occupation as farmer, and the agricultural schedules did not inquire into the nature of their tenure. Nonetheless, as many historians have noted, the manuscript census returns contain systematic anomalies in the enumeration of farm households that can be interpreted as conventions used by census agents to identify tenants.[37] Together with additional information often provided by the agents themselves, it is possible to piece together the complex agrarian social structure in farm communities.

Between one-quarter and one-third of the "farmers" in the two counties were not enumerated in the agricultural schedules and presumably did not operate independent farms. In addition, at least one-third of farmers owned no real wealth in 1860. These "farmers without farms," it has been suggested, were often recent settlers or headed newly formed households. They had either not yet purchased land or had only begun to clear and cultivate their farms.[38]

In the case of Floyd County the census agent identified explicitly the tenure of most household heads in agriculture and so offered a different interpretation

Table 3. Size Distribution of Farms and Shares of Improved Acreage by Improved Acreage Class Farm Operations in DeKalb and Floyd Counties, 1860

	Tenant	1-49 Acres	50-99 Acres	100-199 Acres	200-499 Acres	500 plus Acres
DeKalb						
Percentage of Farmers	11.9	21.1	23.8	30.3	11.4	1.6
Share of Acreage	0.0	6.7	15.5	37.5	28.6	11.6
Floyd						
Percentage of Farmers	25.6	22.3	22.3	17.6	8.4	3.8
Share of Acreage	0.0	6.1	15.2	23.6	24.3	30.8

Notes: Farm operators are those household heads in the sample populations who were enumerated in the agricultural census. In DeKalb County 185 of the sample household heads were matched with those enumerated in the agricultural schedules; in Floyd County, the number of farm operators is 238. Tenants are defined as farm operators enumerated in the agricultural census that reported no improved acreage and farm value; see note 37.

Source: Manuscript Census, Georgia, DeKalb and Floyd Counties, 1860 Schedule II.

of these anomalies. Two-thirds of the landless farmers were enumerated in the agricultural schedules and were clearly designated as "renters."[39] In addition, 10% of the household heads in agriculture were overseers or laborers.

According to the data in Table 2, these categories roughly correspond to the rungs of the agricultural ladder and so define the system of land tenure in the region. Owner-operators were in their mid-forties, and in addition to their farms, owned substantial amounts of personal property, including several slaves. "Renters" or tenants were significantly younger (their median age was 36 years).[40] Although only a few owned even small plots of land, they had accumulated a modicum of personal wealth that was invested in nonland farm capital and in some cases a slave or two. Laborers, with the exception of overseers, were in their late twenties and early thirties and owned little or no wealth at all. Those in the remaining category, landless farmers not enumerated in the agricultural census, clearly occupied an intermediate position between renters and laborers, in terms of their age and wealth holdings, and were perhaps sharecroppers.[41]

In DeKalb County these categories define a similar system of land tenure, although it is not as sharply delineated or complex as the one in Floyd County (see Table 2). Two-thirds of the farmers owned land, and they tended to be older than the other household heads in agriculture. The rest were landless farmers, of whom only one-quarter were farm operators enumerated in the agricultural census. These "tenants" constituted a rather diverse group, including several older individuals with large wealth holdings.[42] Still, their median age was only 35.5 years, and their median wealth holding was $290,

Table 4. Size Distribution of Slaveholders and Shares of Slaveholdings by Slaveholding Class Farm Households in DeKalb and Floyd Counties, 1860

	1-4 Slaves	5-9 Slaves	10-14 Slaves	15-49 Slaves	50 plus Slaves	Percentage of Households with No Slaves
DeKalb						
Percentage of Slaveholders	52.7	25.7	12.2	9.5	0.0	60.6
Share of Slaves	19.1	27.4	20.9	32.6	0.0	
Floyd						
Percentage of Slaveholders	29.8	23.4	11.7	28.7	6.4	60.5
Share of Slaves	4.8	11.4	10.0	43.2	30.6	

Source: Manuscript Census, Georgia, DeKalb and Floyd Counties, 1860, Schedule III.

of which $215 was invested in nonland farm capital. Those landless farmers who were not enumerated in the agricultural census made up the remaining one-quarter of the household heads in agriculture. Whereas they may have been tenants, they were much closer to the class of agricultural laborers in Floyd County in terms of their age and wealth.

Most of the farm operators in the two counties owned their land and cultivated small- to medium-sized farms with family labor, occasionally assisted by a hired hand, tenant or several slaves (see Tables 3 and 4). Tenants independently operated only 12% of the farms in DeKalb County and 26% in Floyd County. Of the remaining owner-operated farms, over one-half contained fewer than 100 improved acres, and only 15 to 17% exceeded 200 improved acres in size, often taken to be the minimum scale of production on plantations. Additionally, 60% of the farm operators in the two counties owned no slaves, and most slaveholders (78% in DeKalb County and 53% in Floyd) owned fewer than 10.

Despite the predominance of "yeoman" farms in the region, there was nonetheless considerable differentiation of farms in terms of their size, measured by improved acreage or the wealth of the operator, and economic function (see Table 5). In DeKalb County on small- and medium-sized farms (those with fewer than 100 improved acres), households devoted their labor and improved acreage primarily to production for household consumption. Most farmers produced just enough corn and other field crops to feed their livestock and families, and occasionally realized a small surplus, which they sold in local markets or used to fatten swine.[43] Along with their wives and children, they produced relatively large quantities of butter and other dairy products, and a variety of manufactured goods.

Table 5. Levels and Composition of Farm Production On Upcountry Farms, 1860

	Tenant	1-49 Acres	50-99 Acres	100-199 Acres	200-499 Acres	500 plus Acres
DeKalb County						
Per Capita Output of:						
Food Crops	44.4	49.2	55.6	66.0	65.0	74.1
Butter	13.3	14.8	11.9	12.4	8.2	15.7
Value of Animals Slaughtered ($)	15.8	12.2	14.0	15.7	14.4	14.4
Value of Home Manufactures ($)	2.3	2.9	1.7	2.5	1.4	0.0
Food Surplus or Deficits	-3.1	6.4	9.3	20.8	20.8	20.9
Percentage Producing Surpluses	40.9	59.0	54.5	85.7	85.7	100.0
Crop Mix	15.5	12.1	18.9	16.8	29.9	26.9
Percentage Producing Cotton	45.5	43.6	70.5	73.2	95.2	100.0
Percentage of Output Marketed	16.0	25.8	28.4	34.1	44.9	40.3
Floyd County						
Per Capita Output of:						
Food Crops	45.6	48.0	83.7	80.4	78.6	111.5
Butter	10.7	11.3	11.4	9.9	6.9	7.8
Value of Animals Slaughtered ($)	21.0	12.7	16.5	16.3	12.2	37.0
Value of Home Manufactures ($)	2.1	3.2	2.7	1.9	0.8	0.6
Food Surplus or Deficits	-1.2	10.4	33.3	38.2	38.9	66.7
Percentage Producing Surpluses	42.6	62.3	69.8	92.9	80.0	100.0
Crop Mix	29.1	29.1	28.8	26.6	46.5	44.9
Percentage Producing Cotton	72.1	62.3	83.0	83.0	85.0	100.0
Percentage of Output Marketed	27.4	37.4	51.1	52.2	67.8	64.8

Notes: Food crops include corn, wheat, oats, rye, peas and beans, and potatoes, and are measured in corn-equivalent bushels based on the nutritional value of each crop relative to corn. For a discussion of the method used to calculate food crop output, food surpluses or deficits, and the value of market production, see Weiman, "Farmers and the Market," especially sections 2 and 3. Crop mix is defined as the share of cotton revenues in the value of field crop output.
Source: See Table 2.

In contrast, production for the market comprised a relatively small share of total household production on these farms. Cotton, the principal staple, was grown on less than half of the tenant and small farms and on three-quarters of the larger farms, and cotton revenues accounted for less than 20% of the total value of field crop production. Even when the value of marketable surpluses of food crops are included, commodity production accounted for only 20 to 30% of total household production.

On the larger farms in the county, producers still supplied the household with its essential food requirements. Market production, however, accounted for an increasing share of farm output, while home manufacturing declined in importance. On almost all farms with at least 100 improved acres, producers cultivated abundant supplies of food crops and realized surpluses above food and feed requirements of 21 bushels of grain per adult consumer. Cotton was produced on most large farms; however, specialization in cotton, as estimated by the crop mix, was greater only on the largest farms in the county, those with at least 200 improved acres. Still, all of these producers were engaged in production for the market, and they sold at least one-third of their farm output.

In Floyd County the extent of self-sufficient and market production varied with farm size in the same way, although producers in this region were more integrated into the market and in particular the cotton economy. Consequently, they devoted larger shares of their farm output to cotton and other cash crops, and there was greater variation in the extent of market production (and in the composition of cash crops) with farm size. Small farmers, those with less than 50 improved acres, produced remarkably similar levels of all outputs, except cotton, to those in DeKalb County. The greater percentage of small farmers producing cotton in Floyd County explains the larger share of output marketed on farms in these size categories. Nonetheless, after controlling for differences in the dependency ratio and in the ratio of farm capital to labor, small farmers in the two counties sold approximately the same share of their total output, between 20 and 30%.[44]

The greater extent of market production in Floyd County occurred on farms with at least 50 improved acres, and market production sharply increased with farm size beyond this point. Floyd County farmers in these size categories produced on average 80 bushels of grains per capita of the farm population, and their marketable surpluses of grains exceeded 30 bushels per capita annually. Over 80% of these producers cultivated cotton, and on the largest farms, those greater than 200 imporved acres, cotton accounted for almost half of the output of field crops. Consequently, these producers sold over half of their total farm output, and on the larger farms the figure was closer to two-thirds.

PATTERNS OF WEALTH HOLDINGS AND MODES OF WEALTH ACCUMULATION IN THE UPCOUNTRY

As the preceding sections show, the extent of economic and social differentiation in Upcountry communities depended on their position within the market system. In those communities on the periphery of the cotton economy, such as in DeKalb County, the local economy and land tenure arrangements were rudimentary. Moreover, specialization in cotton and the extent of commercial production did not increase systematically with farm size, but were greater only on the relatively small number of large farms and plantations in the county. In Floyd County, in contrast, market integration involved urbanization and the further articulation of the agrarian social structure. Household heads in agriculture were differentiated into tenure categories that corresponded to their age and wealth holdings, and among farm operators, the extent of market production and farm size were strongly correlated.

While recognizing the limits of cross-sectional analysis, these results strongly suggest that the structure of rural society in these counties was shaped by distinct modes of wealth accumulation among farm households. Such an hypothesis is implicit in the previous discussion, which considers farm tenure in terms of an agricultural ladder. This hypothesis implies a process of wealth accumulation, in which the extent and composition of household wealth depended on the position of the family in its life cycle. Wealth holdings, in turn, determined the tenure of the household head and the scale and composition of production on the family farm.

To test the first link in this chain, the life cycle pattern of wealth accumulation, regression equations were estimated for farm households in the two samples.[45] Following Atack and Bateman, the specification assumes that the rate of wealth accumulation by households decreased over the course of the life cycle, as measured by the age of the head (AGE), and eventually became negative, when the head neared retirement and presumably transferred wealth to his or her children.[46] The rate of accumulation, it is assumed, also depended on whether the head had a second occupation in addition to farming (DUAL) and the education of the head and other adult members of the household, as measured by the percentage of adults over 20 who were literate (LIT).[47] Because the dependent variable is truncated at zero and a relatively large percentage of households reported owning no wealth, the maximum likelihood tobit model was used to derive unbiased coefficient estimates.

The results of the analysis are presented in Table 5. Equation 1 was estimated over the entire population of farm households. In both counties the estimated coefficients of the age variables have the expected signs and are statistically significant. The coefficients of the remaining variables are also positive, but are not in general statistically significant.

The regression estimates in Equation 1 are consistent with the life cycle hypothesis. They, nonetheless, imply rather different cross-sectional patterns of wealth holdings among households in the two counties. In DeKalb County the relative wealth holdings of households varied greatly with the age of the head. They increased sharply with age, until household heads reached their mid-fifties and then declined. In Floyd County, in contrast, relative wealth holdings varied more gradually with the age of household heads, and declined only when heads reached their early to mix-sixties. In addition, only in Floyd County did household heads with dual occupations have systematically larger wealth holdings. A second occupation may have enabled these household heads to accumulate more wealth than other farmers. Alternatively, they may have come from wealthier families and were provided with a professional education, as well as a substantial inheritance.[48]

The regression estimates capture the differences in land tenure in the two counties (see Table 2) and provide further support for the interpretation of these relations offered in section one. In DeKalb County the farm population was divided into a class of laborers or tenants, who were in their thirties and owned little or no wealth, and owner-operators in their forties and fifties. Although wealth holdings among the latter group varied with age (see Equation 3 in Table 6), the results in Equation 1 clearly reflect this dualism within the population. Moreover, they imply implausibly high rates of wealth accumulation among heads in their thirties and suggest the importance of intergenerational transfers of labor and wealth between these classes.[49]

In Floyd County market integration resulted in the greater differentiation of households by wealth and the further articulation of the agricultural ladder. Consequently, there were intermediate classes of wealth holders between laborers and owner-operators and a smoother cross-sectional pattern of wealth holdings. In addition, age exerted a weaker influence in determining the relative wealth holdings of the household. Not only did household heads with dual occupations have greater wealth holdings regardless of their age, but when estimated over the population of farm operators, the life-cycle regression equation was not statistically significant (see Equation 3 in Table 6).

The weaker correlation between age and wealth in Floyd County can be partly explained by the in-migration of large slaveholders of all ages in the late 1840s and early 1850s that dramatically altered the distribution of wealth holdings among rural households. The effect of these population flows on the cross-sectional pattern of wealth holdings can be seen in Equation 2, which was estimated over the population of farm households excluding large slaveholders, those with at least 10 slaves. In DeKalb County where large slaveholders comprised a small percentage of the population, the coefficient estimates in Equation 2 are almost identical to those for the entire sample. In Floyd County the regression estimates yield a cross-sectional pattern of wealth holdings that is more similar to the one observed in DeKalb County. Among this segment of the population, there was greater variation in wealth holdings with the age of the household head, and wealth holdings declined when heads reached their mid-fifties. The variable for dual occupations, however, is still statistically significant and indicates the importance of this external source of capital.

Table 6. Life-Cycle Regressions

	Equation 1	Equation 2	Equation 3
DeKalb County			
Constant	-12.03	-11.58	1.03
	(3.05)	(3.31)	(6.68)
Age	0.47	0.46	0.27
	(0.12)	(0.13)	(0.06)
Age Squared	-0.0043	-0.0042	-0.0026
	(0.0012)	(0.0014)	(0.0006)
Dual Occupations	3.17	2.1	1.89
	(3.66)	(9.87)	(1.22)
Percentage of Adults Literate	5.94	5.61	-0.17
	(1.35)	(1.45)	(6.56)
Likelihood Ratio Statistic	49.2*	36.8*	16.0*
N	268	250	175
Floyd County			
Constant	-2.88	-3.18	2.24
	(3.34)	(3.43)	(6.56)
Age	0.29	0.34	0.15
	(0.092)	(0.103)	(0.074)
Age Squared	-0.0023	-0.0031	-0.0012
	(0.001)	(0.0011)	(0.0008)
Dual Occupations	2.13	2.15	0.96
	(0.90)	(0.99)	(0.58)
Percentage of Adults Literate	0.79	-0.32	0.75
	(2.74)	(2.71)	(6.33)
Likelihood Ratio Statistic	38.4*	31.4*	8.00
N	285	241	233

Notes: * Significant at a 5% confidence level.
The dependent variable equals the natural logarithm of total wealth. Equation (1) is estimated over the population of household heads in agriculture. Equation (2) is estimated over the same population excluding slaveholders with 10 or more slaves. Equation (3) is estimated over the population of farm operators. Standard errors are given in parentheses. The likelihood ratio statistic tests the significance of the regression equation and is asymptotically distributed as chi-square with degrees of freedom equal to the number of independent variables in the equation.

The further articulation of the tenure ladder in Floyd County also suggests the increased use of contractual arrangements to mediate the exchange of labor services and a more extensive market for labor in this county. This interpretation is consistent with information of farm wages and migrational patterns of young households heads.[50] Although wages for day laborers in both counties were the same and stayed relatively constant throughout the decade 1850 to 1860, this market was largely seasonal, and its geographical scope was limited. More importantly, the wages of full-time farm laborers in Floyd County were 25% higher than those in DeKalb during this period. In 1860, for example, monthly wages in Floyd County were $15 including room and board, as compared to only $12 per month in DeKalb County. This differential signalled the more extensive economic opportunities for household heads who were just beginning their careers in agriculture. As a consequence, a larger percentage of agricultural laborers and younger household heads in general migrated into this county from other states than was true for DeKalb County.[51] Furthermore, these new settlers came directly from Tennessee, North Carolina, and even Alabama, instead of following the more gradual southwestern route into Georgia from South Carolina.

This paper has offered yet another interpretation of rural society in preindustrial America. In contrast to earlier views, the analysis conceives of petty production in agriculture as a mode of wealth accumulation in recently settled areas and so captures the unique economic and social relations of rural society and their transitory nature. Moreover, it shifts the focus of the analysis from individual farm households to the social and economic relations within farm communities that structured their activites. The analysis of yeoman farm communities in the Georgia Upcountry in 1860 reinforces these conclusions. It shows that market integration did not diminish the self-sufficiency of farm households in basic foodstuffs, but rather transformed the local economy and tenure relations in farm communities and increased the extent of economic differentiation among farm operators.

ACKNOWLEDGMENTS

I would like to thank Michael Bernstein, Michael Edelstein, Louis Ferleger, George Grantham, William Parker, Gavin Wright and the participants of the Columbia University Seminar in Economic History for their helpful comments on earlier versions of this paper. I would also like to thank Sarah E. Lawrence for her editorial comments. Financial assistance from the Economic History Association is gratefully acknowledged.

NOTES AND REFERENCES

1. The opposing views in the most recent round of this debate are clearly expressed by Michael Merrill, "Cash is Good to Eat: Self-Sufficiency and Exchange in the Rural Economy of the United

States," *Radical History Review* 3 (Winter 1977): 42-71; James A. Henretta, "Families and Farms: *Mentalite* in Pre-Industrial America," *William and Mary Quarterly* 35 (Jan. 1978): 3-32; Winifred B. Rothenberg, "The Market and the Massachusetts Farmer, 1750-1855," *Journal of Economic History* 41 (June 1981): 283-314; and Jeremy Atack and Fred Bateman, "Marketable Farm Surpluses: Northeastern and Midwestern United States, 1859 and 1860," *Social Science History* 8 (Fall 1984): 371-94. For alternative views on the issue of self-sufficiency and commercial production, see Gavin Wright, *Political Economy of the Cotton South* (New York, 1977), pp. 62-74; and David F. Weiman, "Farmers and the Market: A View from the Georgia Upcountry," *Journal of Economic History* 47 (Sept. 1987).

2. This aspect of rural society is also emphasized by William N. Parker, "From Northwest to Midwest, Social Bases of a Regional History," in *Essays in Nineteenth Century Economic History: The Old Northwest*, ed. David C. Klingaman and Richard K. Vedder (Athens, 1975), pp. 9-17.

3. This point is more fully developed in Weiman, "Farmers and the Market."

4. For a similar perspective, see Wright, *Political Economy of the Cotton South*, esp. ch. 3; Harriet Friedmann, "Household Production and the National Economy: Concepts for the Analysis of Agrarian Formations," *Journal of Peasant Studies* 7 (Jan. 1980): 158-84; and Elizabeth Fox-Genovese, "Antebellum Southern Households: A New Perspective on a Familiar Question," *Review* 7 (Fall 1983): 215-53. Fox-Genovese, however, focuses on the plantation household and so emphasizes the distinct nature of Southern households (pp. 231-249).

5. For an excellent survey of these practices and quantitative estimates of the importance of open-field grazing in the antebellum South, see William K. Hutchinson and Samuel H. Williamson, "The Self-Sufficiency of the Antebellum South," *Journal of Economic History* 31 (Sept. 1971): 595-660. Frank Lawrence Owsley, *Plain Folk of the Old South* (Baton Rouge, 1977), pp. 23-51; Forrest McDonald and Grady McWhiney, "The Antebellum Southern Herdsman: A Reinterpretation," *Journal of Southern History* 41 (May 1975), 147-166; and John Solomon Otto, "The Migration of the Southern Plainfolk," *Journal of Southern History* 51 (May 1985): 183-200 emphasize the importance of open-field grazing to Southern yeomen.

6. The classic work on the subject is still Rolla M. Tyron, *Household Manufactures in the United States, 1640-1860* (Chicago, 1917). For quantitative evidence on the value of home production in newly settled areas, see Richard A. Easterlin, George Allen, and Gretchen A. Condran, "Farm and Farm Families in Old and New Areas: The Northern States in 1860," in *Family and Population in Nineteenth Century America*, ed. Tamara Hareven and Maris Vinovskis (Princeton, 1978), pp. 51-52.

7. See Percy Bidwell and John Falconer, *History of Agriculture in the Northern United States, 1620-1860* (Washington, 1925), pp. 158-159; Allan G. Bogue, *From Prairie to Corn Belt: Farming on the Illinois and Iowa Prairies in the Nineteenth Century* (Chicago, 1963), pp. 47-48; and Otto, "The Migration of the Southern Plainfolk," pp. 186-90.

8. See, for example, John Mack Faragher, *Men and Women on the Overland Trail* (New Haven, 1979), pp. 49-56; Joan Jensen, "Cloth, Butter and Boarders: Women's Household Production for the Market," *Review of Radical Political Economics* 12 (Summer 1980): 15-17; and Julie A. Matthaei, *An Economic History of Women in America Women's Work, the Sexual Division of Labor, and the Development of Capitalism* (New York, 1982), esp. Chapters 1-2.

9. Richard Easterlin, "Population Change and Farm Settlement in the Northern United States," *Journal of Economic History* 36 (March 1976): 63-70, explains the integenerational transfer of wealth by the bequest motive of parents. For an alternative view emphasizing the old-age security motive of parents, see Paul A. David and William A. Sundstrom, "Bargains, Bequests, and Births: An Essay on Integenerational Conflict, Reciprocity, and the Demand for Children in Agrarian Societies," Stanford Project on the History of Fertility Control, Working Paper No. 12 (June 1984), esp. Chapters 3 and 5.

10. See Clarence H. Danhof, *Change in Agriculture: The Northern United States, 1820-1870* (Cambridge, 1969), pp. 73-77, 87-94; Harriet Friedmann, "Simple Commodity Production and

Wage Labor in the American Plains," *Journal of Peasant Studies* 6 (October 1978): 78-79; Henretta, "Families and Farms," p. 7; and Donald L. Winter, "Tenancy as an Economic Institution: The Growth and Distribution of Tenancy in Iowa, 1850-1900," *Journal of Economic History* 37 (June 1977): 386-388.

11. For a formal analysis of "safety-first" behavior by yeomen farmers, see Gavin Wright and Howard Kunreuther, "Cotton, Corn and Risk in the Nineteenth Century South," *Journal of Economic History* 35 (Sept. 1975): 528-536.

12. In the case of Northern agriculture in 1860, see Jeremy Atack and Fred Bateman, *To Their Own Soil* (Ames, IA, 1987), pp. 92-97, 244-246.

13. Lewis C. Gray, *History of Agriculture in the Southern United States to 1860* (Clifton, 1973), pp. 442-443.

14. For evidence of these trades, see Merrill, "Cash is Good to Eat," pp. 53, 55-156; Christopher Clark, "Household Economy, Market Exchange and the Rise of Capitalism in the Connecticut Valley, 1800-1860," *Journal of Social History* 13 (Winter 1979): 173-175; Steven Hahn, *The Roots of Southern Populism: Yeoman Farmers and the Transformation of the Georgia Upcountry* (New York, 1985), pp. 95-99; and John T. Schlotterbeck, "The Social Economy of an Upper South Community: Orange and Greene Counties, Virginia, 1815-1860," in *Class, Conflict and Consensus Antebellum Southern Community Studies*, ed. Orville Vernon Burton and Robert C. McMath, Jr. (Westport, 1982), pp. 16-17.

15. Tyron, *Household Manufactures*, Chapter 6; John Mack Faragher, "Open-Country Community: Sugar Creek, Illinois, 1820-1850," in *The Countryside in the Age of Capitalist Transformation: Essays in the Social History of Rural America*, ed. Steven Hahn and Jonathan Prude (Chapel Hill, 1985), pp. 245-247. According to Danhof, *Change in Agriculture*, pp. 182-183, local smiths did not possess the skills needed to produce new, more complex implements and machines.

16. Lewis Atherton, *The Frontier Merchant in Mid-America* (Columbia, 1971): and Ibid., *The Southern Country Store* (New York, 1968).

17. These bonds of mutuality are emphasized by Merle Curti, et al., *The Making of an American Community* (Stanford, 1959), ch. 6; Hahn, *Roots of Southern Populism,* chapter 2; and Parker, "From Northwest to Midwest," pp. 15-16; and James E. Davis, *Frontier America 1800-1840: A Comparative Demographic Analysis of the Settlement Process* (Glendale, 1977), pp. 42-43.

18. According to Alan L. Olmstead, sharing of equipment was common in commercially developed areas; Olmstead, "The Merchanization of Reaping and Mowing in American Agriculture, 1833-1870," *Journal of Economic History* 35 (June 1975): 334-344.

19. Friedmann, "Simple Commodity Production and Wage Labor," pp. 78-79. See also Winter, "Tenancy as an Economic Institution," pp. 386-388.

20. See Steven Hahn, "Hunting, Fishing, Foraging: Common Rights and Class Relations in the Postbellum South," *Radical History Review* 26 (Oct. 1982): 38-43; J. Crawford King, Jr., "The Closing of the Southern Range: An Exploratory Essay," *Journal of Southern History* 48 (Feb. 1982): 53-70; and Robert C. McMath, Jr., "Sandy Land and Hogs in the Timber: (Agri)cultural Origins of the Farmers' Alliance in Texas," in *The Countryside in the Age of Capitalist Transformation: Essays in the Social History of Rural America*, ed. Steven Hahn and Jonathan Prude (Chapel Hill, 1985), pp. 208-211; and Otto, "The Migration of the Southern Plainfold," pp. 185-186.

21. These informal organizations are discussed in Allan G. Bogue, "The Iowa Claim Clubs: Symbol and Substance," *Mississippi Valley Historical Review* 45 (Sept. 1958): 231-253; and Davis, *Frontier America,* p. 158.

22. Jeremy Atack and Fred Bateman, "Egalitarianism, Inequality, and Age: The Rural North in 1860," *Journal of Economic History* 41 (March 1981): 85-93; and Ibid., *To Their Own Soil,* pp. 87-91. See also Lee Soltow, *Men and Wealth in the United States, 1850-1870* (New Haven, 1975), chapter 6; and Faragher, "Open-Country Community," pp. 247-249.

23. For a discussion of this concept, see Karl Marx, *Capital,* vol. I. (New York, 1977), Pt. 8; Eric J. Habsbawm, "Introduction," in Karl Marx, *Pre-Capitalist Economic Formations* (New York, 1974), pp. 9-65; David P. Levine, "The Theory of the Growth of the Capitalist Economy," *Economic Development and Cultural Change* 24 (Oct. 1975): 52-58; and Carol Heim, "External Spheres and the Theory of Capitalist Development," *Social Concept* 3 (Dec. 1986): 8-12, 23-30.

24. As Albert Fishlow emphasizes, investments in railroads were not built ahead of demand, but followed commercial development; *American Railroads and the Transformation of the Antebellum Economy* (Cambridge, 1965), chapter 4. Speculators, however, may have promoted development through their local investments and advertising; see Robert P. Swierenga, *Pioneers and Profits Land Speculation on the Iowa Frontier* (Ames, 1968), Chapter 9; Paul W. Gates, "The Role of the Land Speculator in Western Development," in *Landlords and Tenants on the Prairie Frontier,* ed. Paul W. Gates (Ithaca, 1973), pp. 58-60, 65-70; and John Denis Haeger, *The Investment Frontier: New York Businessmen and the Economic Development of the Old Northwest* (Albany, 1981).

25. These political struggles cannot simply be attributed to external forces, such as the monopoly power of merchants or large landholders. See, for example, the references in note 20 and Robert Mutch, "Yeoman and Merchant in Pre-Industrial America: Eighteenth-Century Massachusetts as a Case Study," *Societas* 7 (Autumn 1977): 291-295. Rather, they were rooted in the incipient class divisions that grew out of the process of private accumulation and social differentiation, and reflected an inherent tension in farm communities. Thus, the growth of the merchant class depended on the deepening involvement of more prosperous farm households in the market system. This point is also made by Clark, "Household Economy," pp. 181-184.

26. See Morton Rothstein, "Antebellum Wheat and Cotton Exports: A Contrast in Marketing Organization and Economic Development," *Agricultural History* 40 (April 1966): 95-98; Roger Ransom, "Interregional Canals and Economic Specialization in the Antebellum United States," *Explorations in Economic History* 5 (Fall 1967): 16-22; and Parker, "From Northwest to Midwest," pp. 24-25. For an alternative view of the impact of canals on regional specialization, see Albert W. Niemi, Jr., "A Further Look at Interregional Canals and Economic Specialization: 1820-1840," *Explorations in Economic History* 7 (Summer 1970): 499-515 and the response by Ransom "A Closer Look at Canals and Western Manufacturing in the Canal Era," *Explorations in Economic History* 8 (Summer 1971): 501-508.

27. Friedmann, "Household Production and the National Economy," pp. 162-163, refers to this process as "commoditisation." The endpoint of this historical development, she argues, was the individual family farm.

28. For a similar interpretation, see Danhof, *Change in Agriculture,* pp. 75-76. For direct evidence of an agricultural ladder, see Curti et al., *The Making of an American Community,* pp. 199-203; Bogue, *From Prairie to Corn Belt,* pp. 56-58; and Donald L. Winter, *Farmers without Farms: Agricultural Tenancy in Nineteenth-Century Iowa* (Westport, 1978), pp. 82-85.

29. A discriminant analysis, explaining the division between the Cotton Belt and Upcountry of Georgia in 1860, correctly classified both counties in the Upcountry at a one percent confidence level.

30. The sample includes 370 households from DeKalb County and 404 households from Floyd County. For a more complete description of the sampling procedure and tests of the representativeness of the sample populations, see David F. Weiman, "Petty Commodity Production in the Cotton South: Upcountry Farmers in the Georgia Cotton Economy 1840 to 1880," Ph.D. dissertation (Stanford University, 1983), Appendix A.

31. Hahn, *Roots of Southern Populism,* p. 21, presents similar occupation distributions in Carroll and Jackson Counties, also in the Georgia Upcountry. For estimates of the occupational distribution in the rural North in 1840, see Davis, *Frontier America,* p. 139; and in 1860, see Atack and Bateman, *To Their Own Soil,* pp. 43-46.

32. Manuscript Census, Georgia, DeKalb, and Floyd Counties, 1860, Schedule I.

33. Unskilled laborers are defined as those household heads who reported their occupation to be "laborer" and who lived in a town or city. Those laborers who lived in rural districts are assumed to be farm workers and are placed in the farming category.

34. The discussion in the following two paragraphs are developed more fully in David F. Weiman, "Slavery, Plantation Settlement and Regional Development in the Antebellum Cotton South," paper presented to the Economic History Association (September 1985), Sections 2 and 3; and Weiman, "Farmers and the Market." For a similar analysis of the South Carolina Upcountry, see Lacy K. Ford, "Yeoman Farmers in the South Carolina Upcountry: Changing Production Patterns in the Late Antebellum Era," 2 *Agricultural History* 60(Fall 1986): pp. 30-33.

35. Manuscript Census, Georgia, DeKalb County, Schedule I; and Georgia, vol. 9, R.G. Dun & Company Collection, Baker Library, Harvard University Graduate School of Business Administration, pp. 127-136.

36. The population of Rome, Georgia in 1860 was 4010; U.S. Census Office, Eighth Census, 1860, vol. 1, *Population of the United States in 1860* (Washington, D.C., 1864), p. 74. The geographical distribution of nonagricultrual producers and the concentration of wealth among merchants were derived from the Manuscript Census, Georgia, 1860, Floyd County, Schedule I. The role of Rome as a regional marketing center for agricultural producers in northwestern Georgia and northeastern Alabama is documented in U.S. Patent Office, *Annual Report* (Washington, D.C., 1856), pp. 191, 238; and Georgia, vol. 12, R.G. Dun & Company Collection, pp. 151-154.

37. Frederick A. Bode and Donald E. Ginter, *Farm Tenancy and The Census in Antebellum Georgia* (Athens, GA: 1986), chapter 2, survey the studies of tenancy in Southern states and systematically formulate the criteria for identifying tenants in the antebellum South. The criteria for identifying tenants in Northern states are presented in winters, *Farmers without Farms*, pp. 12-14; and Atack and Bateman, *To Their Own Soil*, pp. 107-111.

38. See for example, Winter, "Tenancy as an Economic Institution," pp. 382-383; and *Farmers without Farms*, pp. 18-19.

39. Manuscript Census, Georgia, 1860, Floyd County, Schedule II.

40. An analysis of variance rejects the hypothesis that there was no difference in the average age of landowning farmers and tenants (or laborers) at a 5% confidence level.

41. For a discussion of antebellum sharecropping, see Marjorie Mendenhall Applewhite, "Sharecropper and Tenant in the Courts of North Carolina," *North Carolina Historical Review* 31 (April 1954): 134-149; and Joseph D. Reid, Jr., "Antebellum Southern Rental Contracts," *Explorations in Economic History* 13 (January 1976): 69-83.

42. These household heads may not have been formal tenants, but instead recent settlers, who delayed the purchase of land, or even retired farmers.

43. The implied levels and extent of food deficits on these farms should not be interpreted too literally. The calculations assumed extremely generous levels of feed and food requirements and ignored other commonly used and important sources of feed and food on Southern farms, such as fodder, wild forage and garden products. Despite the relatively large output of food crops per capita on tenant farms, these households realized deficits, because they were assumed to pay one-third of their food crops as rents. For a full discussion of the method used to calculate food and feed requirements and marketable surpluses of food crops, see Weiman, "Farmers and the Market," section 2.

44. Weiman, "Farmers and the Market," p. 13 and Table 7. An analysis of variance controlling for the dependency ratio and the ratio of farm capital to labor, shows that tenant and small owner-operators in the two counties sold on average the same share of farm output.

45. Weiman, "Farmers and the Market," especially sections 3 and 4, demonstrates the relationship between the scale of production, wealth and the composition of farm output. It shows that the extent of market production did not increase smoothly with farm size, but depended on the wealth of the operator as well.

46. Atack and Bateman, *To Their Own Soil*, pp. 93-97.

47. An alternative specification, which included the gender of the household head, was estimated, but because there were few single, female household heads in either county, it yielded similar results. The coefficiency of this variable was positive, but statistically insignificant.

48. I am grateful to Richard Sutch (personal correspondence) for suggesting the latter interpretation.

49. According to my crude estimates, 19% of the tenants worked on the farms of nearby relatives, owner-operators with the same last name. Also, of the 27 agricultural laborers in the county, 20 actually lived in their employer's household.

50. Information of farm wages in the 1850s can be found in the Manuscript Census, DeKalb and Floyd Counties, Georgia, 1850 & 1860, Schedule IV.

51. When broken down by age category, approximately the same percentage of household heads in the two counties were born outside of the state except for those heads who were under 40 years of age. In Floyd County only 50% of the household heads in this age category were born in Georgia, while in DeKalb County the figure was 75%. Moreover, in Floyd County 90% of those heads born outside of the state came from South Carolina, North Carolina, and Virginia, while in DeKalb County, almost all came from these states.

LAND AND THE DEVELOPMENT OF MID-NINETEENTH CENTURY AMERICAN AGRICULTURE IN THE NORTHERN STATES

Jeremy Atack and Fred Bateman

NORTHERN AGRICULTURE IN AMERICA ON THE EVE OF THE CIVIL WAR

This paper is a study of the role played by agricultural land in American economic development in the middle of the nineteenth century. By then, the Industrial Revolution was well underway, but most Americans still lived and worked as farmers. Rural existence remained the typical way of life, and farming the predominant economic pursuit. Only in Massachusetts and Rhode Island did urban residents outnumber rural, whereas elsewhere the ratio of rural to urban population was almost two to one.[1] Moreover, the farm stood at the center of the economic system. It was a major source of demand and the principal supplier of inputs to many of the most important developing industries. The nation's largest single employer of labor, agriculture had a work force two and a half times as large as that in manufacturing.[2] Its role in the complex economic and industrial change then unfolding was fundamental.

Farming acted as a strong magnet, drawing people, capital, and natural resources into its productive processes. The land promised economic and personal independence. Relatively free, unfettered access to this resource formed the linchpin of Jeffersonian democracy, enshrined in the Northwest Ordinances and their successor legislation. For those migrants fortunate enough to be able to buy land for a farm, American agriculture held out financial rewards undreamed of by the centuries of peasants, slaves, serfs, and itinerant workers who had preceded them through history performing the backbreaking toil necessary to produce food. In this New World, the dream was for land ownership, self-sustaining independence, and profit. In the United States, farming could at last become a business.

The lure of the American land, however, like Thomas Jefferson's grand vision, was more than purely economic. Agrarianism incorporated a moral dimension as well. The individual and the family were presumed to gain in moral rectitude when living as a farm unit and to lose important values when part of an industrial environment. Farming provided a way of life, a complete arrangement of family and a social organization.[3] Agriculture's dualistic nature as a complex and successful economic activity that simultaneously provided an engine of social organization produced constraints and trade-offs in agriculture that differed from those in other sectors of the economy. While admittedly not all motivations among farmers were strictly economic, our focus in this paper is primarily on that dimension of American farm life.

The interplay between economic and noneconomic considerations can be seen, for example, in farm labor supply conditions. On the family farm, where family members provided most or all of the work force, allocation decisions sometimes appear irrational unless the low opportunity cost of fixed components of the supply, such as children or grandparents, are factored into the analysis. That such components exist is not totally the result of economic decisions, but to a degree, once the noneconomic element is recognized, its influence can often be given an economic dimension. Furthermore, seemingly surplus (i.e., nonproductive) labor could produce farm capital for which the value is not captured by conventional measures. Similarly, the issue of farm profitability does not lend itself completely to conventional microeconomic analysis. Unlike in a manufacturing enterprise, high profit was not necessarily the overriding goal of the nineteenth century farmer because the farm provided economic security—a minimum annual income—unavailable to urban, nonfarm workers. Even commercially-oriented farmers could hope that their economic survival would be guaranteed during years when surplus production was too small to produce a high market rate of return on their investment. Farmers could also live off their capital, much of it the product of their own labor, longer than industrial producers. And those who tilled a family farm apparently placed greater emphasis on potential capital gains than did investors in nonagricultural pursuits.

A SAMPLE OF RURAL HOUSEHOLDS

Our data are taken from a sample of quantitative information originating in the 1860 federal censuses of agriculture and population. This sample, drawn from a pool of 20 northern states, combines data for 102 townships in 16 states scattered across the northern tier of the United States from New Hampshire to Kansas and as far southward as Maryland and Missouri. These data were chosen as representative of this broad and varied area.[4] All the data from the population and agricultural returns in the sampled townships were recorded, matched, and coded. Farms from the agricultural schedules were linked, where possible, to households in the population manuscripts using the name of the farm operator as the key. The sample for each township thus consists of a number of farms matched with the farm operators' households plus the remaining households in the township. It comprises data for 20,661 households, 11,485 of which were matched with the farms that they operated.[5] In these households lived almost 108,000 free inhabitants and 658 slaves.

The population data include information on the age, sex, color, literacy, occupation, and birthplace of each member of the household and the family's wealth in real and personal estate. The agricultural schedules provide data on the value of the farm, its livestock and implements, the number of improved and unimproved acres, the number of head of various livestock, and the crop production in the 1859 crop year.[6] We have a high degree of confidence in these data, which we believe are certainly more accurate than the published census summaries.[7]

MODELING THE ROLE OF LAND

Central to our argument is the progressive westward push of population in response to the availability of cheap western lands. The availability and cost of these lands were a function of public land policy which, by and large, passively accommodated demands for clear title to property beyond current settlement (and even ahead of survey teams) at ever lower prices and in quantities that offered the common man a chance to bypass the speculator's mark-up. The effects of this policy on national income, its composition and the spatial distribution of population may be analyzed quite simply along the lines set down by Robert Fogel and Jack Rutner (see Figure 1).[8] Their analysis shows theoretically what our data show empirically.

Figure 1. The Distributional Effects of Federal Land Policy:
The Fogel-Rutner Model

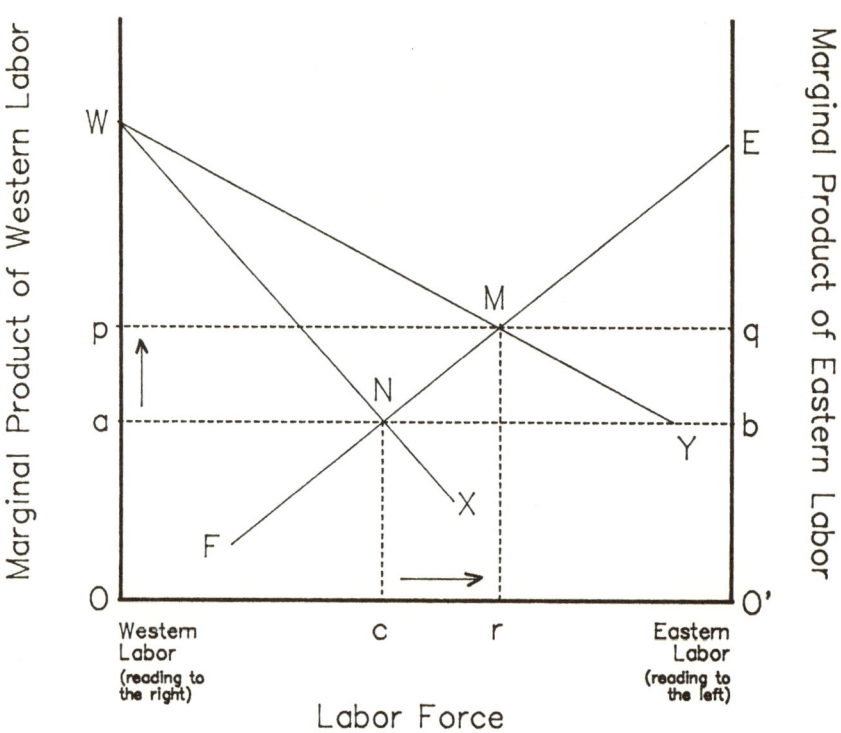

Source: Adapted from Robert W. Fogel and Jack Rutner, "The Efficiency of Federal Land Policy, 1850-1900," in *The Dimension of Quantitative Research in History,* edited by William O. Aydelotte (Princeton, NJ: Princeton University Press, 1972), pp. 390-418.

Land of varying degrees of productivity is located in the intra-frontier "East" and "West." The marginal product of labor is declining. The horizontal axis 00' represents the total available labor supply, and there exists a mapping between the supply of labor and total population. The marginal product of western labor is represented by the line WX and is read against the left axis, the marginal product of eastern labor, EF, is read against the right-hand axis. In the absence of transport costs, the distribution of labor (and population) and national income with its component parts of wages and rents is then determined by the intersection of the two curves at N, where the marginal products of eastern and western labor are equal. Otherwise labor would move from the low wage region to the high wage region. National income is represented by the area 0WNE0' in Figure 1, of which 0ab0' is labor's share with cNb0' going to eastern labor (0'c of labor employed in the East at a wage rate of 0'b) and rental income of aWN for the West and bEN for the East.

Suppose now that the government releases new public lands for settlement. This land lies in the West. If it has the same distribution of fertility as that already settled in the West, then the western marginal product of labor curve, WX, will pivot around W to a new location such as WY.[9] As a result, national income is increased by WNM to 0WME0'. Eastern national income is reduced by cNMr to rME0' of which rMq0' goes to r0' of labor at the prevailing (higher) wage rate, 0'q and MEq accrues to eastern landowners as rents. The eastern loss of income is a transfer to the West associated with the migration of cr of its labor force from eastern to western lands. Wages are increased to $0p = 0'q$.

There is also evidence that suggests that resident population growth and immigration were also influenced by land policy. Western birth rates were higher than in the East. Moreover, immigrants flooded into this country; whether in response to cheap land or high wages is irrelevant as both are a consequence of federal land policy. Interaction between public land policy, and population and labor force growth can be handled within this analysis. Growth of the labor force may be represented simply by the extension of the horizontal axis of Figure 1 which increases national income further. Wages rise by less than in the original case because of the augmented labor supply and the increase in population is divided between East and West. This was most obviously the case with immigrants where the majority stayed in the East. Of the 4.1 million immigrants alive in 1860, 1.4 million resided in just two states: New York and Pennsylvania.[10] There, they may have had the effect of displacing the native-born who in turn moved westward.

THE IMPACT OF LAND POLICY ON WESTERN FARM FORMATION

Theory clearly suggests that federal land policy should have played a role in America's agricultural development in the nineteenth century; this impact upon the structure of western farming is also apparent in the manuscript data. Examination of the size distribution of farms reveals that from Ohio westward disproportionately large numbers of farms consisted of 40, 80, 120, 160, and 200 acres, with the peaks at 40, 80, and 160 acres being the most prominent. These acreages are fractions, 1/16, 1/8, and 1/4, of the Northwest Ordinance land survey section of one square mile (= 640 acres). In the Northeast, by contrast, where settlement predated the Northwest Ordinances, farms were disproportionately concentrated on 50, 100, 150, and 200 acres, units more closely related to the old English county division of Hundreds (see Figure 2).[11]

Figure 2. The Size Distribution of Midwestern and Northeastern Farms, 1860 (Total Acreage, by 10 Acre intervals, centered)

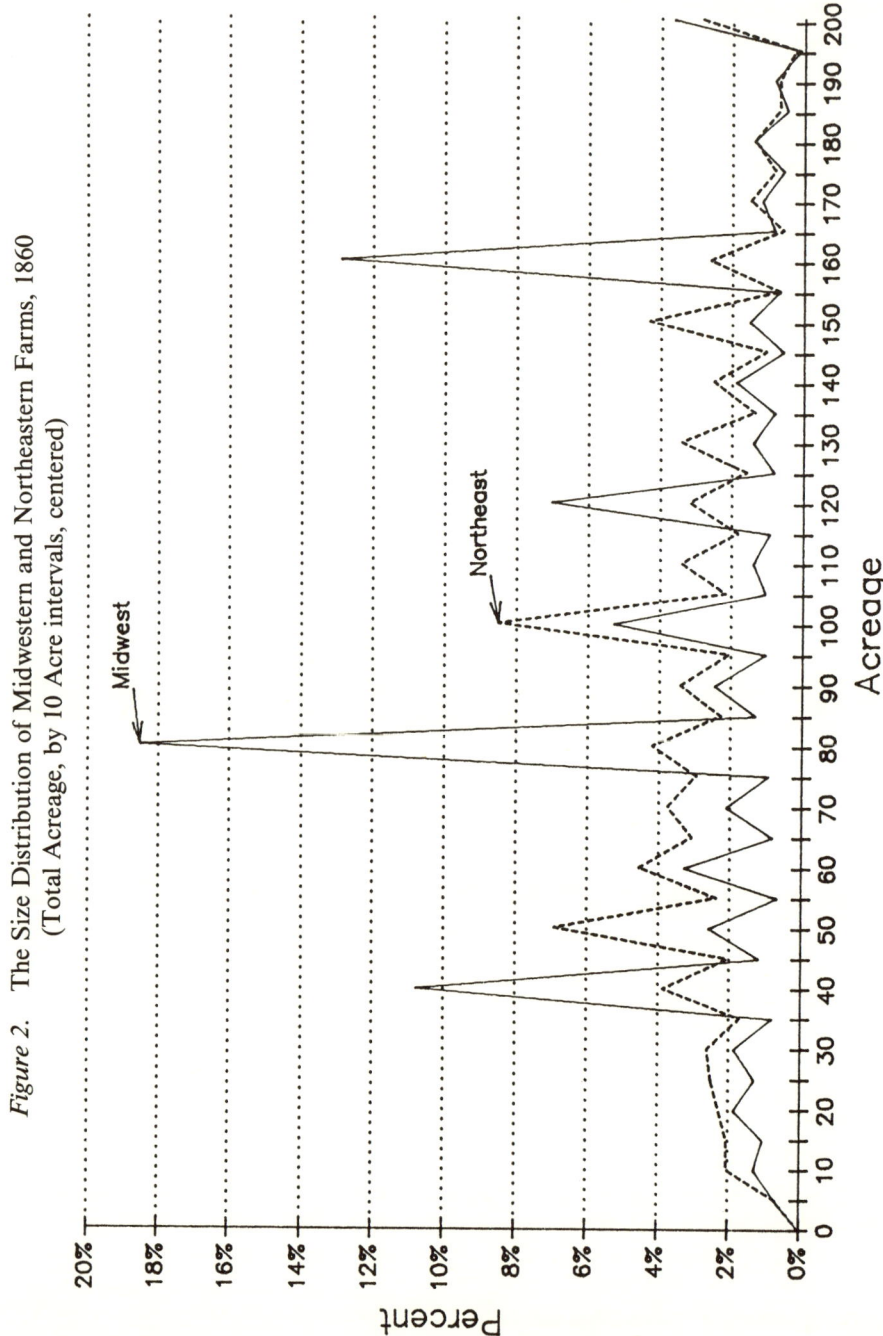

The influence of specific legislative acts is also evident. The Revision Act of 1829 which had set minimum purchase requirements from the federal government at 80 acres (a size which arguably was larger than could be efficiently and fully cultivated using only farm family labor and available technology) had taken effect during the initial settlement of Indiana, Michigan, Illinois, Wisconsin, and Iowa. In each of these states, 80-acre farms were modal in 1859. By the time settlers reached Minnesota and Kansas, preemption was limited to 160 acres and the minimum purchase from the government was set at 40 acres. In both states, 160-acre farms were the most common. Indeed, in Kansas, almost half of the farms were that size in 1859.

EVIDENCE ON WESTWARD MIGRATION

The manuscript census data, by preserving household units, provide superior information on migration patterns. The published census compilations, as well as subsequent researchers, have relied upon Place-of-Birth by State-of-Residence matrices for their findings on migration.[12] This measure is, however, biased against new states of settlement because it reduces the weights of in-migrant decision units (the household) by counting the birthplaces of household members, especially those born in the state of residence after migration.

The sample data on the state of birth of the head of family and the state in which the family was living in 1860 are shown in Table 1. For the Northeast, these data are little different from the published census matrix, except insofar as the sample has proportionately fewer immigrants in the non-urban East where few could afford the entry costs to farming. In the western states, particularly the newer ones, the differences become more substantial because of the exclusion of children born during and after the migration.

Table 1 is arranged so that reading down or across one moves from Northeast to Midwest via contiguous sample states. In this manner not only do the entries show the cultural heritage of the population of each state but they also provide an immediate visual impression of the direction of migration and the distance traveled. The upper diagonal represents a movement to the Midwest; the lower a movement to the Northeast. Along the diagonal, people are still in the states of their birth. These are the "stayers." The further one moves above or below the diagonal the greater the distance a family has moved from the place of birth of the head. Below the table is a reconciliation for the remaining heads of family from other northern states (primarily Massachusetts, although some were from Delaware, Maine, or Rhode Island), southern states (Kentucky, Tennessee, and Virginia being by far the most important sources), or overseas.

Obviously people moved from east to west; the lower diagonal is virtually devoid of entries. Moreover, almost all of the "reverse" migrations took place

Table 1. Nativity and State of Residence of Heads of Family[a], 1860 (percent of all families, reading down)

State/Country of Birth of Heads of Family	Current State of Residence (percent of Heads of Family)														
	NH	VT	CT	NY	NJ	MD	PA	OH	IN	MI	IL	MO	IA	WI	KS	MN
New Hampshire	90	2	1	1	—	—	0	0	0	1	1	0	1	1	2	2
Vermont	3	66	1	4	0	—	0	5	1	3	4	0	2	3	3	4
Connecticut	0	2	85	4	2	—	1	1	0	2	2	1	2	1	2	1
New York	0	3	2	75	8	—	5	4	3	36	11	1	16	21	11	13
New Jersey	0	—	—	1	66	—	2	2	1	1	1	0	1	0	1	—
Maryland	—	1	—	0	0	97	1	9	2	0	1	2	2	0	—	—
Pennsylvania	0	—	—	1	1	—	76	25	8	2	8	2	16	3	10	4
Ohio	—	—	—	0	0	—	0	39	13	3	15	4	23	2	17	5
Indiana	—	—	—	0	—	—	—	0	26	0	4	1	6	1	7	1
Michigan	—	—	—	0	—	—	0	—	0	11	0	—	0	—	1	3
Illinois	—	—	—	—	—	—	—	—	1	—	7	2	1	0	5	1
Missouri	—	—	—	—	—	—	—	—	0	—	0	16	1	0	4	0
Iowa	—	—	—	—	—	—	—	—	0	—	—	—	1	—	0	—
Wisconsin	—	—	—	—	—	—	—	—	—	0	0	—	—	1	—	4
Kansas	—	—	—	—	—	—	—	—	—	—	—	—	—	—	1	0
Minnesota	—	—	—	—	—	—	—	—	—	0	—	—	—	—	—	6
Other Northern States	4	16	1	5	1	—	3	2	1	3	2	0	4	5	4	7
Southern States	0	0	0	0	0	3	1	7	25	1	30	69	12	2	19	3
Total U.S.	98	91	90	91	79	100	89	94	81	63	84	98	85	41	89	55
English-Speaking Foreign	2	8	6	7	14	—	6	5	5	8	11	1	11	36	5	15
Non-English-Speaking Foreign	0	1	4	2	7	—	5	1	14	29	5	1	4	23	6	30
All Foreign	2	9	10	9	21	—	11	6	19	37	16	2	15	59	11	45

Totals (downwards) may not run to 100 due to rounding error.
Zero indicates a move involving less than one-half of one percent of the families.
— indicates no observation of such a move for sample family heads.
[a] All heads of family, including female and other-male headed households.

within New England or the Middle Atlantic states. Thus, for example, 22 of the 791 New Hampshire families in the sample had arrived there from Vermont and 26 had traveled northward from Massachusetts. Some families had returned from the Old Northwest to the Middle Atlantic states, but the number was few and the fraction of the total families very small. No families in the sample made a long distance move from a state west of Indiana to one east of that state. People who relocated to the frontier stayed in the Midwest, although in a few cases they decided that they had gone too far westward originally.

People moved within narrow bands of latitude largely because the majority were farmers who sought to maximize the return on their human and physical capital investments. Although midwestern lands, especially in the first few years of cultivation, were more productive than those in the East, gains could be further increased by farming lands on a similar latitude to that of the migrant's origin. Soils and terrain, for example, were heavily influenced by glaciation, which was latitude dependent. The farmer thus would maximize the value of his human capital (experience) by looking for soils and terrain like those back home. Moving within narrow bands of latitude also maximized the gains from the seed and livestock which the farmer brought with him because of phototropicity (i.e., adaptation to specific hours of sunlight and, therefore, latitude specific).[13]

LAND AND ITS EFFECT ON HUMAN FERTILITY

Investigators have long recognized the existence of substantial East-West fertility differences. Ezra Seaman, for example, in his analysis of the 1840 Census, drew attention to the different proportions of children under 10 to total population in the East and Midwest.[14] In our sample, only one eastern township had a child-woman ratio greater than 1,750 (children under ten per thousand women age 16-44) and in most the ratio was under 1,250. On the other hand, only a few western townships had child-woman ratios that low and many were in excess of 1,750. Not hitherto observed, however, is that eastern and western *nonfarm* fertility rates were approximately of the same orders of magnitude (child-woman ratios on the order of 1,300-1,500) whereas farm fertility rates were radically different, being almost twice as high in the Midwest as in the Northeast (approximately 1,650 versus 950).[15] We attribute this differential to ease of access to land.

Although land declined in relative importance over time, it was the principal form of wealth in most parts of the country in the nineteenth century. Available land represented economic opportunity. Land created employment and with land labor could create capital. Economic opportunity probably influenced the age of marriage and the proportion of women ever married as couples waited upon a "nest egg" before wedding. It would also effect the incentives for married couples to regulate their fertility and influence their choice of completed family size. On a new midwestern farm, work could always be found for family labor; there were fences to build, ditches to dig, and land to clear in addition to the daily routine of farm life. In these circumstances, there were few, if any, incentives to check fertility.

Our data show midwestern women marrying sooner and in greater proportions and having children later into life and with shorter spacing between births than among women in the Northeast. This is consistent with our maintained hypotheses of greater economic opportunity in the Middle West and the absence of strong incentives there to limit fertility. Economic opportunity seems to be the dominant factor in this, because over 40% of the difference in synthetic fertility rates between farm families in the two regions is attributable to the higher proportion of midwestern women who marry, and a quarter of the differential is explained by the earlier age of marriage.

The significance of land availability is borne out in a more elaborate regression model constructed to explain differences in fertility rates between townships.[16] Land availability is measured as the excess demand for land taking into account local available supply and the potential demand from newly formed families. We also included other factors affecting fertility, such as the number of women at risk (the percentage of women age 16-44 who were married with the husband present). A variable was also introduced to measure the percentage of farm units in the township as a proxy for the demand for child labor that had a fairly high value on the farm while simultaneously imposing a relatively low opportunity cost for supervision on mothers in that environment. Wealth was incorporated in the model, although the direction of its effect on fertility is unclear. Because wealth in rural areas was dominated by real estate, it might be expected to have a positive effect on the child-woman ratio through the demand for child labor on farms. Further, if children are considered as consumption rather than as producer goods, more wealth should mean more children. On the other hand, lower fertility is often associated with increasing wealth, the emphasis shifting from quantity to "quality."

Other variables in the model captured cultural background, ethnicity, and religious adherence. For example, we included the percentage of households headed by New Englanders, expecting that migrants from those areas would have lower fertility, as they brought with them the cultural attitudes of an area that had already passed through the demographic transition by 1860 and that had witnessed the effects of population pressure on land. Similarly we included the percentage of foreign-born heads of households as a proxy for the number of families from areas that had not yet undergone demographic transition. We also used a separate variable for the percentage of households headed by Irish persons as proxy for Catholicism in the expectation that this variable would correlate positively with the child-woman ratio. No urbanization or

Table 2. Explaining Inter-Township Variations in the Child-Woman Ratio For All Households and Various Groups, 1 (Standard Error)

Group	Region	Constant	LAND	WEALTH	PCTMAR	PCTNE	PCTIRSH	PCTFORGN	PCTFARM
All Households[a]	Northeast	1027.5* (267.4)	-157.7* (60.9)	-0.05** (0.03)	322.8 (291.6)	-1714.4* (344.0)	-496.3 (460.8)	479.2* (140.4)	656.4* (150.1)
All Households[b]	Midwest	1332.6* (352.3)	-189.1** (105.3)	-0.13* (0.05)	459.9 (465.4)	-363.8* (165.2)	1605.8 (1783.4)	-92.4 (759.2)	2.7 (314.2)
Farm Households[c]	Northeast	1598.4* (254.7)	-135.2 (90.3)	-0.05** (0.03)	231.9 (281.1)	-1740.9* (427.8)	-1348.6* (538.7)	517.5* (198.8)	—
Farm Households[d]	Midwest	1511.0* (360.9)	-317.7* (100.9)	-0.09* (0.02)	329.3 (444.3)	-449.0* (144.4)	4783.1** (2745.6)	-2007.7* (1000.3)	—
Nonfarm Households[e]	Northeast	1111.0* (271.2)	11.8 (68.8)	-0.00 (0.04)	542.9** (319.2)	-303.7 (421.3)	-354.5 (463.4)	334.0* (157.1)	—
Nonfarm Households[f]	Midwest	937.6* (339.8)	-227.3* (93.8)	-0.08 (0.08)	751.5** (406.9)	-93.6 (161.9)	-204.5 (1081.5)	187.8 (678.7)	—
Native Households[g]	Northeast	1474.5* (229.9)	-184.7* (74.1)	-0.07* (0.03)	-181.0 (240.1)	-1122.6* (287.7)	—	—	580.3* (177.9)
Native Households[h]	Midwest	1279.9* (373.5)	-233.0* (87.6)	-0.10* (0.03)	444.4 (478.1)	-364.6* (148.1)	—	—	48.2 (332.0)
Foreign Households[i]	Northeast	951.2* (462.0)	-199.1 (159.4)	-0.00 (0.05)	456.7 (399.5)	—	888.0* (311.0)	—	296.9 (285.5)
Foreign Households[j]	Midwest	563.3* (435.6)	81.0 (139.7)	-0.08 (0.10)	1211.0* (403.7)	—	685.3* (332.2)	—	89.7 (480.2)

[a] $n = 72; R^2 = 0.50; F = 9.13$
[b] $n = 29; R^2 = 0.70; F = 7.13$
[c] $n = 72; R^2 = 0.37; F = 6.25$
[d] $n = 29; R^2 = 0.78; F = 12.81$
[e] $n = 71; R^2 = 0.15; F = 1.83$
[f] $n = 29; R^2 = 0.45; F = 3.05$
[g] $n = 72; R^2 = 0.33; F = 6.64$
[h] $n = 29; R^2 = 0.69; F = 10.10$
[i] $n = 67; R^2 = 0.14; F = 2.00$
[j] $n = 25; R^2 = 0.52; F = 4.07$

* Significant at better than the 0.05 level.
** Significant at the 0.10 level or better.

industrialization variable was introduced in the model because of the rural bias of the sample.

Our model to explain differences in child-woman ratios between the sample townships in the Northeast and Midwest was thus:

CW = f(Land Pressure, Wealth, Percent Married, Percent Farm, Percent New England, Percent Irish and German, Percent Foreign)

and our expectation regarding signs were Land Pressure (−), Wealth (?), Percent Married (+), Percent Farm (+), Percent New England (−), Percent Irish and German (+), and Percent Foreign (+).

The results for farm and nonfarm households and for native- and immigrant-headed households categorized by region are shown in Table 2. The model did not work equally well across all groups. For nonfarm and immigrant-headed households in the Northeast, the regressions failed to explain a significant portion of the variation in fertility between townships and the model also performed relatively poorly in explaining nonfarm fertility in the Midwest. For these groups, however, we would expect it to perform poorly because our model attempts to explain fertility differences in terms of agricultural opportunity. Thus, to the extent that the nonfarm population had free choice regarding their occupational status the failure of the model to conform to their behavior is understandable. Among the foreign-born, relative poverty put farming out of the reach of many.

Land pressure generally had the predicted sign and was usually a significant explanatory variable in the equations. It performed poorly, however, as an explanatory variable among that class for whom it was expected to be the most important determinant of fertility behavior, namely the northeastern farmers. Wealth, whose sign was potentially ambiguous, was found to reduce fertility, significantly so among farm households, suggesting that, other things equal, wealthier communities emphasized "quality" rather than quantity. The fraction of women at risk explained a significant fraction of the fertility rate only among nonfarm households. Among farmers and native-headed households, the fraction of the population drawn from New England significantly reduced fertility. The percentage of foreign-born tended to increase fertility except among midwestern farm families, where it had the opposite effect. The proportion of Irish was important only in explaining fertility among farm households and among the foreign-born and the sign on this variable was sometimes contrary to that expected.

Pairwise comparisons between northeastern and midwestern households in the same group suggests that quite different forces were often at work in the Northeast influencing human fertility from those in the Midwest. This is particularly apparent in the regression for farm households. Land pressure had little explanatory power with respect to northeastern fertility whereas it was the second most important variable explaining that of the Midwest. One reason for this may be that land scarcity in the former region had already forced a change in fertility behavior. And, whereas a greater fraction of Irish reduced northeastern fertility rates, more Irish raised fertility in the Midwest. A greater presence of foreigners had opposite effects in each region.

LAND POLICY IN RELATION TO FARM FORMATION

Public land policy, especially after 1832 when the minimum purchase was reduced to 40 acres at a minimum price of $1.25 per acre, seemed to insure almost universal access to sufficient land to start a family farm in the Midwest. An outlay of $50 was within the reach of 90% of the population. Nevertheless, only 55% of the rural households in the sample availed themselves of the opportunity to operate farms. Among the farmers, land acreage was fairly evenly dispersed (Gini Index of Inequality, $G = 0.41$) and, while real and personal estate were less equally distributed among them, the distribution of wealth among farmers was more even than that among the population as a whole.

One possible explanation for the less equal dispersion of real estate was the barrier to entry posed by the considerable costs involved in farm-making. Although access to the basic resource, land, was relatively unfettered, the initial purchase of land imposed one of the least significant costs in establishing a farm. Clarence Danhof, using contemporary literary accounts, suggested about $1,000 would be needed to establish a fully functional 40-acre farm on the midwestern frontier.[17]

Our estimates based on the census manuscript data are in broad agreement with this figure.[18] In Table 3 we show the sample estimates of the average cost of buying 40-, 80- and 160-acre farms in the midwestern states or on the frontier, as well as the cost of comparable farms in the Northeast, together with the cost of the average number of head of livestock for such a farm and the average value of machinery. For 40-acre farms these costs range from as little as $435 for a farm in Minnesota to $1,549 for the same size holding in Ohio. On the frontier, costs were probably lower, but our sample size for such farms is too small to be reliable. The typical midwestern 40-acre farm, however, cost only half as much as a farm of the same size on the East Coast. The northeastern farmer, selling a 40-acre farm and moving to the Midwest could easily purchase an 80- to 100-acre farm there.

The value of farms in each state, exclusive of implements and livestock, was considerably in excess of $1.25 acre, which suggests that improvements in the way of breaking, fencing and farm buildings had already been made to the land, even on the frontier. These values also contain a premium for proximity to markets.

Table 3. Average Farm and Farm-Making Costs in 1860

State/Region	Number of Farms in Sample	Cash Value of Farm ($)	Farm Cost Components			Total Cost ($)
			Aggregate Value of Implements ($)	Cash Value of Livestock ($)		

State/Region	Number of Farms in Sample	Cash Value of Farm ($)	Aggregate Value of Implements ($)	Cash Value of Livestock ($)	Total Cost ($)
40 Acre Farms					
Illinois	63	756	68	231	1,055
Indiana	302	874	42	216	1,132
Iowa	23	577	34	171	782
Kansas	3	267	37	153	457
Michigan	116	770	47	170	987
Minnesota	13	284	21	130	435
Missouri	52	343	33	215	591
Ohio	23	1,252	50	247	1,549
Wisconsin	29	865	41	108	1,014
Frontier Settlements	3	367	36	253	656
The Midwest	624	786	44	201	1,031
The Northeast	94	1,730	64	256	2,050
80 Acre Farms					
Illinois	152	1,346	101	300	1,747
Indiana	534	1,570	64	293	1,927
Iowa	42	1,093	49	234	1,376
Kansas	29	968	64	319	1,351
Michigan	134	1,296	52	222	1,570
Minnesota	29	556	32	140	728
Missouri	96	739	50	342	1,131
Ohio	48	2,315	71	381	2,767
Wisconsin	53	1,072	60	161	1,293

Frontier Settlements	13	692	26	163	881
The Midwest	1,117	1,384	65	282	1,731
The Northeast	117	2,657	109	377	3,137

160 Acre Farms

Illinois	102	2,691	128	454	3,273
Indiana	242	3,472	110	483	4,065
Iowa	20	2,083	82	303	2,468
Kansas	147	1,686	89	357	2,132
Michigan	37	2,804	95	409	3,308
Minnesota	97	765	46	156	967
Missouri	71	1,461	71	508	2,040
Ohio	28	4,561	99	508	5,168
Wisconsin	34	1,523	81	294	1,898
Frontier Settlements	52	893	52	303	1,248
The Midwest	778	2,398	94	401	2,893
The Northeast	77	3,906	155	593	4,654

The census sample livestock values compare favorably with those given by contempories as desirable levels for the would-be farmer. The midwestern 40-acre farm had at least two draft animals, usually horses. Farms in Iowa, Michigan, Minnesota and Wisconsin fell below that level, but as each had at least one beast of burden, presumably the horse power deficiency for heavy jobs, such as breaking or ploughing, could be made up by cooperative arrangements. In Kansas, Minnesota and Wisconsin most of the power was supplied by oxen, which were often deemed preferable to horses for the new farmer because they were more suited for the heavy job of breaking, subsisted better than horses without supplementary feed and were much cheaper to purchase.[19] In addition, each 40-acre farm included at least one milk cow and some beef cattle and each had a breeding stock of pigs.

The census data do not take account of all the costs included in Danhof's $1,000 figure. Missing are estimates of the cost of provisions for the period before the first crops could be raised (set at $100),[20] estimated at as much as $1-2 per acre or about $25-50 for the average 40-acre midwestern farm.[21] Additionally, an allowance might have to be made for the hire of harvest labor.[22] Neglecting the latter unspecified cost, the average 40-acre farm in the Midwest probably cost about $1,200, but some substantial economies, of about one-third, could be realized by moving to the frontier, substituting oxen for horses, a cart for a wagon, improving fewer acres in the early years and so on. For an 80-acre farm, the cost was likely to have been in excess of $2,000; for a 160-acre holding, in excess of $3,000. These costs compare favorably with those quoted by Danhof. They are higher than estimated by Robert Ankli.[23] But whereas Danhof's estimates expressed the amount that it was desirable for settlers to possess, ours reveal the average amount they actually had.

THE DISTRIBUTION OF WEALTH IN A JEFFERSONIAN DEMOCRACY

With these levels of expenditure it is little wonder that farmers were near the top end of the wealth distribution. Only those with median wealth levels or higher could afford these entry costs. The most important factor, however, accounting for wealth was age. There is strong evidence of a life cycle in wealth accumulation within the data.[24] Wealth increased and became more equally distributed as age increased.[25] Association of higher wealth with age reflects the long term effects of production above family consumption levels; the increasing equality probably reflects an evening out over time of random events, most notably inheritance.

Age was not the only factor accounting for differences in wealth. Race, nativity, literacy, sex, and occupational status contributed to rank in the wealth distribution. To establish the individual importance of these in determining the level of family wealth and to measure their relative importance, we ran a regression estimate of the form:

Family Wealth = g(Age, Age², Race, Sex, Literacy, Occupation, Birth) for each state and subregion as well as for the entire sample. The variables, Race, Sex, Literacy, Occupation and Birth were all 0-1 dummy variables where:

    Race   = 1, if white
                      0, otherwise
    Sex   = 1, if male
                      0, if female
    Literacy   = 1, if literate
                      0, otherwise
    Occupation = 1, if farmer
                      0, otherwise
    and Birth   = 1, if native born
                      0, otherwise.

The variables are represented by the abbreviations: *AGE, AGESQ, RACE, SEX, LIT, OCC,* and *BIRTH*. In some states, the variance of these characterisitics was so low that the variable was not entered in the regression equation.

The raw regression coefficients from these estimates have an immediate and appealing interpretation. They represent the dollar increments (or decrements) to family wealth for each of the social and demographic attributes. The complete results, together with an indication of their statistical significance and the level of family wealth estimated with each of these attributes set at their mean values, are given in Table 4.

Only one of the regressions, that for Vermont, failed to explain a significant amount of the variation in wealth from family to family on the basis of the six social and demographic characteristics that we have identified. In general the coefficient of *AGE* was significantly positive whereas the coefficient of age squared (*AGESQ*), was significantly negative. Thus wealth increases with age, reaching a maximum at age [$AGE/2(AGESQ)$] and declines thereafter. The coefficient of *RACE* was either not significantly different from zero or was significantly positive in six cases. In particular in both regions and in the entire rural North, there is strong evidence of discrimination in the distribution of wealth based on race, such that nonwhite families, either Indian or black, had an average of $1,586 less wealth than a demographically and socially identical white family. This clearly does not tell the full tale of discrimination since the probability that the head of a nonwhite family was either literate or a farmer, or both, was also much smaller than for white families. In fact, the only discrimination with which blacks did not have to contend was that against the foreign-born.

Table 4. The Change in Family Wealth in Response to Social and Demographic Attributes

State	Constant	AGE	AGESQ	RACE	SEX	LIT	OCC	BIRTH	Wealth Level at the Mean Attribute Values
Illinois	-9149.57*	246.68*	-1.98*	1470.28	1067.38	1196.35*	1312.34*	909.81*	26638.33
Indiana	-8612.67*	264.27	-2.27	1141.35	330.18	1158.56*	1255.61*	1185.92*	2388.36
Iowa	-5779.55*	208.24*	-1.74*	—	802.13	1063.92*	597.43*	567.50*	2025.37
Kansas	-4463.52*	154.88*	-1.47*	—	1457.27*	700.17	-163.60	913.09*	1817.57
Michigan	-4385.06*	102.70*	-0.78*	1247.49*	717.78*	610.01*	236.62*	807.22*	1422.45
Minnesota	-6208.26*	220.53*	-2.28**	1236.77**	697.09	702.06	-603.61	1038.27*	1071.66
Missouri	-3015.07*	134.80*	-.037	—	-109.46	1664.71*	1258.62*	-1055.15	2902.38
Ohio	-6567.89*	241.39*	-1.95*	—	169.94	449.32	2426.97*	1136.24*	3032.11
Wisconsin	-6330.59*	267.06*	-2.43*	—	385.34	268.63	—	1395.71*	1803.89
Midwest	-7951.82	213.87*	-1.69*	1578.84*	474.00*	1046.24*	985.58*	1228.46*	2274.23
Connecticut	-3730.79	288.89	-2.91**	221.29	-3409.12*	-2034.31	2098.79*	2198.65	2810.95
Maryland	-2522.51	109.75	-0.86	960.16	-1377.78**	718.15	1980.71*	—	1484.24
New Hampshire	-3681.95*	134.38*	-1.14*	—	528.24	-210.00	719.87*	1433.76*	1965.24
New Jersey	-14565.00*	449.24*	-3.73*	2796.91	879.02	1453.36	2235.61**	1232.12	4037.24
New York	-9580.33*	253.16*	-2.14*	1439.91	752.25*	1132.75*	3011.93*	1519.18*	3284.84
Pennsylvania	-8520.56*	182.25*	-1.29*	2303.07**	683.09**	1251.49*	1431.50*	1465.93*	2762.56
Vermont	-4841.52	187.17	-2.03	—	1027.92	175.27	2309.63**	1529.11	3018.63
Northeast	-8000.78*	220.54*	-1.81*	1623.11*	318.18	1025.04*	2144.69*	1222.16*	2916.15
The Rural North	-8350.68*	220.59*	-1.75*	1585.61*	448.42*	1134.18*	1388.97*	1355.06*	2538.36

* Significantly different from zero at better than the five percent level.
** Significantly different form zero at better than the ten percent level.

The coefficient of *SEX* was significantly negative in both Connecticut and Maryland, a result at variance with the general trend because it implies that female-headed households were wealthier than comparable male-headed households. The general pattern, however, may reflect bias by the nineteenth century census enumerator in most states in presuming an adult male to be head of household whenever one was present.

For the rural North as a whole and in general, the evidence points to significant discrimination against female-headed households, a trend reinforced by the lower probability that women were also farmers. The coefficients of *LIT, OCC,* and *BIRTH* were either not significantly different from zero or were significantly positive and generally were of comparable magnitudes. These results imply discrimination against the foreign-born and in favor of the farmer and the educated.

Although Thomas Jefferson's dreams of equality were not fulfilled perfectly, compared with more recent periods, and with other regions during the same period, wealth indeed was more evenly distributed among the population of the rural townships of 1860, except in the slave-holding township of Costin District in Worcester County, Maryland. Overall, in the North, the richest 1% of the population owned only about 12% of the wealth, which is about half as much as that wealthholding group has held in the United Staes as a whole since the end of World War II.[26]

The distributions of wealth in each of the states west of the eastern continental divide were quite similar, with the Midwest slightly more egalitarian than the Northeast. Except in Minnesota, the Gini index lay in a narrow range from .58 (in Michigan) to .62 (in Missouri), with the richest 5% of the populations holding between 26 and 32% of the total wealth. The range of distributions among the Eastern Seaboard states exceeded that among the states lying westward, the dispersion being most unequal in Maryland where the wealthiest 1% of the population owned more than one-third of the total wealth. Wealth in Worcester County, Maryland, less evenly distributed than in the rest of Maryland, approached the level of concentration estimated for Baltimore by Robert Gallman.[27] Even excluding Maryland because of its slave-status, the distributions for the eastern states ranged from New Hampshire's 0.54 Gini coefficient, which was more egalitarian than that for any of the sample western states, to New Jersey's 0.68, which was at least as concentrated as the most concentrated of the western states.[28]

The Gini coefficient for Maryland, equal to that estimated by Lee Soltow for the South as a whole, indicates an extreme inequality in the distribution of wealth by mid-nineteenth-century northern American standards, although this distribution of wealth differs little from that for the U.S. during the 1920s or for Australia in 1915.[29] In Costin District of Maryland's Worcester County, the richest 10% of households owned more than three-quarters of the total wealth, while the poorest 40% held no wealth whatsoever. This area nevertheless represented the exception to a general wealth equality throughout the rural North in 1860 relative to other areas and times.

SELF-SUFFICIENCY AND THE FAMILY FARM

Another aspect of Jefferson's agricultural ideal was realized. The farmer with 40 acres was self-sufficient and indeed may have produced a small surplus for sale in the market. Three-quarters of the midwestern farms of 40-60 acres produced a dairy surplus, more than half had meat surpluses, and two-thirds had grain surpluses, so that overall fewer than one-third of the farms produced less food than they consumed. Further, about 90% of them could have had positive cash flows from the sale of their crops after allowing for all consumption needs, human and livestock, and seed retained for the next year's planting.[30]

The census reported farm gross production for the year ending June 1, 1860 (i.e., for the 1859 crop year). Some crops and products were, however, neglected such as wood products, poultry, and the sale of surplus livestock. We have made no effort to account for these omitted variables here. From gross production figures, seed allowances were deducted, and the resulting net production figures valued at farm gate prices.[31]

The average marketable surplus among the sample of northern farms was valued at $360, about 70% more than Marvin McInnis found for Canada West farms at about the same time.[32] Like his estimate, this constitutes about 55% of gross production, net of seed allowances, despite the differences in our assumptions. Our estimate includes some items, such as market garden produce and orchard products, not included by McInnis, but excludes some items, such as the value of surplus livestock, that he includes. The surplus being larger in the Northeast than in the Midwest offers one justification for the comparatively higher land prices in the former region. Northeastern farms realized a marketable surplus of $451, those in the Midwest earned $307.

The highest-valued surpluses were in Illinois, New Jersey, New York, and eastern Pennsylvania, where surpluses often exceeded $750 per farm. Surpluses on the northern and western boundaries were typically lower than those elsewhere. Farms in only three townships (in northeastern Michigan, southwestern Minnesota, and southern Missouri) had an average, a deficit that would have required additional sources of income for farm families in order to feed the livestock and put sufficient food on the table. These were all located on the margin of settlement. On the other hand, farms in the Minnesota townships from Polk and Mahnomen counties stood out as exceptions to this generalization. They produced surpluses with cash values of $1,111 and $886 respectively, which were generated by surpluses of both food and nonfood items.

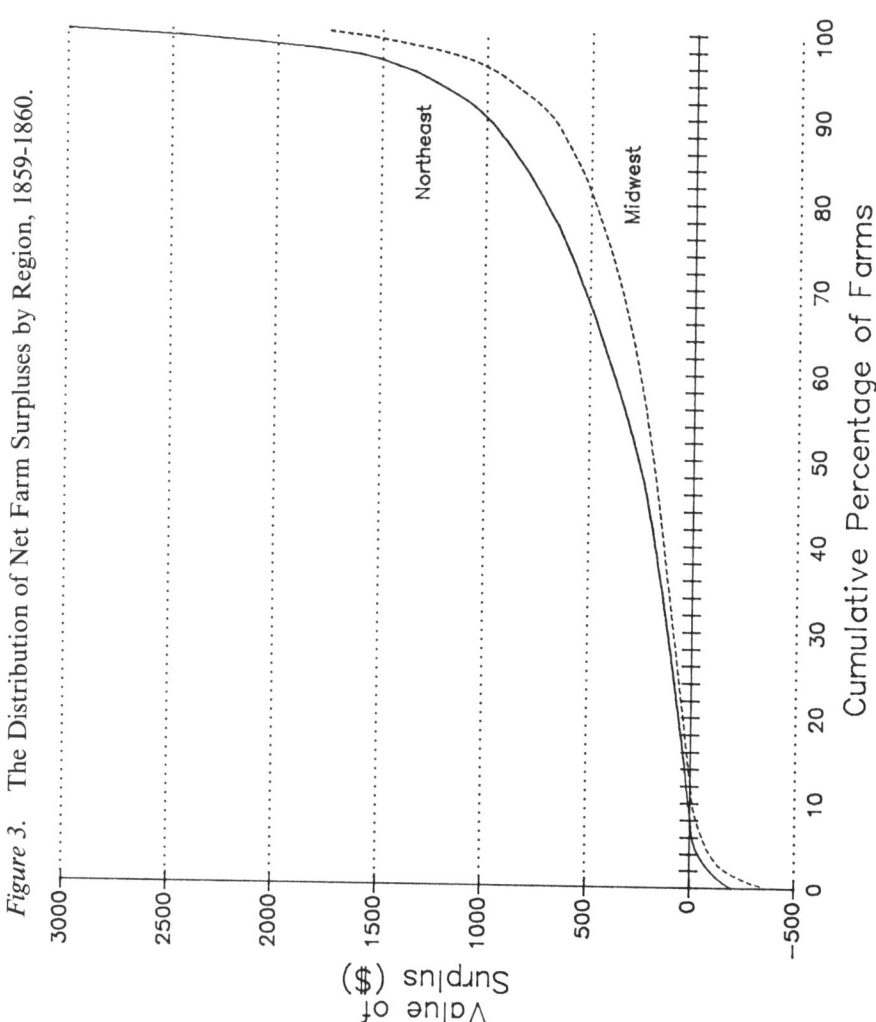

Figure 3. The Distribution of Net Farm Surpluses by Region, 1859-1860.

Table 5. The Value of the Net Marketble Surplus at the Farm Gate, 1859

Location[1]	Average Net Surplus ($)	Average Surplus by Size of Farm (acres)				Percent with Deficits
		30-40	60-80	120-160	160-320	
New England[a]	370	144	267	451	558	4
Middle Atlantic[b]	485	239	405	621	860	8
Northeast[c]	451	222	365	551	765	8
Old Northwest[d]	331	143	228	445	544	9
Recent Settlement[e]	315	134	217	290	434	7
Midwest[f]	307	136	215	379	459	12
Slave States[g]	138	-2	70	178	195	33
With good transport	392	177	275	491	609	9
With poor transport	276	97	208	337	448	14
The Entire Sample	360	156	257	438	566	10

[a] New England: Connecticut, New Hampshire and Vermont
[b] Middle Atlantic: New Jersey, New York and Pennsylvania
[c] Includes Maryland
[d] Old Northwest: Illinois, Indiana, Ohio plus southern Michigan and Wisconsin
[e] Recent Settlement: Iowa, Kansas, Minnesota, plus northern Michigan, northern Wisconsin and the non-slave townships in Missouri
[f] Includes Missouri
[g] Slave: Maryland and the slave-owning townships in Missouri

Regional differences in the distribution of average surpluses among farms are indicated in Figure 3. About 8% of farms in the Northeast had negative net surpluses; in the Midwest about 12% were in that position. The median surplus in the Northeast ($305) was about 50% greater than that in the Midwest ($200). These are neither particularly large nor impressive surpluses, and the low slope of the net farm surplus lines in the graph indicate generally similar conditions on most farms. At least 75% had net surpluses valued at less than $500. In both regions, however, a small fraction of farms produced substantial surpluses. Ten percent in the Northeast earned in excess of $1,000 above and beyond the consumption needs of the livestock and farm family. Only 4.4% of midwestern farms, however, boasted a surplus that large.

Subdivision of the regions into New England, the Middle Atlantic, the Old Northwest, states of recent settlement (Iowa, Kansas, Minnesota, and the northernmost townships in Michigan and Wisconsin), and the two slave states points to some interesting differences and surprising similiarities as the results in Table 5 show. The average surplus was greatest by a considerable margin in the Middle Atlantic states and very low in the slave-owning regions. Surpluses in New England and in the two subregions of the Midwest were of comparable orders of magnitude. The distribution was virtually identical among farms in the Old Northwest and in the areas of recent settlement, except that the top 5% in the Old Northwest had somewhat higher values for their net surpluses. Surprisingly, New England farms were the least likely of all to have a net deficit. By size of farm, net surpluses in New England and the Old Northwest were also very similar but only about two-thirds of the levels realized from farms in the Middle Atlantic states. Surpluses in the slave-owning areas were half, or less, of those in the non-slave townships.

There were also important differences in the value of the marketable surplus depending upon whether a township was served by water or rail transportation or was forced to depend on wagon transportation. Surpluses, where cheap transportation was available were larger, averaging $392 per farm, than those produced by farmers in townships dependent on wagon haulage, which averaged only $276. The most pronounced differences were between the very small or the very large farms. Those with easy, inexpensive access to markets earned twice as much as comparably sized farms without that advantage.

LABOR AND MECHANIZATION ON THE FAMILY FARM

Taking actions to increase land or livestock yields offered one avenue toward the goal of creating "surplus" production for commercial markets. Enlarging output per acre, whereas important for agricultural advance, was not, however, the most obvious solution for farmers' decision problems at mid-century. First, land was not the resource on which most farmers, especially those in the western states, needed most to economize. Second, once cultivators reaped the initial gains in land yields from clearing and settlement, additional advances became difficult given the technological possibilities of the day. The great improvement in yields, in fact, lay almost a century into the future when chemical fertilizers, hybrid seeds, irrigation, and various scientific developments, often made under Department of Agriculture auspices, became available to farm operators. Technological devices designed to raise labor productivity were, however, becoming available during the nineteenth century. Mechanical rather than chemical or biological, these improvements operated primarily through their effect on the usage of labor.

When available, hired hands were scarce and high priced. Farmers depending on casual wage labor lived in constant fear that the labor might not be available when needed at any price that justified its hire. Farm workers were especially scarce in rural areas where population densities were low and where more attractive job opportunities might be available. There was widespread concensus that "manual labor ... [of an] agricultural character, when followed as a necessary means of obtaining a livelihood, is considered by some as a degrading employment throughout our land."[33] A partial solution to the problem was to create a large farm family that provided a pool of captive labor "bound to the entrepreneur by ties of custom, law, fear, and affection" available at an implicit wage below that for hired labor.[34] The wage was lower not simply because of the element of exploitation and the receipt of non-wage benefits but also because the farmer could trade on the discounted present value of the potential inheritance to heirs. As a consequence, the family farm tended to employ more labor and operate at a greater scale for the same costs than a farm which relied on hired workers.

Although the family farm may have used more labor and land than would have been the case if it had paid market wages to its employees, there was still an incentive to mechanize if only for the farm operative to save on his own labor. Mechanization further opened a way to farm the land that had been overbought. As a result, American agriculture tended to operate at the extensive rather than the intensive margin. Land yields were low despite favorable conditions. We have made estimates of yields that, although potentially biased and inconsistent because of the estimation technique that we were forced to use, appear to be both internally consistent and in broad agreement with the published census data.[35] These are lower than those in contemporary sources that are known or suspected to have an upward bias. Our lower yield estimates have the effect of raising William Parker and Judith Klein's estimates of labor productivity growth during the latter half of the century.[36] They also imply greater acreages devoted to grain crops, biasing our figures toward greater reaper use.[37] Nevertheless, few farms outside of Illinois and Wisconsin could have justified ownership of a reaper on the basis of their 1859 wheat acreage. Including all small grain acreage increased the number of farms that were potential purchasers of reapers, but, even so, fewer than a fifth of Illinois and New Hampshire farms exceeded the threshold on this criteria, and less than a quarter of Vermont and Wisconsin farms did so. Dramatic increases in the fraction of farms able to use mechanical harvesters occurred only when their use as mowers was also taken into account, yet the vast majority of farms in most states were still too small to have considered sole ownership of a reaper-mower.

If reaper use had been confined to wheat, perhaps 45,000 farmers would have found sole ownership profitable (making allowance for reaper use in the South and in the excluded northern states, Massachusetts, Rhode Island, and Delaware). Including all small grains, perhaps 100,000 reapers should have been in use in 1859, an estimate not too different from what we could deduce from the contemporary literature.[38]

PROFITABILITY AND AGRICULTURAL EXPANSION

The rapid expansion of the area under cultivation caused by sale of the public land drove down rents. We cannot measure the impact of this at the margin,

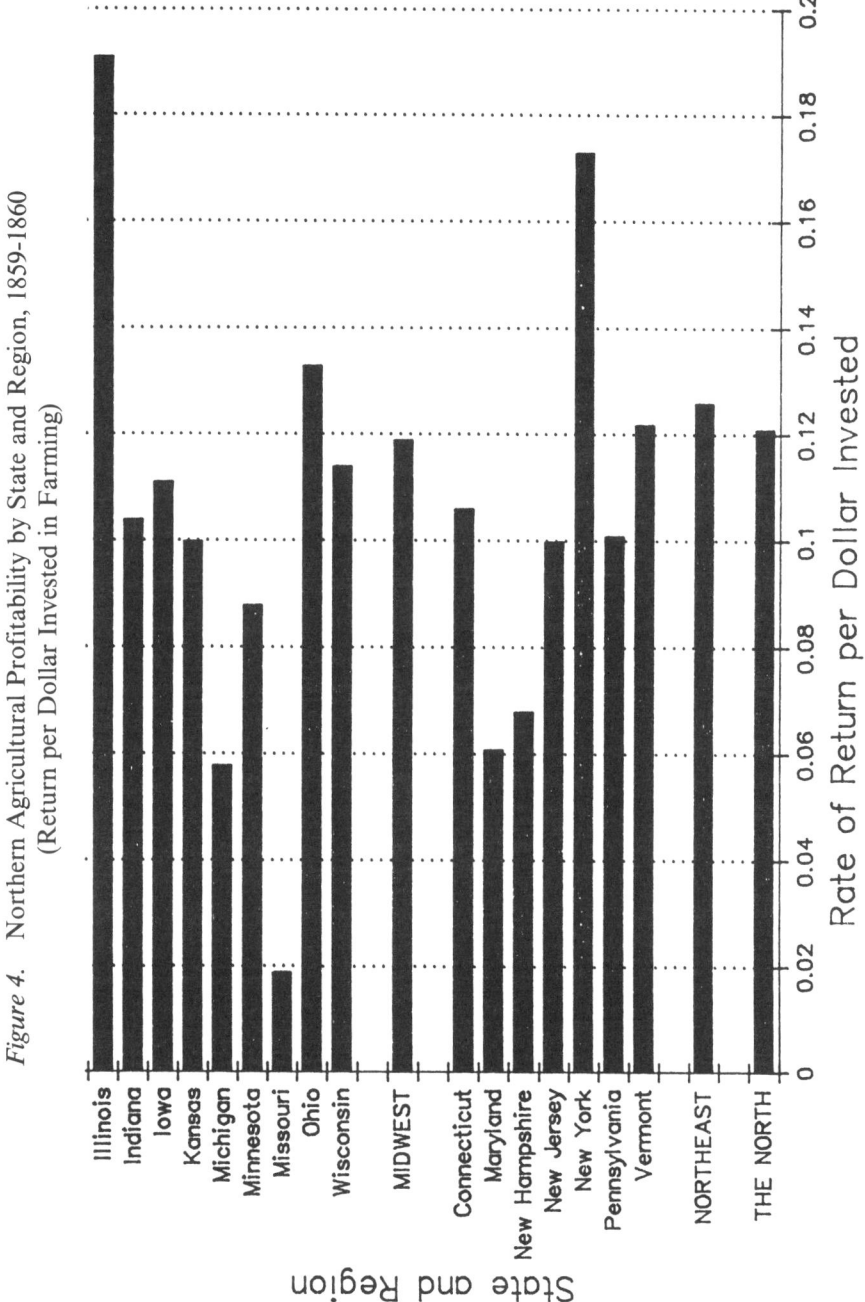

Figure 4. Northern Agricultural Profitability by State and Region, 1859-1860 (Return per Dollar Invested in Farming)

but the effect is discernible in the average noncapitalized rents—farm profits. Our estimate of the average return per dollar invested in northern agriculture, 12% (Figure 4), is quite low relative to that available in such alternative fields as manufacturing or transportation. It is, however, quite close to that being earned by southern farmers at this time and to the traditionally assumed competitive rate.[39] In the two sample slave areas the rate of return was lower.

Although the estimate of the earned rate of return at the regional level is not out of line with expectations, those for the two subregions appear to be at variance with the traditional historical literature. The westward movement of northern agriculture, for example, frequently has been explained in terms of changing relative profit opportunities. Yet our figures indicate a marginally higher return in the Northeast than in the Midwest. This is consistent with the impact of public land policy which would have eroded any scarcity value to midwestern land as a whole. Despite this, however, the rate of return per dollar invested on the Kansas and Minnesota frontier (which might be thought of as the marginal midwestern investments) of between 8.8% and 10% is virtually identical to the rate being earned on bonds at the time.[40] We have no comparable "frontier" figure for the Northeast. Since during the initial investment period in pioneer farming, as in other economic activities, earned profits were more than adequate to stimulate westward migration and interest in western land opportunities.

At the state level, the highest rates of return were being earned by Illinois and New York farmers. Because it accounts for more than one-third of the region's agriculture, New York's high return is in large part responsible for the high rate of profit in the Northeast. And the modest profit rates in Maryland and New Hampshire exert less effect on the northeastern regional average than the lower returns in Michigan and Missouri do on the Midwest. Within regions, the ordinal rankings among states are consistent with historical evidence. Agriculture was most profitable in Illinois and New York; least so in Michigan and New Hampshire.

There is a fairly smooth and plausible gradation of profit rates from east to west and north to south in our data at the township level. The highest profit rates were to be found in a band perhaps 200 miles wide through northern New York State, southern Michigan and northern Indiana, and the northern half of Illinois through into Iowa with peaks in north-central New York and western Illinois. Rates of profit on the northern fringes of the United States, in Michigan, Wisconsin and Minnesota, were negative. They were also negative on the southern edges of the westward expansion.

The rates of return which we discuss above represent the average return per dollar invested in agriculture in a randomly selected township. Farmers, however, invested in farms not in farming. Their return depended critically on the size farm they could afford to buy or rent. Similarly, average farm rate of profit by state or region depends heavily on the size distribution of farms.

Land and the Development of American Agriculture in the Northern States 305

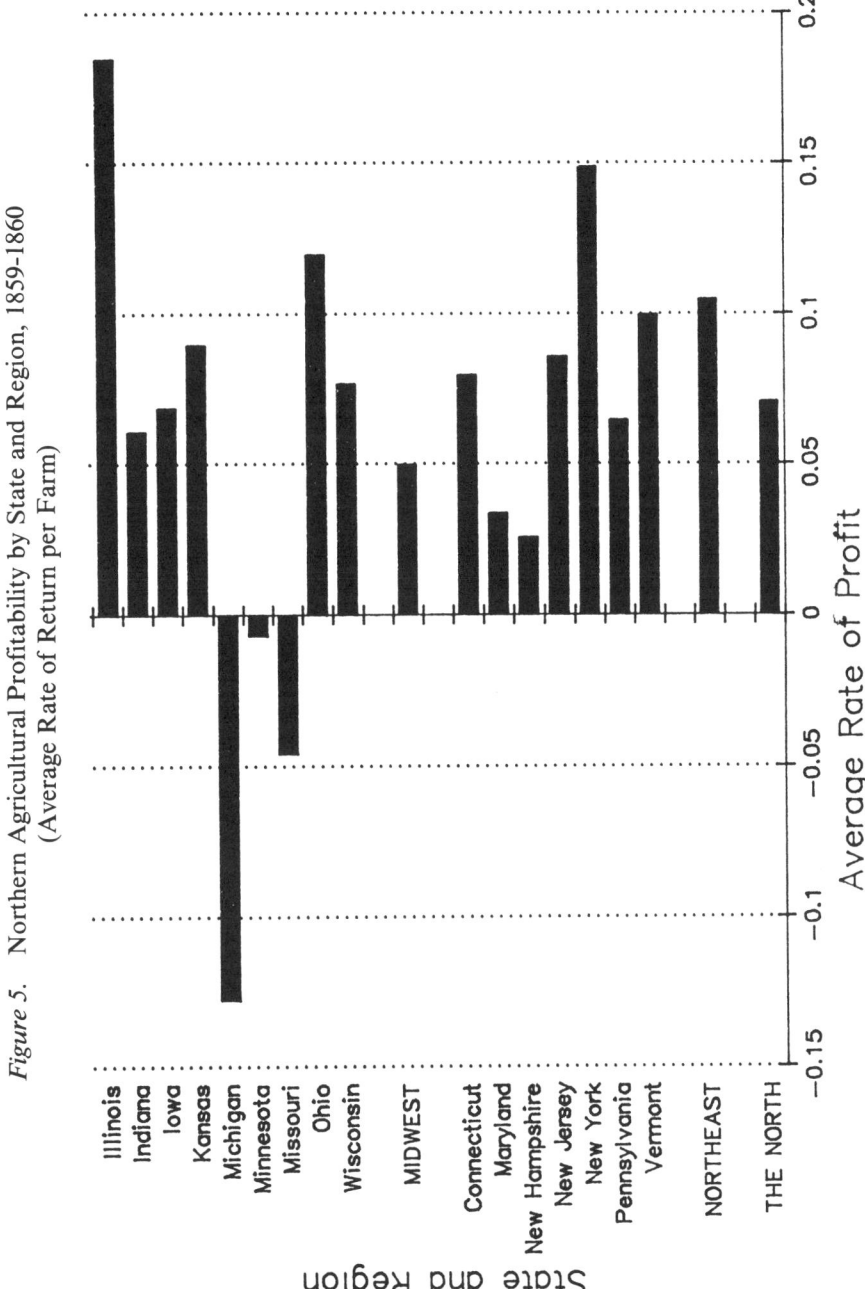

Figure 5. Northern Agricultural Profitability by State and Region, 1859-1860 (Average Rate of Return per Farm)

Big farms were more profitable per dollar invested than small. This finding is the corrollary of our analysis on self-sufficiency which demonstrated that 43% of farms under 40 acres could not feed to the livestock and the farm population the recommended diet, whereas only 19% of those with more than 80 acres fell short of the standard.

The average rate of return per farm in many states averaged about 6% (Figure 5), although it ranged from as much as 17.9% in Illinois to -11.9% in Michigan. In some states, such as Minnesota, Missouri, and New Hampshire, the mean rate of return was very low, but positive, and a farmer must have viewed starting farming there or in Michigan as a very dubious proposition.

Even in the states where they earned low returns, however, farmers who could afford a larger spread could still receive satisfactory rates of return equal to or greater than those offered by, say, bonds. And, moreover, they could live off their capital and invest time and energy in capital improvements that, sooner or later, would be rewarded either through higher productivity or enhanced land values. Thus, even in Michigan where the average "loss" for a farm under 40 acres was 21.3%, the farmer who could afford to buy a farm of 160 acres or larger could expect an average return of 12.5%.

Small midwestern farms were much less profitable than comparably sized northeastern ones (Figure 6), probably reflecting regional differences in agriculture. In the Midwest, the principal cash crop was wheat which was best grown extensively. For the Northeast, truck crops for urban markets and dairy products were important income sources. These activities could be conducted on a much smaller scale than grain farming. The most remarkable feature about Figure 4, however, is the marked relationship between farm size and profitability in each region. Neither was this finding the artifact of a particular state. A systematic relationship between rate of return and scale existed in farming in every state covered in our sample. Notice in particular that a 40-acre family farm was barely, if at all, profitable. To be secure a northeastern farmer probably had to have about 60 acres, while a midwesterner should have had 80 acres or more. In each region, both the modal and median farm size exceeded these levels.

Northern agriculture is less attractive if the basis for our profit estimates is adjusted to one comparable with that used in other sectoral studies by excluding capital gains. By this measure, eastern producers were earning a current rate virtually identical, 10.8%, to that of southern cotton growers. Western farmers, however, were not doing so well, getting only a 5.2 percentage return. This suggests the importance that farmers, particularly those already in the western region or considering migration there, attached to the future, to prospects for realizing capital gains on their land. This has been a commonly expressed opinion among historians. Paul Gates, for example, claimed that, "The pioneer farmer was well aware that in the end his profits would come largely from rising land values."[41] By the 1850s and 1860s, Gates observed,

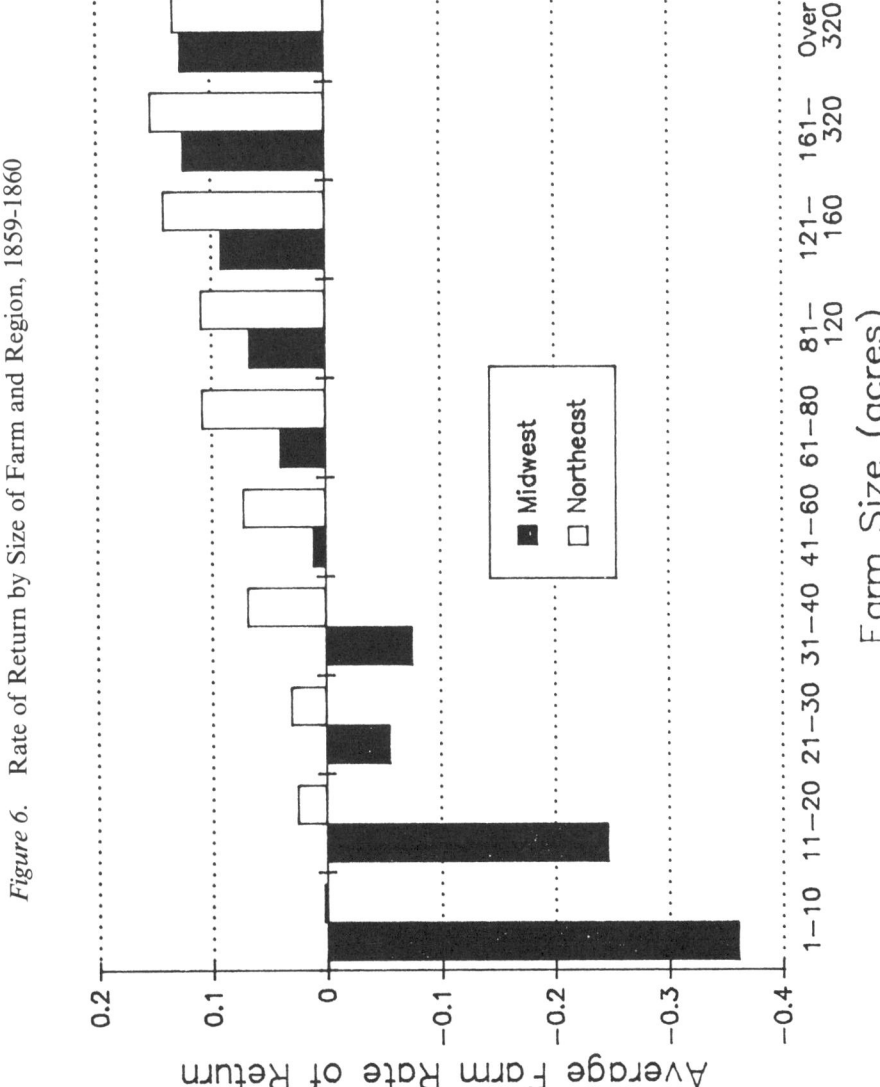

Figure 6. Rate of Return by Size of Farm and Region, 1859–1860

this source of return had diminished considerably in the Northeast, but was still important in the newer western states, an observation clearly substantiated in our analysis of the contributions of each profit component. It is also reflected in land value data. Between 1850 and 1860, the cash value per acre of farmland in the eastern states grew an average of 2.8%, whereas in the West it rose 7.3%.

Still, from the perspective of the national economy, the question remains why agricultural investors in the North and South would be satisfied to earn a relatively low rate of return when a considerably higher one was available in manufacturing, an activity open to even a small investor. Farming represented more than a purely market investment, and presumably most individual western farmers at this time were still able to feed, shelter and clothe their families despite their rather meager return on investment. Nevertheless, even during the postbellum era, when satisfaction with mere survival would seem to have been disturbed by the presence of growing prosperity in the industrial sector, this behavior continued. "Perhaps no development of the nineteenth century," said Theodore Saloutos, "brought greater disappointment to the American farmers than did their failure to realize the prosperity that they had expected from industrialism."[42] Continued Saloutos, "Even before the wholesale transition from a subsistence to a commercialized status, the evidence was rather strong that the financial rewards of farming would be small.[43]

Although low, our estimates for rate of return excluding capital gains are clearly in accord with contemporary observations. If anything, they err on the high side. The wide variation between agricultural and industrial rates was also observed. The Secretary of the Treasury reported in 1845, for example, that "while the profit of agriculture varies from 1 to 8 percent, that of manufacturers is more than double."[44] In this same document from the Treasury, reports of returns on agricultural investments of 3 to 6% were said to be typical for the 1830s and 1840s. Others throughout the period from 1830 until the end of the century report similarly low rates persistently recurring; "overproduction" is often blamed. One additional comment from Saloutos is pertinent:

> Certainly the period from the Civil War to 1897, was not profitable at least from the standpoint of remunerative farm operations ... Part of the answer for the unprofitableness of farming is to be found in the rapid territorial expansion—the land grant, immigration, and irrigation policies that encouraged people to take land without regard for the fact that they accelerated agricultural production beyond all reasonable market demands ... The capacity to produce foodstuffs, contrary to the predictions of Malthus, greatly overstripped the capacities to consume them.[45]

Nevertheless, a substantial portion of the American population, native and immigrant alike, seems to have possessed a single-minded ambition to become a farmer. Farming might indeed have been perceived as a way of life *non-pareil*. It was clearly the fundamental tenet behind American land policy.

ACKNOWLEDGMENTS

This paper is based on Jeremy Atack and Fred Bateman, *To Their Own Soil, Agriculture in the Antebellum North* (Ames: Iowa State University Press, 1987) and a number of our published articles that provide the detailed evidence for our conclusions and arguments.

NOTES AND REFERENCES

1. See U.S. Department of Commerce, *Historical Statistics of the United States From Colonial Times to 1970* (Washington, DC: U.S. Government Printing Office, 1975), Series A202-203.
2. See, for example, the labor statistics in Ibid., Series D153, D156, D170, D174. Comparative figures on sectoral value-added are to be found in Series F239 and F241.
3. See, for example, Thomas Jefferson, *Notes on the State of Virginia* (1782).
4. These data were collected by Fred Bateman and James Foust, with the support of the National Science Foundation under grant AS-27143. The sample is publicly available under the title, *Agricultural and Demographic Records of 21,118 Rural Households Selected from the 1860 Manuscript Censuses*. Some tests of the sample are reported in Fred Bateman and James D. Foust, "A Sample of Rural Households Selected From the 1860 Manuscript Censuses," *Agricultural History* 48 (January 1974): 75-93. More elaborate tests are reported in Atack and Bateman, *To Their Own Soil*. One important *caveat* with respect to the sampling procedure was that all the townships selected were drawn from non-urban counties, where an urban county was defined as one in which at least 90% of the population lived in the largest city. Moreover, a township was rejected if 90% or more of the gainfully employed population reported nonfarm occupations.
5. There were 454 farms unmatched with population and three observations that contain no useful data. There were households in which a member reported his or her occupation as farmer but for whom no farm could be located. The problem of farms without farmers and farmers without farms is one frequently encountered by researchers using the manuscript censuses. See, for example, Allan G. Bogue, *From Prairie to Corn Belt: Farming on the Illinois and Iowa Prairies in the Nineteenth Century* (Chicago: University of Chicago Press, 1963); and Merle Curti, *The Making of An American Community: A Case Study of Democracy in a Frontier County* (Stanford: Stanford University Press, 1959).
6. Copies of the instructions to Assistant Marshals for the collection of data at the Eighth Census, long thought to be lost—see Carroll D. Wright, *History and Growth of the United States Census* (Washington DC: Government Printing Office, 1900)—are to be found in the Library of Congress, the Widener Library at Harvard, the Library of the American Philosophical Society, and the University of Illinois Library. See U.S. Census Office. 8th. Census, *Eighth Census, United States-1860. Act of Congress of Twenty-third May 1850. Instructions to U.S. Marshals. Instructions to Assistants* (Washington, DC: G. W. Bowman, 1860).
7. See, for example, remarks concerning errors in the published census in Atack and Bateman, *To Their Own Soil,* Chapter 7, esp. pp. 114-115.
8. Robert W. Fogel and Jack Rutner, "The Efficiency Effects of Federal Land Policy, 1850-1900: A Report of Some Provisional Findings," in *The Dimension of Quantitative Research in History,* edited by William O. Aydelotte (Princeton: Princeton University Press, 1972), pp. 390-418.
9. If the new soil was more fertile than any of the old, then the new marginal produce curve would lie everywhere above the old; if the best of the new was poorer than the best of the old, then the marginal product curve would be kinked at the point where then best of the new soil entered production.

10. See U.S. Census Office. 8th. Census, *Population of the United States in 1860* (Washington, DC: Government Printing Office, 1864), p. xxix.

11. For histories of public land law and disposal of the public domain, see Benjamin H. Hibbard, *A History of the Public Land Policy* (Madison: University of Wisconsin Press, 1965); and Paul W. Gates, *History of Public Land Law Development* (Washington, DC: Public Land Law Review Commission, 1968).

12. See U.S. Census Office, *Population of the United States in 1860,* pp. 616-623.

13. For a discussion of this point see Richard Steckel, "Migration and Political Conflict During the Nineteenth Century," *Explorations in Economic History* 20 (January 1983): 14-36. For a graphic depiction of yield variations with East-West versus North-South movement, see Illinois Agricultural Experiment Station, "Field Experiments with Corn," *Bulletin* 4, 8, 13, 20, 25, and 31 (1889-1894).

14. Ezra Seaman, *Essays on the Progress of Nations* (New York, 1846).

15. These figures come from a decomposition of synthetic total fertility rates performed in Atack and Bateman, *To Their Own Soil.* For a discussion of the use of synthetic total fertility rates, see Richard Steckel, "Antebellum Southern White Fertility: A Demographic and Economic Analysis," *Journal of Economic History* 40 (June 1980): 331-350.

16. The issue of the role of land abundance on fertility is dealt with by many authors. See especially W. Thompson and P. Whelpton, *Population Trends in the United States* (1953); C. Taeuber and I. Taeuber, *Changing Population in the United States* (1958); Y. Yasuba, *Birth Rates of the White Population in the United States 1800-18609* (1961); C. Forster and G. S. L. Tucker, *Economic Opportunity and White American Fertility Ratios 1800-1860;* Richard A. Easterlin, "Population Change and Farm Settlement in the Northern United States," *Journal of Economic History* 37 (March 1976): 45-75; R. Easterlin, "Factors in the Decline of Farm Family Fertility in the United States: Some Preliminary Results," *Journal of American History* 63 (December 1976): 600-614; Richard Easterlin et al., "Farm and Farm Families in Old and New Areas: The Northern States in 1860" in *Family and Population in Nineteenth Century America,* edited by Tamara Hareven and Maris Vinovskis (Princeton University Press, 1978), pp. 22-84; D. Leet, "Human Fertility and Agricultural Opportunities in Ohio Counties: From Frontier to Maturity, 1810-60," in *Essays in Nineteenth Century Economic History,* edited by D. Klingaman and R. Vedder (Ohio University Press, 1975); and D. Leet, "The Determinants of the Fertility Transition in Antebellum Ohio," *Journal of Economic History* 36 (June 1976). Our measure of land availability is a modification of that adopted by Leet.

17. Clarence H. Danhof, "Farm-Making Costs and the 'Safety Valve': 1850-1860," *Journal of Political Economy* 49 (June 1941): 317-359.

18. For an extended discussion of the following, see Jeremy Atack, "Farm and Farm-Making Costs Revisited," *Agricultural History* 56 (October 1982): 663-676.

19. For example, "Oxen will work in the breaking team and grow fat on the grass they eat at night. They will work in the hottest weather, and they seldom or never loll as they do at the east." Minnesota Commissioner of Statistics, *Minnesota: Its Place Among the States Being the First Annual Report of...* (Hartford: Press of Case, Lockwood and Company, 1860), p. 87.

20. Danhof, "Farm-Making Costs," pp. 350-352. Cf. A. Cunynghame, *Glimpse of the Great Western Republic* (1851), p. 103; John Regan, *The Emigrant's Guide to the Western States of America* (1852), p. 353; and Minnesota Commissioner of Statistics, Minnesota, (p. 87) estimated that $50 would be adequate, while J. B. Newhall (*A Glimpse of Iowa in 1846* [Burlington: W. D. Skillman, 1846], p. 59) put the figure at $75.

21. Danhof, "Farm-Making Costs," p. 349 assumed a 40-acre farm had 24-28 acres under cultivation. *The Country Gentleman* (5 [April 5, 1855], p. 213) set seed costs at $75 for 100 improved acres. Regan set seed costs at $20 for a 40-acre farm, while for ten acres of corn, five of wheat, and five of potatoes, turnips and garden produce, Newhall (*A Glimpse of Iowa in 1846,* p. 59) allowed $5.

22. See Danhof, "Farm-Making Costs," p. 327 and Minnesota Commissioner of Statistics, *Minnesota,* p. 87.
23. See Robert E. Ankli, "Farm-Making Costs in the 1850's," *Agricultural History* 48 (January 1974): 51-74.
24. See Jeremy Atack and Fred Bateman, "The 'Egalitarian Ideal' and the Distribution of Wealth in the Northern Agricultural Community: A Backward Look," *The Review of Economics and Statistics* 63 (February 1981): 124-129.
25. See Jeremy Atack and Fred Bateman, "Egalitarianism, Inequality, and Age: The Rural North in 1860," *Journal of Economic History* 41 (March 1981): 85-93.
26. See U.S. Congress, "Data on the Distribution of Wealth in the United States," Hearings Before the Task Force on the Distributive Impact of Budget and Economic Policies. *95th Cong. 1st. Sess.* (Washington, DC: U.S. Government Printing Office, 1977).
27. Robert E. Gallman, "Trends in the Size Distribution of Wealth in the Nineteenth Century: Some Speculations," in *NBER Studies in Income and Wealth,* Vol. 3, *Six Papers on the Size Distribution of Wealth and Income,* edited by Lee Soltow (New York: Columbia University Press, 1969).
28. For elaboration, see Atack and Bateman, "The 'Equalitarian Ideal'"; and Atack and Bateman, *To Their Own Soil.*
29. This is almost as equal as that found in Australia for the 1960s. See N. Podder and N. C. Kakwani, "The Distribution of Wealth in Australia," *The Review of Income and Wealth* 22 (January 1976): 75-92.
30. The bases for human and livestock consumption estimates and for seed set-asides are developed in Jeremy Atack and Fred Bateman, "Self-Sufficiency and the Marketable Surplus in the Rural North, 1860," *Agricultural History* (June 1984).
31. Our farm gate price estimates are given in Atack and Bateman, *To Their Own Soil,* Chap. 13. Some preliminary estimates appear in Fred Bateman and Jeremy Atack, "The Profitability of Northern Agriculture in 1860," *Research in Economic History,* Vol. 4 (Greenwich, CT: JAI Press, 1979), pp. 87-125. These are drawn from the prices paid by manufacturers to be found in the manuscript censuses of manufacturing, board of trade and chamber of commerce reports, and retrospective price studies published by various Agricultural Experiment Stations drawing their data from local newspapers.
32. See Marvin McInnis, "Marketable Surpluses in Ontario Farming, 1860," Mimeo (Queen's University, September 30, 1983).
33. U.S. Patent Office, *Report 1852,* Vol. 2 (1853), p. 323.
34. William N. Parker, "Agriculture," in *American Economic Growth,* edited by Lance E. Davis et al. (New York: Harper & Row, 1972), p. 395.
35. See Jeremy Atack and Fred Bateman, "Mid-Nineteenth Century Crop Yields and Labor Productivity Growth: A New Look at Parker and Klein," in *Forms and Essays in Economic History: Essays in Honor of William N. Parker,* edited by Gary Saxonhouse and Gavin Wright (Greenwich, CT: JAI Press, 1984).
36. William N. Parker and Judith L. V. Klein, "Productivity Growth in Grain Production in the United States, 1840-1860 and 1900-1910," in *Studies in Income and Wealth.* Vol. 30, *Output, Employment, and Productivity in the United States After 1800,* (New York: National Bureau of Economic Research, 1966), pp. 523-582.
38. The threshold model was developed by Paul A. David, "The Mechanization of Reaping in the Antebellum Midwest," in *Industrialization in Two Systems,* edited by H. Rosovsky (New York: Wiley, 1966). See also the extensions and criticisms of David, especially Alan L. Olmstead, "The Mechanization of Reaping and Mowing in American Agriculture," *Journal of Economic History,* 35 (June 1975): 327-52; and Robert E. Ankli, "The Coming of the Reaper," in *Business and Economic History: Papers Presented at the Twenty-Second Annual Meeting of the Business History Conference,* edited by Paul J. Uselding (Urbana: University of Illinois, 1976), pp. 1-24.

For estimates of the extent of contemporary reaper use, see *The Country Gentleman* 13 (1859): 259-60; and J. J. Thomas, *Farm Implements and Machinery* (New York, 1869), p. 8.

39. See, Alfred H. Conrad and John R. Meyer, "The Economics of Slavery in the Antebellum South," *Journal of Political Economy* 66, 2 (April 1958); Robert J. Evans, "The Economics of American Negro Slavery," in *Aspects of Labor Economics,* edited by Universities—National Bureau Committee for Economic Research (Princeton: Princeton University Press, 1962); Richard Vedder, David Klingaman, and Lowell Galloway, "The Profitability of Ante-Bellum Agriculture in the Cotton Belt: Some New Evidence," *Atlanta Economic Journal* 2 (1974); Richard Vedder and David Stockdale, "The Profitability of Slavery Revisited: A Different Approach," *Agricultural History* 49 (1975); Robert W. Fogel and Stanley L. Engerman, *Time on the Cross: The Economics of American Negro Slavery* (Boston: Little, Brown, 1974).

40. See Frederick R. Macaulay, *Some Theoretical Problems Suggested by the Movement of Interest Rates, Bond Yields and Stock Prices in the United States Since 1856* (New York: National Bureau of Economic Research, 1938).

41. Paul Gates, *The Farmer's Age* (New York: Holt Rinehart & Winston, 1960), p. 399.

42. Theordore Saloutos, "The Agricultural Problem and Nineteenth-Century Industrialism," *Agricultural History* 22,3 (1948): 156.

43. Ibid., p. 159.

44. Report from the Secretary of the Treasury, on the State of the Finances, *29 Congress, 1 Session, Senate Document 2* (December 3, 1845), pp. 12, 245-246, 249, 339. Also see Saloutos, "The Agricultural Problem."

45. Ibid., pp. 161, 162, 163.

THE SIZE STRUCTURE OF FARMING, CANADA WEST, 1861

Marvin McInnis

FARMING NEAR THE END OF A PIONEER ERA

Canada West, the part of Pre-Confederation Canada that became the Province of Ontario, experienced its main period of initial settlement in the years between 1780 and 1860. The first settlements were of refugees from the American War of Independence, loyal to British rule. They were followed in the late 1780s and 1790s by migrants from the United States seeking land in a territory newly opened to settlement. Separate political status was established in 1971 as the British colonial province of Upper Canada. Before the end of the eighteenth century immigrants had also begun to arrive from Britain. The immigrant flow swelled greatly after 1820 and especially in the early 1830s and late 1840s. As well the natural growth of population was very rapid. Immigration continued at a high level in the decade of the 1850s but by the end of that decade land suitable for settlement had been pretty much all taken up. By the following decade the flow of migration had reversed and Canada was experiencing net emigration.

The settlers who came to Upper Canada, or Canada West as it was officially known after the Union with Lower Canada in 1842, found an abundance of good agricultural land in a territory that was remarkably situated for low internal transport costs. Settlement spread out in a thin band along one of the world's best natural waterways. Overland transport was greatly aided by the long winters when frozen ground gave a firm base and an abundance of snow allowed cheap sleighing. Most of the land was originally covered by heavy forest, which may have slowed the process and raised the cost of making farms, but offered some compensation in supplies of timber, abundant fuel and a saleable by-product of forest clearing in the form of potash.

It was an area well-suited to mixed farming. Wheat was the preeminent crop from the earliest days and, eventually after a long struggle to surmount tariff barriers and the high costs of trans-Atlantic transport, gained entry to an export market in Britain. There was no basis for plantation agriculture. Small, family-operated farms predominated, especially in the most recently settled, frontier districts. The province's chief disadvantages as an area of agricultural settlement were that at the outset it lacked strong and readily available external markets for its farm products and that, except in a small and relatively remote area in the southwest, it could not reliably ripen Indian corn. In that regard Canada lacked the highly-productive cheap animal feed that played such a prominent role in the agricultural development of the United States. Except for this lesser role of corn, farming in Canada West was much like farming in the American states of Ohio and Michigan.

There is a strong presumption that what developed in Canada West was an egalitarian type of agricultural settlement. Family farms were almost universal, tenancy was not unknown but owner-occupancy was much more common. There was no large class of landless laborers. Neither was there much in the way of a highly visible elite. This all had come about in spite of government actions, even deliberate policies, in the earliest days of settlement especially, that were directed toward the establishment of a landed gentry. Some large tracts of land were granted by the Crown to a small number of individuals. Political privilege and the concentration of power were cause of unrest in the early years of settlement. By the middle of the nineteenth century, a relatively egalitarian community of most-sized, largely free-hold farms had evolved.

Within this broadly egalitarian agricultural community, however, a discernible size structure of farming had emerged. That is the subject of the present paper. It is important to put the focus of the paper in perspective. This paper examines the distributional aspects of farming in a community where there was no overarching problem of great inequalities. The concern is more with the implications of the size structure of farms for the functioning of the agricultural economy than with distriubtional issue per se. One might express this by putting it that the emphasis is more on the size structure of farming than on the size distribution of farms. As will be shown more explicitly, farms in Canada West in 1861 came in essentially three sizes—small, medium (or standard), and large. The questions of interest relate mainly to the functional role of each size category: In what salient ways were large farms differentiated from standard, medium-sized farms? What was the role of the small farms and how did they fit into the system?

Past writing on historical Canadian agriculture, and especially on farming in Canada West, has been predominantly of an impressionistic sort. Descriptive generalizations have been created out of readings of contemporary accounts and newspaper commentaries, reinforced here and there with some international trade statistics or broad aggregates from the published census tabulations. This paper is based on a systematic use of manuscript census data. It is one of a series of papers developed from the exploitation of a sample of micro-data from the manuscript enumerations of the census of 1861. This body of data has been dubbed the "Canada West Farm Sample, 1861."

THE CANADA WEST FARM SAMPLE, 1861

The Canada West Farm Sample is described more fully and evaluated as to reliability in another paper.[1] This data body has already formed the bases of several studies reported by the author.[2] Only a brief description is given here; just enough to provide an appreciation of the data base which the substance of this paper rests. It is a quite modest-sized sample of 1100 farms and farm households that was originally assembled for the purpose of studying demographic patterns in rural Canada. It was deliberately kept rather small because part of the orginal intention in developing the sample was to explore what could be done with small, specifically-directed, special-purpose samples.

An original sample size of 1200 had been arrived at as the solution to a formal exercise of solving for the desired sample size and design that would minimize certain key variances subject to the constraint imposed by the limited financial resources available at the time to carry out the job. What emerged from that exercise was a stratified, two-stage random sample of persons who gave their occupation as farmer. Stratification was employed to assure adequate representation of recently-settled frontier districts. The townships of Canada West were first organized into five strata according to initial date of settlement. The sampling proceeded in two stages. First a random sample was drawn of townships within each stratum, and then within each sample township a random selection was made of farmers. There are 148 townships in the sample— a number large enough to make it a usable sample of localities. Within each township 7 or 8 farmers were randomly selected. The original design led to the selection of 1131 farms. After editing, 1096 farms form the basis for the results reported in this paper.

The personal and agricultural returns were matched for each sample farm. In addition to the agricultural variables reported in the census, the linked sample file includes data on the demographic characteristics of each member of the farm household and a few variables related to the type of house structure. The census data have also been manipulated and combined with outside information to produce some additional synthetic measures for each farm. These include an estimate of net output for each farm, along with various sub-components of such an estimate. For example, there is an estimated aggregate feed bill and broad components of production such as total field crop output and aggregate dairy and livestock products. The net output measure is actually an index of real product since a constant set of price weights is assumed to apply to each farm. Consumption requirements based on a fixed set of coefficients by sex and age have also been estimated for each farm household. These can be compared with farm output to gauge marketable surpluses for each farm. These features of the sample have been developed and reported in another paper.[3]

An additional feature of the Canada West Farm Sample is that, with the farms distributed over a large number of different localities, variables can be assigned to each farm that represent locality characteristics (such as the date of first settlement in the township, the proportion of occupied land that had come under cultivation by 1861, and proximity to the transport system or to towns and villages).

The data of the Canada West Farm Sample have been thoroughly evaluated and shown to be generally quite reliable. The standard deviations of most variables are acceptably low. The sample replicates quite closely the aggregate tabulations of the published census. There may be a slight overrepresentation of larger farms and an overrepresentation of farms from the eastern districts and underrepresentation of the western districts of the province. These biases, however, are not sufficient to have any serious effect on the conclusions reached in this paper.[4]

THE SIZE DISTRIBUTION ON FARMS

A major attraction of the Canada West Farm sample is that it makes data available at the level of the individual farm. In the past, historical studies of Canadian agriculture have relied on tabulated census data which frequently have been misleading. Averages of acreages of particular crops or holdings of livestock were calculated with all farms in the denominator and without knowledge of the proportion of farms with zero values. Acres of land occupied is the only variable for which the published census provides a size distribution and that distribution is almost maximally inappropriate. The class bounds (less than 10 acres, 10-20, 20-50, 50-100, 100-200, and greater than 200 acres) fall

Table 1. Distribution of Farms by Occupied
Acres per Farm, Canada West Farm Sample, 1861

Farm Size (Acres)	Number of Farms in Sample	Percent of Farms
<10	14	1.3
10-31	39	3.5
32-59	184	16.8
60-69	24	2.1
70-89	67	6.1
90-109	480	43.7
110-139	48	4.4
140-169	60	5.5
170-189	14	1.3
190-209	117	10.6
210-299	28	2.6
300+	23	2.1
Total	1098	100.0

right at the greatest frequencies. This can be seen from Table 1 which is tabulated from the Canada West Farm Sample.

The rather unusual-looking size classes of Table 1 are derived from the full distribution of farms by single acres, a tabulation too cumbersome to attempt to show here. What that full distribution points up, not surprisingly, is that there are heavy concentrations of farms in sizes that are exact fractions or multiples of the standard 100-acre lot of the survey system, and very light frequencies at any of the intermediate values. Indeed, 39% of all farms had precisely the 100 acres of a single lot. Almost 15% had half-lot farms of 50 acres and 9% had exactly 200 acres. There is a natural categorization in the farm size distribution into what might be called small (50-acre), medium or standard (100-acre), and large (200-acre or greater) farms. The most sensible size classification would bracket those clusters. The only remaining issue would be to locate the bounds of those categories. The other categories identified in Table 1 are a result of a search for the breaks in the distribution that indicate where to place the bounds of the size distribution.

The remainder of this paper consists of a comparison of the characteristics of farms of the three "natural" size categories: small, standard, and large. The main evidence to be discussed is presented in Table 2 for farms of 32 to 69 acres (small), 70 to 169 acres (standard), and large farms of 170 acres or more. Before turning to that evidence two other points should be dealt with. One concerns the farms at the extremes of the size distribution. The other point concerns the use of occupied acreage to measure farm size.

Table 2. Farm Characteristics by Size of Holding, Canada West, 1861

Characteristic	Small Farms	Standard Farms	Large Farms
Number in sample	209	654	180
Percent of sample	19.1	59.7	16.4
Acres occupied	50	104	230
Acres cultivated	29	48	92
Cultivated as percent of occupied	58	46	40
Acres in crop	21	33	59
Average value of farm ($)	1169	2145	4303
Value of implements ($)	65	97	170
Crops			
Spring wheat			
percent of farms growing	78.5	89.1	91.1
average acres	6.1	8.2	10.9
yield per acre	18.4	18.3	19.4
Fall Wheat			
percent of farms growing	26.3	35.8	46.7
average acres	7.4	8.7	15.4
yield per acre	18.4	18.3	19.4
Oats			
percent of farms growing	77.0	85.6	83.9
average acres	4.5	6.1	9.6
yield per acre	30.1	30.2	21.2
Peas			
percent of farms growing	65.6	77.2	81.7
average acres	3.5	4.5	7.7
yield per acre	23.2	21.0	21.2
Barley			
percent of farms growing	23.0	27.1	35.0
average acres	3.1	3.8	6.0
yield per acre	22.2	26.8	23.5
Rye			
percent of farms growing	6.2	12.1	12.8
average acres	5.3	6.4	7.5
yield per acre	14.3	14.3	13.1
Indian corn			
percent of farms growing	28.2	27.8	27.8
average acres	2.1	2.5	4.4
yield per acre	30.3	32.2	26.3

Table 2. (*continued*)

Characteristic	Small Farms	Standard Farms	Large Farms
Buckwheat			
percent of farms growing	23.4	22.9	18.9
average acres	2.1	3.1	5.8
yield per acre	21.0	18.5	20.9
Potatoes			
percent of farms growing	88.0	91.1	90.6
average acres	1.3	1.3	1.5
yield per acre	93	105	118
Hay			
percent reporting	81.8	83.8	86.1
tons per farm	5.8	6.8	15.0
Other Products			
Butter			
percent of farms reporting	84.7	87.8	88.9
pounds per farm	176	231	321
Cheese			
percent of farms reporting	7.2	11.1	16.2
pounds per farm	84	210	174
Pork			
percent of farms reporting	76.6	80.4	81.6
barrels per farm	2.8	3.4	4.9
Beef			
percent of farms reporting	21.5	30.4	43.0
barrels per farm	2.2	2.2	2.4
Wool			
percent of farms reporting	58.9	71.3	72.2
pounds per farm	34	47	76
Maple sugar			
percent of farms reporting	31.6	42.4	43.9
pounds per farm	115	124	178
Apple cider			
percent of farms reporting	5.3	9.3	13.9
gallons per farm	167	177	154
Cloth			
percent of farms reporting	56.9	69.9	70.0
yards per farm	24	24	30

(*continued on next page*)

Table 2. (*continued*)

Characteristic	Small Farms	Standard Farms	Large Farms
Livestock			
Horses			
percent of farms reporting	67.9	71.9	78.9
average number	2.2	2.6	4.0
Oxen			
percent of farms reporting	24.9	40.7	52.8
average number	2.3	2.2	2.4
Steers and heifers			
percent of farms reporting	76.6	86.2	89.4
average number	3.5	4.4	5.9
Milk cows			
percent of farms reporting	92.3	93.7	96.1
average number	2.7	3.5	4.5
Swine			
percent of farms reporting	62.6	73.1	73.9
average number	4.6	6.0	7.5
Sheep			
percent of farms reporting	62.6	73.1	73.9
average number	9.8	12.6	22.5
Value of livestock per farm ($)	233	331	517
Value of livestock other than horses—per farm ($)	81	147	242
Synthetic Variables			
Gross value of production ($)	415	584	962
Value of net output ($)	260	378	661
Livestock and dairy products as ($) of net output	41.9	39.7	32.8
Value of Wheat production (net of seed) as percent of net output	53.1	50.1	49.2
Value of net output per cultivated area ($)	9.62	9.02	8.66
Estimated average marketable surplus	116	203	402
Marketable surplus as percent of net output	45	55	61
Percent of farms with no marketable surplus	23	17	12

Table 2. (continued)

Characteristic	Small Farms	Standard Farms	Large Farms
Family and Household			
Average number of persons per household	5.13	5.70	6.36
Males over age 16 per household	1.21	1.42	1.89
Net farm output per adult male	215	266	350

Source: Tabulated from the *Canada West Farm Sample* (1861).

The sample was selected, in the first instance, from household heads who returned their occupation as farmer. A few of those turned out to have very small farms—so small that it can be questioned whether they were genuinely farms. About 5% of the sample had farms of less than 32 acres. Some of those reported only an acre or two but most had about 10 acres. There is no consistent pattern among them. Some were elderly who were clearly retired farmers on small residential plots; a few may have been dairymen or fruitgrowers on the outskirts of towns; whereas others just seem to have been hopeful reporting 10 or 12 acres of land but no agricultural activity. They all stand in sharp contrast to the typical small, half-lot farmer. For the purposes of this paper it seemed most sensible just to leave aside this class of "tiny" (less than 32 acre) farms.

At the other end of the size distribution there is a handful of "elite" farms of vastly larger-than-typical size. They have been left in the analysis as part of the category of large farms because they were indeed a real component of that group. They might, however, be of interest in themselves as indicative of the nature of "elite" farms in Canada West in 1861. In this paper they have not been singled out for separate attention, partly because space does not allow it; partly because there were sufficiently few (only 8 with more than 400 acres) in the sample that it is dubious that any valid generalizations could be drawn about them. One thing that should be noted is that no really grand estates turned up. The largest farm in the sample occupied 2000 acres and it may well have been the largest operating farm unit in Canada West at the time. There were land holdings of considerably greater extent but there may have been no operating farm units of greater extent.[5]

There are some distinct limitations to measuring farm size by occupied acreage. Land was still being settled in Canada West in 1861 and the use of occupied acreage as a basis of delimitation introduces possible distortions. There were some occupiers of 200 or more acres who were doing almost nothing with them. Some were new farmers who had scarcely begun to clear their land. For some purposes, occupied acreage can be a decidedly misleading measure of the distribution of farm size. For many of those purposes it matters what is being done with those acres and any of a number of alternative measures would be a better basis for categorizing farm size. I have in fact examined the distributions of farms by cultivated acreage, by reported farm value, by estimated net output and by size of marketable surplus. For some purposes these alternatives offer preferable indicators of the size distribution of farming operations. They do not, however, address the primary issue raised in this paper—the structure of farming. With regard to that, land was the essential, discriminating asset. The total occupied acreage of the farm was indicative of the class of farm. The size of the farm the operator was able or constrained to acquire represented the grouping within the rural society into which each farm fit. The very discontinuity in the size distribution had meaning. The view of the structure of the agricultural community explored here is thus something rather different from just the size structure of farming.

SMALL, STANDARD AND LARGE FARMS IN CANADA WEST, 1861

The main evidence to be considered on the three size classes of farms is that presented in Table 2. It shows a large number of characteristics of the three size categories identified. Not all of these can be fully discussed within the confines of the present paper. What follows is intended to draw attention to the highlights of Table 2. Because the "standard," 100-acre farm has been identified as a sort of norm it may be appropriate to direct attention to some of the more interesting characteristics of those farms and then to turn to the principal ways in which large and small farms differed.

The medium-sized or "standard" farms comprised 60% of all farms in Canada West. They averaged 104 acres in size, of which 48 acres, or 46% of the area, were under cultivation. As the process of settlement and farm-making was still going on, that proportion of total acreage brought under cultivation was below the 70 to 75 acres a finished 100-acre farm would typically cultivate. In 1861 a little less than 20% of farms in Canada West had reached that "finished" state. Fully one-quarter had only 25 acres under cultivation. There were still many farms in the early stages of development. The standard farm reported a value of $2145, or $20.63 per acre.

An extensive literature on the economic history of Canada West puts great stress on wheat as the "staple" export crop of the region, the key commodity through which so much of the conomic history of the region can be interpreted. In light of that it is interesting to look at wheat as the foremost of the crops grown by the farms of Canada West. A first point to be noted, however, and one that has not had adequate recognition in the literature, is the difference between spring and fall wheat. Wheat constituted two crops, not just one. Conditions of climate, primarily, and soil limited the area in which fall wheat could reliably be grown; yet it was the premium crop. Where it could be successfully grown it yielded more heavily, and it fetched a premium price relative to spring wheat. It was spring wheat, however, that was the ubiquitous crop. Almost 90% of farms grew spring wheat. The standard farm planted about 8 acres to the crop. For a region that was supposed to be specialized in wheat that appears to be surprisingly low. It amounts to only one-sixth of cultivated land and no more than one-quarter of the land actually under crop in the census year. In a sense, then, the standard farm in Canada West appears to have been less involved in wheat production than the historical literature suggests.

Wheat was still predominantly a hand harvested crop and about 10 acres was all that the usual family farm could reap by hand without engaging paid labor. Mechanical reapers had been introduced long before 1861 but few farms in Canada West could have had them. It appears that most farms avoided having to hire harvest labor. Only 5% of standard farms reported more than 20 acres of spring wheat. Farms which were in districts that could grow fall wheat also produced that crop—again 10 acres. Only 36% of standard farms, however, reported any fall wheat.

Oats, primarily for animal feed, was the other nearly ubiquitous crop. Of standard farms, 86% reported oats, averaging 6.1 acres. Peas were also popular, with 77% of farms reporting that crop and an average of 4.5 acres. Hay was produced on 84% of standard farms. Other crops were considerably less common and typically had smaller allotments of land devoted to them. Indian corn, the mainstay of agriculture in the United States, could be reliably ripened only in a confined region in the southwest of the province, and was reported by only 28% of farms. That is about the same proportion of farms that grew any barley at all. There is no indication of any appreciable number of farms specializing in any of the coarse grains. Areas of as much as 20 acres of any of those crops were reported by no more than 1% of farms.

What we see is a sort of mixed farming with wheat in a forefront position. Farms kept a variety of livestock but in amounts geared primarily to the consumption needs of the farm family, or at most the local neighborhood. Milk cows were the most common of livestock, with 94% of farms reporting at least one, and an average of 3.5. Almost as may farms (86%) reported steers or heifers (4.4 on average). Pigs were close to universal, averaging 6 per farm. Again, there are few hints of specialization. Only 10% of standard farms kept 6 or more dairy cows or 8 or more beef cattle. Only 1% of farms reported more than 20 pigs.

The average value of livestock reported by the standard farm was $331 or about 15% of the total value reported for the farm. The net production of each farm was estimated by a complex procedure, described fully in another paper. Broadly speaking the procedure was to weigh the reported production of each crop and the estimated output of each type of animal product by a fixed set of prices and then to deduct an estimated feed bill for the livestock. A number of minor products was necessarily omitted and no provision was made for farm output in the form of additions to capital through clearing, fencing, and draining of land. Hence, the estimates of net farm output are of rather "lean" sort. The average for standard sized farms works out to be $378. Wheat production was responsible for about one half the value of net output. Another 40% was contributed by the total of dairy and meat products.

LARGE FARMS IN CANADA WEST

Large farms, defined as those occupying two or more 100-acre lots, comprised only 16% of all farms. Relatively few (2%) had more than 300 acres, and large farms as a class averaged 230 acres. They tended to have a somewhat smaller fraction of their acreage under cultivation than the standard farms. Commensurate with that, average farm values increased between the size classes by rather less then total acreage. For the most part, large farms were not very different from standard farms. There are few characteristics that would mark them as structurally differentiated. Mainly, they were more diversified; they tended to produce more things. That is in contrast to producing a lot more of each individual product. There is no charactersitic for which the large farms average disproportionally more than standard farms. The ratio of acres occupied by large farms to that of standard farms was 2.21. Large farms reported 2.2 times as much hay production as standard farms, but for no other characteristic is the average for large farms more than double that for medium farms. Most commonly it is considerably less.

This situation is brought out clearly when one focuses on the leading farm product—wheat. Spring wheat was as nearly ubiquitous on large as on standard farms, yet the large farms averaged less than 11 acres, only one-third more than standard farms. That alone may be one of the most interesting findings to come out of the analysis of the Canada West Farm Sample. In a region that was regarded as one of wheat specialization the large farms did not have notably expanded wheat acreage. Relatively few of the large farms could even be said really to specialize in wheat. Only 100% of the farms in the large-size class had more than 20 acres devoted to spring wheat. The large farms were considerably more likely to grow fall wheat than were small and medium farms, and the average acreages of fall wheat on large farms were greater, yet still far from double those of standard farms.

Thus, the large farms of Canada West did not use their greater land area to grow significantly more of the "staple" crop. Instead they grew a greater diversity of crops. They were more likely to produce barley and peas and they produced considerably more hay. That would seem to imply that they were more substantially devoted to dairy and livestock production. In a sense that is indeed so, but it does not show up in quite the way one might expect. They are not clearly and substantially given over to livestock production. The total value of all livestock reported on large farms is only 56% greater than for standard farms. That is partly a consequence of the fact that horses were of considerably higher unit value than any other kind of livestock and farms of all sizes were likely to have at least one team of horses in addition to the total value of all livestock so that the value of livestock exclusive of horses can be calculated, yet that is only 64% greater on large than on standard farms. Similarly, the estimated value of dairy and livestock production is a smaller fraction of net output on large farms than on standard farms, rather than the other way around.

The characteristics for which large farms appear to have the greatest advantage over standard farms are in hay production and in sheep and wool. Large farms were also more likely to have reported cheese production as well. Overall, however, net output on large farms works out only to 75% greater than on standard farms of half the size. As one might have expected, the large farms were operated less intensively; the value of net output per cultivated acre is a little lower than on standard farms. The large farms did have larger households but not to an extent that would permit one to think of them as being characterized by large and complex households in a way that would contrast with standard farms. The situation is a bit different if we consider only adult males, the preponderant source of farm labor for the products considered here. The larger farms had about one-third more males over 16 years of age than standard farms. The household heads and operators of larger farms were a little older; hence, they tended to have larger families on average, with more children over age 16. There was also a considerably greater frequency of nonfamily member adult males on the larger farms. It should be emphasized, however, that this was not a prominent feature of farms in Canada West in 1861. Even in the larger size class fewer than one farm in six had nonfamily labor residing in the farm household.

The appropriate conclusion to reach seems to be that structurally there was no marked difference between large and standard farms. Large farms showed greater complexity and diversity of output, but primarily they were doing the same thing as standard, medium-sized farms. Neither is there any indication that the large farms were doing it any better. There are variations in per acre yield between farms of the three size classes but few of the differences are great enough to be statistically significant; neither do they tend uniformly in one direction.

THE SMALL FARM IN CANADA WEST

Turn now to the small farms, the half-lot units. Where did these fit into the system? How did they differ from the standard farms? For one thing they were more intensive. A higher proportion of the land occupied was under cultivation and an even higher proportion of that was in crop. Small farms had less land in pasture but mainly a lot less land in forest or other wild state. Overall, the small farms average exactly 50 acres, just 48% of the standard farms. Their average value was 54% of that of standard farms.

These small farms comprised a significant element in the agricultural scene. They made up almost 20% of the total of all farms. They performed quite admirably. With only half the land of the standard farm, the small farm displayed most characteristics at 70-80% of the values for standard farms. They were less likely to be raising any of the particular crops than larger farms, with the exceptions that just as many small farms grew Indian corn and a slightly higher proportion raised buckwheat. A decidedly lower proportion of small farms grew fall wheat, but those that did, planted almost as much as standard farms. Acreage of spring wheat was three-quarters that of standard farms. The small farmer might appear to be more committed to wheat than larger farms but, overall, wheat comprised only a slightly larger fraction of net output than was the case on standard farms. That is because the small farms did not have proportionally fewer livestock than standard farms. On average they raised almost as many pigs and beef cattle of standard farms. Hay production per farm on small farms was 85% of that on standard farms. Small farms were operated more intensively than larger farms and squeezed proportionally more output from the limited land at their disposal.

What we would most like to know, perhaps, is whether the small farms were primarily self-contained units or were subsistence plots for persons who supplied labor to the larger farms. To what extent did the small farms have to supplement their incomes by the sale of wage labor? We cannot answer that directly but there are indications that the small farms may have been predominantly self-contained units with no manifest need for the sale of labor of the farm. The average value of net output of the small farms was 69% of that of the standard farms that were twice as large. The average small farm supported a smaller household, though, so output per family member was 77% of that on standard farms. In that sense, without any supplemental income, families on small farms need not have been markedly poorer than those on standard farms. Comparisons of net output with consumption requirements of farm households at fixed average rates of consumption of the products entering into net output indicates that, on average, substantial marketable surpluses were being produced on small farms.[6] The average surplus of $116 was equal to 45% of the value of net output—not all that much below the 55% for standard farms—and more than half the amount of marketable surplus turned out on farms that were twice as large. Further, while almost one-quarter of small farms produced no marketable surplus, that was not dramatically above the 17% of standard farms. Even among large farms, 12% produced no marketable surplus.

Small farms, as they have been defined in this paper, were not patiently distressed farms. It looks as though many farmers in Canada West could have produced enough on a small half-lot farm to have supported a family and probably to have done that without supplementing income by outside work, or at least by doing that to no appreciably greater extent than farmers with considerably more land. If both small and standard sized farms operated with the labor input represented by adult males in the farm household, output per worker on small farms would have been 80% of that on standard farms. That was being acheived with only 60% as much land under cultivation and 70% of the value of livestock. One has to wonder if within that set of relationships there is scope for significant diversions of labor away from the small farms. It is hard to accept that there could have been much. The predominant picture that emerges from the census data is of the small farm as essentially a reduced-sized version of the standard farm, operating more intensively, making up for the smaller endowment of land by using relatively more labor and capital, especially in the form of livestock. That is in contrast to the supposition that the small, half-lot farmer was necessarily heavily dependent opportunities for wage labor on larger farms or elswhere to supplement only a meager output that could be raised on the mere 50 acres available. This does not appear to be the evidence from the census data on small farms. Further the large farms do not give indications of a really extensive dependence on outside labor. Primarily, it appears that in the technical and market circumstances of 1861, at a time when farm-making was still a widespread activity, the half-lot farm was not so small a unit. That is especially the case when it is gauged in terms of land actually being cultivated and when other nonlabor factors of production are taken into account. It is also the case that whereas the half-lot farmers comprised a numerically important group at the small end of the farm structure, there were few representatives of an even smaller category. What has not been addressed in all this is the role and numerical importance of genuinely landless labor in nineteenth-century rural Canada. The census data would have to be used in a different way from that afforded by the Canada West Farm Sample in order to address the question.

SOME CONCLUDING REMARKS

This paper has offered a first, detailed look at some aspects of the size structure of farming in mid-nineteenth-century Onatrio. The retabulation of a sample of manuscript census data has allowed a different perspective and a much more thorough examination of what can be learned about Canadian agriculture from the census data base. The methodology has been exceedingly simple—a direct comparison of the characteristics of three typical size categories. It is an approach, however, that suits the evidence and the kind of clustered distribution that appeared. More could be done, admittedly, in the way of cross-tabulation but the sample is relatively small and connot be pushed far in that direction. Some experimentation has been undertaken with the use of regression analysis to study some aspects of performance but little of that bears directly on the issue of size structure.

Perhaps too much has been read out of one limited body of data relating to one time period. A general caution along those lines is presumed to lie behind the whole of the discussion. This paper is intended as a contribution to an historical literature that has generally erred in the other direction of attempting to say too little and to be insufficiently specific.

The overriding conclusion that seems to emerge is that Ontario agriculture was remarkably homogeneous in structure. It was general—mixed farming with a primary emphasis on wheat—and that characterization applied broadly across the size distribution. Small and large farms were just smaller and larger versions of the same sort of thing and there was little indication of functional differentiation related to size. Neither small nor large farms tended to lean to one or another line of specialization. Right across the size distribution the composition of output was similar. It reflected above all a provision for the consumption needs of the farm households and the nonfarm households of the local community with a rather more substantial marketable surplus of wheat.[7] This is not to say that these were mere subsistence farmers. The estimated marketable surpluses were a sizeable fraction of output, on average, in all size classes of farms.

The small farms in the size structure appear to be predominantly independent farmers, not a dependent class of part farmers, part wage earners. At the same time not many of the large farmers were operating on a scale that would have regularly required large inputs of labor from outside the farm family. The large farms in the sample did not emerge as a differentiated elite. That may be partly due to the use of a sample too small to throw up many examples of a genuine elite. Very large farms did indeed exist but were very scanty in number. It was evidently more common for owners of extensive tracts of land to lease the land to be farmed as 50- or 100- or perhaps 200-acre farms than to operate them as large units. Ownership and tenancy are obviously important characterstics that have not been addressed here. Unfortunately those data were not collected in the census of 1861. The question did get asked a decade later and William Marr has begun to analyse the 1871 census data with an eye particularly to the frequency and role of tenancy.[8] If one can project backward a decade from what Marr has found for 1871 it would appear that while tenancy and part-tenancy were not uncommon, owner-occupancy predominated.

The agriculture of Canada West in 1861 can, then, best be characterized as a relatively homogeneous yeomanry. There was a discernable size structure but it gave very weak indications of underpinnings of a class structure. Neither did it have much bearing on agricultural operations and performance. It would be interesting to make comparisons with the agriculture of the predominantly French province of Canada East that in 1861 had just shaken loose from a feudal system of land holding and is perceived by some writers at least as having a more clearly discernible size and class structure. A time dimension is also very much needed. Was Canada West evolving into a more differentiated structure of farming as, in the years to follow, a greater incidence of tenancy may have emerged, mechanization became more common and permitted more efficient exploitation of large holdings, and were there moves towards more clearly specialized lines of farming? Further exploration of the now readily-available manuscript census data will be needed to answer that.

NOTES AND REFERENCES

1. That is at present not yet published.
2. Marvin McInnis, "Childbearing and Land Availability: Some Evidence from Individual Household Data," in *Population Patterns in the Past,* ed. Ronald D. Lee (New York: Academic Press, 1977), pp. 201-221; Marketable Surpluses in Ontario Farming, 1860," *Social Science History* 8 (Fall 1984): 290-301.
3. Ibid.
4. These matters are discussed fully in an as yet unpublished paper.
5. The sample was designed to look at farms and farmers, whether owners or tenants. There were undoubtedly owners of many farms or of large tracts of land leases in parcels to tenant farmers. What is lacking as large units, operated as single farms. The absence of any really large, plantation-type farms is a consequence of the general scarcity and high price of labor and the lack of a crop that could be produced most efficiently on a plantation basis.
6. In should be made clear that we have no information on actual consumption. This is a comparison of what could have been produced at average rates of conversion of crops into animal products, with what could have been consumed, at assumed average rates of per capita consumption. Whereas this may be a rather artificial calculation it may nevertheless serve to test the presumption that small farmers necessarily depended on supplemental income.
7. This idea is taken up more extensively in McInnis, "Marketable Surpluses in Ontario Farming."
8. Marr has taken the work begun in his contribution to the present collection in a subsequently-written paper: "The Distribition of Tenant Agriculture in Ontario, Canada, 1871," *Social Science History* 11 (Summer 1987): 169-186.

FARM SIZE OF TENANT AND OWNER-OCCUPIED FARMS IN YORK COUNTY, ONTARIO, 1871:
A CASE STUDY

William L. Marr

INTRODUCTION

In the past decade a growing interest in the development and consequences of farm tenancy has developed among economic historians of American agriculture. Whereas the theoretical issues surrounding tenant agriculture are far from settled, the work of Reid, Ransom and Sutch, and Higgs has resulted in the development of theoretical models of tenancy and the collection of a body of information on typical rental and sharecropping contracts that has been utilized to explain the determinants of tenure modes and to measure their effects on agricultural output, efficiency and farm size.[1]

There are three general explanations of the determinants of the contractual mix in farm tenancy: (1) the agricultural ladder, (2) transaction costs, and (3) the distribution of risk. In its basic form the concept of the agricultural ladder asserts that many farmers begin their careers as hired hands and in time become tenant farmers and finally acquire farms of their own. Several reasons have been offered to explain why a farmer might choose to become a tenant. He might want to learn more about the land and climate of a locality before investing in land there; or he might lack savings or sufficient credit standing to finance the acquisition of a farm; or he might lack sufficient information about farming techniques and may thus desire to cooperate in a tenancy agreement with a local landowner. Rapid changes in technology or in the optimal crop mix may induce farmers to opt for tenancy until the new practices become in particular. It has been suggested that foreign-born persons may be particularly subject to these inducements, as they are likely to lack savings and will certainly lack knowledge about the local characteristics of the land and the techniques needed to make it profitable. However, these explanations for the agricultural ladder all rise out of an initial state of disequilibrium that can be expected to disapper as people accumulate the resources, knowledge, and reputation needed to operate an owner-occupied farm.

Reasons for tenancy based on transaction costs have potentially greater permanence. In this literature, transaction costs are typically divided into enforcement costs and supervisory costs. Enforcement costs are the costs of ensuring that parties to an agreement honour their promises. One major problem area in agriculture is the need to secure labour through the crop year. As the costs of securing hired workers over the contract period rises, a landowner has an increasing incentive to substitute tenants for hired workers, using the tenant's claim on the residual income of the farm as the means for inducing self-enforcement of the tenancy contract. Supervisory costs are associated with ensuring that parties to an agricultural contract supply inputs in the stipulated amounts. The use of wage labour implies a degree of supervision and landowners may find it preferable to reduce their supervisory costs by farming their land with tenants, who have a direct incentive to supply the optimal quantity of inputs.

Supervisory costs are closely related to the size of the holding. If large numbers of workers are needed or if the agricultural activity demands constant supervision, there is an incentive to substitute tenants for labourers. On the other hand, labour-saving technical change that allows owners to substitute capital for labour reduces the cost of supervision and may reduce the incentive to farm the land with tenants. Nonlabour inputs themselves have to be supervised; but if an owner supplied capital and livestock, he may want to exercise some control over their use to ensure that labourers do not abuse them. The additional costs of directly supervising labour are likely to be small, making tenancy less advantageous as a means of reducing such costs.

Tenancy has also been explained as a means of dividing the risk of fluctuations in yields and prices between tenant and landowner. Owner-occupiers and lessors on straight money rents bear all of the yield and price risks. As the level of such risks rises, some of them may want to become share tenants in order to share the risks with the owner. This is likely if tenants are more risk averse than landowners.

Canadian historians and economic historians have almost entirely neglected the topic of tenancy in the development of Canada's agriculture. R.L. Jones has written the most thorough study of Ontario's agriculture from a historical perspective. He notes that renting of farmland in Ontario was not the norm, as farmers preferred to own the land they farmed and landowners were reluctant to rent for fear that tenants would not take good care of their land and physical capital.[2] He argues that the prevailing form of tenancy in the middle of the nineteenth century was a kind of share arrangement in which the proportion of output or revenue going to the landowner varied directly with the inputs he provided.[3] The many individual county histories of Ontario are silent on the issue of tenant agriculture.[4]

Marr's paper in *Canadian Papers in Rural History* fills this void in a small way by examining one Ontario county in 1871 and describing the differences between owner-occupied and tenant-run farms.[5] Although the study is limited to York County, it describes a district that contained a large percentage of tenant farms. The study is based on individual microdata files taken from the 1871 Census of Canada. It finds significant and potentially important differences between tenants and owners. For example, tenants tended to be younger, less well-educated (as measured by the ability to read and write) and foreign-born, as compared to owners. There were some productivity differences between tenant and owner-occupied farms, but they tended to diminish when controlled for the age of the head of household. Tenants produced lower yields per acre, but this may reflect smaller farm sizes. The data on the capital stock (livestock and implement) on each type of farm indicates that owners had more capital, but because the Census data referred to "owned" implements and livestock a tenant might have access to these stock items but because he did not own them they were not listed in the Census.

One other difference provides the focus of this paper, namely that owners in York County had larger farms on average than did tenants whether farm size is measured by occupied acreage or improved acreage. This difference was accepted only tentatively because other factors besides tenancy type were not held constant in the earlier study. This paper attempts to do just that while working within the data constraints of the 1871 Canadian Census. First, and as background, the extent of tenant farming in Ontario will be discussed, the farm sample for 1871 in York County will be outlined, and the result on farm size from the earlier study will be described.

TENANCY IN ONTARIO AND YORK COUNTY

Table 1 supplies tenancy rates by the subdivision of a county for the four census years of 1871, 1881, 1891 and 1901. These rates are the total number of tenant occupiers in each county divided by the total number of farm occupiers in the same county. For 1871, 1881, and 1891 the census recorded only two farm groups, namely owners and tenants; however, in 1901, a third category, called owner-tenant, was added. This presumably segregated those who were both owners and tenants. For consistency, the rates of 1901 have tenants only in the numerator. This study is interested in looking at tenancy in 1871, but comparisons with the other three years are discussed briefly here.

In 1871 approximately 16% of all Ontario's farms were tenant-occupied; this compares with 7% in the province of Quebec, 5% in Nova Scotia, and 7% in New Brunswick.[6] For an international comparison, in 1880 the southern United States contained about 36% of farms in one form of tenancy or another.[7] In the northern United States, tenant farming was less common but still important; again in 1880, 26% of all farms in the United States were under tenant control, and in the mid-west, tenancy rates ranged from 9% in Wisconsin to 31% in Illinois.[8] By 1881 in Ontario, the tenancy rate had risen to approximately 18% which is below most but not all of the rates in the states of the United States. Table 1 shows that this upward trend continued in the 1880s to reach about 21% in 1891. Thus, during the 20 years after 1871, tenancy rates on average rose in the province of Ontario during a time when her agriculture was shifting out of grains for human consumption, epecially wheat, into fodder crops and livestock for meat, butter, and cheese. All readily cultivatable land was in private hands and rose in value, especially near cities and towns like Toronto, Ottawa, London, and Hamilton. By 1901, Ontario's tenancy rate appears to be considerably lower than in 1891, but it is unclear how persons who were both owners and tenants were treated in the nineteenth-century censuses; if the rate included owners who are also tenants, then it would be almost 20% in 1901.

Because data for 1871 will be used in the statistical analysis, only tenancy rates in that year are looked at further here. It is clear that the old, established, settled, agricultural districts along the shore of Lake Ontario had a special propensity to adopt tenant agriculture. Near the entry to the St. Lawrence River but still on Lake Ontario are the districts of Lennox and Frontenac which also had relatively high rates: 29.3 and 21% respectively. They are in line with the other Lake Ontario rates and may follow the same pattern. At the other extreme is the St. Lawrence and Ottawa region with an overall tenancy rate of approximately 12%, about 4% below the average for the province. Of course the Northern District had the lowest rates, but it is difficult to characterize because of the almost uninhabited state of that part of Ontario. The St. Lawrence and Ottawa region had been settled, like the Lake Ontario region,

Table 1. Tenancy Rates by County, Ontario, 1871-1901

	County	1871	1881	1891	1901
1.	Essex	.164	.199	.201	.179
2.	Kent	.215	.214	.253	.184
3.	Bothwell	.139	.163	.191	.141
4.	Lambton	.147	.134	.146	.096
5.	Elgin	.145	.186	.189	.136
6.	Middlesex	.142	.176	.233	.129
7.	Norfolk	.16	.192	.23	.191
8.	Oxford	.177	.195	.25	.178
9.	Brant	.199	.242	.219	.176
10.	Haldimand	.163	.174	.213	.105
11.	Monck	.119	.184	.197	.105
12.	Welland	.163	.192	.208	.181
13.	Niagara	.277	.282	.296	.165
14.	Lincoln	.204	.232	.296	.165
15.	Wentworth	.219	.227	.242	.181
16.	Huron	.172	.137	.174	.099
17.	Bruce	.109	.132	.135	.099
18.	Perth	.175	.125	.227	.10
19.	Waterloo	.104	.156	.229	.133
20.	Wellington	.141	.191	.234	.162
21.	Grey	.117	.149	.181	.117
22.	Halton	.248	.212	.224	.172
23.	Peel	.248	.239	.276	.225
24.	Cardwell	.179	.209	.176	.184
25.	Simcoe	.146	.194	.239	.153
26.	York	.295	.331	.36	.329
27.	Ontario	.247	.281	.329	.247
28.	Durham	.253	.287	.298	.260
29.	Victoria	.168	.196	.242	.153
30.	Northumberland	.193	.229	.293	.217
31.	Peterborough	.162	.182	.231	.16
32.	Prince Edward	.111	.143	.196	.15
33.	Hastings	.143	.147	.156	.089
34.	Lennox	.293	.213	.253	.2
35.	Addington	.156	.113	.130	.11
36.	Frontenac	.21	.214	.188	.177
37.	Leeds S.	.129	.179	.183	.144
38.	Brockville	.149	.182	.136	.163
39.	Grenville S.	.104	.144	.183	.107
40.	Leeds & Grenville	.117	.136	.196	.117
41.	Dundas	.166	.171	.171	.165
42.	Stormont	.125	.168	.311	.165
43.	Cornwall	.014	.203	.311	.165
44.	Glengarry	.103	.177	.2	.17
45.	Prescott	.082	.124	.141	.069

(continued)

Table 1. (continued)

County	1871	1881	1891	1901
46. Russell	.103	.14	.163	.08
47. Carleton	.095	.123	.095	.073
48. Lanark	.107	.116	.116	.053
49. Renfrew	.044	.081	.115	.035
50. Nipissing	.026	.109	.067	.026
51. Muskoka	.029	.049	.06	.034
52. Parry Sound	.021	.049	.06	.034
53. Manitoulin	.013	.109	.109	.059
54. Algoma	.237	.109	.109	.059
Total Ontario	.159	.177	.212	.144

Source: *Census of Canada*, 1871, 1881, 1891, 1901.

but the former, being on the Precambrian Shield was less agricultural by 1871. The centre of Ontario's agriculture had shifted west to the area above Lake Erie between Lakes Huron and Ontario. With the exceptions of Kingston and Ottawa, the St. Lawrence and Ottawa region had relatively few urban centres and the completion of the St. Lawrence canals allowed ships to sail right past the region without transhipping their cargoes.

In a sense there was a north-south trend to the pattern of tenancy rates. Some examples will help to make this point. Peterborough had a lower tenancy rate than Northumberland, and Victoria had a lower rate than Durham; Cardwell had a lower rate than either Peel or York, with Simcoe having an even lower rate than Cardwell. In a similar manner, Wellington had a lower rate than any district to its immediate south or southeast, but its tenancy rate was higher than its northern neighbour, Grey district. Beside Grey is Bruce which at 10.9%, also had a relatively low tenancy rate. The census district of Waterloo was somewhat of an anomaly with a rate of only 10.4% in 1871; but it must be wondered if the predominance of Mennonites in that district did not keep the rate at low levels. If it was not the custom for Mennonites to accept or to utilize the tenancy form of landholding, this would explain some of the differential. The extreme southwestern districts had generally lower tenancy rates than areas to their immediate east. The exception, though, is Kent district with a rate of 21.5%.

In order to explain the distribution of tenant farms in Ontario during the late nineteenth century, Marr used data at the microlevel for York census district in 1871 and aggregate data by Census districts (i.e., the data in Table 1) for the southern part of Ontario in the years 1871, 1881 and 1891.[9] The next two pages summarize his conclusions. The hypotheses which were tested fell into four generic "determinants": (1) as a means of economic and social advancement (the agricultural-tenure ladder), (2) as a means of reducing transaction costs, (3) as a risk related device, and (4) as the product of the settlement-development process.

The two data sets support the hypothesis that tenancy was more likely to be found (1) among the foreign-born, (2) among the relatively young, (3) on smaller farms, (4) in areas that are relatively developed, (5) away from urban areas, (6) on farms with fewer milk cows, (7) on farms that are less specialized in wheat production, (8) in areas that had relatively high agricultural wages, and (9) in areas where the value of farm land was relatively high.

What do these findings suggest for the economic history of southern Ontario's agriculture in the early half of the nineteenth century? Tenancy may have acted as a way for the foreign born and the relatively young to gain agricultural experience in agriculture in an area where land prices were rising and "free" land no longer existed for, by 1871, all of the arable land in southern Ontario was in private hands so that a "new" farmer would have found it difficult to start as an owner-occupier. Tenancy allowed him to farm without having to have the capital and the experience to start up such a farm immediately . In the York Census district in 1871, many tenants were over the age of forty-five which suggests that this state of agricultural institution may have appealed to some people. These people were unlikely to rise up the agricultural ladder.

Tenancy was more prevalent in the areas of Ontario which were more agriculturally advanced as measured by the ratio of improved to occupied areas. Whereas this represents in part the response to higher land prices in areas with such characteristics, it may also be an institutional arrangement which the inhabitants of the more settled and older areas found attractive. But, the older settled areas along the St. Lawrence River toward the border with Quebec had relatively lower rates on tenancy. These districts had less fertile land than did the farm areas along Lake Erie and Ontario, and more land was devoted to pasture; therefore, the best agricultural land and areas went hand in hand with tenancy.

The negative relationship (although fairly weak) between urbanization and tenancy suggests that the two were unrelated, and this may seem at odds with the above result that the more settled, more established, and better agricultural areas were associated with more tenancy. The relationship of urbanization with tenancy needs to be interpreted cautiously. If one census district specialized in agriculture and, therefore, had few urban areas whereas another district next to it specialized in urban activities and provided services for the agricultural district, a negative relationship could result from tenancy in a district.

Returning to the present study, York Census district was chosen quite deliberately because of its relatively high tenancy rate in 1871 (29.5%). If tenant and owner-operated farms are to be compared, than the sample of tenant farms must be large enough to allow for meaningful analysis. The three subdistricts of York, namely York North, York West, and York East, had 27%, 31% and 30% tenancy rates respectively in 1871. At that date York Census district contained 6,321 farms of which 4,430 were owner-occupied and 1,865 were tenant run. The hand-written, microfilmed, industrial Census returns provided the data for the comparisons made in this study. In order to keep data collection costs down and because of the characteristics of probability sampling, a one-third sample of all farms in York Census district was taken from the microfilmed data. This proved to be a stratified, systematic sample with the stratifying variables being (1) the spatial regions of the district and (2) the type of farm (owner-occupied or tenant). Thus the sample correctly represents the number of farms in each region and the type of farm both in total and in each region. For each of the approximately 1,700 farm households in the sample, two linked types of information are available. First, personal data on the head of the household and his or her family are provided; this information includes sex, age, birthplace, religion, marital status, ability to read and write of the head of the household, and the number of children with their ages, and whether they attended school. Second, several of the characteristics of the farm operations are available; these include onwership of various implements, acres in some crops (wheat, potatoes, hay), yields of several crops, number of livestock, total occupied acres, and total improved acres. This provides the data set for the anlaysis that follows. The York census district was selected because of its high incidence of tenancy, so that the sample of tenant farms would be large enough to permit meaningful analysis with nontenant farms in the same locality. This means that York was not typical of Ontario in 1871 and therefore generalizations to the province as a whole are risky.

In Marr's study of tenancy in York distict, farm size was investigated because it is of interest in and of itself but also because it can stand as a proxy for some aspects of economic efficiency. The study found that for the entire sample of 1,727 farms in York County, the average acres occupied in 1871 were 83.4 acres and 100.7 acres for tenants and owner-occupiers respectively. For average acres improved, a second measure of farm size, tenants improved 60.6 acres on average while owners had 72.1 acres in 1871.[10] Therefore, in a fairly tight geographical area which subjected each farm to the same economic and institutional forces, tenants had significantly smaller farms than owners. Before the controls for other possible determinants of farm size must be introduced. The next section of this paper discusses that issue.

FARM SIZE AND TENANCY

Following up on these last comments, the variable of interest in this section is farm size as measured by improved areas per farm. As the literature on tenancy has not spent much time describing the relationship of tenancy to farm size, it will be assumed that resource allocation and farm size are related. The latter is one measure of resource allocation. The question addressed here is: Does the form of ownership affect farm size that is taken as the proxy used for resource allocation?

Steven Cheung shows that resource allocation is the same under share tenancy as with owner cultivation; it is not evident that tenant farms should be smaller than owner-occupied farms.[11] He first develops the "traditional" argument that states that resource allocation will be different under the two land holding systems. This argument is that as a tenant receives a fraction of any increment in marginal products, his incentive to invest labour and other inputs will be less than if he were an owner-occupier. The "traditional" view of the size of tenant farms is thus that they ought to be smaller than owner-occupied farms. Cheung argues that this analysis of share tenancy is erroneous because it assumes that the tenant alone makes the decisions about how many resources to allocate to the farm. The owner also has a say on these matters and can stipulate the amount of resources to be allocated to each activity in the share contract.[12] Cheung then develops the optimal resource allocation under share tenancy using the following assumptions: wealth-maximizing behaviour, exclusive and transferable property rights over all resources, homogeneous resources, similar production functions for all farmers producing the same crops, zero transportation costs, and the same relative factor and product prices for all farmers.

Gale Johnson also shows that according to the assumptions of traditional theories of share tenancy, the tenant rents land until its marginal product is zero and production is inefficient.[13] Because this is inconsistent with available data on tenant agriculture, he suggests that landlords probably "encourage" tenants to cultivate to the desired intensity. Leases can stipulate the proper level of cultivation, landlords can share in the cost of other inputs to the same extent as their share of output, or they can use short-term contracts to frequently review their tenant's performance. Although the third method has certain disadvantages by reducing the expected value to the tenant of the marginal product of semidurable inputs and by potentially raising the mobility of farmers, with an attendant loss of knowledge about farming conditions, it may, as Johnson suggests, provide the best means of controlling the level of inputs supplied by tenants. He further argues that on the Great Plains of the United States, the best methods of farming and presumably the appropriate size of the farming unit were discovered only over time, and that tenants adopted prevailing practice out of uncertainty as to the effects of variations in inputs.[15]

Ransom and Sutch in *One Kind of Freedom* have noted that landlords in the southern United States during the late nineteenth century overcame the problems of resource allocation under share tenancy by exerting close control over the land-labour ratio and the crop mix, both of which were stipulated in their contracts with tenants.[16] They argued that "the limitation placed upon farm size effectively lowered the return per worker because each family would have less acreage to cultivate... The effect of acreage restrictions would be to increase the amount of effort the labourer was willing to exert."[17] Recognizing that annual contracting and the resulting insecurity of tenure were used to control the tenants' use of inputs, they nevertheless accept that the practice limited tenants' incentive to invest in their farms. Landlords treated the land as their primary asset and arranged things so as to maximize the value of output per acre.[18] Robinson and Eatwell also argue that "the landlord gains most when the holdings are small and the level of intensity of cultivation so high as to maximize output per acre. From the landlord's point of view, the smaller the holding per tenant the better, provided that it is not so small that the tenant families are unable to live."[19]

Another determinant of resource allocation is the type of production function that the farmer faces.[20] This determines how substitution is possible among the inputs, including land, in the production process. If the technology is such that little or no substitution is possible, then farm size would vary between tenants and owners only because of variations in the availability of other inputs, mainly capital, and would not reflect the type of land agreement in effect.

Historical, empirical studies on North America that examines the relationship between farm size and tenancy are few. Robert Higgs examines the general issue of race and land tenure in the southern United States in 1910, and as part of this study he estimates a regression of the log of total acreage per farmer on the percentage of the improved acreage devoted to cotton cultivation, the percentage of the total acreage improved, a dummy variable for black farm operators, and two dummy variables for type of tenure (fixed rent and share rent).[21] He concludes that "tenant farms tended to be smaller than owner-operated farms, regardless of the farmer's race or the extent of the farm's improvement."[22] Because this finding is not what one would expect from Cheung's model, Higgs tries to show that Cheung's assumptions may not have been true for 1910.

What determines farm size? The dependent variable or farm size can be measured or defined as either the total occupied acres or the total improved acres on each farm in the York County sample. The decision seems to be arbitrary, but since the intention here is to relate farm size to inputs like capital and labour, it seems preferable to use total improved acres per farm as the measure of farm size, because in the production function inputs relate only indirectly to total occupied acres by determining what proportion of these acres are actually cultivated. The dependent variable is the total improved acres per farm in natural logs ($LACRIMP$).[23]

Total improved acres are assumed to be a function of two general types of factors: (1) the type of product that is being produced on the farm; and (2)

Farm Size of Tenant and Owner-Occupied Farms in York County, Ontario, 1871

the availability of inputs to the farmer. The type of products that each farm produced is divided into four crop variables:

1. The log of the proportion of improved land in pasture (*LPRPAST*);
2. The log of the proportion if improved land in orchards and gardens (*LPRORCH*);
3. The long of the proportion of improved land in wheat (*LPRWHET*); and
4. The log of the proportion of improved land in potatoes (*LPRPOT*).

Since these variables are primarily controls to isolate the relationship of farm size to tenancy, their relationship to the dependent variable does not need to be specified. However, common sense or causal empiricism suggest that farms with a higher proportion of land in orchards or gardens and potatoes are likely to be smaller because such activities tend to follow a more intensive form of agriculture.

Each farm's inputs are measured by the following variables:

1. the log of the number of horses (*LNOHORSE*);
2. the log of the number of mild cows, plus horned cattle, plus sheep, plus swine (*LCATTLE*);
3. the log of the amount of capital (farmers simply indicated yes or no to whether the farm owned a wagon, plough, reaper, horserack, thrasher, and fanningmill; this variable in its unlogged form takes only the value of integers between 0 and 6) (*LCAPITAL*);
4. a binary variable with the value of one if the head of the household was from outside of Canada, and zero elsewhere (*FOR*);
5. a binary variable with the value of one of the head of the household could not read, and zero elsewhere (*CANREAD*);
6. the log of the number of children on the farm under the age of 15 (*LCHILD*); and
7. the log of the age of the head of the household (*LAGE*).

It is hypothesized that the first three input-type variables, *LCHILD* and *LAGE* are positively related to total improved acres because more inputs generate or are associated with the need for larger amounts of land; the age of the head of the household also represents the element of time that influences the ability to clear and improve land, and knowledge of skills and the land. Another reason to expect a positive association between improved average and age is that property accumulation is a function of age. But on the other hand, although knowledge of skills and the land increases with age, the physical ability to work the land declines after a certain age. The number of children at home is a crude measure of labor inputs. It is expected that the foreign-born will know less about technical skills and the land, or have less savings, and therefore have a smaller farm. A farmer who cannot read will also have less improved acres.

The log of the proportion of the total occupied acres that are improved (*LFARMED*) is also added as an explanatory variable. This measures the concept of how developed is each farm. A more developed farm presses up against the limits of its occupied acres and, therefore, is more likely to have the means and the inclination to expand, and therefore, has more improved acres.

Finally, a binary variable with a value of one for tenant farms and zero otherwise (*FARMTYPE*) is included. This is the chief independent variable of intent whose relationship to farm size could not be predicted a priori in the earlier part of this section.

Of the 1,727 farms in the sample for York County, the ordinary least squares regressions that follow used the 1,693 that stated total improved acres to be greater than zero. The first result included *FARMTYPE* as the only independent variable:

$$LACRIMP = 3.90 - .15\ [FARMTYPE]$$
$$(12.93)\ (2.96)$$

$$\bar{R}^2 = .005 \qquad F = 8.78$$

In this result and all those that follow, t-statistics are provided in the bracket below each coefficient and the 5% significance level is used. For a two-tailed test, the coefficient on *FARMTYPE* is significant, and the sign on this coefficient indicates that tenant farms were smaller than owner-occupied farms. However, nothing has been controlled; once control variables are introduced for inputs or for the type of products produced, the tenancy variable is never significant. This is illustrated with the following two results which should be taken as representative:

$$LACRIMP = 4.81 - .04\ [FARMTYPE] - .10\ [FOR]$$
$$(108.6)\quad (1.03) \qquad\qquad (2.80)$$
$$- .20\ [CANREAD] + .54\ [LFARMED] + .09\ [LPRPAST]$$
$$(2.61) \qquad\qquad (16.27) \qquad\qquad (13.00)$$
$$- .003\ [LPRORCH] - .06\ [LPRPOT] + .15\ [LPRWHET]$$
$$(.48) \qquad\qquad (7.22) \qquad\qquad (25.94)$$

$$\bar{R}^2 = .454 \qquad\qquad F = 177.0$$

$$LACRIMP = 4.17 + .01\ [FARMTYPE] + .06\ [LPRPAST]$$
$$(18.28)\ (.28) \qquad\qquad (10.00)$$
$$- .01\ [LPRORCH] + .07\ [LNOHORSE] + .48\ [LFARMED]$$
$$(1.92) \qquad\qquad (10.42) \qquad\qquad (16.57)$$

$$+ .09\,[LCATTLE] + .04\,[LCAPITAL] - .07\,[FOR]$$
$$(10.32) \qquad\qquad (6.13) \qquad\qquad (2.00)$$
$$- .11\,[CANREAD] + .09\,[LPRWHET] - .06\,[LPRPOT]$$
$$(1.64) \qquad\qquad (16.47) \qquad\qquad (9.11)$$
$$+ .001\,[LCHILD] + .009\,[LAGE]$$
$$(.46) \qquad\qquad (.16)$$

$$\bar{R}^2 = .590 \qquad\qquad F = 188.2$$

All the variables have the hypothesized signs, but the tenancy variable, the number of children, and the age of the head of the household are insignificant.

CONCLUSION

For York County in Ontario in 1871, a county with a relatively high proportion of tenant farms, the type of land holding and land using arrangement does not seem to have influenced the size of farm as measured by total improved acres. Given type of crop produced and measures of some inputs, any relationship that tenancy may have to farm size disappears in the statistics that are calculated. This seems to result from the fact that tenant farms had fewer horses, livestock, and capital, a greater proportion of land in orchards and gardens, and potatoes than did the owner-occupier, a smaller proportion of land in pasture and in wheat than owner-occupiers, and are more likely to be foreign-born.

Looking at some of these charactersitics in terms of the sample of York farms used here, 46.4% of the owners were born in Ontario while only 34.6% of the tenants were born in Ontario;[24] on the other hand 37.0% and 20.4% respectively of tenants and owners were born in England; in other words, a greater proportion of tenants were foreign-born. With respect to the uses that were actually made of the land, tenants and owners had 46% and 34% respectively of their improved land in potatoes; tenants did put a smaller proportion of their land in wheat than did owners: 12% versus 16%. Owner-occupied farms had an average 3.3 horses and tenants had 2.9 horses; owner-occupied farms had on average 5 milk cows, 5.4 horned cattle, 15.5 sheep, and 7.8 swine; the corresponding averages for tenants were 3.7, 4.8, 12.0, and 6.8. So owner-occupied farms had more livestock on average than the tenant farms. Finally, for all of the implements included in the measure of capital, a larger percentage of the owner-occupied farms had these implements than did the tenant farms. These data on the characteristics of tenant and owner-occupied farms substantiate the regression results that are preferred because they control for other influences when looking at the relationship between each variable and farm size.

In York census district in 1871 there was no difference in the size of farm between owner-occupier and tenant farms, all else the same. Owner-occupiers and tenants differed significantly in the type of product that they produced with the land and in the amount of livestock which they possessed.

ACKNOWLEDGMENTS

Financial support from the Social Sciences and Humanities Research Council of Canada and from Wilfrid Laurier University is gratefully acknowledged. Margaret Weppler provided excellent research assistance.

NOTES AND REFERENCES

1. As examples of some of their writings, see J. Reid, "Sharecropping as an Understandable Market Response: The Post-Bellum South," *Journal of Economic History* 33 (1973): 106-130; Ibid., "Antebellum Southern Rental Contracts," *Explorations in Economic History* 13 (1976): 69-83; Ibid., "White Land, Black Labor, and Agricultural Stagnation. The Causes and Effects of Sharecropping in the Postbellum South," *Explorations in Economic History* 16 (1979); 31-55; R. Ransom and R. Sutch, "The Look—In Mechanism and Overproduction of Cotton in the Postbellum South," *Agricultural History* 49 (1975): 405-425; Ibid., *One Kind of Freedom: The Economic Consequences of Emancipation* (New York: Cambridge University Press, 1977); R. Higgs, "Race, Tenure and Resource Allocation in Southern Agriculture, 1910," *Journal of Economic History* 33 (1973): 149-169; Ibid., *Competition and Coercion* (New York: Cambridge University Press, 1977).

2. R.L. Jones, *History of Agriculture in Ontario, 1613-1880* (Toronto: The University of Toronto Press, 1946), p. 62.

3. Jones, *History of Agriculture,* p. 68.

4. See for example, J. Burtniak, *The History of the County of Welland* (Belleville: Mika Silk Screening, 1972); G.E. Reaman, *A History of Vaughan Township* (Toronto: University of Toronto Press, 1971); W.S. Johnston and H.J.M. Johnston, *History of Perth County to 1967* (Stratford: B-H Press, 1867); J.G. Harkness, *Stormont, Dundas and Glengarry* (Oshawa; Mundy-Goodfellow, 1946); C.M. Johnston, *The Head of the Lake, A History of Wentworth County* (Hamilton: Wentworth County Council, 1958); L.A. Johnson, *History of the County of Ontario, 1615-1875* (Whitby: Corporation of the County of Ontario, 1973).

5. W.L. Marr, "Tenant vs. Owner Occupied Farms in York County Ontario, 1871," *Canadian Papers in Rural History* (1984): 50-71.

6. Canada, Department of Agriculture, *Census of Canada, 1870-1871,* 3, Table 21, p. 100.

7. L.J. Alston and R. Higgs, "Contractual Mix in Southern Agriculture since the Civil War: Facts, Hypotheses, and Tests," *Journal of Economic History* 42 (1982): 330.

8. D.L. Winter, "Tenant Farming in Iowa, 1860-1900: A Study of the Terms of Rental Leases," *Agricultural History* 48 (1974): 130.

9. W.L. Marr, "The Distribution of Tenant Agriculture: Ontario, Canada, 1871," *Social Science History* (forthcoming); W.L. Marr, "Nineteenth Century Tenancy Rates in Ontario's Counties, 1881 and 1891," Department of Economics Working Paper Series (Wilfrid Laurier University, 1986).

10. Marr, *Canadian Papers,* pp. 62-63.

11. S. Cheung, "Private Property Rights and Sharecropping," *Journal of Political Economy* 66 (1968): 1107-1122.

12. Cheung, "Private Property," pp. 1108-1110. Joseph Reid argues that the problem with the "traditional" analysis is that it focuses on only one party, either landlord or tenant, when tenancy is in fact a contract between both parties. Landlords will not passively accept a lower return from sharecropped land because it has alternative uses, that is, alternative to sharecropping. Reid develops his own model to show that sharecropping can be Pareto-efficient. See J. Reid, "Sharecropping and Agricultural Uncertainty," *Economic Development and Cultural Change* 24 (1976): 555-556.

13. D.G. Johnson, "Resource Allocation under Share Contracts," *Journal of Political Economy* 58 (1950): 111-123.

14. Johnson, "Resource Allocation," pp. 118-122.

15. A formal presentation of Johnson's points is found in D.M.G. Newbery, "The Choice of Rental Contract in Peasant Agriculture," in *Agriculture in Development Theory*, ed. L.G. Reynolds (New Haven: Yale University Press, 1975), pp. 113-114.

16. Ransom and Sutch, *One Kind*, pp. 98-103. Several writers have developed models with varying assumptions that show deductively that tenant agriculture need not be inefficient; see, for example, C. Bell, "Alternative Theories of Sharecropping; Some Tests Using Evidence from Northeast India," *Journal of Development Studies* 13 (1976/1977): 317-324; S.J. DeCario, *Agriculture in the Postbellum South: The Economics of Production and Supply* (Cambridge; MIT Press, 1974), 123-130; E.O. Heady, "Optimal Sizes of Farms Under Varying Tenure Forms, Including Renting, Ownership, State and Collective Structures," *American Journal of Agricultural Economics* 53 (1971): 18-24; J. Roumasset, "Sharecropping, Production Externalities and the Theory of Contracts," *American Journal of Agricultural Economics* 61 (1979): 640-644; J.G. Sutinen, "The Rational Choice of Share Leasing and Implications of Efficiency," *American Journal of Agricultural Economics* 57 (1975): 614-618.

17. Ransom and Sutch, *One Kind*, p. 99.

18. G. Wright, "Freedom and the Southern Economy," *Explorations in Economic History* 16 (1979): 100.

19. J. Robinson and J. Eatwell, *An Introduction to Modern Economics* (London: McGraw-Hill, 1973), p. 70.

20. This is suggested in C.H. Rao, "Uncertainty, Entrepreneurship, and Sharecropping in India," *Journal of Political Economy* 79 (1971): 588-589.

21. Higgs, "Race, Tenure," pp. 159-164.

22. Ibid., p. 160.

23. Many of the relationships are tested in linear regressions and these are available from the author on request. The choice of log versus linear was made on statistical grounds; much more of the variation of total acres improved was explained by the former functional form.

24. The statistics in this paragraph are from Marr, *Canadian Papers*.

PART IV

ORGANIZATION AND AGRICULTURAL DEVELOPMENT IN RUSSIA

INTRODUCTION

By contrast with Western Europe and England, agriculture was a weak partner in Russia's industrialization in the last decades of the nineteenth century. In relative terms, Russia fell behind. According to the most recent review of the published data, there was little disparity in per capita income between Petrine Russia (1689-1725) and Europe, but by the time of the peasant emancipation (1861), Russian per capita income was somewhere between one-third and one-half of that of Great Britain, and by 1913 about one-fifth.[1] Russia's relatively poor performance in the century of industrialization is characteristically explained by the residual effects of serfdom and by the preservation of the commune, which maintained control over out-migration, the distribution of land and other decisions affecting production.

From a different perspective, however, improvements in agriculture take on importance. In nineteenth-century Russia, there was a marked increase of land under cultivation and an expanding network of local markets, which led to an increase in agricultural output sufficient to account for a rise in the standard of living, especially after the 1880s. With an annual population growth of roughly 1.6%, total output increased enough to allow personal consumption in rural and urban areas to more than double in the last thirty years of the old regime. The more data that became available, the less justified seems the emphasis on Russia's status in the nineteenth century as one of the poorest countries of Europe.

The main achievement of Soviet and American research in the past few decades is to place more data at the disposal of scholars. Two of the papers below provide new household- and village-level information on manorial agriculture in the north of Russia. Rodney Bohac and Carol Leonard estimate the dimensions of non-agricultural labor and agricultural production in the decades before the emanicipation of the serfs. Bohac's study of the northern province of Tver' explores the effect of growing regional and occupational specialization and of the substitution of earnings from migratory labor and trade for income from agriculture. He traces the intensification of agriculture on large estates as a consequence of greater control over serfs' activity. Leonard's findings point to the same trend in neighboring Iaroslav province, where nonagricultural labor increased in the early nineteenth century to 40% of the working-age male population. However, on large estates, there was also a marked specialization in cereal production with some improvement in yields.

Steven Hoch's research on estate records for a more agricultural region discloses striking evidence of household prosperity. He argues, however, that prosperity was not the consequence of new technology, nor did it imply social and economic stratification, as Soviet scholars, who emphasize the uneven spread of wealth in rural Russia, maintain. Peasant tradition had not changed, he argues; bridewealth and periodic land redistribution by the commune prevented economic stratification.

After the emancipation of the serfs in 1861, peasant holdings were still not entirely separated from the manor, and serfs did not receive real personal freedom. The village obshchina (commune) retained responsibility for dues and later for redemption payments. Apart from the burden that these redemption payments placed on the village community was their perceived unfairness, one of the questions of concern to the intelligentsia in the populist era. Evsey Domar responds to this issue in an attempt to establish the real value of the land that the peasants received.

This is one of many questions that elude an exact answer. For the second half of the nineteenth century, it is difficult to know, for example, how fast the value of land was increasing and how distributional effects were felt. Rapid population growth coupled with restrictions on out-migration drastically affected the land/labor ratio, and peasant indebtedness increased. The poorest peasants are of interest to Soviet scholars, who trace the rise of revolutionary attitudes among the peasantry and the sources of village conflict. Viktor Buganov's paper analyzes the nature and extent of conflict; Ivan Koval'chenko examines its economic basis in social stratification. Using budget estimates of peasant households for several provinces of the blackearth center, he divides households by wealth, distinguishing between them by the intensity of their labor, scale of earnings, and patterns of investment and consumption. Leonid Goriushkin finds even greater distinctions between households in the frontier area of Siberia, where serfdom never developed.

Daniel Field responds to the central issue of stratification with new quantitative evidence for an impoverished region in the Ukraine. For this region, he raises a question about both the degree of development and the presumed effects. Drawing on agricultural census data to estimate stratification of households, with livestock, plowland and sown areas as his indices of wealth, he does produce evidence of differentiation. The results were not significant enough, however, to generate much confidence in the idea of the burgeoning of capitalism in the peasant economy at the turn of the twentieth century.

REFERENCE

1. P. Gregory, *Russian National Income, 1885-1913* (Cambridge, MA: Cambridge University Press, 1985); P. Gatrell, *The Tsarist Economy, 1850-1917* (New York, 1986).

THE DISTRIBUTION OF LAND AND AGRICULTURAL OUTPUT IN NON-BLACKEARTH RUSSIA ON THE EVE OF EMANCIPATION (MALOGA UEZD)

Carol S. Leonard

The boom in eighteenth-century Russian grain prices encouraged the expansion of cereal production in southern Russia, the origin of grain shipped north by the Volga.[1] Improved food supply in turn increased pressure on the land as the population more than tripled between 1719 and 1857, corresponding to the I and X *revizii*.[2] This brought to northern Russia a considerable degree of rural industrial development, and despite seasonal immobility of the labor supply, the expansion of outwork.

The powerful effect of regional exchange was mirrored in the divergence of the institutions of serfdom. Labor services, or *barshchina,* which reduced serfs' allotments and expanded the demesne, came to predominate in the grain-growing regions of the South; in the north-central region around Moscow, by contrast, the demesne was small or nonexistent, and landlords mainly imposed monetary dues, or *obrok.* Over 60% of the serfs in the north-central region in the 1850s paid dues in obrok, averaging roughly half the cost of subsistence per household.[3] Complementary institutional divergence, therefore, reinforced specialization in cereal production in the south and contributed to gradual development of towns in the North.[4] Serfdom, of course, was still an obstacle in the way of the development of a municiple economy based on a permanent labor force available for factory jobs; as a consequence, textiles, for example, remained largely rural.

It is commonly thought that the entrepreneurs in this growing rural economy were the landowners. There is some evidence for the eighteenth century of their interest in agricultural improvements, such as experimental crop rotation; their exodus to the countryside after the grant of freedom to noble servitors to live on their estates (1762) showed their local orientation. There is even more evidence for the nineteenth century in the profusion of technical literature on how to improve yields. These developments were significant, although any assumption about the profitability of serf estates bears a large burden of proof.[5]

Setting aside the issue of profitability and focusing on regional output, one may give large landowners a role in the increased yield in view of the extreme concentration of wealth. In the 1720s those with less than 100 serfs comprised 91.3% of all noble landowners; by the mid-nineteenth century (10 revizii), these were 75.7% of the total; during this time the proportion of serfs owned by this category fell from 41.3% to 20.5%. Table 1 shows the regional distribution of holdings. It should be noted that even the relatively small owner, by comparison with the slaveowner in the U.S. South, tended to own a great number of serfs.[8]

The demesne alone was not responsible for the increased output of grain in the eighteenth and nineteenth century. There is evidence that allotment land contributed a large part of the marketed cereals.[7] In any case, serfs' allotment land on large estates would have shared some advantages with the demesne, for example, in the quality of seed and access to market information. As the data presented will show, it is not essential to show a distinction between them.

The significant distinction for this paper is between large and small. Apart from the general difficulty of determining the effects of distribution of premodern agriculture, for Russian history the task is complicated by the problem of sources.[8] The records of large manors—the most widely used source on serfdom—are inadequate as a sample, because they provide no evidence for any other kind of manor.[9] Historians are misled to generalize from the experience of the Orlovs and Musin-Pushkins, or to assume that other kinds

Table 1. Distribution of Serfs by Region/Landowners
For European Russia, 10th Revizii (1857)

	Categories							
Region	1	2	3	4	5	6	7	8
Central Non-Blackearth	2,168,317	18,530	117	3	18	39	15	25
Central Blackearth	2,117,134	23,274	91	4	17	39	14	27
NW	507,445	7,722	66	5	25	45	14	9
Smolensk	367,115	5,308	69	6	23	40	11	10
Middle Volga	585,7450	4,561	128	2	13	40	18	27
Lower Volga	442,750	3,565	124	2	12	35	15	36
West	1,327,426	10,951	121	2	15	38	14	30
South West	1,484,135	5,449	272	1	6	31	20	43
Ukraine Left Bank	822,910	15,032	55	7	19	34	12	27
South Steppe	500,792	8,844	57	6	28	41	14	11
Urals	262,499	1,069	245	1	6	14	5	75
North	108,222	1,486	73	6	26	43	16	9
Total for 47 provinces in European Russia	10,694,445	106,391	100	3	15	37	15	29

Categories:
1 = Total serf population (males)
2 = Total landowners
3 = Average serfs per landowner
4 = Percent serfs owned by landowners with 1-21 serfs
5 = Percent serfs owned by landowners with 21-100 serfs
6 = Percent serfs owned by landowners with 101-500 serfs
7 = Percent serfs owned by landowners with 501-1000 serfs
8 = Percent serfs owned by landowners with over 1000 serfs

Source: I.D. Koval' chenko, *Russkoe Krepostnoe krest'ianstvo v pervoi polovine XIX v.* [Russian serfs in the first half of the 19th century] (Moscow, 1967), Table 5, p. 59.

of estates were unimportant. During the century-and-a-half of relatively steady growth from 1750 to the end of the nineteenth century, the most important element in commercial specialization may well have been the "plantation" style economy of large estates.[10] But this conclusion cannot be based on records of large estates alone.

A distinction between estates is that the relative poverty of small owners would not have permitted them to pursue elaborate management strategies. Barshchina generally demanded constant supervision, necessitating on large estates costly management. Obrok was also an unreliable form of payment. Obrok estates were remunerative only where dues were collectable; i.e., where an administrative apparatus was present. The difference between large and small estates, therefore, is brought sharply into focus in decisions affecting work schedules and payments, which were critical in the response of serfs and landlords to economic opportunity. This paper examines the relative efficiency of large estates at a threshold size, where management could be introduced to utilize more labor and induce harder work by a different incentive system.

I

The data are a unique collection of village level information for the social and economic history of Iaroslav Province. Three manuscript collections, the "Economic Notes" to the General Land Survey (1778), the "Economic Notes" to the Atlas (1820s-1830s), and the officers' survey (Mende Collection) (1855),[11] furnished information of varying quality but general consistency. The landlords change over time, the villages remain the same. The effect is of panel data, providing a far from complete picture but a dynamic development.[12]

The data show land under culitivation (its quality and type), field allocation, population, serfs dues, and for 1855, crops, yields, farm animals, marketing activity, and other nonagricultural occupations. Information is for 931 parcels (excluding property of the state and crown), or individual parcels making up 310 estates. Reorganized by landowner, the data form 383 entries, of which 115 are without serfs, leaving 268 settled units. In other words, the three data sets coordinated by chronological variables consist of a set with over 900 parts of villages owned by a single individual; a set with 310 estates (the main data set for this paper); and a set with 268 estates organized by landlord (any single entry might represent scattered villages throughout the district, or it might be a single settled allotment owned by a poor noble within a village largely belonging to others).

The data are fragile. What mars them most is potential inaccuracy difficult to pinpoint, such as false answers by landlords evading the imposition of taxes or excessively rough estimates by surveyists about the size of property holdings.[13] Instead of field size, for example, are the categories arable, forest, hay meadows, and waste, categories useful for taxation purposes but inadequate for determining distinctions between allotment land and the demesne, or between fallow and forest. More important, because the land was not remeasured throughout the nineteenth century, it is impossible to determine how much land was reclaimed.[14] As a consequence, the results are a rough replication of the arrangement of land.

II

The district of Maloga from which the data are drawn is in Iaroslav province, north and somewhat east of Moscow. Extremely low yields of 2 and 3:1, and the frequency of harvest failure, meant that no village in Maloga could afford to abandon cereal production, even though most households purchased grain from the Volga merchants.[15] In addition to land, lumber was the most important resource. The location of the district on two main commercial rivers, the Volga and the Maloga, produced a region responsive to needs of transportation, at a cost of perhaps half its forests between the years 1778, the time of the General Land Survey, and the 1850s.[16] Prices rose and landlords profited. Because sawing and construction was done in the winter months, lumber was not an industry in conflict with highly seasonal agriculture. Therefore, even with a substantial portion of males (20%) engaged seasonally in nonagricultural occupations, Maloga remained agricultural, in part also because its rich forests supported the slash/burn method of cultivation and its many rivers provided energy for mills and water for cultivation of its sandy soils. Moreover, although Maloga lay in the non-blackearth region, blackearth could be found in patches nearly everywhere, and fertility was also improved by lush meadows on the banks of the Volga, although the proximity of rivers also meant that nearby settlements lost their winter crop in floods.

Because of its rivers, this region also had longstanding commercial importance. Linked to the fairs of Nizhnii Novgorod and Rostov and to the two capitals, Moscow and St. Petersburg, by the Maloga and Volga rivers, Maloga attracted large settlements in the seventeenth century; by the mid-nineteenth century small population centers had become towns and fairs. Barges carrying grain, iron and salt up the Volga from southern posts to St. Petersburg brought Moscow merchants to local fairs to purchase textiles, nails, dyes, and leather goods. This district, therefore, is representative of most of the northern Volga, where the grain trade had particular impact.

In Iaroslav, the rigidity of agricultural organization under conditions of the intractable, northern soil, make the region a case representing little variation in output per man and woman and per *desiatina* (2.7 acres) over several centuries.[17] Because of the general backwardness of the economy and unusual susceptibility to "shocks," neither cloth production nor metal work activated large-scale industrial enterprise.[18] However, here, like elsewhere in the North, the transfer of labor into rural crafts and industries was significant, and it encouraged some intensification of agriculture.

III

The profile of owners in Maloga shows 28% to have been small holders (less than 700 desiatiny [desiatina = 2.7 acres]); these estates accounted for an insignificant 7% of the land. Most of the land belonged to owners of over 1000 desiatiny (72 of the 383 estates aggregated by landlord), with 67% of the arable and 72% of the forest. As a whole, for all owners the size of property correlated

Table 2. Distribution of Holdings by Serfs and Land
Maloga District, Iaroslav Province, 1855

By Number of Serfs	Categories						
(male and female)	1	2	3	4	5	6	7
Central							
All 310 estates*	222	63,211	1037	318,460	5.20	.09	.36
169 estates							
< 100 serfs	57	8.202	391	65.016	6.28	.19	.29
124 estates							
101-500	199	24,541	702	87,081	3.98	.10	.41
17 estates							
> 500 serfs	1,925	32,894	9,786	166,363	5.11	.07	.58
By land							
257 estates							
< 800 d.	111	26,627	288**	47,918	5.26	.15	.29
53 estates							
> 800 d.	795	36,584	5,104	270,542	4.86	.07	.70
7 estates							
> 9000 d.	4,024	20,121	21,802	152,618	5.34	.04	.73

Categories:
1 = Average number of serfs (male and female)
2 = Total serfs
3 = Average size of estate in desiatiny
4 = Total desiatiny
5 = Arable per *tiaglo* (work unit, usually man and wife)
6 = Garden (serfs' private holding used for vegatables, flax and hay) per tiaglo in desiatiny
7 = Percent property in forest (excluding brush and waste)

Notes: * Estates, called "dachi," as in the survey of 1855 (dach' includes one or more parcels owned by one, sometimes two and three owners)
**Includes 20 estates without serfs

at a coefficient of .92 with forest and .63 with arable, a resource distribution which suggests the commerial potential of large estates. Table 2 shows the distribution of land and serfs.

A few large estates embraced roughly half of the population; half (excluding state peasants) resided on considerably smaller estates. The mean holding was between 800 and 900 desiatiny and probably about 150 to 200 serfs. No estate could be called exactly typical, but two main groups of owners emerge. The distinction between these two is largely one of resources: large estates had huge forests and little of the garden that serfs most prized; small estates had ample garden but considerably less forest. Large estates, with roughly the same tiaglo/ arable ratio, had huge population centers; small estates tended to have small villages, divided even smaller by apportionment to diverse owners. In sum, the economic position of the typically small or middling owner greatly differed from that of the wealthiest owner both by numbers of serfs and by land.

Table 3. Comparison of Editorial Commission List (1859) and
Data Set Aggregated by Landlord (21 estates) (1855)
Maloga District, Iaroslav Prvince*

	Editorial Commisssion (49) Over 100 Souls (males)	Aggregated Data Same estates (21)*[a]
Average serfs (male) per estate	343	457
Arable used by		
serfs	440 d.	1,334 d.
landlords	2,633 d.	1,334 d.
Forests used by		
serfs	89 d.	6,148 d.
landlords	2,107 d.	

Notes: *The Editorial Commission materials are estates owned by single families (excluding jointly owned villages); my data are most of the same list of villages and estates with the same owners, taken from the Economic Surveys (1837 and 1855).
[a] Some villages were excluded because of problems of comparability.

A note should be made that in the published materials most widely used by historians, records of the Commission that prepared the Emancipation Statutes, only estates with over a hundred serfs were listed, on the assumption that this included most of the emancipated serfs.[19] To show what kind of bias this introduces into research, Table 3 is a comparison of my data and the Editorial Commission list.

This Table 3 shows that the Commission erred by omission. There is a discrepancy in size of serf population and in the amount of forest land held. A further implication is that the commission materials should not be used to study typical estates belonging to small or middling owners, who were considerably worse off, as shown in Table 2. Out of the 383 landowners in Maloga, only 49 held over 100 male serfs; they were an elite among landowners.

IV

Did the elite conduct agriculture more efficiently than the rest? There is considerable evidence of a step effect (not a gradual increase of output by scale, but a gap between the largest estates and all others), as measured by specialization in rye and by the yield/seed ratio for rye, the staple winter and sometimes spring crop in northern Iaroslav. Table 4 shows a larger yield per *chetvert'* rye sown (a measure equivalent to a quarter—2.10 hectolitres) for large estates.

Table 4. Crops and Output (Maloga District, 1855)

	Yield/seed ratio			Chetverti sown per tiaglo			
	Winter	Spring	Potato	Rye	Oats	Potato	Barley
All estates (310)	2.90	2.92	2.50	1.64	2.68	.39	.17
Typed by Numbers of Serfs							
< 100 serfs (169)	2.98	2.77	2.29	1.53	2.60	.45	.14
100-500 (124)	3.30	3.13	2.65	1.73	2.74	.39	.20
> 500 (17)	3.41	2.79	3.29	1.87	2.85	.01	.14
Typed by Land Size							
< 50 d. (29)	3.13	2.63	3.26	1.22	2.34	.81	.06
< 800 d. (257)	3.05	2.78	2.40	1.57	2.71	.42	.15
> 800 d. (53)	3.60	3.74	3.12	1.95	2.49	.24	.20
> 9000 d. (7)	5.10	2.70	1.40	3.00	2.60	.00	.22

Table 5. Horses and Cows per Tiaglo (Maloga District, 1855)

	Horses	Cows
All Estates (310)	1.06	1.78
Typed by Numbers of Serfs		
< 100 serfs (169)	1.02	1.70
100-500 (124)	1.12	1.85
> 500 (17)	1.00	1.87
Typed by Land size		
< 50 d. (29)	1.04	1.60
< 800 d. (257)	1.07	1.77
> 800 d. (53)	1.02	1.82
> 9000 d. (7)	1.00	1.60

Other differences can be observed. On small estates, more potatoes were grown; the larger the estate, the more rye as a portion of all crops; on the largest estates, no potatoes were grown. Small estates seem, therefore, to have been closer to subsistence farming than larger estates, which may have been more commercially oriented. In qualification, however, the yield of spring crops does not differ by size of estate, showing an almost unvarying number of oat-consuming cattle per tiaglo (see Table 5).

The number of cattle thought necessary to fertilize a desiatina of land in the North was 6 head; 0.6 was the average in Maloga.[20] This suggests the limits of three- and sometimes two-field agriculture in the North, a limit equally constraining on large and small estates. Why the high yield of rye on the largest estates?

V

The difference between the yields of 5:1 and those of 3:1 is significant.[21] Under the conditions of three-field agriculture and unvarying numbers of cattle, wealthier landlords were apparently able to intensify production with virtually the same arable/tiaglo (land/labor) ratio as in villages of less well-off landlords. One might suggest that wealthier nobles bought better land; but that argument is not supported by Table 6, which shows no striking variation by type of soil. Population size used in Table 6 as a proxy for economic status of landowner (large holdings had larger average serf settlements) indicate that large estates had no advantage in superior soil.

One might suggest, as another hypothesis, that the difference in yield resulted from geographical advantage. The commercial advantage of an estate close to the river might have encouraged improvements in the growing of rye, not

Table 6. Soil Variation, Yield, Population (Maloga District, 1855)*

	Yield/Seed Rye	Av Estate Size (Males)	
Sandy	3.81	56	(N = 19)
Silt/dry	3.00	62	(N = 1)
Silt	3.08	81	(N = 99)
Silt/sand	3.30	315	(N = 27)
Gray silt	2.99	80	(N = 129)
Gray clay	3.80	66	(N = 5)
Sandy/patches of blackearth with iron	4.00	47	(N = 1)
Gray sand	3.50	109	(N = 8)
Clayish	2.79	360	(N = 10)
Gray/silt/sand	4.00	44	(N = 4)

Note: * Soil types determined in 1855 by land surveyors.

entirely cancelled out by the risk of flooding, because there was the added benefit of alluvial soil. In general, confirming intuition, location by river showed a somewhat higher yield, but not enough to account for the lead of large estates. Close to the Volga, the yield was an average of 3:1, and in correlation analysis, proximity of the Volga did not have any relation to yield, average number of horses or crops planted. The significant difference in location might well have been not between the Volga and other rivers, but between, on one hand, the Volga and its tributaries—Maloga, Sheksna, Iana, Iskra, and Pushma—all accessible to traders—and, on the other hand, all other places. But here too, the outcome does not show location by rivers to have been advantageous for the production of grain: estates on any major river— 12 estates—had a yield 2.9, relatively low. One may conclude that overland transportation costs cannot have been a significant barrier to trade.

VI

The failure of yields to vary significantly by soil and location suggests that size of estate should not necessarily be linked with landlords' entrepreneurial interest in agriculture. Because serfs on all size estates provided both the implements and the cattle for their own allotments and for the demesne, landlords, in any case, were constrained in their influence over productivity. This fact and the unvarying average number of cattle show that large landowners were not necessarily buying land in Maloga with an interest in improving it. Other reasons have to be found for the differences observed in mean yields between large estates and small.

There were two main characteristics of the largest estates that have a bearing on output. The first is the elaborate management structure, a hierarchy of well-paid officials, who imposed a highly regulated regime. This presumably achieved some effect by regimentation and rigid work schedules.[22]

A second characteristic is form of dues, which in effect was a scheme of reward and punishment. In the eighteenth century, estates were managed mainly by barshchina or obrok; in the nineteenth century, large landlords introduced a mixed form of dues, which did not inhibit rural industry. Barshchina as a pure system was disappearing, mixed dues were becoming more common. Nearly half of all the estates in Maloga (46%) remained on obrok for the sixty years, 1777-1837; only 29% remained on obrok through 1855. There was a steady decline of obrok and a rise of some barshchina, particularly after 1837. Dividing estates by form of dues (Table 7), although only a third of the estates had mixed dues, they contributed the overwhelming share of output (76%).

Table 7. Form of Dues (Maloga District, 1855)

	Estates (N)	Yield/ Rye	Net Output per Tiaglo	Percent Sum Net Output	Mean Percentage Outworkers among Males
Barshchina	20	2.42	1.77	.53	.06
Obrok	167	3.06	3.66	23.15	.29
Mixed	90	3.60	5.02	76.31	.27

Table 8. Parcel Size (931 cases) and Form of Dues (Maloga District, 1855)

	Barshchina	Obrok	Mixed
1778	36	54	45
1827	46	77	67
1855	52	91	98

On mixed estates, a slightly larger yield and significantly larger seed sown per tiaglo produced a different output by household as well as estate. It seems clear that barshchina estates on the average were small and impoverished (Tables 7 and 8); mixed dues estates had larger settlements (see Table 8) and a greater abundance of seed.

Table 7 shows that although obrok remained the most frequent form of dues,[23] it was not as important for agriculture as the mixed form of dues. 211 out of 901 parcels had a mix of dues; mixed dues rose between 1777 and 1855 from 8.8 to 27% of the 383 cases aggregated by landlord. Clearly the economic effect of mixed dues was visible to contemporaries. This effect was not the same as a return to pure barshchina; landlords did not mix dues in order to reduce serfs' nonagricultural activities and concentrate on agriculture. On mixed dues estates roughly the same percent of the male population was engaged in crafts (see Table 7). In other words, the economic opportunity for the village as a whole was roughly the same on mixed dues and obrok estates.

Mixed dues estates, therefore, achieved greater output by a different kind of effect than regimentation alone would produce. Labor services were disliked by the serfs.[24] It was a punitive system, by which the landlord gained greater authority to demand a faster pace of work and more responsibility in payments. This does not mean that the purpose of mixed dues was the improvement of agriculture. With no evidence of investment in cattle, fertilizer, or implements, it can be assumed that the purpose was to increase monetary revenues, or reduce loss due to nonpayment of obrok. With a management apparatus, the landlord could easily transfer serfs from one form of payment to another; much of the records of large estates consist in these transfers for nonpayment.

A second advantage to mixed dues can be seen in the records of large estates. The Musin-Pushkins, who owned 60,795 desiatiny along the Volga and Iana rivers, or 14% of all the land in the Maloga, imposed mixed dues. By imposing barshchina on indebted peasants, Ivan Iakovlevich Musin Pushkin gained free labor in the winter by demanding that serfs work off debts by hauling loads of wood, "kopani," and constructing barges, sold in the spring in Rybinsk. Musin Pushkin never transferred an entire village to barshchina, although in years of dearth, such as the early 1820s; most of his households had one or two males performing some labor services.[25]

The psychological mechanism was the threat that barshchina posed to household income. Serfs who did not fall into debt were rewarded with permission to leave the village, and because, on the whole, outside earnings could not be captured by an increase in obrok, an amount subject to custom and negotiation, outwork was a source of considerable earnings.[26] Naturally, effort was not a guarantee of remaining on obrok. Threats to serfs' welfare were numerous: harvest failure, a rise in prices, the death of horse or a worker had immediate implications. On the obrok estate, serfs could compensate by outside earnings; on a mixed dues estate, the consequence of a severe loss would be the impoverization of the household under barshchina obligations. It might be argued then, that fear of impoverishment was as great an incentive as the regimentation of labor, and combined, the effect was to raise yields and amount of seed sown and encourage specialization in rye.

What were the possible ways by which serfs increased the yield? One means they might have chosen on large estates was to use landlords' forests for slash/burn agriculture. Or they might have reclaimed more waste, which was abundant on large estates. With no evidence of technological advancement or multiple crop rotation, improvements could also have meant more frequent weeding or double and triple ploughing. Perhaps the landlord purchased better seed for the demesne, bringing a higher yield for the same labor.

VII

In conclusion, in the mid-nineteenth century, distinctions between large and small estates stand out, flagging advances in agriculture in an area where the average yield/seed ratio had remained 2.5:1 and 3:1 for hundreds of years. But output also varied by form of dues, showing a combination of factors. Maloga is not entirely representative of northern Russia, due to its heavily forested terrain and relatively sparse population, but in distribution of wealth, it was indeed typical. Also, like most of northern Russia, the soil was generally intractable, which encouraged the rise of rural industries and outwork.

In regard to the main source of earnings, nonagricultural labor, neither size of estate nor mix of dues made much difference, although in regard to agriculture, these considerations were decisive. However, neither the size of estate nor the form of dues points necessarily to the landlords' entrepreneurial initiative. Much of the history of agriculture and industry in Iaroslav Province lies at the level of the household and in the incentives that impelled serfs to improve yields without adopting new technology.

One implication of these data is that the manorial regime was flexible in response to the needs of rural industry for labor; mixed dues did not restrict nonagricultural occupations. However, the changing economic environment did give birth to a more regimented agricultural arrangement, a mixed form of dues, more restrictive for the serfs, but a savings for the landlord who could afford the costs of supervision.

ACKNOWLEDGMENT

The research for this paper was funded by a grant from the National Science Foundation, Economics Program (329-0215A).

NOTES AND REFERENCES

1. B. Mironov, *Khlebnye tseny v Rossii (XVIII-XIX vv.)* [Grain prices in Russia (18th-19th century)] (Leningrad, 1985).

2. V.M. Kabuzan, *Izmeneniia v razmeshchenii naseleniia Rossii v XVIII-pervoi polovine XIX v.* [Changes in the distribution of the population of Russia in the 18th-first half of the 19th century] (Moscow, 1971), pp., 10-11.

3. In Iaroslav Province, 20-22 silver rubles, the cost of subsistence for an agricultural worker. "Raznye statisticheskie svedeniia," *Gosudarstvennyi Arkhiv Iaroslavskoi Oblasti (GAIaO)* [statistical information, State Archive of Iaroslav Oblast'], *Fond* (F.) [Collection] 642 Gubernskogo statisticheskogo komiteta Iaroslavskoi gubernii, [Provincial statistical committee of Iaroslav], *opis'* (*op.*) [inventory] 1, *delo* (*d.*, or *dd. pl.*) [file] 22457, *chast'* (*ch.*) [part] 1, *listy* (*l.*, or *ll.*) [folios] 45 *ob.* [reverse side]-48; "Svedeniia o tsenakh povol'nomu naimu na zemledel' cheskie raboty v Iaroslavskoi gubernii na khozaiskom prodovol'stvii, 1855-1866 gg.," *d.* 22531, *op.* 1, *ll.* 2-4 [information about prices of hired labor in agriculture in Iaroslav Province]; my data are the source for obrok per tiaglo, an impost on one work unit consisting of a man and woman (16-63 years of age); I.D. Koval'chenko, *Russkoe krepostnoe krest'ianstvo v pervoi polovine XIX v.* [Russian serfs in the first half of the 19th century] (Moscow, 1967), pp. 62-63.

4. B.N. Mironov, *Vnutrennii rynok Rossii vo vtoroi polovine XVIII-pervoi polovine XIX v.* [Internal market of Russia in the second half of the 18th-first half of the 19th century] (Leningrad, 1981).

5. " We have not found that the profitability of Russian serfdom before 1861 was threatened by the rise in grain prices, the growth of population, Paul's Law, or the use of the *obrok* system...These conclusions are based on a number of theoretical assumptions and on empirical data of uncertain quality. They should be treated as highly tentative." E. Domar and M. Machina, "The Profitability of Russian Serfdom," *The Journal of Economic History* 44,4 (December 1984): 949, 919-955.

6. P. Kolchin, *Unfree Labor: American Slavery and Russian Serfdom* (Cambridge, MA, 1987), p. 54.

7. On their land, serfs and state peasants harvested 75% of the grain and potatoes; they produced most of the cattle sold, almost all commercial flax and hemp, Russia's main exports, and 40% of grain traded. See Koval'chenko, *Russkoe Krepostnoe Krest'ianstvo*, p. 384.

8. R. Fogel and S. Engerman, *Time on the Cross: The Economics of American Negro Slavery* (Boston, 1974); see a recent review by E. Field, "The Relative Efficiency of Slavery Revisted: A Translog Production Function Approach," *American Economic Review* 78,3 (June 1988): 543-549.

9. B.B. Kafengauz, *Istoriia khoziastva Demidovykh v XVII-XIX vv.* [History of the Demidov economy in the 17th-19th century], I (Moscow-Leningrad, 1949); Koval'chenko, *Krepostnoe krest'ianstvo;* K.V. Sivkov, *Ocherki po istorii krepostnogo khoziastva i krest'ianskogo dvizheniia v Rossii v pervoi polovine XIX veka* [Essays on the history of the manorial economy and the peasant movement in Russia in the first half of the 19th century] (Moscow, 1951).

10. I.D. Koval'chenko, N.B. Selunskaia and B.M. Litvakov, *Sotsial'no-ekonomicheskii stroi pomeshchich'ego khoziastva Evropeiskoi Rossii v epokh kapitalizma* [Social-economic structure of the manorial economy of European Russia in the era of capitalism] (Moscow, 1982), pp. 4-5; I.D. Koval'chenko and L.V. Milov, *Vserossiiskii agrarnyi rynok, XVIII-nach. XX vv.* [All-Russian agrarian market, 18th- beginning of the 20th century] (Moscow, 1974); B.N. Mironov, "O kriterii edinogo natsional'nogo rynka," in *Ezhegodnik po agrarnoi istorii Vostochnoi Evropy za 1968* g. (EAIVE) [Criteria of a unified national market, Yearbook on the agrarian history of Eastern Europe for 1968] (Leningrad, 1972), pp. 180-189.

11. Inconsistencies in the data for the 1830s reveal that some information for this later period is actually taken from the earlier period. One landowner who died in 1802, for example, is still on the rolls in the 1820s. The data base is drawn from "Economicheskie primechaniia k Generalnomu Mezhevaniiu," *Tsentral'nyi Gosudarstsvennyi Arkhiv Drevnikh Aktov [TsGADA]* [Economic notes to the General Land Survey, Central State Arkhiv of Ancient Acts], F. 1355, d. 2091; "Ekonomicheskie primechaniia k Mezhevym opisam Gen. Mende" [Economic notes to Survey schedules, General Mende] (Maloga, 1855-6), F. 1357, dd. 18/407, 19.408, 20/409; "Ekonomicheskie priimechaniia"(Atlas) [Economic Notes] *Tsentral'nyi Gosudarstvennyi Voenno-Istorichesakii Arkhiv TsGVIA F. Voenno-Uchennyi Arkhiv (VUA)* [Central State Military-Historical Archive, Military-Research Archive], *otdelenie (otd.)* [section] V, d. 19187.

12. Aggregating the data by landlords made it necessary to divide those estates occupied by several owners into equal parts by numbers of owners, although at the time of the land survey, exact boundaries did not exist, and forests, meadows and arable were held in common by the several owners of a single village.

13. In 1787, responding to a question about the size of allotments on the Musin Pushkin estates in Maloga, a village elder reported, "Among us the land is measured by the ancient name of 'pirog' which has 18 desiatiny of land, but this is not correct because the boundaries and *sazheny* [unit of land] of the pirog have never been measured ... *TsGADA*, F. 1270 Musina Pushkina, d. 301. The land survey was completed in 1778.

14. L. V. Milov, "O roli perelozhnykh zemel' v russkom zemledelii vtoroi poloviny VXIII v.," [About the role of fallow in Russian agriculture in the second half of the 18th century] *EAIVE 1961* g. (Riga, 1963), pp. 279-288.

15. On transportation, harvests and population in Maloga, see reports of the Governor, General (Gubernatorskie otchety) for Iaroslav Province, 1804-1861, *Tsentralynii Gosudarstvennii Istoricheskii Arkhiv v gorode Leningrade (TsGIAL)* [Central State Historical Archive in Leningrad], F. 1281 op. 11, dd. 178, 179, 180, 181, 182, 183, op. 4, dd. 22, 40, 52, 61, 145, op. 5, dd. 24, 26, 35, 38, 39, 45, op. 6, dd. 22, 33, 36, 41, 55; F. 1263, op. 1, dd. 621, 796, 865, 984, 1047, 1062, 1182, 1266, 1333, 1416, 1488, 1564, 1638, 1704, 1781, 1858, 1933, 2016, 2018, 2101, 2181, 2251, 2332, 2411, 2477, 2544, 2617, 2617, 2683, 2762, 2829, 2902, 2965; F. 1409, op. 1, dd. 4907, op. 2, 4835, 5865, 6455; F. 1284, op. 15, d. 24, op. 16, d. 24, op. 19, d. 39; "Doneseniia General Gubernatora Alekseia Mel'gunova o Iaroslavskoi i Vologodskoi guberniiakh, 1788-1794

gg.," [reports of the Governor General Aleksei Mel'gunov about Iaroslav and Vologda provinces, 1788-1794] *TsGADA, F.* 16, *d.* 1012, *ch.* I-II; "Opisanie goroda Mologa so vsemi sostoiashchimi v uezde onago dachami s pokazaniem ch'ego oni vladeniia i kakoe kolichestvo zemli v kazhdoi dache kotoryia znachat'sia pod nomerami krasnymi kazennyia i ekonomicheskiia a chernymi raznovladel'cheskie, 1821 g." [Description of the town of Maloga with all the estates in the district and an indication of the owner and the amount of land in each estate, red for state and economic estates, and black for various owners] *d.* 19185; "Topograficheskie opisaniia Iaroslavskoi gubernii" [Topographical description of Iaroslav Province] 1777, 1798, 1808, 1846 gg., *dd.* 19176, 19178, 19179, 19188; "Obozrenie ekonomicheskikh volostei, "Poshekhonsk i Maloga, [Survey of economic regions] *d.* 19181; "Voenno-statisticheskaia opisanie Iaroslavskoi gubernii," [Military-statistical description of Iaroslav Province] 1851 g., *TsGVIA, F. VUA, d.* 19189; I. Vil'son, *Ob"iasneniia k khoziastvennomu statisticheskomu atlasu Evropeiskoi Rossii* [Explanations for the Economic Statistical Atlas of European Russia] (St. Petersburg, 1869), pp. 1-74; *Materialy dlia statistiki Rossii* [Materials for statistics about Russia], *vypusk* (*vyp.*) [issue] 2 (St. Petersburg, 1859).

16. "Topograficheskoe opisanie" [Topographical description], *GAIaO, op.* 1, *d.* 22566, *ch.* 2, *ll.* 148 ob-149.

17. In the south, by contrast, yields may have been larger than has been thought. See Steven Hoch's *Serfdom and Social Control in Russia: Petrovskoe, a Village in Tambov* (Chicago, 1986).

18. J. Mokyr, "Emigration and Poverty in Prefamine Ireland," *Explorations in Economic History,* 19 (1982): 350-384; O. Crisp, *Studies in the Russian Economy* (London, 1976); A. Kahan, "Natural Calamities and their Effect upon the Food Supply in Russia," *Jahrbücher für Geschichte Osteuropas NeuFolge,* bd. 16 (1968): 353-377; and his *The Plow, The Hammer, and the Knout, An Economic History of Eighteenth-Century Russia* (Chicago: The University of Chicago Press, 1985), ch. 2.

19. *Prilozheniia k trudam Redaktsionnykh kommissii dlia sostavleniia polozhenii o krest'ianakh, vykhodiashchikh iz krepostnoi zavisimosti* [Appendices to the works of the Editorial commissions for the creation of statutes on the emancipation of the serfs] (St. Petersburg, 1859-1860), supplementary volumes.

20. *Voenno-statisticheskii sbornik* [Military statistical collection] (St. Petersburg, 1871, p. 230).

21. "A rise in yield from 3 to 4 had the result of increasing the crop grown on the original area by one-third ... The rise in yield has a cumulative effect in that the larger proportion of land that can now be used for food crops is added to it ... This cumulative effect is most notable when the seed/yield ratio is low, for instance when there is a rise from 3 to 4; it is of far less consequence with high seed/yield ratios, e.g. a rise of 11 to 12 or 9 to 12." B. H. Slicher van Bath, *The Agrarian History of Western Europe* (London, 1963), p. 19.

22. See Carol Leonard "Landlord and the Mir: Transactions Costs of Serfdom," in the forthcoming volume of conference papers of the London Conference on the Russian Peasant Commune.

23. Soviet historians have emphasized mixed dues; Domar's work on serfdom ignores them. Domar, "Profitability"; V. I. Krutikov and V. A. Fedorov, "Opisaniia pomeshch'ikh imenii 1858-1859 gg. kak istochnik po istorii pomeshchich' ego khoziastva i krest'ianstva nakanune reformy 1861 g. (po materialam Tul'skoi i Moskovskoi gubernii)," [Descriptions of nobles' estates 1858-1859 as a source on the history of manorial agriculture and the peasantry on the eve of reform in 1861] *EAIVE 1970 g.* (Riga, 1977), pp. 140-155.

24. N.L. Rubinshtein, *Sel'skoe khoziastvo Rossii vo vtoroi polovine XVIII v.* [The rural economy of Russia in the second half of the 18th century] (Moscow, 1957), pp. 13-15; N. M. Shepukova, "Ob izmenenii razmerov dushevladeniia pomeshchikov Evropeiskoi Rossii v pervoi chetverti XVIII-pervoi poloviny XIX v.," [About changes in serfownership in European Russia in the first-quarter of the 18th-first half of the 19th century] *EAIVE 1963 g.* (Vilnius, 1964), pp. 388-408.

25. Among the villages in Maloga belonging to Musin Pushkin, Rozhestveno experienced this change over a few years. In the *podvornye opisi* [household inventories] of 1787 and 1793, all of the households were on obrok and half of them had a lucrative trade in iron ore, bringing in 10 to 50 rubles a year; by the 1820s and 1830s, the serfs had lost this income, along with access to forests and nearby meadows; half had been transferred to barshchina. In 1852, 13 males remained on obrok, 63 were on barshchina. "Podvornye opisi" and "Oklad," *TsGADA, F.* 1279, *dd.* 301, 346, 1086, 1090, 1535, 1658, 2033, 2174, 2173, 2967, 6314, 5351, 4683.

26. Leonard, "Landlord and the Mir."

AGRICULTURAL STRUCTURE AND THE ORIGINS OF MIGRATION IN CENTRAL RUSSIA, 1810-1850

Rodney Bohac

The expanding capitalist markets of the nineteenth and twentieth centuries have challenged the traditional social and economic structures of the peasant community. Many observers and scholars characterize the markets as penetrating forces disrupting or destroying peasant economic security and socioeconomic cohesiveness. In this scenario the frightened peasants unite to defend their community from hostile, external forces. The markets can alternatively be depicted as offering opportunities to the diverse social and sometimes competing social groups within the peasant community.[1] Peasants in early nineteenth-century Russia faced a growing agricultural market and new employment opportunities in rural and urban manufacturing. This paper examines the adaptation of one community of Russian serfs to these changes. Due to serfowner coercion and growing opportunities to work outside the community, the serfs began to supplement their agricultural yields with income from migratory labor and crafts and trades. In this early encounter with an expanding economy it was not the community's poor, but those households enjoying the greatest success in the traditional agricultural sector who were best able to adapt and benefit.

Over one thousand serfs lived in the nine villages of Manuilovskoe estate. Located in the southeastern section of Tver' province, the villages were only eight to twelve miles north of the town of Rzhev, a county seat and port on the Volga river.[2] Moscow lay approximately 150 miles to the southeast. The Manuilovskoe serfs typified those living in the non-black earth region north of Moscow. They were proprietary serfs, bound to land owned by members of the Gagarin family and obligated to pay them rent.[3] Because the Manuilovskoe peasants paid a money rent (*obrok*), the Gagarins and their officials did not supervise the estate directly. Instead an estate manager (*burmistr*), elected by and from the peasantry, carried responsibility for the collection of rent and the administration of Gagarin property.

The absence of direct Gagarin supervision of the estate intensified recordkeeping. From 1810 to 1861 the estate manager sent a steady stream of reports, ledgers, petitions, and household registers (*podvornye opisi*) to Gagarin officials who monitored the estate's activities from Moscow. The household registers, the most important source, list the names of household members, the members' relationship to the household head, and their ages. The registers also often include important economic information concerning grain reserves, landholdings, livestock, and nonagricultural occupations and income.

The registers' data describe the structure of the agricultural economy that shaped the peasant's shift into nonagricultural employment. Using a three-field system of crop rotation, Manuilovskoe peasants planted rye in their winter fields and oats in the spring fields, accompanied by small amounts of barley, buckwheat, and spring wheat. Rye and oats remained the basic crops between 1823 and 1861, as the relative share of each crop in peasant granaries exhibited little change. The peasants, however, modified their selection of supplementary crops. Spring wheat, difficult to grow in the harsh climate and poor soils, disappeared as early as 1851. The peasants replaced spring wheat with flax and hemp, which were increasingly important cash crops in the regions north of Moscow, and turned to growing apples. First mentioned in 1843 reports, apple orchards became a common sight on the estate, as the number of trees rose from 121 in 1851 to 272 a decade later.[4]

The production levels of rye and oats remained relatively stable. The significant fluctuations in total and per capita amounts of each crop seen in Table 1 result from reporting procedures, population shifts, and climatic problems. The November 1826 grain totals, recorded shortly after the harvest, naturally exceed the amounts inspected in February and March. In 1828, the

Gagarins permanently deported 21 households, thereby further radically dropping aggregate production levels. Crop failures explain the rest of the variation. Poor harvests occurred in at least fourteen of the fifty years surveyed.[5]

Frost damage, a recurrent problem due to the short growing season, lowered yields several times. Inadequate drainage and poor soil further hampered crop production.[6] The peasants recognized the need for fertilization, but few owned enough livestock to manure all of their fields. In Rzhev county, home of the estate, the average ratio of seed to grain harvested for rye ranged between 1.0 to 2.5 and 1.0 to 4.0. The yield for oats averaged 1.0 to 3.0.[7]

Periodic redistribution of communal field land, a custom sometimes believed to have limited peasant willingness to invest in new agricultural techniques, did not appreciably hinder productivity. Prior to the 1850s, most references to redistribution concern peasants requesting the village take communal land from them in order to lower the accompanying rent burden. In the 1850s, when the Gagarins may have mandated annual redistribution, households with significant changes in labor strength lost or gained small parcels of land.[8] Most holdings remained intact.

Communal land made up only 48.2% of total holdings. The rest of the land, 5301 acres, was purchased by individuals, groups, and perhaps villages during the preceding century.[9] Such purchases by serfs were rare. Only six other Tver' estates commanded tracts of privately owned land of equal or greater size. The land purchases, coupled with the 1828 deportation of 21 households and slow population growth, created a land surplus. In 1858, Manuilovskoe serfs cultivated only 34% of their privately owned land. They enjoyed mean holdings of 21.1 acres of communal and private field land per male, whereas serfs in Tver' province held an average of 11.6 acres.[10]

The land surplus and slow population growth weakened the impact of the partible inheritance system. Custom dictated the equal division of land and other resources among all male children. Due to demographic and economic constraints only one-fourth of the households parcelled out property to multiple heirs. Those that apportioned inheritance shares successfully employed such methods as postponement and unequal divisions of property to maintain the productive strength of the original household.[11]

The stability of Manuilovskoe agriculture and the weakened impact of the inheritance system bolstered economic stratification. To evaluate household economic standing, I use the number of horses owned as indicators of wealth. Nineteenth-century observers argued that a peasant family of four required two horses for minimum subsistence. Manuilovskoe serfs used this important resource in fieldwork and transport. Other economic indicators, especially grain holdings, even more accurately measure the entire range of peasant wealth, but are not found in all household registers.[12]

Table 1. Household Grain Reserves, 1823-1861 (*Chetverti* Per Capita and Per Worker)

Crop	February 1823	November 1826	January 1829	February 1851	January/ February 1857	March 1860	March 1861
Rye: Total	571.9	1,257.0	911.9	890.0	846.5	690.0	797.0
Per Capita	0.49	1.09	0.94	0.91	0.83	0.64	0.74
Per Worker	2.29	5.02	4.20	3.89	3.60	2.84	3.05
Rye Flour: Total	—	—	—	448.9	378.5	302.6	312.6
Per Capita	—	—	—	0.46	0.37	0.28	0.29
Per Worker	—	—	—	1.96	1.65	1.25	1.20
Oats: Total	1,140.4	1,370.3	—	887.1	934.8	646.6	590.5
Per Capita	0.97	1.19	—	0.91	0.92	0.60	0.55
Per Worker	4.56	5.48	—	3.87	4.06	2.66	2.26
Barley: Total	242.4	430.4	—	286.3	195.5	238.0	211.9
Per Capita	0.27	0.37	—	0.29	0.19	0.20	0.20
Per Worker	0.97	1.72	—	1.25	0.85	0.98	0.81
Barley Flour: Total	—	—	—	133.6	38.2	63.6	33.8
Per Capita	—	—	—	0.14	0.04	0.05	0.03
Per Worker	—	—	—	0.58	0.17	0.26	0.13
Spring Wheat: Total	57.3	46.8	—	—	—	—	—
Per Capita	0.05	0.04	—	—	—	—	—
Per Worker	0.23	0.18	—	—	—	—	—
Buckwheat: Total	5.1	—	—	3.6	40.7	14.0	11.9
Per Capita	0.004	—	—	0.004	0.04	0.01	0.01
Per Worker	0.02	—	—	0.02	0.18	0.06	0.05
Buckwheat Seed: Total	—	—	—	—	8.0	—	0.1
Per Capita	—	—	—	—	0.008	—	trace
Per Worker	—	—	—	—	0.03	—	trace

Agricultural Structure and the Origins of Migration in Central Russia, 1810-1850

Peas: Total	32.8	40.7	—	—	21.8	15.8	13.6
Per Capita	0.03	0.04	—	—	0.02	0.01	0.01
Per Worker	0.13	0.16	—	—	0.09	0.07	0.05
Pea Seed: Total	—	—	—	—	7.7	1.8	0.9
Per Capita	—	—	—	—	0.008	0.002	trace
Per Worker	—	—	—	—	0.03	0.01	trace
Hemp: Total	58.4	132.4	—	87.6	80.2	52.7	52.0
Per Capita	0.05	0.12	—	0.09	0.08	0.05	0.05
Per Worker	0.23	0.53	—	0.38	0.35	0.22	0.20
Flax: Total	—	1.0	—	46.8	47.2	53.2	51.9
Per Capita	—	trace	—	0.05	0.05	0.05	0.05
Per Worker	—	0.004	—	0.20	0.21	0.22	0.20
Spring Crops: Total	1,531.7	2,021.6	1,438.0	1,443.5	1,376.8	1,090.0	974.1
Per Capita	1.31	1.76	1.48	1.48	1.36	1.01	0.91
Per Worker	6.12	8.09	6.63	6.30	5.99	4.49	3.73
Total Crops	2,103.60	3,278.6	2,349.9	2,782.4	2,601.8	2,082.6	2,083.7
Per Capita	1.80	2.85	2.42	2.85	2.56	1.93	1.93
Per Worker	8.41	13.11	10.82	12.26	11.31	8.57	8.01

Crop failures, livestock epidemics, and seasonal marketing all affected the number of horses held. The average number of horses owned per household ranged from 2.5 to 3.2 in the 10 registers. No single household owned the same number of horses in all the registers either. A decrease in the size of the household's herd could reflect only temporary misfortune, a permanent decline in standing, or a problem afflicting the entire community. Terentei Antonov's household, for instance, possessed its largest herd (five horses) in 1813, the best year for all estate households and its smallest (one horse) in 1833, the year of a crop failure. The number of horses his household owned in the rest of the years fluctuated between two and three.

Under these conditions, the best measure of economic standing is the minimum and maximum of horses possessed by a household between 1813 and 1861 (see Table 2). Using this approach, the estate's elite consists of households never possessing fewer than three horses during the period, whereas households in the community's lowest strata never acquired more than three horses. Those whose holdings fluctuated from one or two horses to five or more found themselves in a variety of economic positions. These boundaries among lower, middle, and upper strata are, of course, not rigid. Households in the middle strata, for instance, were sometimes wealthier than the elite households in the upper strata, although most in the middle strata did not remain in high positions for long periods. A small group of households, on the other hand, managed to maintain the wealth and high economic standing they derived from agriculture. The categories serve to demonstrate that Manuilovskoe households did not share common patterns of socioeconomic mobility, but rather moved within separate ranges of economic change.[13]

The elite's abundant material and human resourcees brought many advantages. The wealthy households were better able to withstand crop failures than their poorer counterparts, spend a lower proportion of household income on rent and taxes, and serve more often as estate managers. Their resources also provided the means to trade in regional markets and to become part of the national labor force.

The extent of economic expansion in late eighteenth and early nineteenth-century Russia is still being debated, but exports clearly increased, the number of factories grew, and regional markets began to develop. Due to its position on the major river and land routes between Moscow and St. Petersburg, Tver' province benefited from this growth. Many peasants worked in local industries such as lumbering and construction in the western districts and shoe manufacturing in the northwest. Most peasants, however, had to migrate in order to find employment. Both state and proprietary peasants were required to obtain passports or passes from local government officials to work in locations outside of their villages. Tver' authorities issued 36,122 passports in 1826; thirty years later 64,414 were granted, as well as 133,533 passes permitting more limited travel. One-third of the male serfs in Tver' province were receiving

Table 2. Mean Minimum and Maximum Holdings of Surviving Households, 1813-1861 by Socioeconomic Strata (Per Household and Per Capita)

Economic Strata On Basis of Minimum or Maximum Holdings (1813-1861)	Number of Horses		Amount of Grain			Number of Male Workers (Ages 20-59)	(N)
	Per Household	Per Capita	Per Household	Per Capita	Number of Members		
Lower-strata Households Owning							
Not more than two horses	0.7 - 2.0	.117 - .467	0.0 - 8.5	0.0 - 1.9	4.0 - 8.7	1.0 - 2.0	(3)
Not more than three horses	1.3 - 2.0	.174 - .542	1.3 - 13.1	0.2 - 2.0	4.5 - 9.2	0.7 - 2.5	(25)
One to four horses	1.0 - 4.0	.188 - .721	1.3 - 12.9	0.2 - 2.4	3.0 - 9.8	0.5 - 2.3	(4)
Total	1.2 - 3.0	.176 - .574	1.2 - 12.6	0.2 - 2.1	4.3 - 9.2	0.7 - 2.5	(32)
Middle-Strata Households Owning							
Two to four horses	2.0 - 4.0	.260 - .630	4.3 - 21.3	0.2 - 3.2	5.2 - 10.8	0.9 - 2.7	(16)
Two to five horses	2.0 - 5.0	.288 - .780	9.8 - 36.2	1.1 - 5.3	5.9 - 9.9	0.8 - 2.6	(11)
Total	2.0 - 4.4	.271 - .691	6.5 - 27.4	0.8 - 4.0	5.5 - 10.4	0.9 - 2.7	(27)
Upper-Strata Households Owning							
No fewer than three horses	3.0 - 5.9	.312 - .690	11.8 - 54.8	1.4 - 5.7	6.4 - 13.8	1.4 - 3.99	(18)
No fewer than four horses	4.4 - 6.9	.390 - .780	29.4 - 114.4	2.5 - 10.4	7.5 - 14.9	1.4 - 3.6	(8)
Total	3.4 - 6.2	.348 - .749	17.7 - 73.9	1.7 - 7.2	6.8 - 14.5	1.4 - 3.8	(26)
Mixed-Strata Households Owning							
One to five or more horses	1.0 - 5.1	.101 - .624	1.0 - 29.5	0.5 - 4.7	5.0 - 13.1	0.8 - 3.6	(8)
Two to six or more horses	2.0 - 6.6	.246 - .613	4.1 - 51.3	1.1 - 2.5	6.0 - 14.8	0.8 - 3.9	(8)
Total	1.5 - 5.9	.174 - .619	2.5 - 40.4	0.8 - 3.6	5.5 - 13.9	0.8 - 3.8	(16)
Estate Average	2.0 - 4.6	.248 - .666	7.2 - 37.0	0.9 - 4.4	5.4 - 11.6	0.9 - 3.1	(102)

formal permission to migrate. Only Moscow province issued passports to a larger share of its male serf population than Tver' province.[14]

Manuilovskoe serfs actively pursued the new employment opportunities off the estate. The proportion of households and male workers engaged in such activities grew rapidly from 1814 to 1829, at which point household participation leveled off and worker participation dropped off slightly (see Table 3). The impetus for this new diversification came from two sources: Gagarin pressure on the community to send large groups of its men to work at designated work sites and the peasants' growing awareness of the economic advantages of participating in the nonagricultural sector.

Gagarin-sponsored activities introduced most peasant households to the new sector. Until 1827, the peasants participating in the assigned migration worked on other Gagarin estates. They lumbered and did various carpentry work in Tambov province and worked at a paper mill in Moscow province. The community selected one or two men to supervise the journey to and from these sites, but Gagarin officials supervised the actual work. The officials carefully calculated the money due to peasants by subtracting the number of sick days and holidays and the cost of feeding the workers from the monthly wage rate. Officials claimed to pay the peasants the same wages as workers not owned by the Gagarins. Manuilovskoe laborers never received the money directly. Wages were instead credited to the household of each worker as part of the rent payment.

The Gagarins ordered the migrations to ensure that the annual income from the estate remained constant. The directives calling for Manuilovskoe peasants to migrate to other estates were especially insistent when crop failures led to sharp increases in rent arrears. In September 1824, after the peasants had suffered a fourth consecutive crop failure, the Moscow office directed the peasants to work on another estate. As early as November, the orders of the Moscow office became more specific and threatening. Gagarin officials directed the estate manager to draw up a registetr of all those households unable to pay rent arrears. From this register, the manager and the community were to recruit volunteers to work on other Gagarin estates. If arrears did not disappear after the next harvest, then the community was to order 200 men to work.[15]

The assigned migrations initially faced resistance from the community. The resistance became most visible any time Gagarin officials tried to increase drastically the number of migrants. When in 1814 the Moscow officials wanted only 50 men to work, 50 were found. Ten years later, in January of 1825, Moscow officials called for 180 men to be assigned. The next month they were conceding that only 100 needed to be sent. In the 1840s the officials again requested a very high number of workers. Approximately two-thirds of the 150 assigned actually went.[16]

Table 3. Proportion of Households and Male Workers Employed in the Nonagricultural Sector, 1815-1860

Year	Proportion of Households with Nonagricultural Income				Proportion of Male Workers, Age 20-59, with Nonagricultural Income			
	Gagarin Sponsored Employment	Independent Activities	Total	(N)	Gagarin Sponsored Employment	Independent Activities	Total	(N)
1815*	34.0	5.4	39.4	(147)	20.5	3.3	23.8	(244)
1823	45.9	8.9	50.0	(146)	22.0	5.2	32.0	(250)
1829**	57.9	79.3	81.0	(121)	39.2	79.3	87.6	(217)
1839	53.4	59.2	81.8	(125)	34.7	42.7	70.4	(213)
1860	—	—	—	(125)	44.0	—	—	(260)

Notes: * Data for 1815 comes from the 1813 household register and 1815 reports from the estate manager.
** Data for 1829 describing the number of males in independent activities and the total number working are estimates. The household register lists household occupations in either the singular or plural form of the nouns. All households with employment described in plural form are counted as having two workers.

Peasant resistance appeared in many forms. Wealthy peasants often hired others from the community to take their places in the migration. Another handful chose to run away. Households most commonly expressed their reluctance by sending unfit workers. The estate manager in 1814 had to explain the incapacity of seven migrants, who were either very young or elderly. Despite the Gagarin reprimands, the next year 6 of the 30 nominated migrants were between age of 14 and 18, and 4 were over 50 years old.[17]

The peasants' reluctance to send able-bodied workers to Gagarin estates stemmed primarily from their desire to keep workers at home in the fields. The Manuilovskoe migrants left the estate in late April or early May and usually stayed for five or six months. Participating households thus lost workers for most of the crucial agricultural season. The estate manager defended sending the seven unfit workers on the assigned migration in 1814 by claiming that these migrants were sent, so that able-bodied could stay at home to plant and fertilize. Eleven years later Moscow officials had to order the community to plow for households in which the only male worker was employed off the estate.[18]

Drastic Gagarin actions helped break the long pattern of peasant resistance. Despite Gagarin efforts to get the peasants working off the estate, rent arrears mounted in the 1820s due to a series of crop failures. In 1828 the Gagarins transformed the assigned migration into a more punishing form. They permanently moved 21 households to another estate. The land abandoned by the peasants was used to form a *demesne,* and the majority of the remaining peasants were ordered to remit a labor rent (*barshchina*). The experiment with labor rent lasted only one year, ending when the peasants agreed to pay the remaining debt in three annual installments.[19] After 1829 there are few extant directives calling for intensification of the migration effort. The Gagarins had made their point.

The Gagarins' most effective measure may not have been the deportations or the labor rent experiment, but the switch from assigned work on Gagarin estates to work in St. Petersburg. From 1827 the serfs, except for a brief interval in the early 1840s, went to St. Petersburg to work. The Gagarins no longer supervised the peasants as closely as when they worked on other estates. The community selected one or more foremen to supervise the group and sometimes two or three assistants. The estate manager instructed the foreman to find work for the men and negotiate contracts with employers. He was also to report insolent, disobedient, or drunken workers. The estate manager further admonished the foreman never to give the wages directly to the workers, except for the purchase of food and tools. The foreman instead passed the wages on to a special Gagarin official in St. Petersburg.[20]

Estate peasants had now taken over the supervisory duties of the Gagarin officials and could choose the type of employment. When wages were higher, moreover, the peasants paid all of their rent with the St. Petersburg earnings.

Agricultural Structure and the Origins of Migration in Central Russia, 1810-1850   379

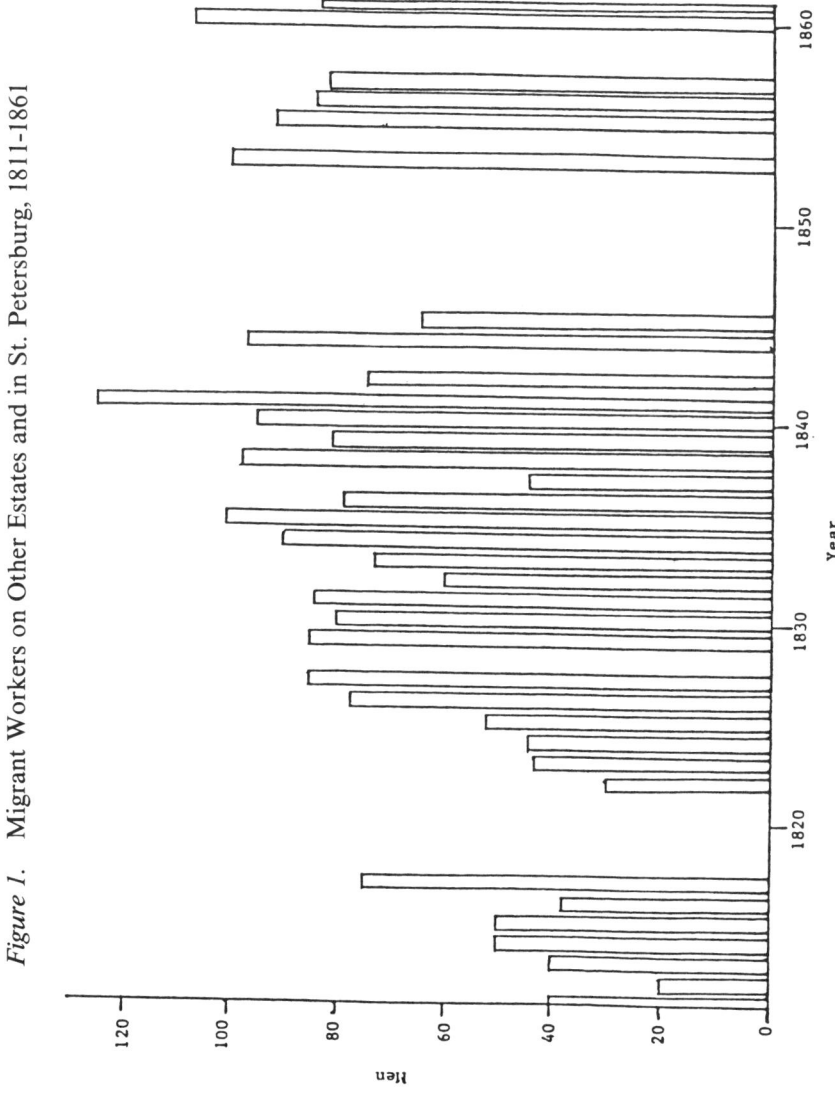

Figure 1. Migrant Workers on Other Estates and in St. Petersburg, 1811-1861

Income from other employment remained their own. Scattered evidence suggests that some households, cognascent of the benefits, sent men and women to St. Petersburg and Moscow outside of the organized migrations.[21]

The switch to the St. Petersburg migration helped end most resistance to the assignments. The community evidently stopped sending the unfit on the assigned migrations, when the men began to go to St. Petersburg. Reports indicate that in the 1830s the young and the old went to work on the estates of nearby serfowners, probably as shepherds and cattle herders.[22]

The increasing numbers migrating after 1828 also reflect declining resistance (see Figure 1). Temporary drops in the number of migrants cannot mask the overall growth in participants.[23] Between 1811 and 1817 an average of 44.7 migrated. Between 1821 and 1827 the average rose to 55.6. In the years from 1829 through 1845 the average increased again to 79.1, and in the 1850s it peaked at 91.7. The percentage of estate males between the ages of 20 and 59 also increased, reaching 44.0% in 1860 (see Table 3). Gagarin policy sped up the transition toward migration, but the serfs' acknowledgment of the benefits turned involuntary labor into an accpeted sector of the economy.

The migration sponsored by the Gagarins made up only part of the serfs' nonagricultural economic activities. Many households supplemented their agricultural income with other types of work they found on their own. It is much more difficult to judge this activity's scope. Managerial reports and household registers reflect the Gagarins' interest in promoting and assessing the results of the migration they sponsored and providve little information about the peasants' independent activities. Only three household registers contain this information, and the last one describes 1839 activities. Two of these registers record the occupations by household and not individuals, so the number of workers must be estimated.

Between 1815 and 1839 the number of households containing men that worked without supervision increased (see Table 3). At least eight men from different households were working and living temporarily in Rzhev in 1816. Others may have been laborers in Rzhev and elsewhere, because all eight men came from the same village. Estate reports mention them due to their arrest for breaking up a tavern.[23] The 1823 household register lists 73 households with outside employment, and for 60 of them carpentry was the sole occupation. Because the term "carpentry" probably designated migrants working on other Gagarin estates, just 13 households definitely found jobs outside of Gagarin sponsored work. More may have done so, as not all the carpenters had to have worked solely for the Gagarins.

Participation increased radically in 1829, when 79.3% of the community's households engaged in occupations other than farming and carpentry (see Table 4). In the 1840 household register the proportion of active households dropped to 59.2% of the total. The labor rent in effect during 1829 accounts in part for the rapid expansion into nonagricultural activities. The desire to

Table 4. Occupations Practiced by Hosueholds Participating in the Nonagricultural Economy, 1823, 1829, and 1840 (Percentage of Households Employed)[a]

Occupation	1823	1829	1840
Carpenter	91.8	71.4	14.9
Carter	1.4	43.9	42.6
Hemp scutcher	11.0	63.3	16.8
St. Petersburg workers	—	—	60.0
Grain and livestock merchants	—	—	2.0
Blacksmiths	—	0.9	1.0
Tailors	1.4	—	3.0
Kitchenware craftsmen	—	—	3.0
Bucket makers	—	0.9	3.0
Gardeners	—	3.1	—
Other	3.2	2.1	1.0

Note: [a] Percentages exceed 100%, because many households engaged in more than one occupation.

erase money rent arrears and quickly end the labor rent increased the time spent working off the farm. The decline after 1829 in the share of households earning nonagricutural income from independent employment resulted primarily from the decision of many households to concentrate their efforts on the lucrative St. Petersburg migration.

The nature of the households' employment also changed over time. Carpentry initially served as an important source of income, but its overall importance declined rapidly once the men stopped working on Gagarin estates (see Table 4). In 1839 nine of the households that still contained carpenters also sent one or more members to St. Petersburg. Carpentry served as the sole occupation for just six households.

A second occupation, hemp processing, functioned as a temporary source of income. Hemp processing involved scutching hemp on the Rzhev wharves for a six-week period in the spring. Merchants employed thousands of peasants in order to finish the work quickly. In 1829 Manuilovskoe peasants flocked to these short-term, easily contracted jobs in order to earn extra money and end the labor rent. The number of peasants going to Rzhev in 1839 declined, because the need for extra income was not great enough to compensate for the back-breaking work and low wages. Crop failures in the late 1850s forced peasants to go to Rzhev in large numbers again. Scutching hemp was short-term, seasonal labor practiced primarily when economic conditions demanded.[24]

Whereas carpentry and hemp processing declined, trades such as cartage grew in importance. Only one household in 1823 transported goods as a means of earning extra income. Six years later, 37.4% did this work, and by 1839 the percentage had risen to 42.6. The sources do not indicate the distances peasants carried freight, but they probably traveled to local trade centers. The estate stood on the main road between Rzhev and another county seat, Staritsa. The road from Staritsa led to Tver', the provincial capital, and to Torzhok, an important upper Volga River port. Another Volga River port and country seat, Zubtsov, was only ten miles from Rzhev.[25]

A small number of peasants engaged in other trades that required varying degrees of skills and some capital. One of the simpler crafts was bucket making. Bucket sales did not produce large incomes. Earning at most 12 kopecks a bucket, one estate bucket maker made only 25 rubles. The craft's advantage was that it could easily be done at home, when there was no fieldwork. Three households produced buckets in 1839. More complex and profitable wooden products were kitchenwares. One of the two households engaged in this craft earned 125 rubles in 1839. Tailoring was also practiced on the estate. The number of tailors grew from one in 1823 to three in 1839. In both years there was one stovemaker as well. A final skilled trade was blacksmithing. In April and May the blacksmith repaired the iron parts of agricultural implements and in the fall made and fit horseshoes.[26] The Manuilovskoe blacksmith also did locksmith work and earned 500 rubles in 1839. In the 1840s the blacksmith opened a dyeworks on the estate.

Trade in products related to agriculture also supplemented income. No data describe how many households were able to sell surpluses of grain or livestock beyond that necessary to pay rent and taxes. Two households in 1839, however, traded in grain and livestock on a large scale. Each household earned approximately one thousand rubles, the estate's highest "nonagricultural" incomes. The Manuilovskoe peasants also sold other products, such as apples and honey, on the local market. The number of hives increased ten times between 1813 and 1857. For 9% of the estate's households, the sale of honey became a steady source of income.[27]

When concerned about finding adequate supplementary income, households often engaged in more than one occupation. In 1823 the 37 households with nonagricultural income had one occupation each. Six years later, only 22 of the 98 households engaged in one occupation. Most households had members who worked in St. Petersburg in the summer and labored elsewhere in the winter and spring. Almost 29% of the working households sent men to scutch hemp in the spring before sending them to work in the national capital. Another 24.3% transported goods in the winter, processed hemp in the spring, and worked in St. Petersburg in the summer.

This pattern began to break down in 1839 as more households began to depend on one type of employment. One-third of the households with nonagricultural income had one occupation. Whereas in 1829 two households depended solely on income from St. Petersburg employment, in 1839, 27 households found this work sufficient. Only two households in 1829 relied entirely on cartage for income, but 17 did so in 1839. Because scutching hemp declined in importance, not one household in 1839 combined scutching, cartage, and work in St. Petersburg. This move toward single occupations partially resulted from a diminished need to earn high incomes quickly. The peasants were no longer seeking to pay off debts and end labor rent. High wages in St. Petersburg may also have made other work unnecessary. The appearance of households employed in only one occupation, finally, coincided with the rise of handicraft industries. Bucket makers, kitchenware craftsmen, and the locksmith first appeared in 1839 documents. The dyeworks soon followed. The rudimentary specialization talking shape explains to a great extent the increasing dependence on a single type of work for supplementary income.

Family size significantly shaped the household's choice of nonagricultural employment. Households with a large number of male workers could afford to send more men for longer periods of time than households with one worker. As a result, households with three or more workers between age 20 and 59 not only enjoyed a higher mean income per household, but also earned a greater number of rubles per capita than smaller households (see Table 5). Small households pulled in low incomes, because their employment options were greatly limited. In 1839, 69% of the small households had their one male working; most in short-term seasonal jobs. All seven households earning their entire supplementary income from scutching hemp, for instance, consisted of one worker. Cartage, another occupation that could be pursued for short periods of time, was the sole employment of nine other small households. A third occupation engaged in on a part-time basis was carpentry, and five of the seven households engaged only in carpentry contained a single worker. Other small households combined some of these trades. Only 14.6% of households with a single worker sent men to St. Petersburg.

Households with two male workers fared much better than those with one worker. Only two of these 47 households contained no migrants, and 66% sent men to St. Petersburg. Almost half (15 of 31) of the households sending men to the capital were able to do additional work, usually cartage during the winter. Seven other households worked in small crafts such as tailoring and producing kitchenware and buckets. Enjoying three or more male workers greatly enhanced a household's ability to work outside of agriculture. All households of this size participated in nonagricultural activities. Three-quarters (77.3%) sent one or two men for the six-month stay in St. Petersburg. Ten of these 17 households also pursued other occupations. Not surprisingly, the households with three or more workers enjoyed the greatest income (see Table 5).

The striking importance of labor availability for the success of nonagricultural activities should not overshadow the need for other types of resources. Cartage, for instance, demanded the ownership of an adequate number of horses, as pairs of horses were usually used in carting goods. The

Table 5. Percentage Distribution of Household Income Earned from Nonagricultural Activities in 1839 by Number of Males Age 20-59

Household Nonagricultural Income (Rubles)	Number of Male Workers Per Household (Age 20-59)					Total (N)
	None	One	Two	Three	Four or More	
0-49	100.0 (8)	58.3 (28)	6.4 (3)	00.0 (0)	00.0 (0)	(39)
50-99	00.0 (0)	31.3 (15)	53.2 (25)	5.9 (1)	00.0 (0)	(41)
100-174	00.0 (0)	10.4 (5)	27.7 (13)	47.1 (8)	20.0 (1)	(27)
175-249	00.0 (0)	00.0 (0)	12.8 (6)	41.2 (7)	20.0 (1)	(1)
250 and above	00.0 (0)	00.0 (0)	00.0 (0)	5.9 (1)	60.0 (3)	(4)
Total	100.0 (8)	100.0 (48)	100.1 (47)	100.1 (17)	100.0 (5)	(125)
Mean Income Per Household (rubles)	00.0	64.6	116.4	221.2	448.0	
Mean Income Per Capita (rubles)	00.0	7.3	13.6	19.3	32.9	

Manuilovskoe carters in 1839 averaged 3.8 horses per household; just one of the households engaged in cartage owned fewer than three horses. Households containing one worker engaged in cartage only when they owned at least three horses. Those small households with fewer than three horses scutched hemp and earned low wages. Skills and financial resources were also critical for the households in crafts industries. The tailors and kitchenware makers possessed three or four horses, and the blacksmith owned six horses.

The estate's agricultural elite, those households never owning fewer than three horses, participated the most actively of all socioeconomic strata in the nonagricultural economy. The community selected these households for the first assigned migrations in 1814 and 1815, when 56% of them sent men to the other Gagarin estates. Six additional elite households refused to send their own men and instead hired replacements from poor households usually containing one worker and one horse. A quarter of a century later, all twenty elite households involved in the first migrations still worked in the nonagricultural sector. Even those who originally hired substitutes now participated. The households they had hired in 1814 and 1815 were not employed in 1839. Many, in fact, had become extinct.

The elite monopolized most of the estate's lucrative occupations in 1839. The two households that traded in grain and livestock naturally commanded large amounts of both. Pavel Egorov's household planted the greatest amount of grain in 1839 and owned 7 horses and 17 head of cattle. As early as 1829, he owned 81 acres of land. The other merchant controlled 162 acres of purchased land. Both households also contained at least one literate person, as their financial resources enabled them to set aside income and some working time to school the young boys. Literacy was important for trade and gave the two housholds another advantage over the rest of the peasants.[28]

Other elite households benefited from their long-term command of abundant material resources. Due to the large number of horses owned, 9 elite households transported goods for supplemental incomes. Another 13 sent men to St. Petersburg and 3 worked as tailors, whereas just 2 scutched hemp. The saga of the entrepreneurial blacksmith best illustrates the advantage of consistent agricultural success. In 1813, Anisem Iakovlev's household was among the estate's wealthiest, owning six horses. His sons started the blacksmith shop as early as 1829 and 10 years later earned 500 rubles a year as blacksmith and locksmith. Using this capital, Iakovlev opened a dyeworks in the 1840s and at the end of decade had founded a second one on an estate owned by the Sheremetev family.

The resources important for agriculture played an important role in the nonagricultural sector. The same shortages of manpower and livestock that limited agricultural success could constrain access to economic opportunities off the farm. Plentiful agricultural resources, in turn, enabled households to engage in crafts and trades or enter the national market as hired laborers. The market's initial penetration of the peasant economy bolstered the community's traditional socioeconomic structure.

NOTES AND REFERENCES

1. The nature of market penetration is considered in such works as James C. Scott, *The Moral Economy of the Peasant* (New Haven: Yale University Press, 1976); Eric Hobsbawm, *Primitive Rebels* (New York: Norton, 1965); Teodor Shanin, *The Awkward Class* (Oxford: At the Clarendon Press, 1972); Samuel L. Popkin, *The Rational Peasant* (Berkely: University of California Press, 1979); and David Goodman and Michael Redclift, *From Peasant to Proletarian* (Oxford: Basil Blackwell, 1981). For an earlier discussion of the Manuilovskoe economy see I. D. Koval'chenko, "Ob osobennostiakh raboty po naimu pomeshchich'ikh krest'ian Rossii v pervoi polovine XIX v.," *Genezis kapitalizma,* ed. S. M. Skazkin (Moscow, 1965).

2. The Manuilovskoe population in 1861 was 1077 persons. All material in the tables and text describing population and household size, structure, and wealth, unless otherwise noted, come from the household registers. Gagarin Family Papers, *Tsentral'nyi gosudarstvennyi arkhiv drevnikh aktov, fond* (collection), *opis'* (inventory), 2, 1813 Register, *delo* (item) 7192, 1823 Register, d. 7215; 1826 Register d. 7226; 1829 Register, d. 7240; 1833 Register, d. 7245; 1840 Register, d. 7256; 1851 Register, d. 7286; 1857 Register, d. 7320; 1860 Register, d. 7335; 1861 Register, d. 7335; 1861 Register, d. 7338. All Gagarin documents are from the same archives, *fond,* and *opis',* and these will no longer be cited.

3. Approximately 44% of Russian serfs lived on estates consisting of 500 or more serfs. In the non-black earth region north and west of Moscow as high as 67% of the serfs paid money rent. Labor rent (*barshchina*) dominated in the black earth region south of Moscow. See I. D. Koval'chenko, *Russkoe krepostnoe krest'ianstvo v pervoi polovine XIX v.* (Moscow, 1967), pp. 59, 62-63.

4. December 1843 Report, d. 7259, *list* (page 1).

5. Due to the abrupt changes in holdings caused by the deportations and to inadequate data on grain prices for most years, I have decided to present only the raw data for grain stored.

6. V. I. Pokrovskii, ed. *Istoriko-statisticheskoe opisanie Tverskoi gubernii v sel'sko-khoziaistvennom otnoshenii,* 2 vols. (St. Petersburg, 1879), pp. 66-67; V. I. Pokrovskii, *General'noe soobrazhenie po Tverskoi gubernii izvlechennoe iz podrobnogo topograficheskogo i kameral'nogo po gorodam i uezdam opisaniia, 1783-1784 gg.* (Tver', 1873), p. 128; V. A. Preobrazhenskii, *Opisanie Tverskoi gubernii v sel'sko-khoziaistvennom otnoshenii* (St. Petersburg, 1854), p. 62; November 3, 1826 Report, d. 7228, 1. 67; December 1843 Report, d. 7259, 1.4; October 1822 Petition, d. 7214, 11.91 *obratnaia* (*verso*); August 27, 1823 Report, d. 7214, 1. 168; June 12, 1833 Report, d. 7244, 11. 67-67 ob.

7. Preobrazhenskii, pp. 268-71; Pokrovskii, *Soobrazhenie,* pp. 119, 128; December 1843 Report, d. 7259, 1. 4.

8. January 26, 1815 Petition from Varvara Gavrilova, d. 7200, 1. 8; Rent Assessment Register, May 10, 1860, d. 7324, 11. 8-15 ob.

9. Excerpts from Gagarin Land Survey Books, March 22, 1828, d. 7296, 11. 6-8.

10. Tver' Provincial Committee on the Betterment of the Condition of the Peasantry, Description of Estate of Prince L. N. Gagarin, July 17, 1858, d. 7325, 11. 31 ob.-32.

11. For a fuller discussion see Rodney D. Bohac, "Peasant Inheritance Strategies in Russia," *Journal of Interdisciplinary History* 16 (Summer, 1985):23-42. As suggested in Robert Brenner, "Agrarian Class Structure and Economic Development in Pre-Industrial Europe," *Past and Present* 97 (November, 1982):16-113, population pressures and land shortages did not play a role in the shift toward nonagricultural employment. On Manuilovskoe estate, however, the partible inheritance system did not overwhelm the tendency to accumulate as Brenner argues (p. 36).

Agricultural Structure and the Origins of Migration in Central Russia, 1810-1850   387

12. Preobrazhenskii, p. 335, Pokrovskii, *Opisanie,* p. 214; Koval'chenko, *Russkoe krepostnoe,* pp. 44-47. Grain reserves in many respects even more precisely reflect household wealth, but extant data describe only holdings in the 1820s and 1850s. Land also cannot be used as an indicator of wealth, because the community recorded holdings only in the 1820s.

13. Rodney D. Bohac, "Family, Property, and Socioeconomic Mobility: Russian Peasants on Manuilovskoe Estate, 1810-1861" (Ph.D. dissertation, University of Illinois, 1982), pp. 234-237, 244-252.

14. Koval'chenko, *Russkoe krepostnoe,* p. 89; V. A. Fedorov, *Pomeshchich'i krest'iane tsentral'no-promyshlennogo raiona Rossii kontsa XVII-pervoi poloviny XIX v.* (Moscow, 1974), pp. 4-135, 304-305. Jerome Blum, *Lord and Peasant in Russia* (Princeton: Princeton University Press, 1961), pp. 286-291; Olga Crisp, *Studies in the Russian Economy Before 1914* (London: MacMillan, 1976), pp. 12-17, 68-69.

15. September 30, 1824 Report, d. 7218, l. 1; November 1, 1824 Directive, d. 7218, l. 4 ob., November 18, 1824 Directive, d. 7218, l. 6; January 19, 1825 Directive, d. 7218, l. 21.

16. May 14, 1814 Report, d. 7199, l. 36; January 15, 1825 Directive, d. 7218, l. 20; February 10, 1825 Directive, d. 7218, l. 26; January 16, 1844 Report, d. 7267, ll. 14-16.

17. June 3, 1814 Report, d. 7199, l. 28; June 15, 1825 Directive, d. 7218, l. 20; February 6, 1824 Petition from Egor Romanov, d. 7218, l. 10; February 10, 1825 Directive, d. 7218, l. 26.

18. June 3, 1814 Report, d. 7199, l. 26; March 24, 1825 Directive, d. 7218, l. 24.

19. January 30, 1829 Report, d. 7240, l. 21-21 ob.; April 28, 1832 Directive, d. 7243, l. 75 ob.

20. April 26, 1829 Directive, d. 7232, ll. 32-33; May 12, 1831 Report, d. 7242, l. 59.

21. January 25, 1828 Report, d. 7240, l. 33; May 12, 1831 Report, d. 7242, ll. 59-60; February 16, 1854 Report, d. 7306, l. 26.

22. April 30, 1830 Report, d. 7235, l. 8 ob; May 1, 1834 Report, d. 7246, l. 72.

23. The numbers of workers for the years 1840 and 1841 may be exaggerated, as these were the numbers assigned for migration. There is no assurance all were actually sent. Two years earlier, however, 98 men traveled to St. Petersburg, so the data for 1840 and 1841 are probably correct.

24. Pokrovskii, *Soobrazhenie,* pp. 118, 121; Tver' Provincial Committee on the Betterment of the Condition of the Peasantry, Description of Estate of L. N. Gagarin, July 17, 1858, d. 7325, ll. 24-45.

25. Preobrazhenskii, p. 240.

26. Ibid., pp. 425, 450-451.

27. The number of hives rose from 14 in 1813 to 113 in 1857, while the number of households with hives rose from five to eleven.

28. Barbara A. Anderson, *Internal Migration during Modernization in Late Nineteenth-Century Russia* (Princeton: Princeton University Press, 1980), pp. 181-182 utilizes literacy as an indicator of modern attitudes. Provinces with high literacy rates tended to send migrants to urban centers. The Manuilovskoe evidence suggests that literacy may be closely connected with wealth and economic standing.

BRIDEWEALTH, DOWRY, AND SOCIOECONOMIC DIFFERENTIATION IN RURAL RUSSIA

Steven L. Hoch

In an agricultural society with a very low level of technology and more than adequate amounts of arable lands—as in Petrovskoe (the serf estate under examination in this study) and in much of the central agricultural region in imperial Russia—labor was of the utmost value and the primary determinant of output. Other than draft animals, additional capital inputs were extremely limited. But in Russia, the climate uniquely affected the structure of field labor organization. As a consequence of the extremely short growing season, five-and-a-half to six months instead of the eight to nine months in western Europe, the harvesting of winter and spring cereals and the plowing and sowing of the winter field all came in quick succession within the span of six weeks. From mid-July to the end of August was the harvest season, the *stradnaia pora* as the Russians called it; literally the time suffering. It was an agonizing period of exertion demanding that numerous tasks be accomplished simultaneously. A work team, a *tiaglo* (a husband and wife together), proved to be the best allocation of labor resources. A single male simply could not complete all the necessary field work if he were to allow the cereals to mature fully while avoiding the danger of an early frost.[1]

There thus emerged in Russia a clear differentiation of field labor by sex. During the harvest season, women used sickles to cut rye, winter wheat, if any, and sometimes oats, whereas the men reaped the other spring cereals with scythes. The women then tied the grain into sheaves for drying; the men began plowing the winter field. While they sowed next year's crop, the women started to cart the sheaves from the fields and, if time permitted, were assisted by their husbands. In general, plowing, harrowing, sowing, cutting hay, and harvesting with a scythe were men's field work; tending to the kitchen garden and hemp field, raking hay, cutting stalks with a sickle, tying them, and transporting them to the threshing floor were women's field work.[2]

A partnership was essential. Single or widowed females were never part of a work team, and rarely did males carry a full tiaglo alone. Of all males age 15-19, the interval during which they first assumed some estate field labor obligations receiving in return a land allotment, 38% carried no tiaglo, none of whom were married; 32 carried a half-tiaglo, of whom only 4% were married; and 29% carried a full-tiaglo, of whom at least three-quarters were married.[3]

To maximize output on the Petrovskoe estate the bailiff had to maximize the number of work teams. In practice, this meant the distribution of corvee obligations had to be synchronized with internal changes in household composition resulting from marriage and death so as to avoid the underutilization of labor. When a young couple married it immediately formed a new tiaglo which further increased the productive capacity of the estate. The earlier serfs married, the sooner this economic benefit to the estate would be realized.[4]

But if the young couples would have had to establish their own households, early marriage would then have necessarily confronted both the problem of capital accumulation and parental concerns regarding the premature loss of an adult laborer. In contrast, had the serfs of Petrovskoe found it necessary to delay marriage seven to eight years, until the mid- or late-twenties as in western Europe, then the productive capacity of the estate and all serf households would have been reduced by anywhere from 17% (assuming all single males over age 19 carried a half-tiaglo) to 35% (if males had no corvee obligations until marriage).[5] Roughly speaking, a figure of 20% seems reasonable as the amount of gross grain production that would have been lost if marriages had followed the "European" pattern. Gross income would have suffered comparably.

Overcoming these problems was accomplished, first, by tying the execution of estate labor obligations to the right to use an allotment of peasant arable land, a practice common throughout all of the central agricultural region and much of Great Russia as well. This provided a new couple with immediate access to a plot of land, the most crucial capital input for its maintenance. Arable land was thus constantly being redistributed to reflect marriages, retirements, and deaths. Second, virilocal postmarital residence not only obviated the need for much additional capital accumulation, but constituted a windfall for the bridegroom's household. Often, the mere addition of a daughter-in-law increased the number of tiaglo in a household from one to two or two to three, thereby increasing a *dvor's* total arable land by 50 to 100%. Parents thus had a strong economic incentive to see that their sons married young. "Get married at eighteen in order to settle on a tiaglo" (*V vosemnadtstat' let zhenit'sia, chtob na tiaglo sadit'sia*) was common advice given to young males.[6] Third, the payment of a substantial brideprice (or bridewealth) known as *kladka,* given by the grooms's head of household to the bride's enticed dvors to part with their unmarried, mature female laborers. Kladka, in effect, redistrubuted wealth among households without upsetting patriarchal authority within them.

Kladka had both characteristics of a bridewealth, the permanent movement of resources from the groom's household in exchange for rights to the bride, and indirect dowry, gifts of "money indirectly contributed by the groom to the endowment of the bride."[7] The distinction is important, even if blurred within the custom of kladka itself, for bridewealth was a "circulating societal fund," a redistribution of resources limiting socioeconomic differentiation among households, whereas an indirect dowry did not necessarily entail the permanent alienation of any property from either household. Indirect dowry with virilocal postmarital residence resulted in all wealth remaining in place.[8]

Marriage almost everywhere involves the transmission of property, but in most of Great Russia supplying a newly married couple with a conjugal fund by direct or indirect dowry was not important. At Petrovskoe, the estate provided arable land through the repartitional land structure, and the groom's family, an established household. Little else was needed except clothing. In fact, the custom of direct dowry (*pridanoe,* which also means trousseau), "a type of pre-mortem inheritance to the bride"[9] from her family was of little or no consequence where the repartitional land commune existed.

Between 1871 and 1874 a special government commission concerned with the reorganization of the township courts (*volostnye sudy*) investigated peasant customary practices in 15 provinces of European Russia, including all 12 districts (*uezdy*) of Tambov guberniia. In Borisoglebskii district where Petrovskoe was located, 10 of the 29 townships were studied, although the Petrovskoe estate, a *volost'* by itself, was not one of them. Nevertheless, in two of the townships adjacent to Petrovskoe the commission noted that "a dowry (pridanoe) is not given, but the bridegroom pays a kladka for the bride (*zhenikh platit za nevestu kladku*)." In seven of the eight remaining townships, dowries were "never given," and in the eighth, closest to the district seat of Borisogleb, they were given "very rarely."[10]

Many nineteenth-century ethnographers were quite surprised to discover that peasants did not give their daughters direct dowries, but the evidence is overwhelming. Observers for the Imperial Russian Geographic Society found the practice of kladka widespread in regions where the repartitional commune existed.[11] Direct dowries were common only in the far north and in Little Russia where lands were held in perpetuity. In fact, after the introduction of the repartitional commune in Arkangel' guberniia, direct dowries declined in importance.[12] To quote the ethnographer V.P. Mukhin; "the custom of giving a kladka for the bride is very strictly observed in those areas where it is not usual to give a dowry; thus kladka in this case is like a surrogate dowry, coming from the side of the groom."[13] In 1874, Aleksandra Efimenko, another student of peasant life, noted that where kladka was part of the marriage contract, no conditions were set for a bride's dowry.[14] There was nothing, however that prohibited the bride's household from giving their daughter or new in-laws small gifts or from contributing directly to the wedding feast, and this was sometimes done.

Kladka was essentially a payment of money from the groom's household to the bride's, the amount being set at the time of betrothal. Often a fur coat or other clothes for the bride were also specified in the marriage agreement. Neither livestock nor, of course, land was ever exchanged as kladka although these were common endowments where direct dowries existed. Some, and occasionally all, of the kladka money went to cover the costs of the bride's trousseau, wedding expenses (*stolovye den'gi*), and gifts, usually clothes, to the future husband and in-laws. This is what is meant by the indirect dowry aspect or portion of kladka, for no redistribution of wealth was involved; it all returned to the groom's household with the bride, minus, of course, the expenses of the actual festivities.[15] But kladka payments were usually very substantial, frequently far exceeding the expenditures required of the bride's family. Table 1 presents information on the customary amount of kladka paid in the middle of the nineteenth century for regions where it was common. Most of the figures come from responses to a questionnaire sent out by the Imperial Russia Geographic Society in 1848 on the investigation of the "ordinary Russian person." Contributions were primarily village priests, local landlords, doctors, statisticians, teachers, and seminary students—"the wide mass of the rural intelligentsia," as one archivist describes them.[16] Abstracts of many of the responses from 36 guberniias, Arkhangel' through Saratov, were published.[17] For 14 guberniias of European Russia, this was not done. In addition, from some of the 36 provinces came only a few responses, and frequently authors did not specify the amount of kladka. Not many figures were available from other sources. Thus, the absence of a guberniia from Table 2 should not necessarily be interpreted as signifying absence of the custom of kladka.

Table 1. Customary Amount of Kladka

Province	Uezd	Year	Amount of Kladka (rubles assignats)
Arkhangel'	Shenkurskii	1854	20-35
Vladimir	Muromskii	1849	17-35
Voronezh	Pavlovskii	1850	Not more than 20
	Korotoianskii	1850	50-100
Viatka	Elabuzhskii	1850	35-105
Kazan'	Zakamskii krai	1850	25-45
Kaluga	Medzynskii	1856	40-140
	Zhizdrinskii	1849	9
Kursk[a]	Oboianskii	1862	3-24 and more
Nizhegorod	Sergachskii	1850s	up to 50
	Sergachskii	1850s	7-14
	Not specified	1849	15-50
	Vasil'skii	1849	40-100
	Kniaghininskii	1849	20-40
	Kniaghininskii	1849	10-60
	Arzamaskii	1850	15-30
	Alizhegorodskii	1848	up to 100
	Likoianovskii	1850	5-80
Novgorod	Cherepovskii	1850	up to 50
Penza	Not specified	1850	15-20
	Kerenskii	1857	up to 50
	Saranskii	1853-54	35-85
Perm	Verkhoturskii	1848	20-30
	Shadrinskii	1849	10-210
Riazan'	Zaraiskii	1867	20-35
	Mikhailovskii	1876	5-50
	Spasskii	1854	7-50
Iaroslavl'[b]	Molozhskii	1853	20-40
Simbirsk[c]		1840	Rarely more than 150
Simbirsk[d]		1862	3-105
Vladimir and Nizhegorod[e]		1853	50-100
Iaroslavl[e]		1853	20-40
Kaluga, Kursk, Tambov[e]		1853	70-245
Great Russia[f]		Second half of the eighteenth century	15-150

[a] Mashkin, "Byt krest'ian Kurskoi gubernii, Oboianskogo uzda," *Etnograficheskii sbornik* 5 (1862):23.

[b] A. Preobrazhenskii, "Prikhod Stanilovskii na Siti, Iaroslavskoi gubernii, Molozhskogo uezda, *Etnograficheskii sbornik* I (1853):141-45.

[c] V. B., "Simbirskie obychai pokupat; nevest,"*Otechestvennye zapiski* 9 no. 7 (1840): 28-29.

[d] N. Aristov, "Ocherk krest'ianskoi svad'by," *Volga,* no. 13 (1862): 49-50.

[e] A. Afanes'ev, "Kritika: Etnograficheskii sbornik," *Otechestvennye zapiski,* nos. 9-10, part 4 (1853):25.

[f] V.I. Semevskii, "Domashnii byt i nravy krest'ian vo vtoroi polovine XVIII v.," *Ustoi,* no. 2 (1882):76.

Source: Unless noted, D.K. Zelenin, *Opisanie rukopisei uchenago arkhiva Imperatorskogo russkogo geograficheskogo obshchestva,* 3 vols. (Petrograd, 1914-1916), passim.

Table 2. Dynamic Study of Peasant Mobility,
Village of Petrovskoe (1813-27)

Number of Tiaglos	Number of Households in 1813	Number of Households in 1827		
		Fewer Tiaglos	Same No. of Tiaglos	More Tiaglos
0.0	2	—	—	2
1.0	22	3	9	10
1.5	2	—	—	2
2.0	10	5	2	3
2.5	4	3	1	—
Total	40	11	12	17

Number of Horses	Number of Households in 1813	Number of Households in 1827		
		Fewer Horses	Same No. of Horses	More Horses
0	1	—	—	1
1	2	—	—	2
2	11	1	3	7
3	9	3	2	4
4	9	3	1	5
5	7	2	1	4
6	1	1	—	—
Total	40	10	7	23

Source: TsGADA, f. 1262, op. I, ed. khr. 1495: op. 4, ch. I, ed. khr. 41, 59, 121, 186, 344, 357.

It is not clear how much of the kladka the bride's family was required to spend on gifts, but her household generally kept a sizeable portion of the kladka for itself, this being the bridewealth or wealth equalizing aspect of the exchange. Simply put, because the repartitional land commune immediately provided the bridegroom's household with a unit of peasant arable land upon the formation of a new work team, the bride's household required compensation for the loss of its female laborer and any decline in its economic and social status resulting from her departure. Kalachov noted that a girl's parents, concerned about the loss of a female worker, would stipulate in the marriage agreement that either she spend the stradnaia pora at home or "that the family of the bridegroom pay a redemption for her, known as kladka."[18] Pakhman saw the dual nature of kladka, both a payment to reduce wedding costs and to compensate for the person of "the bride herself, as a laborer the family is losing by the girl marrying out."[19] According to Efimenko, "in some southwestern steppe guberniias the payment for the bride is determined by simple competition," with the highest bidder getting the girl, and the price reflecting true market demand.[20] Muhkin found that the amount of kladka was greater in regions where a female's labor was more highly valued. In Nizhegorod guberniia, women involved in bast production could do exactly the same work as men, and thus a bride's family could demand a high bridewealth for her.[21] Bridewealth also had its counterpart: "groomwealth." On the rare occasion when the male became part of the bride's household, usually because it had no other working-age males, his parents required compensation for the loss of his labor.[22] In sum, to quote another nineteenth-century ethnographer: "Dowries do not play a large role in peasant life; frequently the bridegroom not only does not receive a dowry, but even further he has to compensate the parents of the bride for their loss of her free labor."[23]

The acquisition of a daughter-in-law was a major expenditure, and the bridegroom's household had to be sure it acquired a good worker in order to recoup its investment. A bad choice could ruin a household for the additional allotment of peasant arable land and the extra worker had to offset not only the costs of the kladka, but an extra mouth to feed, higher taxes, and increased obligations. Marriage was too important for the household seeking either to minimize its losses or recoup its investment, the commune having to pay taxes, and the estate trying to maximize production to permit the young persons involved to play any significant role in mate selection. Marriage rituals included the mutual inspection of households by the parents (*smotrina* or *osmotr*) and differed little from the transaction of property. The matchmaker, often a relative, having been sent by the boy's parents, would usually greet the father of the potential bride saying, "we have a buyer, and you have the goods" (*U nas est' kupets, a u vas tovarets*) to signify the reason for the visit. Love was not a factor in marriage and was even thought to be harmful. The grooms' family was concerned solely with the bride's health, skills, and ability to work; the girl's, with being sure it would receive a fair kladka. Terms were set orally by a marital agreement (*brachnyi sgovor*), made binding by a *rukobit'e*, a ritual clapping of hands by the two fathers or heads of household, occasionally sanctified by a priest, and celebrated by a bout of heavy drinking (*zapoi* or *propoi*).[24]

Young, unmarried females were in a very ambiguous position in their natal households. Whereas their labor was valued, they were viewed as temporary members of the dvor. They had no claim to land where agriculture was the primary pursuit, although their departue would bring in a kladka, which should allow a brother or male cousin to marry. Marriageable daughters, granddaughters, and nieces were both consumers and laborers yielding small, short-run benefits, but having no prospects for substantial long-run benefits, but having no prospects for substantial long-run gains for their elders like unmarried males. Thus peasants were constantly balancing the mean age at marriage with the customary size of kladka, an equilibrium that would vary with changing economic circumstances.

Economic motives were clearly in the minds of the Petrovskoe serfs when they arranged marriages. Household serfs required the permission of the central estate office in Moscow to marry, and the archives of the estate hold many of the parent's petitions. The language was formal, undoubtedly having been composed by a scribe, but the reasons were plain. Karneia Abramova, a widow with four daughters, sought to marry off her eldest, Praskov'ia, 18 years old, "in order to avoid my having to support [her].[25] Arkhip Aglovin, the father of six children, including a 22-year-old daughter, Elena, with an illegitimate infant, requested permission for her to marry a free man for exactly the same reason.[26]

Parents were also often desperate for their sons to marry and bring a daughter-in-law into the household as the following petition reveals:

> Having two sons, of whom Savelii is in Moscow on a passport, and Fedot lives with me, and both have come of age, [but] are not married. And as my wife and I have gotten old and fallen into decrepitude, and with all this moreover, I have at home a daughter who is constantly afflicted by illness, because of this I suffer a great need of bedclothes and other domestic items, so I dare to trouble the Main Office with my most humble request to be favorably disposed to pay merciful attention to our extreme situation to allow our son Fedot to enter into marriage. For this we should pray to God for the health of Your Excellency and the director of the Main Office.   Ivan Smetanin[27]

Economic concerns even affected the seasonal pattern of marriages. The limited evidence available suggests that most first marriages took place in the fall, between September and November, somewhat less often in January and February following the prohibition of Advent, much less frequently in the spring, and almost never in the summer. Peasant sentiments were summed up by the sayings: "A betrothed girl in the household—a corpse at the table (*Nevesta na dvore–mertvets na stole*)," or, the reverse, "All winter I fed her, so let her work for me this summer (*Zimu, Ia ee prokormil, tak pust' mne eto letom zarabotaet*)."[28] Thus, the very timing of a wedding itself was a mechanism for the redistributrion of wealth.

But it was primarily the abundance of land, its constant redistribution, and the bridewealth aspect of kladka that prevented socioeconomic differentiation from developing in much of Great Russian peasant society, as in Petrovskoe. Bridewealth provided for "a double dispersal of property." Money passed in one direction; the bride and land in the other. Moreover, the bride's new household was where the children would be, and they would further dissipate the wealth resulting from the added unit of arable land.[29] Kladka was a "circulating pool of resources" in the sense that "what goes out for a bride has to come in for a sister." Thus, it served essentially "as a regulator of marriage and not as a means of increasing the father's wealth."[30] In contrast, the intent behind a bride's dowry is to endow a woman "with property to attract a husband of the same rank." Dowries exist in societies with substantial socioeconomic differentiation for their purpose is to preserve the status of the family into the next generation. A daughter with a dowry would not have to marry down, and this reinforces stratification in the society. "Dowry differentiates, just as bridewealth tends to homogenize."[31]

In Russia, bridewealth had no concern with the future status of the household. Rather, it merely facilitated marriage, greatly easing economic constraints. "The distribution of wives" was "very closely related to the distribution of sisters." In effect, kladka constantly moved toward creating an economic equilibrium. As long as villages had adequate amounts of arable "to satisfy the needs of *net* additional numbers of married couples" or other ready means of earning a living, wealth would flow in both directions.[32] In addition, these land reserves served to overcome any sex imbalance in the offspring of individual households. Furthermore, because of the high bridewealth payments, children were very dependent upon the head of the household or father to arrange marriages and to negotiate properly regarding the kladka. A bad deal, accepting too low a kladka, for example, might leave the household with too little money to find a bride for its own unmarried males. Bridewealth, therefore, directly affected the social and material well-being of the present generation, whereas necessity for correct patriarchal management of marriage enhanced the authority of the elders in the household.[33]

Boserup has argued that bridewealth is common in rural societies where very primitive systems of field cultivation are used and where "the major part of agricultural work is done by women." In contrast, "where plough cultivation predominates and where women do less agricultural work than men... a dowry is usually paid by the girl's family."[34] Goody has suggested that bridewealth and dowry were "related less directly to women's contribution to agriculture and more to the problem of 'status placement' in societies with varying degrees of socioeconomic differentiation." Goody does note, however, that more advanced plow cultivation allows for much greater stratification to develop than primitive slash/burn, digging stick, and hoe techniques which were practiced where population densities were low and land was not usually scarce.[35]

According to these interpretations, the presence of bridewealth in much of Great Russia would be rather difficult to explain. Whereas population density was lower than in the rest of Europe, the three-field system of plow agriculture was well in place in Great Russia by the early nineteenth cneutry, more primitive tillage systems existing only on the periphery.[36] Nevertheless, the theses of Boserup and Goody have something to contribute to the understanding of life in Petrovskoe and much of Great Russia.

But first, what was the extent of socioeconomic differentiation at Petrovskoe? Certainly some serfs' households were better off than others. "The majority of the field peasants are in good economic condition; among them there is a part middling and poor," the bailiff noted in the spring of 1844.[37] Soviet historians have seen stratification almost everywhere in serf society in Russia throughout the first half of the nineteenth cnetury, the process quickening in the 1830's and sharpening the crisis of the feudal system until its collapse in 1861. This viewpoint is virtually a cliché in Soviet historical literature. Koval'chenko, in examining data from Petrovskoe, concluded that between 1813 and 1856 "the characteristic feature of the stratification of the peasantry at the Petrovskoe estate was the rapid growth of the stratum of the poorest peasants," that is, households having less than three horses.[38]

To examine stratification in a peasant society requires a dynamic analysis of household mobility. Socioeconomic stratification is not the uneven distribution of wealth at a single point in time, but is differentiation over time giving rise to separate strata with distinct members, each stratum having its own economic interests, social orientation, strategies for survival, and means for maintaining or improving its status. An analysis of stratification, however, cannot be done solely on the level of the household, ignoring possible changes in its size and structure. Often per capita measures are more useful and accurate.[39]

At Petrovskoe, until 1825 partial redistributions of peasant allotments, demesne obligations, and tax burdens, all of which were apportioned by tiagla, took place annually in the spring; thereafter, once every two years. There was never a need for a general repartition as the on-going process of readjustment took care of all serf marriages, recruitment levies, flight, migration, retirements, and deaths. With the repartitional system, the total area of a household's arable depended on the number of tiagla, which was essentially a function of household size (see Figure 1). Larger households thus had more land; however as Figure 2 shows, land holdings per capita were quite equal regardless of the number of tiagla or members in a dvor. Eighty-two percent of the population in the village of Petrovskoe lived in households of 6 to 14 persons. In these dvory, the average holding by household size fluctuated from 1.46 to 1.70 *desiatinas* per capita, a range of only 16%. Very large households, those with more than 14 members and with 8% of the village population, had slightly lower average per capita holdings, varying from 1.22. to 1.70 desiatinas. Finally, households of less than six persons were subject to wide statistical variance, but they were neither uniformaly richer nor poorer than larger households. The communal process of annual or biennial partial repartitions was, therefore, extremely effective in providing an equal access to arable land based on labor capabilities and consumption needs.

There were few additional sources of revenue at Petrovskoe that could have given rise to substantial economic differentiation. Cereal cultivation was the primary pursuit of the peasants, whereas wealth in livestock was derived from the land. The serfs had very limited access to extra land, the estate renting out only 243 acres of reserve arable land to both its own and non-estate peasants, the bailiffs preferred letting the reserves lie fallow. Handicrafts and cottage industries were poorly developed in this region, and the Petrovskoe peasants did not engage in such pursuits. During the winter, the peasants spent

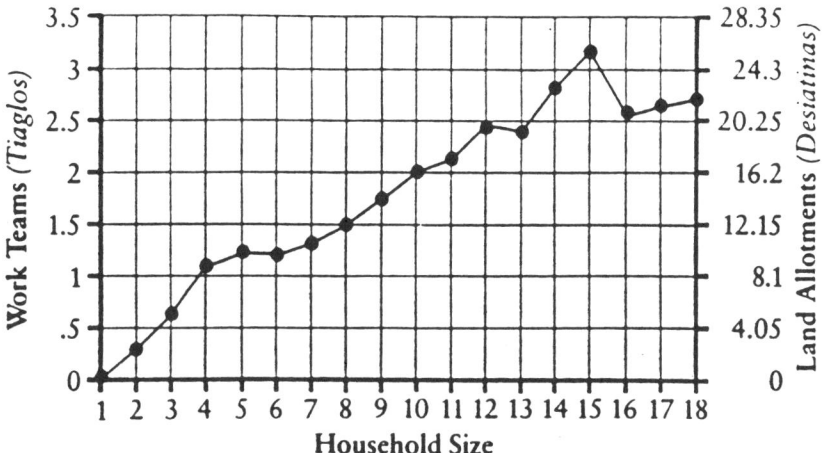

Figure 1. Work Teams (Tiaglos) and Land Allotments (Statutory Desiatinas) by Household Size, Village of Petrovskoe (1813-27)

Source: TsGADA, f. 1262, op. 1, ed. khr. 1495; op. 4, ch. 1, ed. khr. 41, 59, 121, 186, 344, 357.

much of their time threshing grain and transporting it to market, although they were able to undertake some private carting. Distribution of this work, however, depended in large part on the distribution of horses, which was rather equitable. Estate records do indicate that four serfs rented the fishing rights to the lake on estate property, presumably providing them with some additional income, but there are no references to other similar arrangements.[40]

Studies of many preindustrial societies have found a positive correlation between household size and wealth per capita. According to a number of empirical investigations, larger households tend to have higher capital/worker ratios and seem to benefit "from more efficient use of productive factors as a result of the larger scale of production."[41] Nevertheless, the data from Petrovskoe shows that if there were any accumulation of advantages by larger households that might have functioned collectively as a societal centrifuge separating the peasants into distinct economic layers, these advantages were confronted with strong egalitarian and levelling mechanisms.[42] In fact, Figure 2

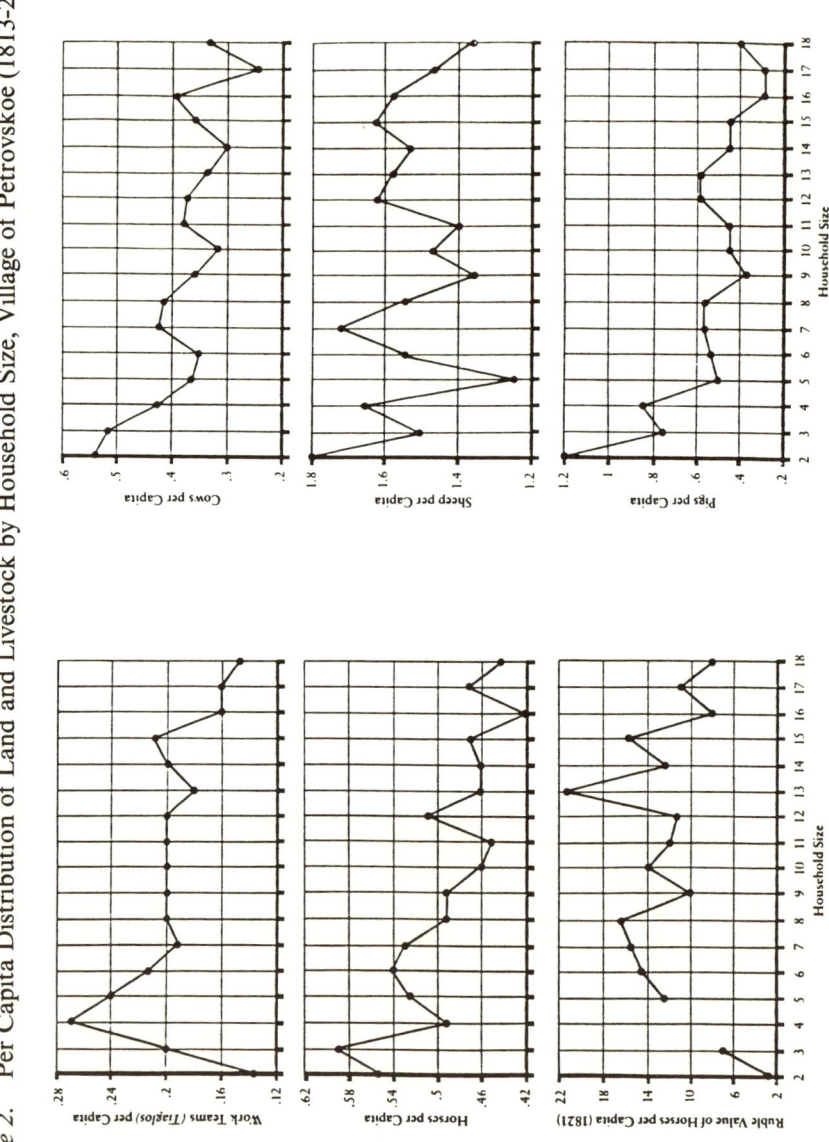

Figure 2. Per Capita Distribution of Land and Livestock by Household Size, Village of Petrovskoe (1813-27)

Sources: TsGADA, f. 1262, op. 1, ed. khr. 1495; op. 4, ch. 1, ed. khr. 41, 59, 121, 186, 344, 357.

suggests that in Petrovskoe, as households increased in size they were slightly poorer per capita. Actually, because larger households were those that had recently experienced higher fertility and consequently had a greater proportion of children, their consumption requirements per capita were somewhat lower, reducing, if not offsetting, the apparent advantages in wealth for smaller households.

This does not imply that there were not substantial differences among individual households in wealth per capita. Compare the following two households in the village of Petrovskoe in 1813. The first, dvor number twenty, was headed by Fedor Ivanov, age 45 and his wife Afim'ia Egorove. They had three children: Ivan, whose wife Afim'ia Nazarova lived with them; Andrei, age 12 and retarded; and Alena, age 3. In all there were 6 persons with 2 tiagla, 3 horses, 2 cows, 15 sheep, and 5 pigs. The second, dvor number twenty-five, headed by Peter Nazarov and his wife Arina Federova, was much worse off. Peter had three daughters of his own, a widowed sister-in-law, and her three unmarried children all living with him. Peter and his wife comprised the only tiaglo in the dvor and had to support 12 persons with half the land and virtually the same livestock holdings as Fedor Ivanov.[43]

But such differences were not the result of customary, legal, or institutional factors favoring socioeconomic differentiation. At Petrovskoe, wealth did not depend on inheritance, family status, or the ability to command a disproportionate amount of productive resources. The biological life cycle of households and luck determined much of the differentiation. For Peter Nazarov, it was unfortunate that his parents died leaving him with three unmarried sisters, that his brother died leaving him with four dependents, and that all of his own children were as yet unmarried. In contrast, fate was generous to Fedor Ivanov by giving him four adult workers in his household of six persons. "Far from being extraordinary occurences, crises and strokes of luck formed an integral part of peasant life," and they "must, therefore, have caused market socioeconomic mobility among peasant households."[44]

Fate could indeed be generous, but only temporarily. At Petrovskoe, whether due to biological or random factors, the rich got poorer, and the poor, richer. A dynamic analysis of peasant households, excluding those that underwent partitioning, merger, or extinction (these substantive changes being inherently levelling mechanisms)[45] reveals the presence of very strong equalizing tendencies in the village. Table 2 traces the fate of the 40 households in Petrovskoe that did not experience any substantive changes between 1813 and 1827. They comprise 63% of all households. The table shows that the more tiagla (and allotted arable land) a household had in 1813, the greater the likelihood that it had less in 1827. Of the 14 households that had two or more tiagla in 1813, 8 (57%) had fewer work teams by 1827, 3 (21%) had the same number, and 3 had more. Conversely, of the 26 households with less than two tiagla, 14 (54%) had more, 9 (35%) the same, and only 3 (12%) fewer in 1827.

The distribution of horses is the measure most frequently used by Soviet historians. The results for Petrovskoe are somewhat masked by an aggregate shift upward, an increase of 40 in the total number of horses owned by the households, the consequence of an estate program assisting the peasants in the purchase of horses. Nevertheless, the pattern was the same. Households with fewer horses (0-2) in 1813 were on the whole in a better position in 1827. Those dvory with many horses (5-6) in 1813 were poorer, relatively speaking, fourteen years later. Finally, it should be noted that mobility for households not undergoing substantive changes has a built-in upward bias caused by population growth.

At Petrovskoe, all indices indicate that wealth was distributed on an extremely equitable basis, limited only by biological and random fluctuations over which the serfs, the commune, and the estate had little or no control. Moreover, there was no permanent or definitive socioeconomic differentiation, no kulaks or *bedniaks* (poor peasants) only households that were in a constant state of flux. Household mobility was endemic, stratification nonexistent. Social status, if it were to exist at Petrovskoe, could not have been defined by land, the most valuable asset in the society, because it was not in the serfs' hands, regularly redistributed, and allotted according to the ability to work it. Livestock, although a potential source of status, depended on cereal cultivation and communal pastures, and consequently mirrored their distribution. Beyond land and livestock, there was little of value.

Thus, Goody's argument that bridewealth reinforces economic equality and is practiced in societies "relatively homogeneous" with little socioeconomic differentiation and little concern for status placement holds true for Petrovskoe. Bridewealth, however, does not require a primitive level of agricultural technology for elaborate mechanisms as the repartitional commune, biological life cycles, the pattern of household division and extinction, and random multidirectional mobility may provide the same agalitarian socioeconomic structure. Further, Boserup's suggestion that bridewealth is common in rural societies where women make a substantial contribution to field labor is also valid, although ecological and not just technological reasons may explain the high value priced on female agricultural labor.

Kladka complemented other levelling practices and tendencies at Petrovskoe by limiting the economic differentiation that would necessarily have resulted from marriage and the addition of a new work team to the bridegroom's household. Bridewealth favored universal marriage by evenly distributing daughters and daughters-in-law, by exchanging one for the other. The economic costs of not participating in the process, of having an unmarried daughter instead of a kladka to attract a daughter-in-law or to keep for oneself were extremely high. "In Russia, the organization of the repartitional commune is such that there are always more married male peasants, than unmarried, that it is seldom possible to meet an unmarried man there. And this striving to marry for economic motives has led in some places to monstrous consequences."[46] According to the author of this statement, there were ludicrously early ages for boys at marriage, sometimes as young as six or seven years old, and *snokhachestvo,* sexual relations between the father-in-law and daughter-in-law. Neither of these seem to have been problems at Petrovskoe. But given the availability of arable land, kladka and the repartitional system are linked with early marriage because they facilitated the creation of new wealth, increased productive capacity, broadened the commune's tax base, and most importantly, implied the sharing of this new wealth between the bride and bridegroom's households. These benefits were obviously desired as soon as possible, as soon as the young couple could assume the necessary responsibilities.

The egalitarian distribution of wealth among households according to their size or number of tiagla, the balance of land, labor, and livestock, was also the optimal use of resources. Any imbalance would have lowered total production for too many horses in one dvor given its land and labor and too few in another meant the estate and both households would have suffered. Consequently, bailiffs and landlords were very conscious of the need for the equitable distribution of wealth. Sir Donald Mackenzie Wallace, on his travels through Russia in the 1870s, noted that serfowners, "for evident reasons of self-interest, as well as from benevolent motives" prevented the development of socioeconomic differentiation. With the emancipation in 1861, however, "the Communal equality thus artificially maintained" by serfowners was weakened as enterprising individuals sought to better their status.[47]

During the course of the nineteenth century, estate managers came to realize that merely increasing the number of tiagla or the size of the demesne did not necessarily increase revenues. In fact, such policies could ruin an estate by undermining the peasants' well-being and exhausting their livestock. High revenues rested on the ability of an estate administration to make each tiaglo equally capable of cultivating the land.[48] Nasonov found that on the estates of the Iusupov family, poor management resulted in economic differentiation among the serfs. In other words, the bailiff had to intervene directly in peasant affairs to prevent stratification, even that caused by luck or the biological life cycle of households. Enforcement of the constant redistribution of plowlands and the assurance of equal access to communal pastures and meadows for all dvory were of the utmost importance. But the bailiff also had to prevent the serfs from renting out their allotments to one another, to restrict their sale of grain and livestock, and to assist poorer households in acquiring draft animals.[49] Of course, maximizing the number of tiagla and the size of the demesne were still important, but they could be carried to excess. The vigorous pursuit of the equalization of wealth had no inherent economic dangers.

Many anthropologtists and sociologists have noted that the constant fear of subsistence crises has, in most precapitalist peasant societies, given rise to what might be appropriately termed a subsistence ethic. This moral outlook, it has been suggested, was shared by the French, Russian, and Italian peasants in the nineteenth century and is present in many developing countries today.[50] The subsistence ethic meant that, economically, peasants were risk-avoiders, whereas socially they sought relationships that would provide assistance in times of crisis. But more importantly, it entailed "the right of all to a subsistence niche," and "in normal times it assured the 'survival of the weakest.'"[51] Communal lands, open fields divided into strips, and even periodic redistributions of arable land were all techniques of the subsistence ethic. Essentially, a community shared the risks of an uncertain environment, and there is no reason to suspect that this attitude was not present at Petrovskoe. But this moral outlook required only a limited reallocation of wealth to provide "a minimal subsistence insurance," not the limitation of socioeconomic differentiation as much as possible.[52]

At Petrovskoe, more than simply a subsistence ethic was involved. The remarkable egalitarian distribution of wealth was a vital part of the social and political order on the estate. The forces levelling economic differences along with early marriage and stable forms of domestic groupings served to structure and distribute power among the serfs and to uphold the central purpose of the institution of serfdom, income for the landlord. All these characteristics of serf life were fundamental supports in a system of control that rested on the collusion and cooperation of the bailiff and patriarchs, the heads of household.

Investigations into social stratification within peasant communities have usually centered on the differentiation of households by wealth and status. Small landholders, tenant farmers, and landless laborers are generally contrasted, or peasants with a similar relationship to the productive process are distinguished on the basis of land and livestock holdings per capita. Certainly, this method of analysis would be fruitless for Petrovskoe, for there were no such differences. But a patriarchal society is also highly stratified. There exists a sharp, intergenerational division that cuts across all households, limiting their role as symbols of self-identification and providing a foundation for interhousehold control.

A patriarchal society at its foundation entails nothing more than the movement of wealth and power from the young and toward the old. With the patriarchal structure in Petrovskoe, the household was more than anything else the unit of exploitation used not only by the noble landlord as a member of the political elite, but by serf patriarchs as well. A patriarch sought to better himself not by claiming a disproportionate share of wealth or productive resources in the village, not by competing with other households, but by exploiting more effectively the members of his own household. Status was defined by position with the dvor, the ability to control economic and fertility decisions, and the power to maintain advantages over other household members.

The egalitarian distribution of land, labor, and livestock not only maximixed estate and peasant production of cereal at Petrovskoe, raising the standard of living for all, it minimized conflicts between households, limiting disputes over wealth and power within the political leadership of the village. What emerged was a ruling stratum of peasants in which membership was primarily a function of age. This ruling elite, the heads of households, shared with the estate management a number of concerns, and together they functioned in a social system that advanced and protected their common interests. By upholding the large patriarchal family either by directly controlling household fission of by granting village elders the right to regulate household size, the bailiffs supported the very foundation of patriarchal authority. And, this authority assured the estate of a strong ally in the battle to get the remainder of the serf population to work productively and behave properly.

The immediate economic advantages of early and universal marriage to both patriarchs and the estate have already been discussed. In essence, for the male's household, a marriage never worsened and almost always improved its consumer/labor ratio and its allotment size/capita, to the benefit of all family members but the new couple. Equally important, the high fertility that resulted from this marriage pattern was the only means by which a patriarch and his wife could avoid destitution in their old age, given the high level of mortality. Moreover, high fertility made it possible for serf elders to be freed from their field work responsibilities by their mid-fifties, thereby avoiding some of the drudgery of peasant life. After age 55, most patriarchs were simply managers, while others in the household worked. But even before this, it is likely that heads of household enjoyed a privileged position in the nature and amount of work they performed. Stable high fertility and large households considerably enhanced the managerial functions of the patriarchs. They were called the *bol'shak,* the big one, the boss, the one who gives orders; their wives, the *bol'shitsa* or *bol'shukha.*

Nineteenth-century Russian ethnographers frequently commented on the strict, almost despotic control that patriarchs exercised in their household.[53] At Petrovskoe, households worked an average of 42 acres of arable, including the demesne, all in scattered strips. The bol'shak was responsible for allocating and overseeing his labor and livestock to get the most out of the land. Larger households also permitted some degree of specialization of labor. This was especially true for women, some cooking year-round, others tending the livestock and watching the children, and in the spring and summer working the fields and taking care of the kitchen garden. It was for the bol'shitsa to see that the household benefitted as much as possible from the proper division of these tasks.

In other peasant societies with stable high fertility, the advantages for patriarchs have included not only the choice of work, but better food and clothing, precedence in feeding, and privileged use of house space and facilities.⁵⁴ In Russia, the bol'shak clearly had preferential use of space in the *izba*. In the winter, the bol'shak and his wife slept on the *polati* (sleeping platforms) directly over the stove, the warmest place in the hut. In the summer, it was the other married couples who had to move out and into various outbuildings and storerooms. The so-callled beautiful, holy icon corner (*krasnyi, sviatoi, obraznnoi ugol*) was also the elder's (*starshii*) corner. In this corner was a table where the family ate its meals with the place beneath the icon reserved for the head of household. He relinquished his place only on the wedding day of a son, when the newly married couple sat under the icon during the celebration feast.⁵⁵

The spiritual owner of a peasant dvor and a symbolic idealization of the patriarch was the *dedushka-domovoi,* the grandfather house-spirit, thought by peasants throughout Great Russia to share a similar economic fate with the household in which he lived. Every household had its own domovoi, who lived behind the hearth beneath the bed of the bol'shak and was often addressed as "khoziain," head of household. If the domovoi looked favorably upon the family, its horses were strong and healthy; if he became angry, the animals became thin and died. The domovoi saw to all trifles in the dvor. He liked fertile domestic fowl and livestock and was intolerant of needless expenditures. In a word, the domovoi was laborious, thrifty, economical, and painstaking, and the peasants took great care not to offend him in anyway.

The domovoi was thought to be a good-natured, elderly being with a grey beard and stooped pasture. He would only communicate with the eldest member of the dvor if he wished to inform the family of some good or evil to come. If a family moved into new izba, the patriarch would ask the domovoi to accompany them and bring his favor to the new hut. As an invitation, a few hot cinders were taken from the sotve of the old hut and were buried in the elder's or beautiful corner of the new izba under the icon, where the head of household normally sat. The domovoi always accepted. Fights between different households were seen as one house-spirit trying to better his dvor at the expense of the other. A domovoi could not live with another house-spirit, and if two households merged there was fighting between the domovoi as they clashed for control of the house. Such was the great power of the domovoi that families often found it impossible to stay together.⁵⁶

Whether peasant patriarchs were better fed and clothed than other members of their dvor is unknown. But stable high fertility clearly brought considerable power and benefits to the heads of household. Lower fertility and smaller households would have undermined quite substantially the position of the patriarchs. In essence, a reproductive pattern was "needed to support the economic one and to maintain the existing gradations of material advantage within the family."⁵⁷ Stable high fertility at Petrovskoe was also one of the key factors that stabilized household structures, greatly compressing the duration of household life cycles and providing for the constancy of the three-generation, multiple family dvor. This, coupled with the egalitarian distribution of wealth, meant that patriarchal power within a household varied little over time as the bol'shak did not have to adapt to greatly different familial patterns, labor and livestock resources, and levels of well-being.[58] In sum, the power of the patriarchs, supported by the entire economic and social structure of life, was unequaled and unchanging.

The stability of households and the maximization of production benefited not only the estate and the heads of household, but every serf at Petrovskoe. Nevertheless, the estate and the patriarchs derived the greatest share of wealth and power based on a conjuction of interests. As a result, intergenerational antagonism was structurally endemic at Petrovskoe, with the patriarch and his wife on one side and the exploited members of the dvor on the other. This structure of authority helped maintain the social and economic order.

NOTES AND REFERENCES

1. N. Kalachov, "Iuridicheskie obychai krest'ian v nekotorykh mestnostiak," *Arkhiv istoricheskikh i prakticheskikh svedenii, otnosiashikhsia do Rossii*, vol. 2 (St. Petersburg, 1859), p. 25; M.N. Kishkin, "Dannye i predpolozheniia," p. 226; A. Smirnov, *Ocherki semeinykh otnoshenii po obychnomu pravu russkogo naroda* (Moscow, 1878), pp. 76-81; and A.N. Nasonov, "Iz istorii," p. 518. See also Olga Crisp, "The pattern of Industrialization in Russia, 1700-1914," *Studies in the Russian Economy before 1914* (London, 1976), p. 21.

2. The weekly reports of the bailiff of Petrovskoe to Moscow usually noted the tasks assigned to men and women during the previous seven days, and these documents reveal this division of labor. See also Mashkin, "Byt," pp. 95-96, 101; A. Preobrazhenskii, "Volost' Pokrovsko-Sitskaia," pp. 79-80; and D.I., "Zametki o krest'ianskoi sem'e v Novgorodskoi gubernii," in *Sbornik narodnykh iuridicheskikh obychaev*, vol. 2, in *Zapiski Imperatorskogo russkogo geograficheskogo obshchestva po otdeleniiu etnografi*, vol. 18 (St. Petersburg, 1900), p. 166.

3. TsGADA, f. 1262, *op.* 1, *ch* 1, *ed khr.* 1495; *op* 4, *khr.* 41, 59, 121, 186, 344, 357; *ch.* 2, *ed. khr.* 822. Of this last group, in all likelihood, more than 75% were married because the nominative lists often failed to distinguish between single males and those who had been widowed shortly after their first marriage. A recently widowed male age 15-19 would have formed a full tiaglo upon marriage and was formally obligated to fulfill his responsiblities until the next redistribution of land and corvee duties. Nevertheless, young, single males from families with no other working-age males did on occasion carry a full tiaglo, with a mother, sisters, or younger brothers assisting in the field work. See also I. Tuitriumov, "Krest'ianskaia sem'ia. Ocherk obychnogo prava," *Russkaia Rech'*, vol. 7 (1879), pp. 135-137.

4. D.I., "Zametki," pp. 262-263; Kalachov, "Iuridicheskie obychai," p. 25; Kishkin, "Dannye i predpolozheniia," p. 226; Nasonov, "Iz istorii," p. 518; A. Gerschenkron, "Agrarian Policies and Industrialization: Russia 1861-1917," in *The Cambridge Economic History of Europe*, vol. 6, part 2 (Cambridge, 1965), p. 749; and P. Czap, "Marriage and the Peasant Joint Family in the Era of Serfdom" in *The Family in Imperial Russia*, ed. by David L. Ransel (Urbana: University of Illinois Press, 1978), p. 115.

5. These figures are based on the total number of working person-years lived for all males between 19 and 54, the latter being the mean age of retirement for surviving males, assuming the estimate of expectation of life at birth determined above. Coale and Demeny, *Regional Model Life Tables*, part 2, p. 7.

6. P. Efimenko, "Sem'ia Arkhangel'skogo krest'ianina po obychnomu pravu," *Sudebnyi zhurnal* (July-August, 1873), pp. 97-98. Efimenko is referring here to customary practices in central Russia, not in the far north. V. Dal', *Polovitsy russkogo naroda*, p. 362. Tiaglo in this case means the unit of allotted land associated with the formation of work team and the assumption of corvee. On the benefits of early marriage for peasant elders, see Brzheskii, *Ocherki iuridicheskogo byta*, pp. 180-181; Zvonkov, "Sovremennyi brak," pp. 30-31; Efimenko "Sem'ia," p. 97; P. Efimenko, *Pridanoe po obychnomu pravu krest'ian Archangel'skoi gubernii* (St. Petersburg, 1872), pp. 39-41; A. Zaloskin, "Khoziaistvennye statisticheskie zamechaniia po selu abakumovo, Riazanskoi gubernii, Pronskogo uezda, Pomeshchika G...na," *Zhurnal zemlevladel'tsev*, vol. 2., no. 6 (1858), p. 41; N. Lebedev. "Byt krest'ian Tverskoi gubernii, Tverskogo uezda," *ES*, I, p. 186; K. Myl'nikova and V. Tsintsius, "Severno-velikorusskaia svad'ba," *Materialy po svad'be i semeino-rodovomu stroiu naradov SSSR*, vol. 1 (Leningrad, 1926), pp. 24-27; N. Otto, "Iz narodnogo byta: Novgorodskaia svad'ba," *Severnaia Pchela*, no. 137 (1862), p. 545; and Pr V. E-iu, "Opisanie sel'skoi svad'by v Sengileevskom uezde, Simbirskoi gubernii," *Etnograficheskoe obozrenie*, vol. 42, no. 3 (1899), pp. 108-109.

7. J. Goody, "Bridewealth and Dowry in Africa and Eurasia," in *Bridewealth and Dowry* (Cambridge, 1973) pp. 1-5.

8. Ibid., pp. 2, 46.

9. Ibid., p. 1.

10. *Trudy kommissi po preobrazovaniiu volostnykh sudov*, vols. 1-7 (St. Petersburg, 1873-1874), I, pp. 389-486.

11. D. K. Zelenin, *Opisanie rukopisei uchenogo arkhiva Imperatorskogo russkogo geograficheskogo obshchestva*, 3 vols. (Petrograd, 1914-1916), *passim;* V.P. Muhkin, *Obychnyi poriadok nasledovaniia u krest'ian* (St. Petersburg, 1881), pp. 88-90, 132-136; Tuitriumov, "Krest'ianskaia sem'ia," pp. 155-156; A. Efimenko, "Narodnye iuridicheskie vozrenia na brak," *Znanie*, no. 1 (1874),p. 15; Smirnov, "Ocherki semeinykh otnoshenii," pp. 182-183; [no author], "Sloboda Trekhizbianskaia," *ES*, II., p. 7.

12. P. Chubinskii, "Ocherk narodnyky iuridicheskikh obychaev i poniatii v Malorossii," *Zapiski Imperatorskogo russkogo geograficheskogo obshchestva po otdeleniiu etnografi*, vol. 2 (1969), pp. 690-691; Efimenko, *Pridanoe*, pp. 8-17.

13. Mukhin, *Obychnyi poriadok*, pp. 135-136.

14. Efimenko, "Narodnye iuridicheskie vozreniaa," p. 15. See also S. V. Pakhman, *Obychnoe grazhdanskoe pravo v Rossii*, 2 vols. (St. Petersburg, 1877), II, p. 68; and A. Afanas'ev, "Kritika: Ethnograficheskii sbornik," *Otechestvennye zapiski*, vol. 90, nos. 9-10 (1853), part IV, p. 25.

15. Zelenin, *Opisanie*, passim; Muhkin, *Obychnyi poriadok*, pp. 113-116, 123-134; Rudnev, "Selo Golun'," pp. 107-108; Efimenko, "Narodnye iuridicheskie vozreniia," p. 14; Efimenko, *Pridanoe*, p. 7; Semenova, *Zhizn' Evana,"* p. 3; Troitskii, "Selo Lipitsky," p. 89; Tuitriumov, "Krest'ianskaia sem'ia, p. 155; M.E. Mikheev, "Opisanie svadebnykh obychaev i obriadov v Buzulukskom uezde, Samarskoi gubernii," *Etnograficheskoe obozrenie*, 3 (1899), pp. 146-147; N. Aristov, "Ocherk krest'ianskoi svad'by," *Volga*, 13 (1862), pp. 49-50; N. Vinogradov, "Narodnaia svad'ba v Kostromskom uezde," vol. 8 (1917), pp. 74-79; and N. Kostrov, "Svadebnye obriady Minusinskikh krest'ian," *Illiustratisiia* 176 (1861), p. 10.

16. Akademiia nauk SSR. Geograficheskoe obschestvo, *Russkie geografy i puteshestvenniki. Fondy arkhiva Geograficheskogo obshchestva* (Leningrad, 1971), p. 9.

17. Zelenin, *Opisanie*, I-III, passim.

18. Kalachov, "Iuridicheskie obychai," p. 24. See also Tuitriumov, "Krest'ianskaia sem'ia," p. 137 for a virtually identical statement.

19. Pakhman, *Obychnoe grazhdanskoe pravo*, vol. 2, pp. 60-62.

20. Efimenko, "Krest'ianskaia zhenshchina," pp. 194-198.

21. Muhkin, *Obychnyi poriadok*, pp. 17-19.

22. Semevskii, "Domashnii byt," p. 77.

23. Tiutriumov, "Krest'ianskaia sem'ia," pp. 155-156. See also Afanas'ev, "Kritika," p. 25 and Smirnov, "Ocherki semeinykh otnoshenii," p. 122.

24. Descriptions of marriage and wedding rituals are numerous. See A. Efimenko, "Krest'ianskaia zhenshchina," pp. 77, 197-198; Smirnov, "Ocherki semeinykh otnoshenii," pp. 228-242; P. Efimenko, *Pridanoe,* pp. 39-41; A. Efimenko, "Narodnye iuridicheskie vozrenie," pp. 1-22; P. Efimenko, "Sem'ia," p. 32; Aristov, "Ocherk," p. 49; Pr. V.E.-iu, "Opisanie sel'skoi svad'by," pp. 110-111; Tiutriumov, "Krest'ianskaia sem'ia," pp. 123-129; Otto, "Iz narodnogo byta," p. 545; Mikheev, "Opisanie svadebnykh obychaev," pp. 144-146; Vinogradov, "Narodnaia svad'ba," pp. 74-79; Myl'nikova, "Severno-velikorusskaia svad'ba," pp. 35-36; A. Nikolaev, "Krest'ianskaia svad'ba v Zvenigorodskom uezde, Moskovskoi gubernii," *Severnaia Pchela,* 209-210 (1863), pp. 921-925; N.F. Sumtsov, *O svadebnykh obriadakh, preimushchestvenno russkikh* (Kharkov, 1881), pp. 22-34; E.G. Kagarov, "Sostav i proiskhozhdenie svadebnoi obriadnosti," in *Sbornik Muzeia antropologii i etnografi AN SSSR,* vol. 42 (1899), pp. 160-163; V.A. Aleksandrov, "Vologodskaia svad'ba," *Biblioteka dlia chteniia,* no. 5 (1863), pp. 6-13; N.R.-v, "Svadebyne obychai v Ostashkovskom uezde v polovine XIX veka," *Tverskaia starina,* no. 2 (1913), p. 39; and V.P., "Simbirskie obychai pokupat' nevest," *Otechestvennyie zapiski,* no. 7 (1840), pp. 28-29.

25. TsGADA, f. 1262, op. 4, ch. I, ed. khr. 649, 1.255 (December 22, 1854).

26. Ibid., 1.150 (October 18, 1954).

27. TsGADA, f. 1262, op. 4, ch. II, ed. khr. 866, 1.24 (January 12, 1959).

28. Czap, "Marriage," pp. 107-108; Mashkin, "Byt," p. 23; Mukhin, *Obychnyi poriadok,* pp. 121-122; N. Lebedev, "Byt krest'ian Tverskoi gubernii, Tverskogo uezda," *ES,* I, p. 186; N. Galentorn, "Svad'ba v Saltykovskoi volosti, Morshanskogo uezda, Tambovskoi gubernii," in *Materialy po svad'be i semeinorodovomu stroiu narodov SSSR,* vol. 1 (Leningrad, 1926), pp. 171-173; and N. Shternberg, "Novye materialy po svad'be," in ibid., p. 10.

29. Goody, "Bridewealth," p. 13.

30. Ibid., p. 5.

31. Ibid., pp. 17-25, 47.

32. Ibid., p. 18, and Gerschenkron, "Agrarian Policies," p. 749. Emphasis in Gershenkron's original.

33. Goody, "Bridewealth," p. 5.

34. Boserup, *Women's Role in Economic Development* (London, 1970), p. 50.

35. Goody, "Bridewealth," pp. 23, 46.

36. M. Confino, *Systemes agraires et progrès agricole* (Paris, 1969), pp. 26-55.

37. TsGADA, f. 1262, op. 4, ch. I, ed. khr. 615, 1.11 (December, 1843-April, 1944).

38. Koval'chenko, *Krest'iane,* pp. 205-208. For other scholarship echoing the same interpretation regarding stratification, see Koval'chenko, *Russkoe krepostnoe kres'tianstvo, passim;* Fedorov, *Pomeshchich'i krest'iane,* pp. 251-253; Grekov, "Tambovskoe imenie," pp. 489-491; and P. A. Zaionchkovskii, *Otmena krepostnogo prava v Rossii* (Moscow, 1968), pp. 21-24.

39. T. Shanin, *The Awkward Class* (Oxford: Oxford University Press, 1972), pp. 45-80.

40. TsGADA, f. 1262, op. 4, ch. I, ed. khr. 615, 1.10-11; ed. khr. 649, 1.93; and ch. II, ed. khr. 862, 1.6,7.

41. Shanin, *The Awkward Class,* pp. 63-68.

42. Ibid., pp. 63-121.

43. TsGADA, f. 1262, op. 4, ch. I, ed. khr. 41.

44. Shanin, *The Awkward Class,* p. 115.

45. Ibid., pp. 81-94.

46. Cited in A. Efimenko, "Sem'ia," pp. 107-113. See also Semevskii, "Domashnii byt," p. 74.

47. Sir Donald Mackensie Wallace, *Russia on the Eve of War and Revolution,* ed. by Cyril E. Black (New York, 1961), p. 342.

48. A.N. Shishkov, "Mysli o khoziaistve i otchetnosti," *ZLOSKh za 1855,* part 2 (1856), pp. 142-146; Nasonov, "Khoziaistvo krupnoi votchiny," p. 345.

49. A.N. Nasonov, "Iusupovski votchiny v XIX-om veke," *Doklady A.N. SSSR,* series 5 (1926), pp. 1-3.

50. James C. Scott, *The Moral Economy of the Peasant* (New Haven, Connecticut, 1976), p. 2.

51. Ibid., pp. 3, 41, 43. See also Jere R. Behrman, "Supply Responses and the Modernization of Peasant Agriculture: A Study of Major Annual Crops in Thailand," in *Subsistence Agriculture and Economic Development,* ed. by C.R. Wharton, Jr. (Chicago, 1969), p. 236; J.W. Mellor, "The Subsistence Farmer in Traditional Economies," in ibid., p. 214; H. Myiant, "The Peasant Economies of Today's Underdeveloped Areas," in ibid., p. 103; and K. Polanyi, *The Great Transformation* (Boston, 1957), pp. 163-164.

52. Scott, *The Moral Economy,* p. 5.

53. Zvonkov, "Sovremennyi brak," pp. 24-27; Tiutriumov, "Krest'ianskaia sem'ia.".

54. J.C. Caldwell, "A Theory of Fertility: From High Plateau to Destabilization," *Population and Development Review,* 4 (1978), pp. 555-557, 560-561.

55. Sumtsov, *O svadebnykh obriadakh,* pp. 186-187; Malykhin, "Byt," pp. 210-211; Semevskii, "Domashnii byt," part I, pp. 110-112; and Troitskii, "Selo Lipitsy," pp. 83-84.

56. Bondarenko, "Pover'ia krest'ian Tambovskoi gubernii," pp. 116-120; A. Afans'ev, "Dedushka-domovoi," *Arkhiv istoriko-iuridicheskie svedenii otnosiashikhsia do Rossii,* vol. I (Moscow, 1850), pp. 16-22; and M. Dobrozrakov, "Selo Ul'ianovka, Nizhegorodskoi gubernii, Lukianovskogo uezda," *ES,* I, pp. 57-59.

57. Caldwell, "A Theory of Fertility," p. 566.

58. Ibid., p. 565.

THE RUSSIAN PEASANT MOVEMENT IN THE EIGHTEENTH AND NINETEENTH CENTURY

Viktor Ivanovich Buganov

The history of Russian political and economic structure in the late stages of feudalism and during the transition to capitalism is related to the development of the manorial economy and the confrontation of two classes: the peasantry and the landed nobility.

The peasant movement has been a continual object of interest to historians. Since the nineteenth century, historians have treated peasant protest within two contexts: the emerging peasant economy and the place of the peasant in society. The study of old Russia is limited by sources, many of which, especially official records, have not survived. For the seventeenth and eighteenth century the material is better, and for the nineteenth century, abundant. There are documents directly attributable to peasants or relating to them (petitions and resolutions of the peasant commune, or *mir*) and about the landed nobility (surveys of estates, stewards' correspondence); there is official material (reports, statistics, surveys from ministeries, committees, zemstvo and other local institutions, legislative acts, clerical correspondence, and so forth).[1]

There is no need to enumerate all the accomplishments of archeography;[2] but we may single out a landmark, the series edited by N.M. Druzhinin, four volumes on agrarian protest from 1796 through 1861[3] and another four on the post-reform struggle of the Russian peasantry.[4] The historiography is also rich. A team of scholars, including N.M. Druzhinin, I.D. Koval'chenko, N.L. Rubinshtein, and V.A. Fedorov have reviewed the early nineteenth-century economy, Druzhinin, A.M. Anfimov, and others, have studied the second half of the nineteenth century.[6] In addition, there are articles and books by region, period, and topic.[7] Of particular importance on the eighteenth century are works by V.I. Semevskii and V.V. Mavrodin;[8] and on the early nineteenth century, articles by I.I. Ignativich, I.I. Linkov, and V.A. Fedorov;[9] B.G. Litvak's book and articles by N.M. Druzhinin and V.A. Fedorov also encompass the whole period.

Priority is still given to the first half of the nineteenth century.[10] As a consequence, the peasant movement of the latter half of the nineteenth century, has been studied far more superficially than that of the first. Also, the materials, although plentiful, require classification. Finally a great deal of material is yet to be discovered, especially in regional archives. While studying the peasant movement on an estate in central Russia, for example, V.A. Fedorov determined (using data obtained from central and regional archives) that between 1801-1860 there were 1,119 instances of peasant unrest at separate manors;[11] from central archives, Druzhinin had found 494 cases—238% fewer.[12] In his work on peasant protest from 1855-1864, B.G. Litvak wrote that regional exaggerated instances of unrest by roughly a third for the second half of the century. According to Litvak,

> Since the central archives have been studied rather thoroughly, the likelihood of adding significantly to our knowledge is extremely slight. But then in the years that witnessed the revolutionary situation (from the end of the 1850s to the beginning of the 1860s—V.B.) and in the years that followed, the scope of regional institutions connected, one way or another, with the "peasant question" expanded greatly. The information collected settled into regional records.[14]

Such skepticism about the possibility of knowing more about peasant unrest in the first half of the nineteenth century has not been justified. Despite disagreement, however, specialists do concur that the existing studies and publications have not explored all the relevant material.

The sources are flawed and incomplete. In their reports, agents of the Ministry of Internal Affairs, the Third Department of His Imperial Majesty's Privy Chancellery, and other institutions, sought to conceal repressive measures taken against the peasantry, although both anti-feudal and antigovernment demonstrations were included in official figures on crime. As a result, both before and after the 1917 revolution, historians used gross estimates in calculating peasant disturbances, and only since the end of the 1950s (beginning with the Tallin session of the Symposium on Eastern European Agrarian History) have these data been subjected to well-founded criticism. Gross figures lead to misinterpretation of qualitative distinctions between individual manifestations and to exaggeration of scale (because the researchers had been operating on purely quantitative unsystematized evidence). The distortion was such that, in the words of Druzhinin, "quantitative description of the peasant movement fully concordant with reality" might be impossible to achieve; facts surrounding the agrarian protest have not been preserved.

For the purposes of analysis, N.N. Liashchenko proposed, as I.I. Ignatovich before him, that the peasant disturbance be considered the descriptive unit—i.e., open insubordination by a more or less significant group of state or manorial peasants in violation of the regulations. Litvak rightly considers such a definition amorphous and inadequate; several peasant disturbances involved no violation of the law whatsoever (for example, the struggle against "exploitation by the landlords"). Violation was by nobles who increased peasant dues beyond all reasonable bounds, compelled cohabitation with female peasants, and so forth). Once the principal forms of peasant struggle have been defined, each specific instance may be categorized as one form or a composite of several. It seems that Litvak's proposal would enable us to conduct more thorough and detailed research on the peasant movement, providing the necessary quantitative and qualitative base of description.[13]

It is safe to say that the universally recognized cause of the peasant movement was the deterioration of the peasants' situation from the end of the eighteenth through the first half of the nineteenth century: increased pressure from the landlords and repression by theTsarist regime. During the reforms, the cause of agrarian protest was the peasants' struggle for improvement in size of holdings (peasants refused to accept temporary arrangements or to sign regulatory charters, demanded a reduction in redemption payments and dues, an end to exploitation by landlords and representatives of the Tsar). Naturally there were also specific precipitating events (rumors of freedom, rumors concerning the activities of various secret committees on the "peasant question," and the promulgation of decrees and manifestoes).

The first half of the nineteenth century witnessed the crisis of the feudal system as represented by the contradiction between serfdom and the emergence of capitalism. Serfdom powerfully retarded capitalist development. The industrial revolution, approximately the 1840s to the 1880s, introduced the textile mill and machine production to factories. Growing productive capacity was evident in textiles. But it was only after the reforms of 1861 that capitalist production expanded particularly rapidly, as is demonstrated in Lenin's *The*

Development of Capitalism in Russia and in other scholarly works from the late nineteenth century on.

Before 1861, the influence of serfdom on industry could be felt in the extensive use of servile labor, especially in mining and metallurgy, where serfs comprised 80% of the workforce on the eve of the reform. This contributed to the production decline in the Ural mountains. Unfree labor hindered capitalist reorganization of these branches of industry. Those branches that make broad use of hired labor—such as the cotton industry—developed far more rapidly.

To an even greater degree, retardation affected agriculture, which played a dominant role in the national economy, because the peasantry constituted the majority of the population (90% in 1795; 86% in 1857). New significant socioeconomic processes encouraged the expansion of production and linked peasant and manor to the market system. The nonagricultural, urban population placed an increased demand on agricultural production; and more and more peasants engaged in various trades and seasonal work (several hundred thousand at the end of the eighteenth century). But restrictions imposed by the state authorities and by the nobility greatly impeded these trends. Nobles preferred serf labor to improve the output of their land; they cut back peasant allotments (at the beginning of the eighteenth century, peasant allotments were typically 2 to 2.5 desiatiny per male peasant [5.4 to 6.75 acres]; by the mid nineteenth century, allotments averaged the minimum); they increased quit-rent and work hours for labor service (at the end of the eighteenth century, peasants divided their time equally between services owed to the landlord and work on their own allotments; in the mid-nineteenth century, time spent in labor services typically exceeded work on the allotment by a factor of two, and quit-rent had increased several times over). As a result of the new imposition, serf's output declined sharply in the central and western regions of the country (in net grain harvest per person). As Koval'chenko wrote, "By the mid-nineteenth century, opportunities for improving production through servile relations had been exhausted..these relations, had become obsolete."

Meanwhile, the peasant economy occupied a more prominent position in agricultural production, constituting the foundation of capitalist relations in agriculture. Manorial and state peasants produced 71% of all crops (36% and 35% respectively); landlords 21%. The manorial economy sometimes preserved a natural economy. By contrast, on the serfs' own land and where there was quit-rent or state land, rural life progressed towards bourgeois stratification, although this process was impeded both by landlords and by the debased status of the serf and peasant. The relationships born of serfdom greatly affected the development of capitalist relationships.

Commodity production based on unfree labor, as developed by landlords on their estates, was not profitable for society as a whole, although it was profitable for the landlord, because it brought him considerable revenues (assuming the absence of expenses for replacement of the labor force, minimal expenses for tools and work animals). K.D. Kavelin, the renowned state school representative and historian of the mid-nineteenth century, wrote: "In the performance of labor services, a peasant will work at least twice as poorly as at home, on his own fields."[14]

During the post-reform era, the rapid development of agrarian capitalism, still hampered by remaining manorial restrictions, by temporary obligations of freed peasants to "work off" their dues, and by the debased status of peasants) gave particular importance to peasant holdings and to "depeasantisation," or stratification, which proceeded rapidly after the reforms.

In the years before 1861, the peasant movement was directed mainly against serfdom and was motivated by a desire for freedom; after the reforms, it was directed against what remained of serfdom and toward the free development of the peasant economy on the model of the American family farm. Competition between the two evolutionary paths—the Prussian and the American—constitutes the core of the agrarian development of reform-era Russia.[15]

The suppression of the last peasant war in the history of pre-reform Russia (Pugachev's rebellion from 1773-1775) by no means put a stop to agrarian protest. Protest took various forms—throughout the seventeenth and eighteenth centuries. As before, banditry was common. Frequently, bandits were part of a criminal element. But government records no doubt concealed the elements of social struggle implicit in some forms of banditry. From the 1770s through the 1790s for example, bandit parties raided the lands of the Volga (the famous cases described by D.L. Mordovtsev and others), the regions of Nizhnyi Novgorod and Vologda. Typically, these bandit gangs, sometimes former participants of the Pugachev rebellion, strove to recreate that bygone insurrection.

Then there were the disseminators of rumors and tales about Pugachev, purportedly leaked by agencies that had held him. Among the disseminators were such former Pugachevists as Pyotr Khripunov, who began to speak out in 1783 in Altai. He asserted that Pugachev was alive and that he had been summoned to continue the struggle against the nobles and the officials. The following year he was arrested. Two years later, he made an unsuccessful attempt to escape to the Cossacks and died shortly thereafter. Ivan Sokolov, a townsman from Tiumen', spread "harmful talk" about the "past disorders" at the Zlatoustov factory in the Urals. According to Sokolov, Pugachev and his army were waiting near the Black Sea and would bring "peace to all." The government called such rumors "falesehoods about Pugachev."

Forty-four cases involving disseminators have survived from a single Secret Senate Expedition investigating political crimes from 1774-1793. Those arrested were of diverse background, peasants, soldiers, townspeople, workers, Russians, non-Russians—Tatars, Ukrainians, Bakshirs, Kalmyks.

Also during this period, there were roughly 150 Pugachev impostors, including former *atamans* and other participants in the rebellion, hoping to "reawaken the spirit of the Pugachev revolt" and to "pursue the nobles." One of these in the Volga area was a Don Cossack named Maksim Kanin, a former ataman under Pugachev. He claimed the throne as Peter III and maintained that Pugachev and his colonel Ovchinnikov were alive and in Holstein. Kanin planned to stir up a new peasant war from the Urals to the Zaporozh cossacks and to take Moscow and St. Petersburg and exterminate "all the high and mighty" (1778-1780). In 1782 or 1783, about seven years after the Peasant War, Anton Korovka, who had in his time given shelter to Pugachev, met with peasants near the city of Suma. He assured them that Pugachev was alive, undefeated, and eager that they join him in Iaik for a new uprising.

Some pretenders used the name Peter III, others that of his son, Paul Petrovich, and still others Prince Ivan (Ivan VI Antonovich). They spread rumors throughout the country (including Siberia) that Peter III was on his way to both capitals to "hang all the lords," he would bring about the happy time when "there would no longer be noblemen," and he would "take back all the lands." The tsar would save the people from the bondage of serfdom and from taxes and all obligations, including conscription.

By the beginning of the nineteenth century, imposture began to die out, ceasing to be the banner of class protest. But faith in the goodness and mercy of the tsar lived on for a very long time. Belief in impostor sovereigns gave way to faith in the promised land of truth, freedom, one's own fields and faith. Utopian aspirations led some to seek such a land in Belovod'e Anapa, "city of Ignatius," or somewhere in the East.

As before, the peasants petitioned and sent their envoys to the officials. Alone and in groups they fled to frontier areas and abroad, hoping to escape poverty, tyranny of the landlords, starvation and hard labor, and humiliation. Landlords viewed this mass as a scourge. Peasants attempted to find "a single hour of freedom" to "escape from the lord," and "just to spend a little bit of time somewhere without a master (*barin*)."

The most active protests of the time took the form of disturbances and uprisings. Peasants rebelled against landlords, pillaged estates, destroyed documents, refused to fulfill obligations or pay quit-rent, and disavowed their serf status. They wanted to become state peasants and achieve "freedom." Armed uprisings took place in Novgorod, Tver, Riazan, Orlov, Kazan, and Viatka provinces. Twenty rebellions broke out in the southern Ukraine during this period. Rebellions occurred among workers (state peasants) at factories in the Urals and serf workers at the textile mills in Moscow province.

Some movements, such as uprising at Stakanovo village in Livensk District of Eletsk province (1776), in Porkhovskii District in Novgorod province (1777-1780), and in the Ukrainian village of Turbai (1789-1793), were of long duration. Armed, the peasants repulsed military detachments sent to suppress

Table 1. Peasant Disturbances by Year and Type

Year	Active Resistance by Serfs	Complaints by Serfs	Active Resistance by Other Peasants	Complaints by Other Peasants	Total
1796	53	2	2	—	57
1797	118	57	1	1	177
1798	9	2	1	—	12
1799	5	1	2	2	10
1800	8	1	4	3	16
1801	3	1	2	1	7
1802	12	3	6	3	24
1803	11	7	7	1	26
1804	12	2	6	—	20
1805	20	2	6	1	29
1806	12	—	2	1	15
1807	6	1	5	—	12
1808	22	—	6	1	29
1809	17	7	3	3	30
1810	9	—	7	1	17
1811	17	—	13	—	30
1812	39	4	21	1	65
1813	125	6	4	4	29
1814	8	3	7	2	20
1815	20	5	9	4	38
1816	16	6	8	—	30
1817	23	22	11	—	56
1818	31	28	9	14	82
1819	55	43	4	5	87
1820	20	21	2	5	48
1821	14	15	2	5	36
1822	41	22	5	1	69
1823	33	42	6	7	88
1824	22	33	5	10	70
1825	28	19	9	5	61
1826	113	54	5	6	178
1827	33	13	5	2	53
1828	14	3	7	1	25
1829	18	9	5	3	35
1830	46	7	15	8	76
1831	34	20	14	5	73
1832	20	21	5	5	51
1833	28	26	8	8	70
1834	35	16	13	3	67
1835	29	18	5	5	48
1836	41	12	32	7	92
1837	41	19	3	15	78
1838	46	37	5	2	90
1839	63	9	5	1	78

(continued)

Table 1. (continued)

Year	Active Resistance by Serfs	Complaints by Serfs	Active Resistance by Other Peasants	Complaints by Other Peasants	Total
1840	45	5	5	2	55
1841	38	10	11	—	59
1842	61	12	14	3	90
1843	40	25	11	5	81
1844	44	20	8	—	72
1845	91	9	11	5	116
1846	44	15	3	2	64
1847	74	10	4	—	88
1848	160	30	10	2	202
1849	37	20	4	2	63
1850	73	24	8	4	109
1851	62	12	10	4	88
1852	79	20	6	2	107
1853	75	19	2	2	98
1854	68	16	4	2	90
1855	54	4	9	3	70
1856	66	6	5	—	77
Total	2342	876	427	188	3833

them. Sometimes the peasants secured concessions both from their landlords and officials, who pursued a cautious policy from the late 1770s to the early 1790s warning nobles against "strong measures in hard times." The authorities tried to clarify the cause of peasant dissatisfaction, talk to the landlords, and express their dissatisfaction with the conduct of officers who allowed, as the government saw it, excess brutality. The Pugachev influence was undoubtedly of great importance. Its shadow would continue to hang over the ruling class in the years that followed.[16]

Historians of the peasant movement note the continuation of the Pugachev tradition, possibly into the nineteenth century. Historians of the nineteenth century have worked to understand this link. They have found materials in regional archives, which, despite their incompleteness, constitute an impressive foundation for a quantitative and qualitative description of Russian agrarian protest in the period that interests us.

Annual data on peasant disturbances between 1796 and 1856 is presented Table 1.[17] Despite fluctuations, one can see their increase towards the mid-nineteenth century. One observes peaks, or spurts, for specific years. For each case, there are causes and precipitating events. Thus, in 1797 there were 177 disturbances (by contrast only 57 in 1796 and 12 in 1798). This may be explained by Paul's decision to invite even serfs to his coronation in 1796. His decree of December 12, 1796 and the manifesto of April 5, 1797, authorized personal petitions, aroused discussion and generated rumors. One landlord from

Table 2. Number of Disturbances, 1801-1860

Years	Number of Disturbances
1801-1805	85
1806-1810	89
1811-1815	153
1816-1820	159
1821-1825	165
1826-1830	216
1831-1835	126
1836-1840	202
1841-1845	231
1846-1850	314
1851-1855	158
1856-1869	852
Total	2,750

Vologda described a "powerful rumor" in "these parts" that "today they crown the Sovereign; tomorrow they won't support the landlords." Peasant hopes for freedom were widespread. But the ultimate result was an increase in disturbances, instances of insubordination, collective complaints and protests, and demands for transfer to the state. The legal recourse to complaint enabled the peasants to present petitions to the tsar.

During the Patriotic War of 1812, there was a revival of disturbances. There were disturbances after 1817 (in connection with the creation of a committee on land ownership and serfdom in the Don area), in 1826 at the accession; and in 1848 with the inventory reform in the western provinces. From 1821 to 1831 and in 1839 and 1848, there were uprisings attributable to poor harvests and famine, and from 1853-1856, to the Crimean War.[18]

The data in tables 2 and 3[19] bear witness to a steady rise in manorial disturbances over 5-, 10- and 15-year periods and to an increase between the first and second third of the nineteenth century. Of the total 2796 disturbances occurring between 1796-1856, 85% (23342 disturbances) were on manorial estates. During the decade 1830-1840, the ratio of manorial to state peasants was 1:7, and the ratio of their protests was 1:.16.[20] Note indices of average annual increase (from 28 disturbances between 1796-1825 to 62 for 1826-1856) and a general increase in the number of disturbances by 15 year periods: from 1812-1856 there was little increase in comparison with 1796-1811 (407 to 447, or 19,8%); but from 1826-1840 there were 1.6 times as many as in 1812-1825 and between 1841-1856, 1.5 times as many as in the preceding 15 years. Finally, there was a jump in the number of disturbances for the 5-year period (1856-1860) before the reform of 1861:

Table 3. Active Peasant Disturbances

Years	Manorial	Other	Total	Yearly Average
1796-1811	334	73	407	25
1812-1825	345	102	447	32
1796-1825	679	175	854	28
1826-1840	597	132	729	49
1841-1856	1066	120	1186	74
1826-1856	1663	252	1915	62

852 disturbances (170 disturbances per year) as opposed to 158, 165, 159 and 158 for the preceding five years.

Including complaints and collective petitions to the tsar, the increase becomes even more explicit. In the first quarter of the century, peasants submitted a total of 368 complaints; in the second half, 903; between 1850 and 1860, 1276 (with 1108 of those submitted between 1856 and 1860). For all forms of protest (uprising, disturbances, murder and attempted murder of landlords, petitions) the period 1850-1856 saw 649 acts of struggle, while the period 1857-May 1861 saw 3,382, or, over five times as many (the first five months of 1861 saw over half the total number of disturbances of this 4.5 year period). In nearly one thousand cases, these peasant disturbances were suppressed by military force.[21]

Let me add that in addition to the forms of struggle previously mentioned, there was an uninterrupted continuation of other, ordinary manifestations of protest, refusal to perform labor services or pay quit-rent, theft of wood belonging to the landlord, and other forms not easily quantifiable. These were a kind of active, or as Koval'chenko put it, "open" peasant disturbance, events "of great social significance."[22]

Fedorov also emphasized the significance of everyday protest, which he labels "economic." "It took place on all estates on a massive scale." Serfs inflicted "serious economic damage upon the manorial system," creating "an atmosphere of tension, making the likelihood of peasant disturbance all the greater; the disturbances themselves turned out to be especially dangerous for the landlords.[23]

Litvak, who, by his research virtually rebuilt the methodological foundation for statistical study of peasant struggle, proposed that a diffentiated and detailed approach be taken to analyze data on all forms of peasant struggle. His approach is more promising than the "gross estimate method used in the past. Litvak organized the material for his estimates and tables by the following classification. He counted 48 forms of struggle, divided into 4 groups: (1) vengeance and passive resistance (complaints and petitions, attacks on and murder of manorial administrators and landlords), and arson; (2) small-scale economic actions against the landlord (collective theft of the landlords' wood, damage to property, refusal to pay dues, bring in the harvest, relocate, and so forth); (3) larger-scale economic action (insubordination, arrest of the landlords, refusal to acknowledge officials, demand that they be replaced); and (4) anti-government acts (refusal to submit to officials, resistance to military detachments, naive attempts at agitation (imposture, dissemination of counterfeit documents), and uprisings.[24]

The above data show that agrarian defiance and protest peaked on the eve of the abolition of serfdom. It was during those years that the authorities began the process of loosening the peasants' shackles by establishing restrictions of the arbitrary rule of the landlords, that peasant protest increased, assuming its more virulent, intensified character. Manorial peasants waged a persistent and prolonged armed struggle, which, in the opinion of A.A. Preobrazhenskii, sometimes assumed the character of "minor peasant war." State peasants protested the police innovations of the great reforms. Serfs who paid quit-rent (obrok) (as opposed to those on labor services) were the most active: they had a more profound understanding of the value of the relative freedom they enjoyed, and they struggled patiently and decisively toward complete freedom from the landlords' will. Of course freedom, land, and improved economic conditions were what all peasants wanted, rich and poor, manorial, state and appanage.[25]

Before emancipation, the peasant movement had little or no organization. The proletariat and bourgeoisie, which might have given the peasants organization and political consciousness, were still in formation. However, the movement preserved and augmented the tradition of struggle, and intensified it every day and everywhere. The secret reports of the Third Department reported on the aspirations of peasants. According to one, the peasants "await their liberator, just as the Jews await their Messiah, and they have given him the name "Metelkin' [the broom] (the prototype was I.P. Zaprometov, a deacon's son and fugitive soldier, active in 1775 in along the Volga— V.B.) They say among themselves, "Pugachev scared the lords, but Metelkin will sweep them out" (1827). According to another report, "the simple folk are not what they were 25 years ago. Their whole spirit is focused on one aim— liberation" (1839). The peasantry began to produce men conscious of the society's problems, men who wrote "projects" and "essays." For example, an essay "News about Russia," written in 1849 by an anonymous seasonal worker, advanced demands for universal equality and election of government officials on basis of "talent" not birth.

The peasantry's ideology, the complex of notions, demands, and opinions reflecting the essential interests of the class, rested on freedom, equality, and rejection of serfdom. Their realization would have brought the destruction of feudal society, the elimination of the rights and privileges enjoyed by the nobility and other privileged estates, and equal rights for all. The theoretical basis for the peasant's slogans was religious. Faith in God and the Tsar went together. His authority and goodness, the single, unifying basis of the state, justified to the peasant anti-manorial slogans and actions. Thus, the peasant movement combined many disparate elements; in its ideology—hatred of serfdom and aspiration for land and freedom, yet faith in the Tsar; in its pattern—no real program, no political consciousness and sporadic outbreak.

In the nineteenth century, although there were no peasant wars the peasantry acted decisively and collectively to attack serfdom. Among their demands, land and freedom became a single question—freedom from servile dependence would give them not only their own allotments, but manorial land as well. Here one may note a difference from the seventeenth and eighteenth centuries, even taking into account the movements of Pugachev and Razin. The significance of impostures declined at the end of the eighteenth and beginning of the nineteenth centuries: elements of imposture still evident at this time (for example, during the disturbances in the Urals in the 1840s) seem modest in comparison to the Pugachev era or the Time of Troubles of the early seventeenth century.[26]

The peasant movement in the first half of the nineteenth century also had new goals, the right to choose a trade and free enterprise. Although the main force of disturbances was still the poor, now the village elite also played a significant role. Despite the discrepancy between rich and poor, social struggle on that count did not develop to any significant degree; one connot speak of a "second social struggle" in the village of the pre-reform era. Diverse propertied groups within the peasantry waged war in common against serfdom.[27]

The peasant movement of the late 1850s and early 1860s became an integral part of the revolutionary situation of the period. In essence, the peasant movement became the leading cause of the appearance of the revolutionary situation. According to Lenin, a revolutionary situation is characterized by: (1) the inability of the ruling classes to preserve their situation unchanged (it is generally insufficient that "the lower classes don't want to," and also the upper classes should not be able to live by the old order; (2) intense poverty; and (3) a significant increase in protest activity.[28]

Toward the middle of the nineteenth century the activity of the Russian peasant, resulting from intense want and need, did indeed result in the discrediting of the old order. The original program of reforms had envisioned personal emancipation, but preserved the system of dependency. As before, the peasant would receive an allotment in return for dues. In response to protest, officials changed this program to give peasants land in return for redemption payments.

The literature notes a sharp rise in the development of the peasant movement from the late 1850s to the early 1860s. In 1859, a temperance movement overwhelmed 32 provinces—over half the country. Peasants of all categories demonstrated against the state spirits monopoly, and the following year, the government repealed the monopoly. The peasants felt that the success of this struggle readied them for "settling accounts with the landlords."

It is for this period 1855-1863, that 48 forms of peasant struggle (previously discussed) were recorded. Litvak categorized disturbances that were within legal bounds (complaints, petitions, etc.) across regions. His data reveal a rise at the junction of the 1850s and 1860s. The unity and massive scale of the peasant movement was also visible in the peasant's refusal to sign the regulatory charters that set the conditions of reform. Thus, in six provinces within the central black soil belt (Voronezh, Kursk, Orlov, Riazan, Tamb, and Tula), over 1.15 million peasants took part in the 1861-1863 boycott of the regulatory charters (only 62.4 thousand took part in other kinds of struggle).

The movement achieved scale in the central black soil belt provinces: the Volga and the Ukraine. These uprisings were sometimes supressed by force; during the implementation of the reform in 1861, 64 infantry and 16 cavalry divisions, and 7 independent battalions were dispatched altogether. Executions and repression (as, for example, in Bezdna village in Kazan province and Kandeevka in Penza [where hundreds were murdered or wounded]), allowed the government to handle the peasants with dispatch. But the peasants protested the "new *kabala*" (a form of Tatar slavery) and the "new serfdom," (as they termed the reform). They fought for "genuine" freedom, for redistribution of manorial lands, for liquidation of manorial land-holdings, for an end to the salary paid to the nobility, and for self-government independent of the nobility and the authorities. But unity of aspiration was not reinforced by unit of action, and the peasants were defeated.[28]

The reforms of 1861, though flawed as far as the peasants' interests were concerned, signified the "beginning of a new, bourgeois Russia, born of the servile epoch"[30]; this was manifest in all aspects of life during the reform era, including agrarian protest by the peasantry, which underwent fundamental change due in part to the peculiarity of the reform causing peasant dissatisfaction, and in part to new forces acting on the peasantry, economic growth and rural stratification. Therefore, although protest related to the desire for freedom disappear, new forms appear. For example, the transition to redemption, completed in the 1890s, provoked mild forms of protest, such as the refusal to convert to the rental system and more violent forms. Agricultural strikes occurred at this time and anti-kulak demonstrations. But, as before, the principal antagonists were the peasants and the nobles.

Although historical conditions had altered, the peasantry as before protested in a united front against the landlords and the state despite social antagonism within the peasantry itself. From the reform era to the early twentieth century, the struggle was strongly influenced in content and form by the earlier movement against the signing of regulatory charters.

The peasant also continued as a small producer to work for better conditions. Data on this is from redemption payments. Peasants sought reduced allotments, increased payments, and suitable apportioning of lands. There was a slump after 1863. That year witnessed 509 disturbances: 1864 had 156, 1865 had 135, 1866 had 91, 1867 had 68, 1868 had 60, and 1869 had 65. That is 575 disturbances in a 6-year period, slightly more than in the single year 1863. The next six years (1870-1875) yield 252 demonstrations: the five years from 1876-1880 had 147 disturbances. Troops were less frequently called in. The movement was no longer concerned with the critical, cardinal questions that had constituted the pre-reform agenda but with more personal questions concerning daily life and communal management. Peaceful, legal means of struggle were suited to the resolution of these problems. Moreover, the breakdown of peasant society had begun; once its former unity was destroyed, its solidarity evaporated.

Nonetheless, the revolutionary capacity of the peasantry, never extinguished, came into play during the later struggle. In the mid 1860s, peasants protested against reapportionment as envisioned in the reform. The peasants fought for land against excessive dues and against the violence and caprice of the representatives of the tsarist adminstration. As before, with their faith in the tsar, they awaited *"Chernyi peredel"* (elimination of private, nonpeasant property in land and sharing out among peasants-CSL) and possession of manorial lands. Rumors lasted until the 1880s and 1890s.

In the new revolutionary situation of 1879-1881, the government reacted to the disaffection of the peasantry by retracting the redetermination of dues as prescribed in the emancipation legislation of February 19, 1861. The government also simultaneously canceled payments of all peasants temporarily obligated to their landlords (15.3% of the total former serfs), abolished accumulated arrears, reduced payments within the inner Russian provinces, revoked the soul tax, and began organization of land-credit. To a certain degree the condition of the peasantry improved.

But the peasants' struggle against the landlords continued throughout the 1880s and 1890s: the years 1881-1890 witnessed 629 demonstrations; 1891-1900 witnessed 515. The rate of uprisings increased; in the 1870s they constituted 43.1% of all disturbances (172 out of 399); the 1880s constituted 67.3% (424); and the 1890s constituted 77.3% (398). The proletarian class struggle exerted influence on the peasantry (expressed in the greater organization of peasant movements near industrial centers, the appearance of proclamations and appeals from the cities, which peasants helped disseminate).

The main target was the landlord. But a second social war was developing in the village—that of the poor against the kulaks; the turn of the century witnessed organized farm-labor strikes. However, the data cited at the beginning of this paper show the scale of this social struggle as insignificant as compared with the continuing conflict with landlords. See the data in Table 4. The

Table 4. Disturbances, 1881-1900

Years	Agrarian Anti-Landlord	Agrarian within Peasantry	Strikes of Hired Laborers	Political	Total
1881	35	2	5	9	51
1882	45	2	—	15	62
1883	67	3	2	23	95
1884	93	3	—	24	120
1885	38	2	1	19	60
1886	37	—	—	21	58
1887	46	1	—	28	75
1888	18	—	1	28	47
1889	19	—	—	19	38
1890	32	2	2	9	45
1891	27	1	1	8	37
1892	31	2	—	20	53
1893	24	2	—	8	34
1894	25	—	—	6	31
1895	27	—	—	1	28
1896	107	—	1	5	113
1897	80	—	—	3	83
1898	49	—	1	1	51
1899	50	—	—	2	52
1900	31	—	—	1	32

heading "demonstration" covers seizing of meadowland, theft of wood, and damage to boundaries; "disorders" covers disturbances and disputes within the commune; "political activity" is famine-caused disturbances, epidemics, resistance to the land decrees, nonpayment of judicial retainers, and unauthorized resettlement. As is appparent, although further research should be done, social stratification was a relatively insignificant cause of revolt.

The peasant movement grew considerably in the early twentieth century. Among numerous demonstrations, one in 1902 drew 39,000 peasants from 174 village societies in the Poltav and Kharkov provinces. They pillaged 105 manorial estates and were suppressed by ten thousand soldiers. Within a few years, this massive peasant movement became an integral part of the first Russian Revolution, prompting historians to speak of a peasant war in early twentieth century Russia.

The persistence of features of manorial life and the beginning of acute socioeconomic discrepancies within the village engendered the aphorisms, "1861 begot 1905," "reform begot revolution."[31] United with and guided by the proletariat, the peasantry took an active part in the later revolutions, encouraged by such slogans as liquidation of manorial ownership, nationalization of the land, and democratization of the sociopolitical life of the nation. And the very poorest element of the peasantry assumed the role of a driving force of the revolution.[32]

The data examined earlier led us to conclude that the Russian peasantry's agrarian protest from the end of the eighteenth through the nineteenth century was an essential component of the overall development of the nation, exerting considerable influence on the evolution of feudalism in its late stage and on the transition to a capitalist system. The peasants' uninterrupted protest, in various forms and on various scales, the pressure they exerted and concessions they exacted resulted in the abolition of serfdom. And the struggle undertaken with the proletariat against the autocracy resulted in the rebuilding of the country just over a half century after the peasant reform of 1861. The ruling class, as its spokesman Emperor Alexander II explained, supposed that with their "revolution from above," they had staved off the "revolution from below." But in October, 1917, it was the workers and peasants who, "from below," decided the principal question unresolved after 1861, the issue of land.

NOTES AND REFERENCES

1. I.D. Koval'chenko, ed., *Istochnikovedenie istorii SSSR* [*Source Study on the History of the USSR*] (Moscow, 1981); B.G. Litvak, *Ocherki istochnikovedeniia massovoi dokumentatsii XIX-nachala XX vv.* [*Essays on Source Study of Quantitative Documentation for the 19th and Early Twentieth Century*] (Moscow, 1979); B.G. Litvak, *Opyt statisticheskogo izucheniia krest'ianskogo dvizheniia v Rossii XIX v.* [*Attempt at a Statistical Study of the Peasant Movement in Russia in the Nineteenth Century*] (Moscow, 1967).

2. The most important source publications of the nineteenth and early twentieth century are, *Materialy po istorii krepostnogo prava v Rossii za 1836-1856 gg.* [*Materials on the History of Serfdom in Russia, 1836-1856*] (Berlin, 1872); E.A. Morkhovets, ed., *Krest'ianskoe dvizhenie, 1827-1869. [The Peasant Movement, 1827-1869*], issues No. 1-2 (Moscow, 1931); see also E.S. Paina, *Krest'ianskoe dvizhenie v Rossii v XIX-nachale XX vv.* [*The Peasant Movement in Russia in the 19-20th Century*] (Moscow, 1963); V.A. Fedorov, *Krest'ianskoe dvizhenie v tsentral'noi Rossii, 1800-1860 gg.*[*The Peasant Movement in Central Russia, 1800-1860*] (Moscow, 1980), pp. 4-6 ff.

3. *Krest'ianskoe dvizhenie v Rossii v 1796-1825 gg.* [*The Peasant Movement in Russia 1796-1825*] (Moscow, 1961); *Krest'ianskoe dvizhenie v Rossii v 1850-1856 gg.* (Moscow, 1962); *Krest'ianskoe dvizhenie v Rossii v 1857-mae 1861 gg.* (Moscow, 1963).

4. *Krest'ianskoe dvizhenie v Rossii v 1861-1869 gg.* (Moscow, 1964); *Krest'ianskoe dvizhenie v Rossii v 1879-1880 gg.* (Moscow, 1968); *Krest'ianskoe dvizhenie v Rossii v 1881-1889 gg.* (Moscow, 1960); *Krest'ianskoe dvizhenie v Rossii v 1890-1900 gg.* (Moscow, 1959).

5. N.M. Druzhinin, *Gosudarstvennye krest'iane i reforma P.D. Kiseleva* [*State Peasants and the Reform of P.D. Kiselev*], vols 1-2 (Moscow, 1946-1958); I.D. Koval'chenko, *Russkoe krepostnoe krest'ianstvo v pervoi polovine XIX v.* [*Russian Serfs in the First Half of the Nineteenth Century*] (Moscow, 1967); N.L. Rubinshtein, *Sel'skoe khoziaistvo v Rossii vo vtoroi polovine XVIII v.* [*The Agricultural Economy in Russia in the Second Half of the Eighteenth Century*] (Moscow, 1957); V.A. Fedorov, *Pomeshchich'i krest'iane tsentral'no-promyshlennogo raiona Rossii Kontsa XVIII-pervoi poloviny XIX v.* [*Private Serfs of Central Industrial Russia at the End of the Eighteenth-first Half of the 19th Century*] (Moscow, 1974).

6. N.M. Druzhinin, *Russkaia derevnia na perelome, 1861-1880 gg.* [*The Russian Countryside in Transition, 1861-1880*] (Moscow, 1978); A.M. Anfimov, *Krest'ainskoe khoziaistvo Evropeiskoi Rossii, 1881-1904* [*The Peasant Economy of European Russia, 1881-1904*] (Moscow, 1980).

7. E.A. Morkhovets, "Opyt bibliograficheskogo ukazatel'ia po istorii krest'ianskogo dvizheniia v Rossii," *Vestnik sotsialisticheskoi akademii* [*An Attempt at a Bibliographic Guide to the History of the Peasant Movement in Russia, Messenger of the Socialist Academy*] (Moscow-Prague, 1923), Book 3, pp. 415-420; Book 4, pp. 465-472.

8. V.I. Semevskii, *Krest'iane v tsarstvovanie imperatritsy Ekateriny II* [*Peasants During the Reign of Empress Catherine II*], vols. 1-2 (St Petersburg, 1901-1903); Semevskii, *Krest'ianskii vopros v Rossii v XVIII i pervoi polovine XIX v.* [*The Peasant Question in Russia in the Eighteenth and First Half of the Nineteenth Century*], vol. 1 (St. Petersburg, 1884). V.V. Mavrodin, *Klassovaia bor'ba i obshchestvenno-politicheskaia mysl' v Rossii v XVIII v. (1773-1790 gg.)* [*Class Struggle and Social-Political Thought in Russia in the Eighteenth Century, 1773-1790*] (Leningrad, 1975).

9. I.I. Ignatovich, *Krest'ianskoe dvizhenie v Rossii v pervoi chetverti XIX v.* [*The Peasant Movement in Russia in the First Quarter of the Nineteenth Century*] (Moscow, 1963); I.I. Linkov, *Ocherki istorii krest'ianskogo dvizheniia v Rossii v 1825-1861 gg.* [*Essays on the History of the Peasant Movement in Russia 1825-1861*] (Moscow, 1952); I.I. Linkov, *Krest'ianskoe dvizhenie v Rossii vo vremia Krymskoi voiny, 1853-1856* [*The Peasant Movement in Russia During the Crimean War, 1853-1856*] (Moscow, 1940); V.A. Fedorov, *Krest'ianskoe dvizhenie v tsentral'noi Rossii, 1800-1860* [*The Peasant Movement in Central Russia 1800-1860*] (Moscow, 1980); N.M. Druzhinin, V.A. Fedorov, "Krest'ianskoe dvizhenie v Rossii v XIX v.," *Istoriia SSSR* 4 (1977): 106-126.

10. From remarks at a conference of Soviet and American historians in September, 1975, I.D. Koval'chenko, "Antikrepostnicheskoe dvizhenie v Rossii do 1861 g." I express my deep gratitude to I.D. Koval'chenko for giving me the opportunity to use data from his paper.

11. V.A. Fedorov, *Krest'ianskoe dvizhenie*, pp. 44.

12. The central industrial region included Moscow, Vladimir, Tver' Iaroslav, Kostroma, Nizhnyi Novgorod, and Kaluga provinces.

13. I.I. Ignatovich, "Krest'ianskie volneniia," in *Velikaia reforma*, vol. 3, p. 42; B.G. Litvak, *Ocherki*, pp. 23-29, 42-43.

14. K.D. Kavelin, *Sochineniia* [*Works*], vol. 2 (St. Petersburg, 1898), pp. 14-15.

15. See Druzhinin, Koval'chenko, Fedorov, Anfimov, Koval'chenko's paper of 1975.

16. Mavrodin, *Klassovaia bor'ba*, pp. 119-154.

17. Litvak, *Opyt*, p. 10.

18. Litvak, *Opyt*, pp. 7-9, 11-12; Fedorov, *Krest'ianskoe dvizhenie*, p. 42; V.I. Buganov, A.A. Preobrazhenskii, Yu A. Tikhonov, *Evoliutsiia feodalizma v Rossii, sotsial'no-ekonomicheskie problemy* [*Evolution of Feudalism in Russia, Social and Economic Problems*] (Moscow, 1980), p. 286.

19. Druzhinin, Fedorov, "Krest'ianskoe dvizhenie," p. 107; Koval'chenko, 1975 paper, p. 20.

20. P.G. Ryndziunskii, "Voprosy izucheniia melkotovarnogo uklada v Rossii XIX v.," *Istoriia SSSR* [*Problems of Studying Petty Commodity Structure in Russia in the Nineteenth Century, History of the USSR*] 4 (1963): 105; Litvak, *Opyt*, p. 14.

21. Druzhinin, Fedorov, "Krest'ianskoe dvizhenie," p. 108; Buganov et al., *Evoliutsiia*, pp. 286-287.

22. Koval'chenko, 1975 paper, pp. 22-23.

23. Fedorov, *Krest'ianskoe dvizhenie*, p. 40.

24. Litvak, *Opyt*, pp. 30-54, 64-74, 116. Also see Fedorov, *Krest'ianskoe dvizhenie*, pp. 40-108.

25. Koval'chenko, 1975 paper, p. 20; Litvak, *Opyt*, p. 14; Ryndziunskii, "Voprosy izucheniia," p. 105; Druzhinin, Fedorov, "Krest'ianskoe dvizhenie," p. 113-114; Buganov et al. *Evoliutsiia*, pp. 287-288.

26. Druzhinin, Fedorov, "Krestian'skoe dvizhenie," pp. 111-113; Buganov et al., *Evoliutsiia,* pp. 288-290; Koval'chenko, 1975 paper, pp. 23-27; Fedorov, *Krest'ianskoe dvizhenie,* pp. 148-161.
27. Fedorov, *Krest'ianskoe dvizhenie,* pp. 108-120.
28. Lenin, V.I., *Polnoe sobranie sochinenii,* vol. 26, p. 218.
29. Druzhinin, Fedorov, "Krest'ianskoe dvizhenie," pp. 115-121. Litvak *Opyt,* pp. 15-22, 55-64, 74. Fedorov, *Krest'ianskoe dvizhenie,* pp. 125-148; Koval'chenko, 1975 paper, pp. 30-32.
30. Lenin, *Sochinenii,* vol. 20, p. 174.
31. Lenin, *Sochinenii,* vol. 20, p. 177.
32. Druzhinin, Fedorov, "Krest'ianskoe dvizhenie," pp. 121-125; Litvak, *Opyt,* pp. 53-54, 65, 81-83; Fedorov, *Krest'ianskoe dvizhenie,* p. 112.

WERE RUSSIAN SERFS OVERCHARGED FOR THEIR LAND BY THE 1861 EMANCIPATION?
THE HISTORY OF ONE HISTORICAL TABLE

Evsey D. Domar

>*Ah, don't say that you agree with me. When people agree with me I always feel that I must be wrong.*
>—Oscar Wilde, *The Critic as Artist*

>*It were not best that we should all think alike: it is difference of opinion that makes horse races.*
>—Mark Twain, *Pudd'nhead Wilson*

If five economies are said to hold six opinions about a current event, how many opinions should be expected from five historians about an event that took place over a hundred years ago? I am referring to the allegedly excessive prices charged the former Russian serfs for the land allotted to them by the provisions of the 1861 Emancipation. That these prices were found excessive by several historians is not surprising—what else could have been expected from the gentry-dominated tsarist government of the time?—but that these historians would agree on the *exact magnitude* of the overcharge does appear a bit strange. The data shown in Table 1 (taken here from Gerschenkron) has been presented time and again.[1]

The reasons for this unusual unanimity are not far to seek: the historians must have taken these figures from the same source—a paper published by A. Lositskii in St. Petersburg in 1906. They accepted his figures on faith, without examining the origin of his data and the nature of his assumptions. They did not even check his arithmetic.[2]

Obviously, to calculate the alleged overcharge for the allotted land, we must establish the correct magnitudes of three variables: (1) the quantity of land allotted to the peasants, (2) the amount they were charged for it, and (3) the amount that they should have paid at "free market prices." The Emancipation was an extremely complex operation lasting some twenty years. The quantity of land allotted to the peasants and the amounts charged for it in the various areas were adjusted and readjusted many times. Therefore, any composite figure, even as simple as the quantity of land or the charge for it, may be subject to a good margin of error. Although my own research in this area has been confined to market land prices, I shall make a few brief remarks about the other two variables.

Lositskii gave very few sources of his data. All I could do with the quantity of the allotted land was to correct his additions and to compare his figures with those published by the Soviet historian Zaionchkovskii in 1958. In cases of disagreement, I decided to use the latter's figures because Zaionchkovskii knew of Lositskii's work and seemed to have done a more thorough job. A comparison between the two sets of data and the effect of substituting Zaionchkovskii's figures for Lositskii's are presented in Table 2.[2]

As shown in column 3, the quantity of allotted land for the whole country increased by some 5%. A comparison of the last columns of Table 1 and Table 2 shows that the total overcharge was reduced only from 34 to 28%, but in the black-soil zone the reduction was considerable—from 20 to 13%, by a third. On the other hand, the largest overcharge—in the non-black-soil zone—fell by only 9 percentage points, from 90 to 81%. In the Western provinces, the quantity of allotted land was slightly reduced; however, the changes in provincial weights produced a slight discount in the peasants' favor. But before the reader concludes that Lositskii exaggerated the overcharge he should read the rest of this paper.

I have been unable to check Lositskii's figures on the total cost of land charged the peasants;[4] hence, for the purpose of this paper, they are accepted. Of the several totals that he gave I chose the ones that looked most reliable.[5]

Table 1. The Basic Data

	Allotment Land in Thousands of Dessyatinas* (1)	Value of Allotment Land at Free Market Prices in Millions of Rubles		Value of Allotment Land at Redemption Values (4)	Column (4) as Percentage of Column (3) (5)
		1854-1858 (2)	1863-1872 (3)		
Non-black-earth Provinces	12,286	155	180	342	190
Black-earth Provinces	9,841	219	284	342	120
Western Provinces	10,141	170	184	183	100
Total	32,268**	544	648	867	134

Notes: * One desiatina (spelled by Gerschenkron as dessyatina) = 1.09 hectares.
** For some reason the total of column (1) (32,268) is missing from Gerschenkron's table.

Source: A. Gerschenkron, "Agrarian Policies and Industrialization: Russia, 1861-1917," *The Cambridge Economic History of Europe* (Cambridge, 1965), vol. 6, part 2, p. 738.

Table 2. The Quantity of Allotted Land*
(Thousands of Desiatinas)

	From Lositskii (corrected) (1)	From Zaionchkovskii (adjusted) (2)	Percentage Difference Between Column (2) and Column (1) (3)	Recalculated Column (5) of Table 1 (4)
Non-black-earth Provinces	12,286.5	13,002.6	5.8	181
Black-earth Provinces	9,876.9	10,771.1	9.1	113
Western Provinces	10,141.1	10,133.5	-.3	98
Total	32,304.5	33,887.2	4.9	128

Note: * Additional explanations of these figures are given in note 3.
Sources: A. Lositskii, *Vykupnaia operatsiia* [*The Redemption Operation*] (St. Petersburg, 1906), pp. 38-39; P.A. Zaionshkovskii, *Provedenie v zhizn' krest'ianskoi reformy 1861 g.* [*The Actual Conduct of the Peasant Reform in 1861*] (Moscow, 1958), pp. 431-443.

Our next task—of greater interest to an economist—is finding those "free market prices" that the peasants should have paid. Table 1 evalutes the land allotment in two sets of prices: for 1854-1858 and 1863-1872 periods. Gerschenkron's use of the 1863-1872 prices for the calculations presented in column 5 of Table 1 suggest that he considered them more relevant than the 1854-1858 prices. He was probably right, but unfortunately the reliability of the 1863-1872 prices does not support the trust he placed in them. They were described by D.A. Rikhter, the author of an important paper on land prices and a recognized expert on the subject, as fragmentary and incomplete:

> The number of statements relating to [land sales in] the 1863-72 period is insignificant and the statements themselves are subject to doubt because there is no indication that they are based on concrete cases [of land sales]. It can be surmised that they are recorded on the basis of accidental recollections of the correspondents.

He also mentioned that the data were assembled in 1883 and 1889, that is, some ten or twenty years after the land sales had supposedly taken place.[6] On reading this evaluation of the 1863-1872 prices, I lost further interest in them.

Having rejected the 1863-1872 land prices as unreliable, Rikhter then proceeded to bring to his readers' attention another set of price data—for 1854-1858 (published in 1859)—which he regarded highly and that, judging by the title of his paper, must have been forgotten by that time (1897).

Because these data were described and analyzed in considerable detail in a recent paper I can be brief here.[7] They consist of reports of actual land sales classified by provinces (*gubernii*) and counties (*uezdy*) for that 5-year period and divided into sales of populated land (with serfs) and of unpopulated land. The main obstacle to deriving prices of populated land lies in the difficulty of separating the value of land from the value of serfs. Lositskii attempted no such separation; he simply assumed that prices of populated and of unpopulated land (in each area) were equal.[8] A formal statistical test rejected (on the 5% level) this assumtion. Rather surprisingly, populated land turned out to have been much cheaper than unpopulated land.[9] If so, the peasants might have been overcharged much more than Lositskii and his followers have suggested.

To find the prices of populated land a regression was run of the values of the populated estates against the number of *desiatinas* and the number of serfs on them, in each area. Unfortunately, the rather high correlation between these two variables may have made the estimates of them imprecise and the heterogeneous character of land may have imparted a downward bias to the estimated land prices.[10]

Perhaps a rough idea of the magnitude of the overcharge imposed on the peasants can be obtained by other, less sophisticated, methods. It had been estimated that the total value of all serf estates in the country amounted to some 2,100 million rubles and that they contained about 98 million desiatinas of land.[11] The 33 million desiatinas received by the peasants thus constituted some 34% of land owned by their former masters while the payments 856 million rubles—41% of the value of the estates. A sizeable overcharge is already in sight. But the estates contained not only land but also serfs. (The peasants were not supposed to pay for their own freedom.) If we could find the fraction of the market value of the estates embodied in land we could easily calculate the market price per desiatina, compare it with the price charged to the peasants and thus estimate the magnitude of the overcharge.

The sales reports also contain the official prices of land and of serfs (by provinces) used by the government for granting loans secured by the estates. The Editor explicitly warned the users of the reports that these official prices were set below market prices, but said nothing about the *relative* understatement of land and of serf prices.[12] As an experiment, let us assume that these prices were understated in the same proportion, so that the *ratios* between the prices of land and the prices of serfs in a given province remained reasonably correct. Now by evaluating the estates in the sales reports at these official prices (in a given area) we can find the fraction of the values of the estates represented by land. The results are presented in Column 1 of Table 3.

They are a bit surprising. According to the traditional view, land constituted the major part of a serfowner's wealth in the South (the black-earth zone), but not in the North (the non-black-earth zone) because in the South the combination of soil and climate favored agriculture, while in the North a good part of the master's income came from the nonagricultural pursuits of his serfs.[13] Our calculations do not confirm this view: the fractions of the values of the estates in the sales report represented by land turned out to be very similar in the several zones; if anything, the non-black-soil figure is a bit higher than the others.[14] It is possible that the official prices of land and of serfs were set by the governmental lending institutions so arbitrarily that even the price ratios used in the present experiment make little sense. On the other hand, grain was cheap in the South and expensive in the North, particularly before the construction of railroads, and it is the value of the harvest rather than its quantity that is reflected in the price of land.[15] These results are certainly insufficient to reject the traditional view, but they may be good enough to plant a seed of doubt about it in the reader's mind.

Columns 2-5 in Table 3 show the several steps involved in the calculation of the market price of a desiatina of land (in each zone) that the peasants should have paid. The last column gives the ratio between the actual price paid by the peasants and this calculated market price. These ratios, whether taken by themselves or compared with Lositskii's estimates given in Table 1, are amazing, to put it mildly; on the average, the peasants were overcharged more than three times; in both black-earth and non-black-earth zones they overpaid more than four times, and only in the West were they lucky to escape with a modest double price!

Table 3. An Estimate of the Overcharge*

	Value of Land on Serf Estates as Percentage of Their Total Value at Official Prices (1)	Estimated Value of All Populated Estates in the Country in Millions of Rubles (2)	Total Value of Land on Serf Estates in Millions of Rubles (1) x (2) (3)	Total Land Area on Serf Estates in Thousands of Desiatinas (4)	Average Market Price per Desiatina on Serf Estates in Rubles (3)/(4) (5)	Price per Desiatina of Allotted Land Charged to Peasants in Rubles (6)	Overcharge Ratio (5)/(4) (7)
Non-black-earth Provinces	37.9	570.1	216	35,211	6.14	26.30	4.28
Black-earth Provinces	32.1	850.6	273	35,992	7.57	31.75	4.19
Western Provinces	36.5	671.4	245	27,048	9.07	18.09	1.99
Total and Weighted Averages	35.4	2,090.9	740	98,251	7.53	25.58	3.40

Notes: *The data in this table differ from those in Tabes 1 and 2 because of the exclusion here of the three unimportant provinces of Don, Ufa, and Astrakhan' for which full data were not available.

Sources: Column (1): From the reports on land sales by the method described in the text.
Column (2): Estimated by the method described by E.D. Domar and M.J. Machina, "On the Profitability of Russian Serfdom," *The Journal of Economic History* 44 (1984); 948.
Column (3): By mutiplying column (1) and column (2). The zonal values do not add up to the total exactly because each was estimated separately.
Column (4): From Domar and Machina, "On the Profitability of Russian Serfdom," p. 940.
Column (6): From Tables 1 and 2.

That the overcharges in the first two zones were nearly the same again contradicts the accepted view that the peasants in the north suffered more.[16] A different method of estimating land market prices, still based on official prices, gave similar, if more conventional, results; the overcharge ratio was *at least* 4 in the north, 3.3 in the South and 1.9 in the West.[17]

But it is unlikely that even the tsarist regime, acting as it did in the interests of the serfowners (the *pomeshchiki*) could have perpetrated such a fraud. There must be some other explanations of these fantastic ratios. Indeed, there are.

1. Any calculation based on official prices may be simply wrong.
2. Our basic source of information is the reports of land sales. How good a sample do these reports constitute?
3. The reported sale values of serf estates must have been grossly understated (to reduce transfer duties). In fact, in a number of provinces the values of estates as reported were below those calculated on the basis of official prices.[18] If the reported prices had been correct it would have paid some enterprising members of the gentry (if there were such) to buy up serf estates, mortgage them and never repay the loans. But if the values of the serf estates were so understated it is likely that the prices of unpopulated land used by Lositskii had been reported truthfullly?
4. A sharp recent drop in the values of serf estates, not yet reflected in the official land and serf prices, might have been caused by the rumors of the forthcoming Emancipation.[19]
5. There might have also been more permanent reasons for the depressed prices of serf estates. Probably the most important one was the legal restriction on their purchase and ownership to the members of the nobility (*dvorianstvo*), a class well known for lack of cash and absence of business sense.

It is also likely that the Russian habit of evaluating an estate in terms of the number of serfs on it (which determined the owner's social status) rather than in terms of its land area contributed to the low market prices of populated land.

So far I have not considered the possibility that the land allotted to the peasants might have differed in quality broadly defined, from the rest of the populated land. There is much anecdotal evidence that some masters contrived to allot their former serfs poorer land. On the other hand, the law required the allotments to consist of "serviceable" land (*udobnaia zemliu*) only.[20] This would imply that the peasants received their farmstead, arable and some meadows, to the exclusion of waste, pasture and forest. Was a desiatina of allotted land more or less valuable than the average desiatina on the serf estates?[21]

There is one more qualification. The market prices of land (like most prices) are the results of marginal transactions involving small fractions of the total stock of land (only .7% per year in the present case). Do these market prices really apply to the giant land transfer engineered by the Emancipation? Suppose that the compulsory transfer of land from the masters to the former serfs never took place, and that instead the peasants were lent the same 870 million rubles to buy land on the free market. What prices would they have paid and how much land would they have acquired?[22]

* * *

What conclusions does this paper lead to? Were the peasants overcharged for their land? They most probably were. Perhaps they were overcharged much more than anyone has ever suggested. And perhaps much less, or not at all. The five historians with whom my story began could well afford to express six opinions. And even more than six.

ACKNOWLEDGMENTS

Thanks are due to Marina Goldberg, then an undergraduate student at Yale University, for her assistance in the early stages of this paper, to the National Science Foundation (Grant No. SES-7709307) for financial support, and to Professor Mark Machina for helpful comments.

NOTES AND REFERENCES

1. Here are a few examples: G. T. Robinson, *Rural Russia under the Old Regime* (Berkeley, [1932] 1960), p. 88; M. N. Pokrovskii, *Russkaia istoriia s drevneishikh vremen [Russian History from Ancient Times]*, vol. 4 (Moscow, 1934), p. 93; A. G. Mazur, *Russia Past and Present* (New York, 1951), p. 164 (he cites the figures in the text instead of using a table); P. I. Liashchenko, *Istoriia narodnogo khoziaistva SSSR [History of the Peoples' Economy of the USSR]*, vol. 1 (Moscow, 1956), p. 584; A. Gerschenkron, "Agrarian Policies and Industrialization: Russia 1861-1917," *The Cambridge Economic History of Europe*, vol. 6, part 2 (Cambridge, 1965), p. 738. There are probably other historians who used this table, but I stopped looking after I found five.

2. A. Lositskii, *Vykupnaia operatsiia [The Redemption Operation]* (St. Petersburg, 1906). Actually, he was more concerned with the excessive interest rate charged to the peasants for the money lent to them than with the inflated prices for the land.

3. P.A. Zaionchkovskii, *Provedenie v zhizn' krest'ianskoi reformy 1861 g. [The Actual Conduct of the Peasant Reform in 1861]* (Moscow, 1958), particularly pp. 431-443. In eight provinces, the data for one county each is missing. I added the missing figures by assuming that the quantity of land allotted to the peasants in each missing county was proportional to the quantity of populated land (serf estates) in that county.

Lositskii's work is rather sloppy and his assumptions are not always consistent. He might have used the wrong weights in obtaining provincial land prices from county data. My experiments with alternative sets of weights changed some provincial figures but had little effect on regional totals. The details of my corrections and adjustments are not discussed here because they are not important for this paper.

4. Lositskii mentioned the *Report of the State Bank* for 1893 as the source of his data, but our search in the 1892 and 1893 reports turned up nothing. It is likely that he referred to a special publication of the State Bank in 1983, but no such report was found by us in the Widener and the Union catalogues.

According to him, the financial records of the redemption operation were kept so badly that two ministers of finance (S. Greig and N. Bunge) left office before they could get an exact report.

5. In the text of the paper (p. 431), the total amount charged the peasants is 897 million rubles; in his summary table (p. 16) (from which our Table 1 must have been derived) it is 866.6, and a recalculation of the addition in his detailed table (by provinces, pp. 38-39) produced 870.2. No explanation for these discrepancies is given. Fortunately, they are small. Until a professional historian, skilled in archival research, finds something better, I shall use the corrected figures from that detailed table but because some of the relevant data are lacking for three provinces—Don, Ufa, and Astrakhan'—both the quantity of land allotted there and the charges for it are excluded from figures used in the subsequent discussion and in Table 3. This omission is of very little importance.

6. D. I. Rikhter, "Zabytyi material po statistike prodazhnykh tsen na zemliu" ["Forgotten Materials on the Statistics of Sale Prices of Land"] *Trudy Imperatorskogo Vol'nogo Ekonomicheskogo Obshchestva* [*Works of the Imperial Free Economic Society*], vol. 2, Book 4 (1897), pp. 1-23.

7. See E. D. Domar and M. J. Machina, "On the Profitability of Russian Serfdom," *The Journal of Economic History* 44 (1984): 919-955. A detailed list of sources is given there. The report on the 1854-58 prices entitled "Svedeniia o prodazhnykh tsenakh na zemli ["Data on Selling Prices on Land"] was published in the *Zhurnal ministerstva vnutrennikh del* [*The Journal of the Ministry of Internal Affairs*], Book 7 (1859), pp. 1-46; Book 8, pp. 95-118.

8. This assumption was made by serveral historians in spite of a specific warning against it. See Domar and Machina, "On the Profitability of Russian Serfdom," pp. 940-941.

9. Ibid., pp. 949-955.

10. Ibid., pp. 943-944.

11. The sources and methods are given in ibid., p. 948. All these figures exclude the provinces mentioned in Note 5.

12. Ibid., pp. 939-941.

13. See Gerschenkron, "Agrarian Policies and Industrialization," p. 730.

14. There was also little variation in this ratio among the several regions comprising each zone. The two highest ratios were in White Russia (47.7%) and in the Lake Region (46.4%), neither region belonging to the Black-earth zone. In the other regions, the ratios were around 35%.

15. The weighted average official price of land (in the sales reports) in the black-earth zone was only 3% above that in the non-black-earth zone.

16. See our Table 1 and Gerschenkron's discussion, "Agrarian Policies and Industrialization," pp. 739-740.

17. Perhaps a bit of simple algebra will clarify the nature of both methods. For every serfowning unit (an estate, a country, a province, and so forth) there is the identity

$$V = P_S S + P_T T, \qquad (1)$$

where V is the value of the unit, P_S and P_T are market prices of serfs and of land respectively, S is the number of serfs and T—the number of desiatinas of land. To find the magnitude of P_T we need a second relationship between the two prices. The first method provides it by the assumption that

$$\frac{P_S}{P_T} = \frac{P_{SO}}{P_{TO}}, \qquad (2)$$

where P_{SO} and P_{TO} are official prices of serfs and of land respectively, so that the ratio P_{SO}/P_{TO} is a given constant for a certain unit (or area). The substitution of (2) into (1) quickly determines the magnitude of P_T.

The second method also starts with the identity (1), but instead of using (2) it assumes (as asserted by the Editor of the sales reports) that $P_{SO} \leq P_S$. Therefore,

$$P_T \leq \frac{V - P_{SO}S}{T} \qquad (3)$$

In other words, the use of the official price for serfs gives us the *maximum* magnitude that the price of land can attain.

The lower overcharge for the West obtained by all three methods undoubtedly reflects the desire of the Russian government to earn the support of the peasants, many of them Greek-Orthodox, against their Catholic masters.

18. To complicate things further we should note that the values of certain estates—the patrimonies—might have been overstated.

19. Alexander II's famous announcement of March 30, 1856, that the end of serfdom was in sight, took place right in the middle of the 1854-1858 period.

20. See Zaionchkovskii, *Provedenie v zhizn' krest'ianskoi reformy 1861 g.*, pp. 142-145.

21. There is also a point made by Gerschenkron ("Agrarian Policies and Industrialization," pp. 740, 745-756) that the restrictions imposed on the ownership and use of the allotted land made it less valuable for the peasants.

22. When one American corporation takes over another, the stockholders of the latter are usually paid some 20-30% more than the market price of their shares. See M. C. Jensen and R. S. Ruback, "The Market for Corporate Control: The Scientific Evidence," *The Journal of Financial Economics* 11 (1983): 5-50.

THE GENERAL AND THE SPECIFIC IN SIBERIAN AGRARIAN DEVELOPMENT IN THE SECOND HALF OF THE NINETEENTH AND BEGINNING OF THE TWENTIETH CENTURY

Leonid Mikhailovich Goriushkin

The history of Siberia bears close comparison to that of European Russia, outlying areas of Imperial Russia and colonized areas of many other countries. Yet interpretations of Siberian development have tended to contrast the general and specific traits of the agrarian history of Siberia from those of the rest of the Russian empire. At the end of the nineteenth and beginning of the twentieth centuries, Siberian scholars, headed by G.N. Potanin, denied a common experience between Russian and Siberian development and even advanced the idea of a specific Russo-Siberian nation.[1] Contemporary American scholars such as D. Treadgold and R. Snow share this view of Siberia's exceptionalism.[2] By contrast, Soviet historians sometimes underestimate the uniqueness of Siberian agrarian development and emphasize only the difficult position of Siberian peasants and the presence of serfdom.[3]

There is one principle important for studying Siberia, that due to its historical position, placing it geographically, economically, culturally, and demographically indissoluably part of the Russian empire, along with the rest of the country, after the abolition of serfdom, it acquired a capitalist structure. Therefore its development was defined by laws common to all of Russia. At the same time there was some variation. Unlike European Russia, which was settled in ancient times and was, therefore, comparatively developed by the second half of the nineteenth century and beginning of the twentieth, Siberia was undeveloped, that is, neither entirely settled nor entirely agricultural. As a frontier area, it had the features of a colony in the economic sense: there was available land, division of labor promoting specialization of agricultural production, and importation of industrial goods.

In central Russia capitalism developed deeply, maturing within densely settled territorty. In Siberia capitalism spread widely, as capitalistic relations began to form in new territory. Siberia had almost no experience with private land ownership, which was widespread in European Russia. In this remote area the main landowners were the state and the crown, which leased the land to peasants. There were other differences: Siberia's natural features—a prolonged, especially cold winter, a short growing season, large wide-open spaces, and greater forestation. There was a distinctive note to agrarian-capitalistic evolution in Siberia.

A main feature of agrarian evolution in Siberia was colonization. From 1861 to 1914, 3,249,000 people migrated eastward, a number surpassing the total population of Siberia at the beginning of the 1860s (under 3,000,000).[4] At the end of the nineteenth century, Siberia was the principal frontier of Russia, constituting approximately four-fifths of all migration from the center. Migration affected the development of production, having an impact on population growth, the expansion of land under cultivation and livestock raising. Demographic movements in Siberia and European Russia were practically the same, but migration was the source and governed the rate of population growth in Siberia while natural fertility affected European Russia. Starting in the 1890s, migration increased even more, accounting for nearly two-thirds the population growth, and as a result, Siberia started to grow faster than European Russia. In 1858 Siberia's population was 26,915,000; by 1914 it had grown to 102,634,000.[5]

Along with its position as a frontier went a larger allocation of population resources to agriculture than in European Russia, a higher ratio of men to women and a greater proportion of workers between age 20 and 40. There was a movement from west to east in Siberia, from settled to unsettled, and the percentage of children in the rural population declined while the percentage of adults increased due to the hardships of taming new lands in remote areas. Siberia was characterized by its landed peasantry among whom were a substantial number of native Siberians.

Despite rapid population growth, Siberia had a relatively low population density, particularly in northern Siberia. The main belt of settlement in the nineteenth century stretched from the Urals to the Siberian highway and along the highway, 200 kilometers north and south. This "colonized basin," comprising more than 1.5 million square kilometers, was the center of Siberian agriculture, stretching north to Tobolsk province at 60 degrees latitude, to Tomsk province at 58 degrees, to Yenisei and Irkutsk provinces at 56-57 degrees, and to Yakutsk at 64-65 degrees. Peasants settled these regions. Due to their labor, at the beginning of the twentieth century, Siberia became one of the leading grain-producing areas of the country.

Because of the vast migration, the absence of landowners, the plentitude of unoccupied land, and the animal husbandry, Siberian production began to grow more rapidly than Central Russia. The supply of grain and livestock per 100 persons in the rural population was greater. The pace of production in Siberia was improved after the construction in the 1890s of the trans-Siberian railroad, which helped migration, opened up Siberia to domestic and foreign investment and consolidated its ties with Russian and world markets. Oil manufacture and the importation of agricultural machinery increased. Land under cultivation grew from an average of 3.6 million *desiatiny* (1 desiatina equals 2.7 acres) in 1901-1905, to 6.7 million desiatiny in 1911-1915, or by 75%, while in European Russia the increase was 14.6%.

The development during the period of Siberia's colonization was capitalistic. The peasants were differentiated into rural bourgeoisie and proletariat. The main contradictory features of this process were common to all of Russia, polarization of the peasantry in market relations in the context of remaining vestiges of feudalism (nonpayment of taxes and arrears), and exploitation of the peasantry through hired labor. The polarization of the peasantry was a process that is inherent in capitalistic commodity production; the work force becomes the commodity.

The signs of development of new social strata were the same for European Russia and Siberia. The rural bourgeoisie dominated and combined commercial agriculture and commercial-industrial enterprise: they hired farm workers, especially temporary laborers, exploited resources to improve the economy, and developed lending operations. The rural proletarian consisted of the hired workers, indigent peasants who were either without land or had a small allotment. They had only what fell by the wayside and could not subsist without selling their labor. Theirs was a miserable existence.[7]

The polarization of the peasantry in European Russia and Siberia was affected by the vestiges of serfdom, the influence of the previous ownership of property by landlords. Under feudalism, the division of class and estate coincided. Individual classes were simultaneously estates. As capitalism developed, new social strata emerged in rural areas, breaking up estates and forming new fissures within rural society. Yet the peasantry as a whole still maintained some estate awareness and as such en masse opposed the autocracy, the landlords, the system of taxation, and other remains of feudalism both in European Russia and in Siberia.

By the end of the 1880s and in the 1890s new social strata were beginning to form.[8] The polarization of the peasantry was enhanced by the development of a railroad, by the further development of the extraction industry (made possible by the influx of colonizers), and by the import of agricultural machinery and capital. The stratification became more widespread.

The materials of the agricultural census of 1916 for Tomsk province show that the peasants, averaging 4 desiatiny of arable (and one or two or no horses, in some areas three) comprised 47% of all households but only 15% of all land under cultivation; the rural bourgeoisie or kulaks (having ten or more desiatiny under cultivation and more than five horses) had 18% of all farms while their share of land under cultivation was more than 46%.[9]

The process of the polarization of the peasantry was distinctive in Siberia. The absence of private ownership of land and a less dense population than that of European Russia created better conditions for the development of agrarian-capitalistic relations in Siberia. Owing to the seizure of unoccupied land and the exploitation of the colonizers' and exiles' cheap labor, the kulaks gained a foothold in Siberia. The proportion of kulaks within the peasantry was higher here than where there had been private ownership. The kulaks in Tomsk province in 1912-1913 who had no competition from noble landowners, held 56% of the total value of peasant property and 60% of all capital and noncapital income. For the poor these figures were 10.7% and 9.8%.[10] The proportion of kulaks and middle-class peasants in Siberia was higher and as a whole the peasantry was more prosperous than in European Russia.

In Siberia the development of agrarian relations was under the influence of the colonization which bore and strengthened polarization. The colonizers were of all social strata. Until about the 1890s middle-class peasants predominated but later poor peasants were a majority. Already on the move and without financial resources they hired themselves out to prosperous colonizers and these relations continued after their arrival in Siberia. Many settlers hired themselves out in order to be able to buy farms. At the end of the nineteenth century in Tomsk province 61-64% of all settlers on crown land rented their homes while nearly 82% of those living on state land rented.[11] In Altai a settler had to work for a kulak for more than 8 years to save up enough money to buy a farm. The constant influx of colonizers, which broadened the use of hired labor, furthered the process of the polarization of the peasantry. The census taken by the military in 1908 and 1912 shows that in provinces having the largest influx of settlers—Tomsk and Yenesei—the polarization of the peasantry was much sharper than in other areas of Siberia.[12]

In European Russia there was new stratification among the native-born peasants, but in Siberia among both natives and new residents. In Tomsk province according to data for the years 1912-1913, there is no evidence of the homogeneity of the process. Among the settlers who preserved a social structure similar to that in European Russia, the number of poor was higher, the percent of wealthy peasants higher, and polarization and spread of the means of production, income and property between groups was greater than among the native-born Siberians. As a whole, however, the native-born and immigrant economies of Siberia did not exist in isolation from each other and in general the process of agrarian evolution was the same.

Perhaps capitalistic development and the growth of new social strata was most clearly reflected in the use of hired labor. Conditions were basically the same for European Russia and Siberia, that is, in the types of hired labor, wages and the position of rural workers. The separation of the peasantry from the means of production served as the classical basis for the formation of the job market. This pattern of market formation in Siberia however is changed by the colonization variable, that is, by the influx of settlers to the hinterlands. One might also mention the exile of criminals. But this played no significant role in the colonization of Siberia. The census of 1897 shows that exiles made up only 5% of Siberia's population, and their role in the formation of the job market was even less according to the census of 1900. Meanwhile the significance of migration, especially from 1907 to 1913, rose sharply.

In contrast to European Russia, there were few landowners among rentiers and as a consequence, no indentured workers on landowners' farms; sharecropping was rare. The tenant's productivity determined to a large extent his income on kulaks' farms. By our calculations the number of permanent farm workers in Siberia grew from 127,000 in 1897 to 220,000 in 1913. The number of people who were working as hired hands (including dayworkers and pieceworkers) just before World War I exceeded 600,000, or 12% of the total peasant population.[12]

The use of farm machinery grew along with the development of commercial-capitalistic farming. In Siberia the spread of machinery began after the construction of the Trans-Siberian railroad. Just as in the center of the country, the wealthy peasants used most of the machinery and others did not use it at all. Data from the registration of implements in 1910 and the all-Russian census of 1917 show that European Russia had fewer threshers, reapers and machines for mowing hay than Siberia.[14] The two regions had approximately the same number of plows and winnowing machines per 100 desiatiny of sown land; Siberia had fewer seeders. The comparatively wide distribution of machinery is explained by the rapid growth of multicrop farms and the conditions of farm production (the short span of time involved in sowing and especially harvesting activities).

Tools that were used in tilling the hard local soils had their own specific history in Siberia. In the nineteenth and even at the beginning of the twentieth century peasants were still using the Siberian wooden plow. It could turn the top soil so that the lower layer would be below the furrow, which was necessary before virgin and long fallowed lands could be plowed. The Russian plow chopped up the soil more which is why the settlers refused to use it in Siberia. Also, the Siberian plow went less deep than the Russian plow, and the peasants preferred a shallow plow because plowing deeply quickened the depletion of the soil. So it went with other farming implements, which were adapted to local conditions.

In a quantitative sense, the Siberian countryside was dominated by middling producers, who comprised over half of the peasant households, and during the growth of capitalism, constituted a petty bourgeoisie. In their level of economic security, productivity, and use of machines and hired labor, they were like kulaks of the Russian center. More than one-third of the land under cultivation belonged to them and nearly the same amount of the means of production.

Under conditions of agrarian-capitalistic evolution the structure of the middle-class peasants was not homogenous. Prosperous, well-to-do peasants made up the first group (approximately one-third) who used hired labor and under favorable conditions enlarged the ranks of kulaks. The majority had a tendency to slip in status, occasionally at first but later more systematically selling their labor and dropping down into the lower class. This reflected the instability and contradictory nature of the middle-class and showed the process of the peasantry's decline. Middle-class peasants were subjected to exploitation by the bourgeois-capitalist state, which taxed them heavily, by commercial business firms, exporters of peasant goods, suppliers of farm machinery, and moneylenders and wholesale buyers.

Almost all the owners of dairies had commercial shops and often traded milk for goods with the peasants, raising the price 10-50% higher than the market price.[15] The high cost of farm machinery (in 1912 a seeder cost 230 rubles, hay mowers 152 rubles, reapers 200 rubles when the full value of the average middle-class peasants property was 500 rubles) was compensated by loans from state funds and commercial firms, which required the buyer to pay one-third up front and the rest over two years at 6% interest. If a payment was late the next payment was another 8% on the overdue amount. Depending on the owner, on market conditions, and on the harvest a middle-class peasant often could not repay his debt and had his property seized and sold at auction. In 1911-1914 defaults on state loans alone amounted to 23,500 and the debtor's property was confiscated.[16]

The construction of the Trans-Siberian railroad heightened the role of capital investment in rural bourgeois farms (sale of farm products, use of machinery, hired labor, and so forth), and limited the activity of moneylenders but did not completely eliminate them. In 1913 approximately one-third of peasant farms in western Siberia marketed their produce to moneylenders and wholesale buyers. Offering a lower price, giving advances on the basis of the next harvest, cheating and swindling, they drained peasant farms of revenues. The instability of peasant farms was especially apparent in times of bad harvests. In Siberia, as in European Russia, this was not infrequent (1870, 1874, 1878-1879, 1883, 1900-1902, 1911-1912, and 1916).

During the famine of 1911-1912 peasants of Tobolsk province in an attempt to save their cattle from starvation, drove them 100 versts into the Tomsk province, sold them for next to nothing or slaughtered them for meat, losing from one-third to one-half of all cows and horses. Debtors to state and cooperative institutions, required to pay interest of 50-100%, saw four-fifths of their farms in Tobolsk province sold at auction. These were lower- and middle-class households with an average debt of 113 rubles per household.[17] It is not surprising that during harvests failure many peasant farms were ruined.

Although their relative percentage in the Siberian population declined, the absolute number of middle-class peasants increased dramatically. The relative reduction is explained by the fact that the ranks of the poor rapidly increased as a result of migration of settlers, who, at the end of the nineteenth and beginning of the twentieth centuries, were mainly poor peasants. Yet migration increased the absolute number of middle-class peasants: before the 1890s the central figure among settlers was the middle-class peasant settlers who first acquired some property and then lost some; a part of the poor settlers also acquired the position of wealthier peasants; new regions were taken into the zone of small and middle-scale production by the development of capitalism and commercial relations.

Poor peasants worked parcels of rented land, had one or two horses and 3-4 desiatiny of land, satisfied their demands, and did not hire themselves out. As a rule they did not produce surpluses, yet had close ties wth the market. In the fall when grain was cheap, they sold a part of their food stores in order to pay off their debts. Their own grain would last until the middle of winter when they would have to buy more at inflated prices. In the final analysis they lost considerably in this exchange.

Material needs forced poor peasants to take out loans from kulaks at 25% interest yearly. The transactions were usually concluded early in the spring when the poor peasant had run out of seed and money to pay taxes for the first half of the year. Productivity of their labor was lower when working off loans; a debtor could be called to work at any time. Sometimes poor peasants would work as the kulak plowed and sowed his own plot with the kulak's seeds (which is a variety of work in exchange for tools and seeds). Just as in Russia, this "working off" of loans represented an undeveloped form of hired labor. The difference is that in Siberia indentured labor was closely associated with colonization of the frontier (most of the debtors were settlers). They did not work on landowners' farms but on kulaks'. Indentured labor in exchange for land was rare in Siberia as was sharecropping. In the Siberian hinterlands, which were being settled, the patriarchal system was preserved more widely than in Central Russia. Patriarchy was reflected in Russian peasant farming in the taiga, mountainous and virgin steppe areas, cut off from the cities, railroads and highways as well as cattle-raising and semi-nomadic farming of the natives. At the end of the nineteenth century Lenin listed Siberia as among those regions where there were still strong remnants of the patrirarchal system.[18] After the construction of the Trans-Siberian railroad there were fewer regions like this although they remained relatively widespread. Most of Siberia's territory remained undeveloped. Two-thirds of income and expenditures on farming in 1911 and 1912 at some distance from the railroad was not in money, but in kind.[19]

More than thirty ethnographic groups populated Siberia. They experienced both social and colonial oppression under tsardom. The positive economic and cultural influence of Russian workers, who worked here along with them, turned out to be a decisive factor in their fate. Following the example of the Russian work force, the people of Siberia developed haymowing and grain-sowing, acquired farm machinery, built farm structures and houses, and learned the skills necessary for leading a settled way of life. In cooperation with Russians, the Siberian natives made a huge contribution in the economic settling of the area. Their population increased from 173,000 in 1662 to 230,000 in 1763, 363,000 in 1796, 648,000 in 1858, 780,000 in 1897, and 973,000 in 1911.[20] They were part of the development of commercial-capitalistic relations, which were prevalent among the Buryats, Yakuts, Tuvints, Khakass, and Altais, at an early stage of where commercial and moneylending capital became interwoven with precapitalist economic forms. On the whole, patriarchal-feudalistic relations and a natural remained characteristic of natives of Siberia.

The development of the commercial-capitalistic economy defined the character of land use. Capitalism transformed various forms of land ownership and land use. Under the tsars, Siberian peasants used land by squatter's rights or with a government allotment of 15 desiatiny per male. In Siberia capital penetrated by the renting of land for profit, concessions of mineral rights, exploitation of the forest and agricultural production by kulaks, which noticeably altered property relations. Yet by 1917 the modification of property relations had not reached the dialectical transition, and therefore the bourgeois-democratic revolution in the Siberian countryside was still to come.

The fact that the State and the crown did not engage in agricultural production does not mean that they were a judicial invention. The government was a property owner, compelling peasants to work government land (seventeenth century), then to pay taxes on that land, and from the 1760s on charging them rent. At the end of the nineteenth century the state introduced a new tax on government and crown land, which was both feudal and capitalist, demanding from the peasant payment for use of the land. The tax system in Siberia showed the exploitation of the peasantry in a system was permeated by the fiscal interests of the State rather than capital or the profitability of farms. Poor peasants paid a higher rate of taxes than more prosperous peasants. Tax increase caused arrears among poor peasants and led to the destruction of the peasantry.

The tax system in Siberia had its specific features; responsibility for the escort guard for criminals. There was the "Yasak" which the crown levied against "wandering and nomadic foreigners." There was a large number of natural conscripts, which is explained by the lack of settlement, remoteness, and lack of means of communication in the region. As a whole the tax burden in the hinterlands by all appearances was less than in European Russia where, besides regular taxes, until 1905 peasants owed redemption payments for their land.

A distinctive feature of agrarian relations in colonized Siberia was the absence of peasant property or the concept of equal distribution of land; what dominated was the forced settlement by the enserfing state. In Siberia, the commune began to play a greater role toward the end of the nineteenth and beginning of the twentieth century in defending the interest of the peasant and acquiring land. It owned the land used by the peasants, regulated its distribution and transfer by inheritance, rented it, and sold it to other communes. By contrast with the center of the country, the peasant obshchina in Siberia gave great freedom to the peasant's economic initiative. This was manifested in the absence of forced crop rotation and in the rare redistribution of land, which was usually not accompanied by the transfer of farms wtih land under cultivation. The Siberian commune, dependent on peasant and other managers, was not directly dependent on landowners. From the end of the nineteenth century on, the tsarist government launched a campaign to reorganize land distribution, during which it limited the peasant's plot to 15 desiatiny. However, at the beginning of the twentieth century substantial remnants of forcible land seizure remained. As is evident from research on migrants in 1911-1912, out of 413 villages, forcible land seizure remained in 205, for the most part in eastern Siberia.[21] Forcible land seizure and land-leasing encouraged the emergence of kulaks.

The realization of landed property came about by the lease of state and crown lands, their sale or transfer by concession, and the collection of quit rent (*obrok*) paid by a peasant for the use of land alloted to him. In comparison with European Russia, the sale of land was not widespread, because the peasants by law could not sell it openly whereas the small privately-owned plots they were allowed to sell were small. The sale of land for farming, disguised as grants for new settlers, was more widespread than in Central Russia, where it was almost unknown. It is associated with the massive influx of settlers to Siberia. The fee for registering with the village societies (at the beginning of the twentieth century as high as 200 rubles) signified that in effect the peasants were buying land for farming.

The leasing of land in Siberia, encountered as early as the eighteenth century, became more widespread after the construction of the Trans-Siberian railroad. This aided the massive migration and the growth of agricultural enterprise, which in turn encouraged out-migration from the commune. Migrants not registered with the village societies in 1910 numbered about 600,000 people.[22] The granting of land to enterprises limited peasant land-use and increased the State's and Siberian Cossack troops' rent fund. On the eve of World War I this fund exceeded 5 million desiatiny, approximately one-third of all arable land cultivated by Siberian settlers. In Siberia enterprises encompassed two-thirds of all rented land belonging to the State and the Crown.[23]

It is possible to distinguish the following types of entrepreneurs: owners of petty capitalist farms wtih an average of 15 to 16 desiatiny of cultivated land on one estate, employing hired lands and farm machinery; large entrepreneurs, renting from 300 to 3000 desiatiny or more; owners of large amounts of cultivated land, herds of fine-fleeced sheep, thoroughbred horses, and pedigree cattle; cattle breeders renting the land on the outskirts of town for grazing, suppliers of horses to the army; renters of fishing grounds and land for minnig of construction materials and mills, dairies, tanneries, and wineries. Nonagricultural rented lands were also used for markets, docks, storage, mines, and so forth. In Siberia, farming was the predominant use of rented lands.

As the 1916 census shows, the second most extensive use of cultivated lands was for the middling peasants' enterprises; the third was rental to the poor for crops. Among those renting, the affluent comprised 18% and rented 56% of all land, the middle class 41% and 29% respectively, and the poor 41% and 15%.[24] The State and Crown forced settlers who occupied State and Crown land to pay rent. A common result was subrental, where owners rented large areas of land cheaply in three-acre plots, giving the poor scraps of land at a greater price and turning land into the object of speculation. As in the middle of the country, land rental contributed to its concentration in the hands of the rural bourgeoisie, whose share in Siberia reached 40% of the parceled land and 60% of all rented peasant lands. Rental payments received by the State and Crown represented capitalist rent, and was the landowner's preferred method of conducting business.

In Siberia, land sales were not as widespread as in European Russia. This was due to the lack of peasant ownership in the territory, a ban on the sale of parceled land, as well as the presence of free lands and the right of seizure, which made it unnecessary for wealthy peasants to buy land. Those participating in rental transactions were different as well. In Siberia, long-term residents and migrants alike rented land, and not from landowners, but from the State and Crown. Rental rates in Siberia were 5 to 10 times lower than in the country's center. Sharecropping and earned rent on the part of the kulaks comprised about 10% of rented lands primarily in Eastern Siberia, and was more the exception than the rule.[25]

Rental relations gave an impression of widespread development of capitalism. Yet capital investment for the improvement of rented properties was not made by the State and Crown. Short-term transactions, enhancing the mobility of the population, served to strip rental relations of stability. In contrast to other landholders, the State and Crown not only had the power of land, but great political power as well, which opened the possibility of arbitrary rule. They could break rental agreements and give the land over to more profitable renters, taking against rental payments or back rent part of the crop yield, seize belongings, and so forth. Those renting small forests were required to guard the plots and the surrounding area for fifty meters on all sides, and if they were incapable of detaining violators, to bear material responsibility.[26]

As for the evolution of capitalism, there stood before Russia but one road for bourgeois development. At the beginning of the twentieth century capitalist relations were predominant in both the peasant and landowner economies.[27] But this development could take various forms: the presevation of landowner latifundia that slowly developed into junker-bourgeois properties, the lack of landowner properties, or their elimination in the Revolution when the peasantry, as the sole agent of agriculture evolved into the capitalist farmer.

Under separate conditions similar to the Prussian path of capitalist evolution, elements of farming actually existed in Russia as well. In regions with strong remnants of serfdom, where the Prussian course predominated, elements of farming, checked by the landowners' latifundia, were weaker than in Siberia. In Siberia there were no privately owned latifundia, and the transition from patriarchal peasant farming to capitalistic comprised the main content of the development, and evolution of the farming type predominated. This is the most important characteristic of rural Siberia.

In the outlying regions the institution of independent farming did not take shape. It was hindered by the autocracy, the landowners, and other remnants of serfdom. In the center of the country and in Siberia, neither of the two paths—Prussian and American—was successful. A sharp struggle resulted between the peasantry and the landowners, comprising the main content of social life in rural Russia after the reforms of 1861. Despite the different forms of agrarian evolution in European Russia and the outlying regions, their main result was the same. The low and progressively falling percentage of landowner properties in the farming industry provided proof of the impossibility of success for the Prussian path. Governmental colonization, built on semi-serfdom, reached an impasse as well. Its fate was sealed with the revolutionary destruction of the autocracy and the subsequent inevitable transition of the bourgeois-democratic revolution to a socialist revolution.

The remnants of the feudal and serf systems found expression in the agrarian issue. Just as with the development of capitalism, the agrarian issue affected all of Russia. Its essence lay in the revolutionary destruction of the landed class and all remnants of the serf-feudal systems in the agricultural and political systems of Russia. Despite this, the form and severity of the agrarian issue were not the same in European Russia and colonized Siberia.

In Siberia, it appeared in the restraining influence of serfownership which posed an obstacle to the colonization of the outlying regions; in the policies of tsarism (affecting migration, land development and taxes), contaminating the serf-based outlands; in the dominance of State and Crown and Cossack owned (in Siberia in 1917 there were 122,000 landless farms, 40% of all villages were on government land, and 57% on Crown owned land did not receive forests during land development);[28] in the unequal guarantee of land to peasants of different classes (Cossacks, long-term residents, and migrants), and the new social strata of poor and kulaks; in the unsatisfactory system of migrations; in the massive return of those who were unsuccessful to European Russia.

Agrarian tension was less severe in Siberia than in the center of the country, although it was marked. The tsarist government's attempt to thin out the attachment to land via migrations, and thus protect the landed from destruction only led to the spread of the agrarian crisis to Siberia as well (curtailment of the norm of land use, growth of the number of unregistered migrants and those without land, and so forth). Thus the issue of colonization of Siberia was dependent on the agrarian issue in Russia in general. The agrarian issue in Siberia was not a matter of the lack of land (as opposed to European Russia, where there was a large resource for colonization), but by the peasantry's lack of means to accomplish the breaking in of new lands because of the obstacle of State and Crown ownership and because of policies on migration.

This constitutes the "the colonization issue"[29] as Lenin described it, the liquidation of feudal forms in the agricultural and political system of Russia and of the old methods of colonization dependent on them in the growth of agricultural production. It describes the unity of European Russia and Siberia in their agrarian evolution, the decisive meaning of the agrarian issue in European Russia and the subordination of the issue of colonization to it, and the interest of the Siberian peasantry in the destruction of the autocracy and the landed class.

In the Russian peasant movement there were two struggles: the peasantry against the feudal remains and the poor peasantry against the rural bourgeoisie. The preconditions of revolt in the center of the country and in Siberia were similar. The basis of the first is clear; and for the second, it was the decline of the peasantry in the evolution of capitalism and the exploitation of the rural poor by kulaks. In Siberia, as in other regions of the country, the two struggles were interwoven with each other. The content and direction of each of these struggles were common. Even in the Siberian outlands, as the chronicles of the peasant movement from 1861-1917 show, the peasant struggle with lags expanded, and the union of the peasantry and the working class took shape.

Agrarian relations conditioned the peasant movement in Siberia. Here it was considerably weaker than in other regions of the country, which was related to the lack of noble landholdings and the relative weakness of the remaining constraints of serfdom. It is not coincidental that the peasant movement was more massive and active on Crown owned land than elsewhere, because here were the vestiges of feudalism. As for the second peasant struggle, in Siberia this was fierce, because the conflict with kulaks was not obscured by the local struggle with noble landowners.

The history of Russia was one with world history, where the defining feature is changes in the means of production. The patterns of history emerged in Russia and Siberia in concrete settings of time and place. Capitalist agrarian evolution, similar in essence in European Russia and Siberia, were different in form. This is the substance of describing the general and specific aspects of agrarian development. It is impossible to delineate features of development entirely separated from their context. Yet, the specific is a partial manifestation of the whole. The capitalist agrarian evolution of Siberia can be understood only in the organic unity of the general and the particular, with an account of the determinant historical patterns of the second half of the nineteenth and beginning of the twentieth centuries in Russia and other capitalist countries.

REFERENCES

1. G. N. Potanin, *Oblastnicheskaia tendentsiia v Sibiri* (Tomsk, 1907).
2. D. W. Treadgold, *The Great Siberian Migration* (Princeton, 1952).
3. A. P. Borodavkin, *Reforma 1861 goda na Altae* (Tomsk, 1972); A. T. Topchii, *Krestianskie reformy v Sibiri (1861-1899 gg.)* (Tomsk, 1979).
4. N. A. Turchaninov, *Itogi pereselencheskogo dvizheniia za vremia s 1896 po 1909 gg. (vkliuchitel'no)* (St. Petersburg, 1910), pp. 52-56; I. Imazin, *Pererselencheskoe dvizhenie v Rossii s momenta osvobozhdeniia krest'ian* (Kiev, 1912), p. 12; N. A. Turchaninov and A. Domrachev, *Itogi pereselencheskogo dvizheniia za vremia s 1910 po 1914 gg.* (St. Petersburg, 1916), pp. 48-69.
5. *Statisticheskie tablitsy Rossiiskoi imperii, izdavaemye po rasporiazheniiu ministra vnutrennikh del*, vyp. I (St. Petersburg, 1863); *Statisticheskii ezhegodnik Rossii 1914 g.* (Petrograd, 1915).
6. *Sel'skoe khoziaistvo Rossii v XX veke* (Moscow, 1923), p. 89, 170-173.
7. V. I. Lenin, *Polnoe sobranie sochinenii*, vol. 3, pp. 169-170.
8. *Materialy dlya izucheniia ekonomicheskogo byta gosudarstvennykh krest'ian i inorodtsev zapadnoi Sibiri*, vyp. I-XXII. (St. Petersburg, 1888-1898); *Materialy po issledovaniiu zemlepol'zovaniia i khoziastvennogo byta sel'skogo naseleniia Irkutskoi i Eniseiskoi gubernii*, Vol. 1 (Irkutsk, 1889); vyp. 2-5 (Moscow, 1890); Vol. 6 (Irkutsk, 1893); Vol. 4, vyp. 1-6 (Irkutsk, 1893-1894).
9. *Materialy perepisi 1916 g. po Tomskoi gubernii (iz opyta obrabotki na EVM)*, ed. L. M. Goriushkin (Moscow, 1969).
10. *Pereselentsy, priselivshiesia k starozhilam, i starozhili Altaisko-Tomskoi chasti Sibiri. Materialy statistiko-ekonomicheskogo obsledovaniia* (Tomsk, 1927), pp. 193, 196-199, 203-204, 221, 225.
11. A. A. Kaufman, *Khoziaistvennoe polozhenie pereselentsev, vodvorennykh na kazennykh zemliakh Tomskoi gubernii*, vol. 1, chapter 1 (St. Petersburg, 1896), pp. 238, 334; *Materialy po*

issledovaniiu mest vodvoreniia pereselentsev v Altaiskom Okruge, vyp. 2 (Barnaul, 1899), pp. 4-5, 20-21.

12. *Statistika Rossiiskoi imperii,* vol. 52; *Voennokonskaia perepis' 1908 g.* (St. Petersburg, 1910); *Voenno-konsskaia perepis' 1912 g.* (Petrograd, 1914).

13. L. M. Goriushkin, *Agrarnye otnosheniia v Sibiri perioda imperializma (1900-1917 gg.)* (Novosibirsk, 1976), p. 236.

14. *Statistika Rossiiskoi imperii,* vol. 79; *Sel'skokhoziaistvennye mashiny i orudiia v Evropeiskoi Rossii i Aziatskoi Rossii v 1910 g.* (St. Petersburg, 1913); *Pogubernskie itogi Vserossiiskoi sel'skokhoziaistvennoi i pozemel'noi perepisi 1917 g. po 52 guberniiam i oblastiam, Trudy TsSu,* vol. 5, vyp. I. (Moscow, 1921).

15. *Obzor Tomskoi guberniiu za 1916 g. v sel'skokhoziaistvennym otnoshenii* (Tomsk, 1921), p. 97.

16. L. M. Goriushkin, *Sibirskoe krest'ianstvo na rubezhe dvykh vekov* (Novosibirsk, 1967), pp. 119-120.

17. *Gosudarstvennyi arkhiv Tiumenskoi oblasti v. g. Tobol'ske,* f. 152, op. 45, d. 273, f. 335, op. 605, d. 53, f. 417, op.1, d. 443.

18. V. I. Lenin, *Polnoe sobranie sochinenii,* vol. 3, s. 328.

19. *Sbornik statisticheskikh svedenii ob ekonomicheskom polozhenii pereselentsev v Sibiri,* vyp. I (St. Petersburg, 1912), p. 169.

20. *Aziatskaia Rossiia,* vol. 1. *Liudi i poriadki za Uraloom* (St. Petersburg, 1914); *Entsiklopedicheskii slovar' Granat,* vol. 38.

21. *Sbornik statisticheskikh svedenii ob ekonomicheskom polozhenii pereselentsev v Sibiri,* vyp. 1 (St. Petersburg, 1912), p. 79.

22. *Poezdka v Sibiri i Povolzh'e. Zapiska P. A. Stolypina i A. V. Krivosheina* (St. Petersburg, 1911), p. 28.

23. *Sbornik statisticheskikh svedenii ob ekonomicheskom polozhenii pereselentsev v Sibiri,* vyp. 1, pp. 94, 125; *Pereselentsy, priselivshiesia k starozhilam, i starozhily Altaisko-Tomskoi chasti Sibiri,* s. 193, 203.

24. *Materialy perepisi 1916 g. po Tomskoi gubernii (iz opyta obrabotki na EVM),* ed. L.M. Goriushkina (Novosibirsk, 1969).

25. *Sbornik statisticheskikh svedenii ob ekonomicheskom polozhenii pereselentsev,* vyp. 1, p. 128.

26. *Gosudarstvennii arkhiv Tiumenskoi oblasti v g. Tobol'ske,* f. 185, op. 1, d. 11, 1, pp. 98-99.

27. I. D. Koval'chenko, N. B. Selunskaia, B. M. Litvakov, *Sotsial'no-ekonomicheskii stroi pomeshchich'ego khoziaistva Evropeiskoi Rossii v epokhu kapitalizma. Istochniki i metody izucheniia* (Moscow, 1982), pp. 217-218.

28. *Pogubernskie itogi Vserossiiskoi sel'skokhoziaistvennoi i pozemel'noi perepisi 1917 g. po 51 guberniiam i oblastiam. Trudy TsSU,* vol. 5, vyp. 1 (Moscow, 1921), pp. 64,73,76,85; *Tsentral'nyi gosudarstvennyi istoricheskii arkhiv,* f. 468, op. 45, d. 66, 1, p. 107.

29. V. I. Lenin. *Polnoe sobranie sochinenii,* vol. 17, pp. 68, 70.

THE PEASANT ECONOMY IN CENTRAL RUSSIA IN THE LATE NINETEENTH AND EARLY TWENTIETH CENTURY

I.D. Koval'chenko

Despite rapid industrialization in the late nineteenth century, Russia remained largely an agrarian country. The peasant economy produced a great part of the gross as well as marketed agricultural output, and it is, therefore, naturally at the center of Soviet research. Soviet historians study the peasantry in order to understand the broad and specific trends leading to the bourgeois-democratic and socialist revolutions and the revolutionary role played by the peasantry, the ally of the working class.

Research on the peasantry has been considerable, although there is still a great deal to be done by Soviet historians before they can provide a thorough analysis of rural development under capitalism. Most important, they have not yet adequately clarified the degree of capitalist development in Russia before the revolution. The development of capitalism in agrarian life, and not only agrarian life, begins with the economy. One seeks the social division of labor and the involvement of the peasants in commodity production in the market, "the regulator of social production."[1] The regulatory influence of the market gave the peasant economy an internal balance and economic rationality, and with this balance and rationality the economy functioned according to socially imperative conditions and demands, preserving its competitive position and profits. This is the structure we have studied by tracing the development of rural capitalism.

The involvement of petty producers in commodity production led first to economic and then to social stratification, that is, to the formation of a rural proletariat and bourgeoisie: a bourgeois social structure. There emerged political antagonisms inherent in bourgeois society, struggle between the rural proletariat and bourgeoisie, and in a moral, ideological, and psychological sense, daily contradictions between the proletariat and the middling stratum.

Soviet historians approach these issues separately; my analysis is general. I deal with the structure of the peasant economy and the basis of commodity-based capitalist relations.

I introduce data on the structure of peasant society, tracing the dependence of peasants' economic activity on certain conditions and demands. In the late nineteenth century, conditions and demands were determined by the capitalist agrarian market, which had by the early twentieth century reached an extremely high level, although a national market for land had not yet been formed.[2]

The laws of the capitalist market differed from those of the simple commodities market. In the simple commodities market "producers of goods stood in opposition to one another."[3] On the capitalist market "goods are exchanged not simply as goods, but as products of capital."[4] In the sample market prices were determined by the cost of goods, i.e., by socially necessary expenditures for their production; in the capitalist market the main factor in price determination was production cost that equals "production expenses plus an average profit."[5]

Costs of production became the regulator of market prices only with the rise of capitalist production in the country's economy, i.e., from the time "when it exists not only sporadically, but dominates the means of social production."[6] From that time on, all types of commodity-producing households, including those where hired labor played a less than decisive role or none at all, fall subject to the laws inherent in the capitalist market. One basic characteristic of capitalist means of production is the extraction of a surplus through the exploitation of hired workers. As soon as this means of production was established, its laws determined the structure of all types of commodity-producing enterprises.

Deriving equal profit from equal capital expenditures is one of the indicators of how closely tied producers of goods are to the market, and how subject their enterprises are to the laws of development. Therefore, our task is to show the degree to which production expenditures of groups of peasants, differing in their economic status, first corresponded to socially necessary expenditures, and second, brought equal income for equal expenditures.

Unfortunately, there are few good sources. What exists are isolated budget surveys of the peasant economy, which embrace for the entire capitalist period only several thousand peasant households in regions of European Russia. Because this means only several hundred units per province, as a whole, this selection of sources cannot be considered representative for quantitative correlations of various types of peasant households. Nevertheless, the budgets help describe the various groupings and the inherent features of the peasant economy, because the main goal of the authors of budget surveys was to describe in detail the types of households and their economic activity.[7]

The budgets are a unique source because they contain a wide range of information on the peasant economy not found elsewhere, and they are complimentary to the extensive census data on the peasant economy.

This paper is based on the largest budget surveys conducted, those covering the peasant economy from the mid-chernozem (black earth) region. This region, overwhelmingly agricultural, developed slowly in comparison with other regions of the country. This means that commodity production would have been at its lowest level, an important point for evaluating the level of social stratification reflected. The first budget data we examined were for Penza province, where we begin our anlaysis of the structure of the peasant economy.

The budget survey of peasants in Penza Province, carried out in 1913, is unique even among budget surveys.[8] It is the only survey that gives a monetary figure for peasants' labor on their own land, how much labor they hired, and how much they expended elsewhere. With this information, we group household economies based on a calculation of the correlation between expenditures of their own labor on their own farm and the purchase of hired labor. We determined four groups of household economies.

The first group, consisting of 89 households, includes those that expended more labor on others' household land than on their own. This was a rural proletariat that had a meager agricultural production on a small allotment.

The second of the four groups includes 92 households that hired some workers but released greater number to other households and spent most of their labor on their own land.

The third group (49 household economies) includes households where there was no hiring of outside labor and less than 10% of the labor capacity of the household released for work on others' lands. The fourth group (31 household economies) comprised households that hired more labor than they released or expended from their own household on their land.

Table 1. Correlation of Working for Hire and Hiring Labor among Peasant Households in Penza Province

	Farm Groups				Total
	1	2	3	4	
Households	89	92	49	31	261
Total expenditures of own labor (per household)	224.7	178.5	174.5	142.1	189
On own land	25.4	73.3	97.7	94.4	60.0
Work for hire	74.6	26.7	2.3	5.6	40.0
Hired labor as percentage of own labor on land	14.9	3.2	1.0	44.6	10.4

The criteria used for isolating the groups are relative, but they facilitate the separation of groups by the hiring of labor. A quantitative correlation of the groups, which can differ with different grouping criteria, is not of major significance in this case.

As Table 1 shows, the first group, the rural proletariat with a small allotment and great expenditure of labor (76.4%) on others' land, is in contrast with a fourth group of households which characteristically expended roughly half (44.65%) of their labor on their own land. And although the households in this group as a whole were not yet capitalist in the true sense, because they expended more labor on their land than they hired, still, they were a middling stratum that would give rise to a class of agrarian capitalists.

The second and third groups are the middle strata. The second clearly exhibited a tendency to evolve socially in the direction of the first, the proletarian. In the second group over one-fourth of the expenditure on labor went toward hired labor. The third group was most characteristically "peasant." The purchase and sale of labor did not play a significant role in the household economy.

We will now consider how the peasant economy of the previously discussed groups differed in terms of size (see Table 2). By size of household and number of workers, the first three groups did not differ greatly. The proportion of males and workers among prospserous households was only somewhat less than for the others. The other characteristics of the peasant economy show an increase by group. Overall, the prosperous households had approximately twice as much as the poorest in total land, cultivated land, implements, livestock, capital expenditures, and gross revenue as the poorest group. It is evident that the social differences between the types of households is wholly determined by size of these variables.

Table 2. Sizes of Different Groups of Peasants in Penza Province

Per household	Groups				Total
	1	2	3	4	
Persons of both sex	7.02	7.47	6.90	6.84	7.13
Male workers	2.88	2.79	2.78	2.49	2.78
Total land owned in desiatiny*	6.76	9.99	12.20	13.60	7.66
Cultivated land	4.25	6.00	7.23	8.90	5.98
Costs of agriculture and other inventory (ruble value)	46.10	62.90	62.80	92.40	60.6
Cost of total livestock and poultry (rubles)	152.70	217.70	231.00	286.60	206.20
Cost of total personal property (rubles)	197.00	207.20	206.60	249.30	208.60
Total expenditure of production capital (rubles)	255.40	359.30	425.90	500.90	353.20
Total gross income (rubles)	692.20	850.50	1089.00	1465.00	914.30

Note: * Desiatina = 2.7 acres.

Crop cultivation was the main type of farming in all groups (see Table 3). It accounted for 39 to 47% of the general revenue. Other branches of agriculture (livestock raising, poultry raising, and bee-keeping) combined under the heading "livestock raising," accounted for 8-10% of all income; that is, they were not well developed. Peasants in all groups received approximately half of their total revenue from agriculture. Trade and industry, naturally accounted for a significant portion of revenue in the groups of prosperous peasantry (groups 3 and 4: 23-25%).

In all groups the peasants' own economy accounted for the greatest portion of their overall revenue. However, in different groups, the significance of this item varied. In the first group it accounted for a little more than half of the income. In the second group it accounted for two-thirds, and in the third and fourth groups, approximately three-fourths of revenues.

In the first group the release of labor for hire in agriculture and industry accounted for roughly half, or the major part of income. It was an essential source of income in the second group also.

In all groups, the household economy was connected with the market. Naturally, the degree of market involvement varied. It was most significant in crop cultivation (26.3%), livestock raising (71.6%), and in agriculture as a

Table 3. Sector Structure and Market Capacity of the Peasant Economy in Penza Province

	Groups				Totals
	1	2	3	4	
Total gross income					
(rubles per household)	692.2	850.5	1089.0	1465.0	913.3
Crop cultivation	39.3	47.3	42.6	41.4	43.1
Livestock raising	10.4	8.5	8.4	8.0	9.4
Total agriculture	49.7	55.8	51.0	49.4	52.5
Nonagricultural					
enterprises	2.0	10.0	25.4	22.9	13.8
Total from					
household	51.7	65.8	76.4	72.3	66.3
Monetary portion of					
receipts in income (%)					
Crop cultivation	16.8	16.9	21.2	26.3	19.5
Livestock raising	18.1	7.0	8.0	71.6	21.2
Total agriculture	17.0	15.2	19.0	33.7	19.8
Nonagricultural					
enterprises	90.0	96.1	98.8	84.5	96.5
Total gross income	48.0	42.3	50.9	53.3	47.8

whole (33.7%) for the more prosperous peasants, but least significant in the first and second groups (17 and 15.2%). However, the overall level of market ties for the peasant economy was extremely high. Thus, the monetary portion of the total gross income was 42-53%; it was lowest in the second group (42.3%) and highest in the fourth group (53.3%).

We now turn to productive capital expenditures for different groups (see Table 4). The results are surprising. Of the nine determinants, only inventory and livestock in the third group and expenditures on crop cultivation in the fourth group diverge more than 10% from the average. In all other aspects, variation is insignificant. Generally, households differed in expenditure of agricultural and total capital only by 3-4%.

What about income? It is obvious that when development of the capitalist agrarian market reached an extremely high level, the peasants' equivalent production expenditures should have produced approximately equal revenues. That was exactly what did happen (see Table 5).

The profitability of peasants' households in all groups was very similar in all ways, in crop cultivation and livestock raising as well as in agricultural production as a whole. The differences that existed were insignificant.

Table 4. Productive Capital and Expenditures by Peasant Households in Penza Province

	Groups				Total
	1	2	3	4	
Cost (rubles)					
Inventory per cultivated desiatina	10.8	10.5	8.7	10.4	10.1
Total livestock per desiatina land (ruble value)*	22.6	21.8	18.9	21.1	21.2
Draft animals per cultivated desiatina (ruble value)	13.0	15.5	15.4	15.1	14.8
Expenditures on draft animals and inventory (ruble value)					
Per cultivated desiatina	11.7	10.8	10.8	10.6	11.0
Per ruble of inventory and draft animal	0.49	0.41	0.45	0.42	0.44
Crop cultivation expenditures per cultivated desiatina (rubles)	23.7	22.8	22.5	29.7	24.2
Maintenance expenditures for productive livestock (rubles) per ruble of total livestock cost	0.41	0.38	j0.40	0.44	0.40
Total expenditures of agricultural capital (rubles)					
Per land held	24.1	23.7	24.0	24.6	24.0
Per cultivated desiatina	38.4	39.4	40.5	37.6	39.1

Note: * The cost of poultry and bees are included in the total livestock cost.

It is very significant that peasants in all categories received approximately the same return on expenditures, as shown by household income per ruble of expenditure. They also had an approximately equal total gross income per ruble of production and personal expenditure. It constituted between 1.13-1.20 rubles, or, on the average, 1.15 rubles. This means that the overall profitability of the peasant economy in different groups was approximately equal, meaning that peasants' individual consumption depended on production conditions and levels.

Table 5. Profitability of Peasant Households of Penza Province

	Groups				Total
	1	2	3	4	
Gross income from crop cultivation (rubles)					
Per cultivated desiatina	64.0	67.0	64.2	68.2	65.9
Per ruble of draft animal and inventory expenditures	5.5	6.2	5.9	6.4	6.0
Per ruble of total expenditures on crop cultivation	2.7	2.9	2.9	2.3	2.7
Gross income from livestock (rubles) per ruble of livestock expenditures	0.49	0.40	0.38	0.39	0.41
Total income from agriculture (rubles)					
Per ruble of agricultural capital expenditures	2.10	2.10	1.90	2.20	2.10
Per ruble of total agricultural expenses	1.39	1.39	1.38	1.27	1.37
Income from all aspects of own farm (rubles) per ruble of expenditure on own farm	1.44	1.43	1.43	1.30	1.39
Total gross income per ruble of total expenditures	1.20	1.13	1.16	1.15	1.15

Therefore, the peasant economy in all categories made approximately equal profit not only on relatively equal productive capital expenditures, but also on equal total capital expenditures. This situation was a result of vital fluctuations characteristic of individual household economies.

Thus, we see that total income and expenditure and relative investment in resources by different peasant groups conformed to laws of the commodity-based capitalist market. How did households differ? This becomes clear when labor expenditures, capital, and labor productivity of different groups are considered, as in Table 6. When labor expenditures in different categories differed significantly, there was an approximately equivalent relative difference

Table 6. Labor Expenditures, Capital and Labor Productivity of Peasant Households in Penza Province

	Groups				Total
	1	2	3	4	
Labor expenditures in agriculture (ruble value)					
Per cultivated desiatina	22.4	17.0	13.1	12.7	16.6
Per ruble of agricultural capital expenditures	0.58	0.43	0.32	0.34	0.43
Total expenditures of labor (ruble value)					
Per ruble of production capital expenditures	1.29	0.72	0.57	0.58	0.80
Per ruble of total capital expenditures	0.91	0.51	0.41	0.40	0.57
Expenditures per ruble of household income					
Inventory and draft animal cost per unit of agricultural labor expenditures	1.07	1.53	1.84	2.01	1.50
Agricultural capital expenditures (rubles) per unit of agricultural labor expenditures	1.71	2.32	3.10	2.96	2.34
Total productive capital expenditures per unit of all labor expenditures (ruble value)	0.78	1.40	1.77	1.72	1.25
Portion of productive capital expenditures in overall labor and capital expenditures	0.45	0.59	0.64	0.64	0.56
Income from agriculture (rubles) per unit of agricultural labor expenditures	3.6	4.5	5.9	6.4	4.8
Gross income (rubles) per unit of all labor expenditures	3.0	4.6	6.2	7.2	4.6
Per person (rubles)					
Household income	51.4	76.6	120.7	155	85.1
Gross income	98.6	113.9	157.8	214	123.1

of productive capital. These differences show an increase in expenditures from the higher to the lower groups. Thus, agricultural labor expenditures in agriculture per cultivated desiatina and per ruble of agricultural capital investment were almost twice as high in the first group as in the fourth. Overall labor expenditure on the household land per ruble of production and total expenditures were more than twice as high in the first group as in the fourth (1.29 and .58; .91 and .40 respectively).

In general, the poorest peasants had to invest approximately twice as much labor as prosperous peasants (the third and fourth groups) to get the same revenue per equivalent expenditure of material and monetary capital. A reduced amount of capital, i.e., the material and technical worth of the poorest peasants' labor, was the cause of this.

Therefore, inventory and draft animal cost per unit of agricultural labor expenditure was twice as low in the first group as in the fourth (1.07 and 2.01 rubles respectively). This was confirmed by data on expenditure of all agricultural capital as well. The overall productive capital expended per unit of total labor expended was 2.2 times lower in the first group than in the fourth (0.78 and 1.72 rubles respectively). All of this is evidence of the existence of vital differences in the structure of capital investment by different peasant groups, which was higher in prosperous groups. The portion of productive capital expenditures in labor and capital was the same for the first group at 45% but 64% for the third and fourth groups.

Significant differences in capital investment was caused by lower labor productivity in the lower peasant groups and consequently a lower general income. Revenue from agriculture per unit of agricultural labor expenditure was 1.8 times lower in the first group than in the fourth (3.6 and 6.4 rubles respectively), and the total gross income per unit of all expenditures was 2.4 times lower (3.0 and 7.2 rubles). The per capita income from the household economy (profitability) was 3 times lower in the poorest group than in the most prosperous group (51.4 and 155 rubles). The differences in total gross income per capita were somewhat lower (98.6 and 214.2 rubles, i.e., 2.2 times lower). This was because income from labor was included along with total gross income excluding household receipts. This amount was very significant, as evident from the first group.

Thus, although it was necessary for all categories to secure a certain production level, the poorest rural stratum did this by intensifying its own labor, whereas the prosperous peasantry did it by capital investment.

One may contrast the relatively equal productive income in material and monetary resources of the four groups and the equal income earned on equal capital expenditures with significant differences in labor capital and productivity and therefore in profitability. The less prosperous rural strata labored more but had a lower income. This inevitably affected material standing and opportunities for further agricultural advancement.

Table 7. Intensity of Labor and the Position of the Peasants in Penza Province

	Groups				Total
	1	2	3	4	
One worker's expenditures of own labor	78.0	64.0	62.8	57.1	68.0
Food consumption (ruble value per capita)	29.2	31.5	34.2	41.1	32.3
Total personal expenditures (rubles per capita)	46.4	46.9	51.8	67.2	49.9
Total personal expense percentage of gross income	47.0	41.2	32.8	31.4	38.9
Total expenses by household percentage of total income	36.3	47.0	53.4	55.5	47.7

As Table 7 shows, one worker's expenditures of his own labor were 1.4 times greater in the first group than in the fourth group (78.0 and 57.1 respectively). This indicates that the poorest peasants labored approximately 1.5 times more intensively than the prosperous peasants. At the same time, the poorest peasants were much more poorly fed than the prosperous ones. Per capita food consumption was 1.4 times lower in the first group than in the fourth (29.2 and 41.1 rubles). Overall expenditures on personal necessities were also 1.4 times lower in the first group than in the fourth (46.4 and 67.2 rubles). Food and personal expenditures among the most prosperous peasantry (the fourth group) differed significantly not only from those of the proletarian and poorest groups, but also from the prosperous middle stratum (the third group).

In general, the situation of the lowest peasant group, as expected, was significantly worse than that of the higher groups, especially the most prosperous. Opportunities for advancement varied among the different peasant groups.

As Table 7 shows, the share of the total gross income on personal expenses was significantly higher in the poorest groups than in the prosperous (47.0% and 31.4% for the first and fourth groups respectively). Opportunities for maintenance and development of household economies were significantly worse for the first group than for the second. Total expenses on household constituted a decreasing portion of the gross income from the more prosperous to the poorer groups (it equalled 36.3 and 55.5% in the first and fourth groups).

It is clear that the poorest peasants could maintain their household economies at the level demanded by the commodity-based capitalist market. They did this mainly by intensifying their labor while the prosperous rural strata had significantly greater capital to increase investments and productivity. These are the results of an analysis of the budget survey for Penza in 1913.

* * *

We turn now to other parts of the mid-chernozem zone. We have 1887-1896 budget data on 230 household economies in Voronezh Province (published in 1900 by A. F. Shcherbina). We grouped the peasant economy by size of gross income per household, i.e., by the end result of the peasant's activity.

Four household groups were distinguished with the following incomes:

Group 1: Up to 300 rubles (31 households)
Group 2: 301-600 rubles (58 households)
Group 3: 601-1000 rubles (56 households)
Group 4: Over 1000 rubles (34 households)

The groups differed significantly by amount of land cultivated by farm, approximately 10 times greater for the fourth than the first group (2.48 and 24.31 des.). Compared to the first group, the fourth group had an average per household 8.7 times higher in agricultural activity, 13.6 times higher in total livestock and poultry, and 9.4 times higher in gross income. Agriculture was the predominant sector of the peasant economy in Voronezh Province. Crop cultivation and livestock raising accounted for 55-61% of gross income (see Table 8).

Market involvement for all types of the peasant economy was extremely high, producing a characteristically large proportion of monetary expenditures in agriculture (81-87%). The peasants' wealth was almost identical for all groups in inventory and draft animals (16-19 per des.) and total agricultural expenses per cultivated desiatina ranged 23 to 26 rubles.

Therefore, the level of wealth in productive capital and agricultural expenditures calculated by commensurate units was approximately equal for all types of the peasant economy, although gross revenues differed.

Thus, returns on crop cultivation and on crop cultivation and livestock raising together per cultivated desiatina were almost equal for all groups. The total gross income per ruble of agricultural expenditure also was very close in all groups (2.5-2.7 rubles). The total gross income per ruble of total expenditures was almost identical in the first three groups (1.07-1.13 rubles). It was a bit higher in the prosperous group (1.23 rubles).

Table 8. Structure of the Peasant Economy in Voronezh Province at the End of the Nineteenth Century

	Groups			
	1	2	3	4
Total gross income				
(rubles per household)	175.3	428.9	772.6	1641.0
Percent from				
Crop cultivation				
and livestock raising	55.2	63.5	65.7	60.0
Monetary portion of				
gross income (%)	51.5	46.0	43.7	44.0
Monetary				
expenditures				
in household				
expenses (%)	86.6	84.4	81.9	81.0
Draft horses and				
inventory per				
cultivated desiatina				
(ruble value)	17.1	18.6	17.0	16.0
Draft horses and				
inventory per capita				
(ruble value)	9.0	17.7	20.2	27.0
Economic expenditures (ruble value)				
Per cultivated				
desiatina	26.4	23.1	25.4	25.0
Per capita	13.9	22.0	30.2	42.0
Income from crop				
cultivation per				
cultivated desiatina	26.4	25.9	29.2	27.0
Income from crop				
cultivation and				
livestock raising per				
cultivated desiatina	39.2	36.5	41.7	40.0
Total gross income (rubles)				
Per ruble of				
economic				
expenditures	2.68	2.48	2.50	2.0
Per ruble of total				
expenditures	1.07	1.10	1.13	1.0
Per capita	37.3	54.6	75.5	113.0

Therefore, for Voronezh Province the dependency of the peasant economy in all categories on the commodity-based capitalist market is very evident, as is the bourgeois nature of the peasant household.

The variations between the different types of households in Penza Province were caused by inequality in productivity of capital and labor. Thus, there were three times more draft animals and inventory per capita in the fourth group than in the first (9 and 27 rubles respectively) (see Table 8). In the fourth group all per capita agricultural expenditures were three times greater than in the first group (13.9 and 42.2 rubles).

The lower elasticity of labor in the poorest peasant household groups was responsible for their lower productivity, and therefore their general profitability. The total gross income (see Table 8) per capita was three times lower in the first group than in the fourth (37.3 and 113.5 rubles).

It is clear that the main features of the structure for the peasant economy in Voronezh Province are basically the same as those for Penza Province.

* * *

In 1913, budget surveys were carried out in Simbirsk Province for 220 households of different types. In comparison to the Penza and Voronezh Province budget surveys, however, for Simbirsk there is no estimate of monetary worth for categories of the budget, a shortcoming because such data facilitate the determination of peasant market ties. The following four groups were isolated according to the area of land under cultivation:

Group 1:   Up to 5.0 des. (29 households)
Group 2:   5.1 -10.0 des. (86 households)
Group 3:   10.1-15.0 des. (50 households)
Group 4:   Over 15 des. (55 households)

Compared to the poorest group, the more prosperous households (the fourth group) had 5 times more land, 5.6 times more under cultivation, 5 times more production expenses, and 3 times more income. The prosperous peasants made relatively great use of hired labor. In this group hired laborers constituted 22.4% of labor on their land.

The production structure of the groups was as follows (see Table 9). Agriculture was the peasants' main occupation in the second through fourth groups. It accounted for 67-85% of the total gross income. In the first group it accounted for only 35.3% of the income, with individual enterprise the main source (61.2%). For the poorest peasants this most often meant working for hire. This accounted for the greater part of their income.

Production expenditures calculated per desiatina were almost identical for all groups (9.5-11.2 rubles), but calculated per cultivated desiatina, groups one, three and four were extremely close (18.4-20.5 rubles), and group two only a little lower (16.6 rubles). On the whole, the level of production expenditures was approximately identical in different household categories.

Table 9. Structure of the Peasant Economy in Simbirsk Province (1913)

	Groups			
	1	2	3	4
Total gross income per household economy (rubles)	269.1	324.5	513.2	804.0
Percent from				
Agriculture	35.3	66.9	80.7	85.4
Individual enterprise	61.2	23.9	10.7	8.5
Production Expenses (ruble value)				
Per land tenure desitiana	11.2	9.5	11.1	11.1
Per cultivated desiatina	20.5	16.6	18.9	18.4
Per agricultural laborer	23.1	33.4	50.9	59.7
Production expense percentage of total expenses	30.8	42.9	53.0	56.2
Peasant incomes (rubles)				
From crop cultivation per cultivated desiatina	17.2	21.2	25.7	25.5
From livestock raising per land tenure desiatina	4.6	4.2	4.4	4.5
Total from agriculture				
Per production ruble spent	2.0	2.6	2.5	2.3
Per agricultural laborer	28.0	57.7	89.5	107.4
Total gross income (rubles)				
Per ruble of total expenditures	1.09	1.11	1.16	1.1
Per laborer (total laborers)	71.6	78.6	107.1	122.6
Per capita	41.5	43.6	64.2	80.8

The revenues from crops per cultivated desiatina were the same for the third and fourth groups, but for the first and second groups, they were noticeably lower. The level of revenues from livestock raising was approximately the same. Overall agricultural revenues per expended ruble in the second through fourth groups differed insignificantly (2.3-2.6 rubles), but were considerably lower for the poorest peasants (2.0 rubles). Thus, the great majority of peasants (191 households out of 220) received approximately equal revenues for equivalent production expenditures. The poorest peasants received an income considerably lower than average. This proves that the households of peasants receiving their basic income working for hire could not withstand competition, and there was a trend toward their decline.

The gross income per ruble expended, the profitability of the household, fluctuated between 1.09 and 1.18 rubles among the groups; i.e., it differed slightly. The differences in the structure among individual types of households were similar to those in Penza and Voronezh Provinces. Production expenditures per laborer were 2.6 times less in the first group than in the fourth (23.1 and 59.7 rubles), largely because of differing levels of labor productivity. Revenues from agriculture per laborer were 3.7 times greater in the highest group than in the lowest (28.9 and 107.4 rubles). The overall profitability of the peasants' economic activity also varied. The gross income differed by 1.7 times per laborer between the extreme groups (71.6 and 122.6 rubles) and per capita by 1.9 times (41.5 and 80.8 rubles). Moreover, the differences increased more dramatically from the lower groups (1 and 2) to the higher groups (3 and 4).

As a whole, the data for Simbirsk Province shows that the structure for different types of the peasant economy was similar to that in Penza and Voronezh Provinces.

Turning to another mid-chernozem zone province, we examine the extensive budget survey data published for Starobel'skii District of Khar'kov province (1910) that embraced 101 households. The four groups differed significantly by amount of cultivated land. The gross income was 10 times greater in the fourth group than in the first (see Table 10).

Agriculture was the main occupation in all peasant categories. It accounted for 73.4% of all income in the first group and 88-90% in the second, third, and fourth groups.[9]

One distinction for Khar'kov was the importance of animal husbandry. In all groups, but especially in the first three, income from it was greater than from crop cultivation. The wealth of the peasant household economy in inventory and livestock was approximately equal in all categories. Only the wealth per cultivated desiatina by inventory and livestock was somewhat lower for poor peasants. However, crop expenditures per cultivated and land were approximately the same for all groups. All groups had roughly the same income from crop cultivation per cultivated desiatina and per ruble, from animal husbandry per ruble, and from the total agricultural production per ruble (see determinants 8-11, Table 10). The total gross income per ruble was also basically the same (1.19-1.25 rubles).

Table 10. Structure of the Peasant Economy in Starobel'skii District of Khar'kov Province (1910)*

	Group by Cultivation Amount per Household (*desiatina*)			
	1 Up to 3.00	2 3.01- 7.50	3 7.51- 15.00	4 Over 15.00
Total gross income per household (rubles)	326.8	843.3	780.7	3263
Percent from				
Crop cultivation	33.0	38.8	39.3	43
Livestock raising	40.4	48.7	50.0	46
Inventory and total livestock cost per cultivated desiatina (ruble value)	46.1	55.4	52.4	52
Total economic expenditures (ruble value) per				
Cultivated desiatina	33.0	29.6	31.1	32
Arable land desiatina	42.4	48.0	47.3	48
Laborer	74.5	114.9	175.3	269
Peasant Income (rubles)				
From crop cultivation per cultivated desiatina	61.3	58.9	60.3	61
From crop cultivation per ruble spent	1.86	1.99	1.94	1
From livestock raising per ruble spent	2.96	3.22	3.15	2
Total per ruble of production expenditures	1.23	1.27	1.24	1
Total gross income (rubles)				
Per ruble of total expenditures	1.25	1.22	1.19	1
Per capita	75.1	134.3	190.0	286

Source: *Data for calculations taken from *Biudzhety krest'ian Starobel'skogo uezda* (Kar'kov, 1915), p. 10 ff.

The differences between the groups in capital, labor productivity, and general profits were significant. Production expenditures per laborer were 3.6 times greater in the fourth group. Accordingly, gross per capita income is 3.8 times greater in the fourth group than in the first. On the whole, these results are the same as those for other provinces.

* * *

Finally, we will examine data for Tula Province, located in the northern part of the mid-chernozem zone. We have budgets for 655 households from 1911 to 1914.[10] We have combined some ten groups to make up the following four (by land under cultivation):

>Group 1: Up to 4.0 des. (279 households)
>Group 2: 4.1 - 8.0 des. (224 households)
>Group 3: 8.1 - 15.00 des. (121 households)
>Group 4: Over 15.00 des. (21 households)

Data on the structure for these groups is shown in Table 11.

As for the other provinces, the household types, distinguished by size, differ significantly. On the average, total land in tenure was 5.6 greater, cultivated land was 8.8 times greater, and total gross income was 4.4 times greater per household in the fourth group than the first.

Market involvement was extremely developed for all household categories: Agriculture played a major role in the peasant economy. Economic

Table 11. Structure of the Peasant Economy in Tula Province (1911-1914)

	Groups by Cultivated Land per Household (*desiatina*)			
	1	2	3	4
Total gross income per household (rubles)	542.0	827.6	1288.0	2361.3
Monetary portion (%)	48.7	39.5	39.4	40.2
Portion of gross income from agricultural receipts (%)	73.3	83.9	89.0	89.4
Material expenditures among total expenditures (%)	37.0	43.5	49.7	57.3
Material expenditures (ruble value)				
Per owned desiatina	41.7	38.4	43.0	45.6
Per laborer	56.8	74.7	106.5	193.6
Revenues from agriculture (rubles)				
Per desiatina land owned	91.3	87.8	92.4	86.9
Per ruble spent in material	2.20	2.28	2.15	1.9
Gross income (rubles)				
Per ruble of total expenditures	1.11	1.18	1.20	1.22
Per laborer	170.5	203.3	257.2	413.2
Per head	133.0	158.7	200.6	315.8

expenditures calculated per desiatina were approximately the same for all groups, and peasants got equal returns. Income from agriculture per desiatina came to 88-92 rubles, but per ruble of general expenditures, 1.91-2.23 rubles, that is, on the whole an insignificant difference. The total gross income per ruble of expenditures ranged from 1.11 to 1.22 rubles.

Consequently, all types of households in Tula Province received an approximately equal income by household for equivalent production expenditures and an equal gross income per equivalent total expenditures. Capital and labor productivity and total revenues determined by them differed significantly by group. Economic expenditures calculated per laborer were much greater for the higher than for the lower group. The gross income, calculated per laborer and per head, was 2.4 times greater in the fourth group than in the first. The structure of the peasant economy in Tula Province was characterized the same as other localities of the mid-chernozem zone.

* * *

In conclusion, we can see from the data that at the end of the nineteenth and beginning of the twentieth century, the household economy of the peasantry in the mid-chernozem zone of European Russia had common features. These were determined by the demands of the commodity-based capitalist market. In order to withstand competition and gain a minimal profit, any size household involved with the market should maintain a technological potential and level of necessary expenditures corresponding to the average social expenditures for given production conditions. An identical level of wealth in productive capital, relative to scale of production, and of expenditures on household necessities by all groups confirms the presence of such a regularity in economic development.

Another expression of the link of the peasant economy to the commodity-based capitalist market was the fact that all peasant household categories received an approximately equal income on equal expenditure of material and monetary capital. This income included an average norm of capitalist profit because prices on the capitalist market were determined by production expenses plus an average profit. In other words, all resources that were used in the peasant economy acted as capital, as a self-increasing cost.

Therefore, these data prove that the structure of different types of the household economies had an objective commodity-based capitalist nature—it was bourgeois. However, the bourgeois nature of the peasant economy does not in any way mean that there was a general similarity in socioeconomic and production structures. Although all household categories derived an average profit, the size of which was determined by general conditions of the capitalist market, this was achieved differently by different households. Prosperous peasants did so by capital expenditures, by increasing material resources; poor peasants increased their labor. The result was a fundamental difference in the labor productivity of the higher and lower groups and in the outcome of production: income. Income was several times lower for the poor than for the prosperous.

In all, both the position and the opportunity of peasants differed by category. Under conditions of intensifying competition, only the most prosperous peasants could improve their technology and labor productivity, and, therefore, withstand competition. A decline in the level of the poorest rural strata was unavoidable, because they had only limited opportunity to intensify their labor and little means of improving their technology. These peasants were able to forestall their final decline for a certain period of time by reducing the amount of production or by investing into it some of the capital gained from working for hire. The ruin and transformation of the poorest peasantry into a proletariat most often involved the proletariat who had some allotment land but meager household resources. It was precisely under commodity-based capitalist conditions that the bourgeois structure of the peasant economy became evident, expressed in the rise of a small stratum of prosperous households and the ruin of a mass of poor households, and in the absorption of small households by large ones. In rural areas without exception the following law was clear, "greater productivity means greater stability of the large peasant household." This led to "the displacement of the middling and poor peasantry by the peasant bourgeoisie."[11]

An essential feature of capitalist development in rural Russia was the slowing tempo of growth, conditioned by the continuing influence of a fedual past. Usury, various kinds of debt-slavery (kabala), and oppression were widespread in rural areas. As a result, the proportion of the poorest peasants was very high, and the transformation of prosperous peasants into landed capitalist peasants occurred extremely slowly.

The main factor in this was the preservation of a quasi-serf-owning nobility at the same time that peasants experienced an ever-pressing need for land. The peasants spent huge amount of capital on redemption payments and on the purchase and rent of land. In 1905, the peasants paid 2.5 billion rubles on redemption payments. From 1863 to 1920 the peasantry spent 1.9 billion rubles on land purchases from private landowners. At the end of the nineteenth century, the peasantry spent 150 million rubles each year on land rent, and in the beginning of the twentieth century, 200-250 million each year, i.e., the peasantry spent even more on land rent than on redemption payments and land purchase.[12]

These are huge sums, especially considering that in 1905 the value of noble landholdings in European Russia came to 4.8 million rubles, with a total value was 20.2 million rubles for the country. Therefore, the interest of all strata of peasants in liquidating noble landownership and eliminating other vestiges of serfdom is obvious. Only the revolution could eliminate the oppression of the peasantry. The course of agrarian development in the beginning of the twentieth century inevitably led to revolution. It put the solution of the peasant question first on the social and economic agenda.

NOTES AND REFERENCES

1. V.I. Lenin, *Polnoe sobranie sochinenii* [*Full Collection of Works*], vol. 1 (Moscow, 1958-1965), p. 66.
2. I. D. Koval'chenko, L. V. Milov, *Vserossiiskii agrarnyi rynok XVIII–nachalo XX vv.* [*All-Russian Agrarian Market in the 18th-19th century*] (Moscow, 1974).
3. K. Marx, F. Engels, *Sochineniia* [works], vol. 25, chapter 1 (Moscow, 1956), p. 213.
4. Ibid., p. 192.
5. Ibid., p. 172.
6. Ibid., vol. 26, chapter 3, p. 436.
7. The general features of the peasant budget in A. Chayanov, G. Studenskii, *Istoriia biudzhetnyh issledovannii* [*History of Budget Research*], 2nd ed. (Moscow, 1922); A. Chayanov, *Biudzhetnyie issledovaniia: istoriia i metody* [*Budget Research: History and Methods*] (Moscow, 1929); N. N. Kornievskaia, *Biudzhetnyie obsledovaniia krest'ianskikh khoziaistv v dorevoliutsionnoi Rossii* [*Budget Research on Peasant Households in Prerevolutionary Russia*] (Moscow, 1954).
8. *Itogi otsenochno-statisticheskogo obsledovaniia Penzenskoi gubernii 1909-1913 gg.* [*Summary Totals of Price-based Statistical Research on Penza Province 1909-1913*], ser. 3, chapter 3, no. 1 (Penza, 1923).
9. Incomes from crop cultivation and livestock raising include all income from agriculture.
10. *Prodovol'stvie krest'ianskogo naseleniia Tul'skoi gubernii (po dannym monograficheskogo opisaniia 1911-1912 gg.* [*Production by the Peasant Population of Tula Province, From Data From Monographic Descriptions, 1911-1912*] (Tula, 1917).
11. Lenin, *Sochinenii,* vol. 3, p. 66.
12. I. D. Koval'ehenko, "O burzhuaznonm kharaktere krest'ianskogo khoziaistva evropeiskoi Rossii v kontse XIX—nachale XX v., *Istoriia SSSR* [*The Bourgeois Character of the Peasant Economy of European Russia at the End of the 19th–Beginning of the 20th Century*] (1983), n. 5.

THE POLARIZATION OF PEASANT HOUSEHOLDS IN PREREVOLUTIONARY RUSSIA:
ZEMSTVO CENSUSES AND PROBLEMS OF MEASUREMENT

Daniel Field

For Russian peasants under the old regime, life was hard. The historian wants to know, hard like what? Were the peasants in thrall to retrogressive social and political forces, including some of their own making? Or were they victims of the restless and deeply alien forces of nascent capitalism? Both propositions are true, to some extent, for most peasants. The great task for historians of Russia, and the great ground of dispute among them, is to locate and to render the balance point between the elements of stagnation and the forces for change. This task is worth pursuing and holds a particular interest for our Soviet colleagues. If it is understood that stagnation and the remnants of serfdom prevailed in the Russian countryside, then the revolt of the peasants against tsarism and its social analogues, in 1905-1907 and in 1917, becomes fully intelligible. If that was the case, however, if the forces of capitalist development in Russia were still weak, then a city-based socialist revolution in 1917 was premature, it was (as the Bolsheviks' Marxist critics charged at the time) "adventurism."

To particularize, for Soviet historians, it is an article of faith that in the revolutionary years rank-and-file peasants were engaged in a social war on two fronts, one against the old oppressor (the squires), the other against the new (the rural bourgeoisie, or *kulaks*). Many western historians, following the lead of Chaianov and Shanin,[1] find the concept of a "second social war" untenable because one of the contending forces did not exist; they hold that differences of wealth and productive power among peasant households were evanescent and, indeed, cyclical, and that these cycles occurred by the peasants' deliberate arrangement. This picture conforms to much of what we know about peasant attitudes and institutions, but is as hard to demonstrate as the doctrine of transubstantiation.

What we want is a measure with which to plot the fever chart of rural Russia in the period of 1861-1917. The measures that come first to mind—household income, for example, or participation in the market—will not do either because they cannot be determined or because they do not measure what most interests us. The best single measure, best because it registers both social and economic phenomena, is *rassloenie*.

Rassloenie refers to the transformation of a once-homogeneous peasantry into distinct socioeconomic layers and, ultimately, into distinct classes; poor peasants become a rural proletariat, rich peasants become a rural bourgeoisie, and only a diminishing middle segment continues to live and work as peasants used to do. The term is formed from *ras-*, meaning "apart" and *sloi* meaning "stratum." It is sometimes translated as "stratification" but in this context "polarization" is better.[2]

Rassloenie describes a transition from one mythical state to another. There were no days so good and so old that everyone was a middle peasant. There was never a peasant community in which all productive resources were concentrated in a few rich households. Yet rassloenie remains the best single measure of the extent of capitalist development in the postreform countryside, as Russian historians since the 1890's have emphasized.[3]

Historians usually register rassloenie in a format, superficially quantitative but acutally verbal, like this: "in year X, the middle peasantry (defined by ownership of draft animals) represented 62% of the households and 51% of the population in village A; they held 42% of the plowland and worked 36% of the sown area." This format registers an authentic phenomenon, but does not permit systematic comparisons between village A and another village or any other unit.

The Gini index has much to offer the historian studying stratification.[4] It reckons with *all*[5] units (e.g., households—Russian *dvory,* singular *dvor*) and the asset holdings of *each* unit (e.g., horses).[6] It yields a single number, which permits comparison to other villages, cantons or districts, and also to other years, and so opens the way to correlation and other forms of statistical analysis.

Given their love of quantitative methods, and given the importance Lenin attached to rassloenie in his *Development of Capitalism in Russia* and elsewhere, it is surprising that Soviet historians have not applied the Gini index to the prerevolutionary peasantry.[7] To the historian of the prerevolutionary village, the Gini index does present theoretical and practical problems, which I shall now explore.

ZEMSTVO CENSUSES

There are two broad classes of published quantitative data on the prerevolutionary peasant village, those produced by the central government and those produced by the various *zemstva.* The latter, for those provinces and district in which they were conducted, are more comprehensive and reliable.[8] The zemstvo, an elective agency of local administration, conducted household censuses at its discretion and, (to the despair of the historian, as we shall see) each was free to follow its own design. Some 56 zemstvo household censuses were conducted in 311 districts between 1880 and 1913; most of them register the distribution of one or more assets among peasant households, opening the way to the calculation of Gini indexes.[9]

Consider Table 1. One may, without being an obscurantist, complain that the Gini indexes in Table 1 are not eloquent and that, given the economic diversity of the districts involved, these statistics hold no surprises. This

Table 1. Distribution of Horses, Selected Districts—Gini Indexes
All Peasant Households (*Nalichnye-pripisannye dvory*)

ID	Year	District	Province	Total dvory	Mean horses per dvor	Gini index
2032	1900	Viazma	Smolensk	14425	1.5	.342
2076	1897	Murom	Vladimir	20428	0.6	.572
2088	1894	Orel	Orel	22032	1.0	.497
2090	1900	Zadonsk	Voronezh	6469	1.1	.473
2096	1894	Petrovsk	Saratov	32698	1.2	.437

Source: Z.M. Svavitskaia and N.A. Svavitskii, *Zemskie podvoryne perepisi, 1880-1913: Pouezdnye itogi* (Moscow, 1926), pp. 92, 100-101, 114, 122-123, 136, 144-145.

complaint is appropriate. The average of horses per household means something, or seems to; the absolute values of Gini indexes are not evocative. They take on meaning when used in systematic comparisons over time or between territorial units. To conduct such comparisons we turn to Poltava Province.

HOUSEHOLD CENSUSES IN POLTAVA PROVINCE

The examples below are drawn from the household censuses carried out by the Poltava Provincial Zemstvo in the 1880s, in 1900, and in 1910. Data are available for all three censuses at the canton (*volost'*), district (*uezd*), and province levels.[10] The Poltava zemstvo censuses, particularly that of 1900,[11] are among the richest and most rigorous of their kind. Subsequent discussion will focus on the census data for the fifteen districts of the province and, in order to carry out comparisons among censuses, on the data concerning the forty cantons of the two easternmost districts of the province, Konstantinograd and Poltava.

Contemporary statisticians and later historians have agreed that zemstvo censuses are much more reliable than other data and, in particular, more reliable than the ongoing records of population and landholding maintained by the cantonal administrations (*volostnye pravleniia*); these records underlay most of the central government's statistical publications concerning peasants. Among the zemstvo statistical bureaux, the one in Poltava Province was regarded as exemplary. Thanks to a possibly unique coincidence, we have in print the *volostnoe pravlenie* data for the same year (1900) as the second of the three zemstvo censuses. These data show, for Konstantinograd District, a peasant population equal to 97.0% of the zemstvo figure, 94.0% of the zemstvo total of households, and 88.3% of the zemstvo total of land in peasant hands. For Poltava District, the corresponding figures are 104.5%, 92.5% and 90.8%. These discrepancies, which range more widely for particular cantons, are disturbing, but it does seem that the historian should cleave to the zemstvo data as the best available.[12]

GROUPING

The absolute value of a Gini index depends on the grouping used. The point may seem obvious, but it is worth raising because misunderstanding has arisen on this count. If one wanted to show that income is distributed equally in the United States, one would group the data by states; to show the opposite, one

Table 2. Gini Indexes, Holdings of Own Plowland, Reported Values Konstantinograd District, 1900

	All Holders			Holders 0-50 des.		
(1)	Total dvory (2)	Gini (per dvor) (3)	Gini (per capita) (4)	Total dvory (5)	Gini (per dvor) (6)	Gini (per capita) (7)
All unprivileged	34363	.604	.527	33919	.508	.421
Cossacks	3580	.718	.653	3440	.627	.562
Ex-serfs	17514	.555	.496	17412	.503	.442
All households	34891	.729	.662	34311	.513	.427

Source: Poltavskoe gubernskoe zemstvo, Statisticheskoe biuro, *Obezpechennost' pakhatnoi zemleiu khoziaiastv Poltavskoi gubernii: Dopolnenie k "Materialam podvornoi perepisi 1900 goda," Konstantinogradskii uezd* (Poltava, 1907), pp. 2-43.

would choose census tracts or some smaller unit, because rich and poor tend to live in different neighborhoods. The Gini index for distribution of plowland in Konstantinograd District in 1900, reckoning all "unprivileged" households, is .581. Here households are grouped in ascending order according to their holdings, that is, "households holding no plowland," "households holding 0-1 *desiatiny*," "households holding 1-2 des.," and so on.[13] Using exactly the same data for households and plowland, but using a grouping by cantons, the Gini index is .188. In the first instance, one is measuring distribution among household groups—indeed, among sloi—while in the second, one is measuring distribution among cantons. (Because groupings defined by ascending order of asset holdings are used throughout this paper, the absolute values of Gini indexes necessarily will be high). It is obviously necessary to choose a sensible grouping and to use the same grouping in making comparisons between years or territorial units. Table 2 introduces us at once to three important issues that arise when using Gini indexes with zemstvo censuses.

PER CAPITA OR PER HOUSEHOLD?

For prerevolutionary Russia, it is rarely possible to find per-capita data about peasants. It is rarely worth trying to find them, since the household was the basic unit of both consumption and production and, until the Stolypin reforms of 1906-1911, held legal title to land and other productive assets. For one asset, own plowland, and for one census, 1900, the sources underlying Table 2 enable us to see how much per capita measurement deflates the Gini index. Compare column 3 with column 4 and column 6 with column 7. (Table 3 permits the same kind of comparison for the districts of Poltava Province.) This deflation is just what we would expect since, in the traditional Russian village, the most

Table 3. Distribution of Own Plowland Poltava Province, 1900
All Values Reported

District (1)	Total dvory (2)	Population (3)	Gini (per dvor) (4)	Gini (per capita) (5)	Column 4 minus Column 5 (6)
A. Unprivileged Households Holding 0-50 des.					
Gadiach'	23,272	138,601	.564 (12)	.490 (12)	.074
Khorol	27,099	165,722	.603 (9)	.531 (10)	.072
Kobeliaki	34,840	206,694	.664 (2)	.611 (2)	.053
Konstantinograd	34,919	221,874	.521 (15)	.434 (15)	.087
Kremenchug	29,408	173,205	.663 (3)	.608 (3)	.056
Lokhvitsa	26,145	145,289	.584 (11)	.530 (11)	.053
Lubny	21,261	128,369	.627 (6)	.555 (7)	.072
Mirgorod	26,181	150,212	.629 (5)	.565 (6)	.063
Periaslavl'	32,707	182,317	.596 (10)	.542 (8)	.054
Piriatin	26,870	160,523	.529 (14)	.470 (14)	.059
Poltava	29,409	167,748	.662 (4)	.605 (4)	.056
Priluki	32,640	185,796	.538 (13)	.486 (13)	.051
Romny	29,601	175,734	.608 (8)	.532 (9)	.075
Zen'kov	24,896	135,662	.681 (1)	.627 (1)	.054
Zolotonoshna	39,585	224,325	.621 (7)	.572 (5)	.049
Province	438,833	2,562,071	.608 (—)	.545 (—)	.063
B. All Unprivileged Households					
Gadiach'	23,351	139,517	.587 (13)	.514 (13)	.074
Khorol	27,259	167,384	.649 (8)	.581 (8)	.068
Kobeliaki	35,144	209,406	.712 (1)	.663 (1)	.049
Konstantinograd	35,364	226,513	.614 (12)	.538 (12)	.076
Kremenchug	29,593	174,943	.700 (4)	.647 (4)	.053
Lokhvitsa	26,248	146,256	.615 (11)	.562 (11)	.052
Lubny	21,424	130,190	.667 (5)	.597 (6)	.070
Mirgorod	26,300	151,457	.653 (6)	.589 (7)	.063
Periaslavl'	32,824	183,359	.616 (10)	.563 (10)	.053
Piriatin	26,960	161,373	.561 (14)	.503 (15)	.057
Poltava	29,593	169,529	.710 (3)	.657 (2)	.053
Priluki	32,721	186,508	.559 (15)	.508 (14)	.050
Romny	29,715	176,887	.638 (9)	.566 (9)	.072
Zen'kov	25,021	136,816	.710 (2)	.657 (3)	.053
Zolotonoshna	39,706	225,414	.649 (7)	.602 (5)	.047
Province	441,223	2,585,552	.647 (—)	.587 (—)	.060

Note: The rank of each district is shown in parentheses to the right of the corresponding Gini index.

Source: Poltavskoe gubernskoe zemstvo, Statisticheskoe biuro, *Obezpechenost' pakhatnoi zemleiu khoziaiastv Poltavskoi gubernii: Dopolnenie k "Materialam podvornoi perepisi 1900 goda." Itogi po gubernii.* (Poltava, 1907), pp. 26-31.

important single productive asset was adult laborers. A populous household was almost always more prosperous than its neighbors, whatever assset is used to measure prosperity and even if prosperity is measured per capita. Conversely, a fragmentary household—say, a single adult male, and his elderly mother and his two children—was almost always a pauper household.

STATUS

In prerevolutionary Russia, statistics were usually presented in terms of status groups—"estates of the realm," or *sosloviia*. Table 2 also shows the importance of maintaining uniform status groups, although this importance diminishes if (as with columns 5-7) one imposes a ceiling so as to limit consideration to small holders—peasant households and those akin to them. Conversely, a Gini index covering all status-groups and with no ceiling will, for prerevolutionary Russia, be drastically skewed by the estates, some of them vast latafundia,[14] of the nobility. Such an index would tell us something about the overall distribution of landed property—something we already knew very well—but nothing about relationships within the peasant communities.

The inclusion in our calculation of a mere 528 privileged households (essentially, the nobility or *dvorianstvo*) increases the value of the Gini index reckoned per household by .125 compared to the value for "unprivileged" households (a category essentially coextensive with the peasantry); the increase per capita is even greater. But notice also the very high values for cossacks; they serve to remind us that rassloenie was a function not only of the development of capitalism, but also of centuries-old patterns of land allocation. Cossack communities tended to practice hereditary household tenure and to have a high proportion of pauper households, the descendents of the *golytba*, and so were more likely to have a larger proportion of households at both extremes of the spectrum than were communities of ex-serfs or former state peasants.[15]

THE PROBLEM OF CEILING

Whatever his ancestry or *soslovie*, the owner of 1000 des. of land was not, either socially or economically, a peasant; in the left-bank Ukraine, he probably did not even live in the village, but in a separate farmstead (*khutor*). However, the zemstvo statistician would usually include such a person with his brethen by status. It is desirable and legitimate to segregate holders (or sowers) of more than 50 des., so as to tabulate *real* peasants only.[16] To do so presents problems of estimation (discussed below) and also problems of comparison. If, in a particular canton, twelve households acquired enough land between two censuses to pass over into the 50+ category, and if the distribution of land among the other households remained much the same, then the Gini index for the second census (reckoned for holders of 0-50 des. only) will be lower, even though the extent of rassloenie will be higher. One can get around this problem by calculating two Ginis: one for households holding 0-50 des., and another for all unprivileged households.

ESTIMATION

To calculate the Gini index, we need to know the absolute number of households (or persons) in each grouping and the absolute amount of assets held by each grouping. The Gini indexes in Tables 2 and 3 are based on absolute values reported in the sources. Sources of that kind, however, are rare. As a rule, in zemstvo census publications, absolute asset values are not stated, and we must estimate Y-values using the size of intervals. We know that in 1900, 118 households in Karlovka Canton held between 2 and 3 des. of plowland. What was the total area held by these households? We must assume that the mid-point of the interval is the mean, multiply the population (118) by the mid-point (2.5) and so estimate the area as 295 des. This kind of estimation enjoys the blessing of both Lenin and Blalock[17] and works well so long as the interval is narrow. But if the interval is "15-50 des.," it is silly to suppose that the true mean is 32.5. And if the top interval is open-ended (50+ des.), there is no mid-point and no basis for an estimate. For the distribution of plowland and sown area, Y-values can be estimated as follows: taking the mid-point of each interval as the mean, estimate the total holdings of all intervals through 15 des., sum these estimated values, subtract this sum from the reported total for all intervals, and then subtract the reported holdings of households with more than 50 des. The residue is the estimated total held by households holding 15-50 des. and, divided by the number of such households, produces an estimated mean for 15-50 des. interval.

There is worse to tell. For most cantons and districts, this estimation procedure yields a gratifying result of 18-20 des. as the mean for households holding 15-50 des. For some, however, the result is impossible (9.7 des.) or even negative. The reason is not far to seek. The true means (which we can ascertain only for the category "own plowland" and only for the census of 1900) fall below the mid-point, and fall further in the upper intervals. Table 4 shows that, in the 20 cantons of Konstantinograd District, for the 6 intervals between 1-2 des. and 15-50 des, there are only 9 instances out of 240 where the reported mean equals or surpasses the midpoint; in the 15 districts of Poltava Province, there are none.

Table 4. Reported Means, Household Holdings of Plowland, 1900

	Groupings						
	0-1 des.	1-2 des.	2-3 des.	3-6 des.	6-9 des.	9-15 des.	15-50 des.
	Midpoints						
	0.5	1.5	2.5	4.5	7.5	12.0	32.5
	A. Cantons of Konstantinograd District						
Belukhovka	0.538	1.476	2.303	4.124	7.377	10.939	21.789
Berestoven'ka	0.000	1.576	2.238	4.188	7.533	11.576	20.981
Dar Nadezhda	0.593	1.400	2.438	4.079	7.210	11.090	26.946
Ganeboe	0.733	1.422	2.492	3.955	6.921	11.985	24.250
Karlovka	0.565	1.493	2.203	4.044	7.170	11.156	21.179
Kegichevka	0.667	1.482	2.330	4.045	7.056	11.095	25.319
Mashevka	0.509	1.450	2.476	4.142	6.920	10.900	26.184
Natal'ino	0.683	1.387	2.315	3.996	7.236	11.118	23.245
Nekhvoroshcha	0.489	1.646	2.655	4.418	6.982	10.607	23.641
Novo-Tagamlik*	0.523	1.297	2.297	4.103	7.345	11.124	26.749
Paraskoveia	0.500	1.403	2.512	4.223	7.026	10.833	23.647
Peschanka	0.667	1.375	2.345	4.295	7.272	11.038	21.797
Petrovka	0.747	1.599	2.376	3.957	6.938	10.452	21.429
Riasskoe	0.698	1.257	2.429	4.325	7.083	11.200	24.688
Runovshchina	0.686	1.500	2.191	4.194	7.056	11.285	23.644
Staroverovka	0.000	0.000	2.550	4.940	7.494	11.388	19.323
Tagamlik	0.556	1.355	2.220	4.025	7.124	11.038	23.031
Velikie Buchki	0.593	1.402	2.393	4.006	7.353	11.729	23.153
Zapechilovka	0.655	1.413	2.290	3.942	6.879	11.398	25.390
Zhirkovka	0.600	1.457	2.386	4.131	7.148	10.833	25.490
	B. Districts of Poltava Province						
Gadiach'	0.540	1.342	2.287	4.033	7.012	11.043	21.951
Khorol	0.521	1.308	2.268	3.957	7.013	11.260	23.035
Kobeliaki	0.539	1.318	2.300	4.097	7.064	11.201	24.075
Konstantinograd	0.615	1.443	2.363	4.152	7.164	11.223	24.220
Kremenchug	0.519	1.288	2.239	3.999	7.045	11.182	23.346
Lokhvitsa	0.546	1.363	2.322	3.991	7.013	11.086	22.339
Lubny	0.550	1.373	2.313	4.038	7.136	11.282	23.812
Mirgorod	0.522	1.307	2.281	3.972	7.021	11.129	23.113
Periaslavl'	0.555	1.373	2.318	4.062	7.086	11.178	23.324
Piriatin	0.581	1.345	2.240	3.889	6.910	10.945	22.379
Poltava	0.528	1.298	2.264	4.012	7.095	11.144	23.296
Priluki	0.582	1.377	2.301	3.956	7.015	11.002	21.965
Romny	0.522	1.354	2.288	4.027	6.989	10.961	22.689
Zen'kov	0.513	1.304	2.263	3.986	6.986	11.047	22.973
Zolotonoshna	0.546	1.340	2.290	3.977	6.977	11.068	22.769

Note: *Malo-Pereshchipina included with Novo-Tagamlik.
Sources: Poltavskoe gubernskoe zemstvo, Statisticheskoe biuro, *Obezpechennost' pakhatnoi zemleiu khoziaiastv Poltavskoi gubernii: Dopolnenie k "Materialam podvornoi perepisi 1900 goda." Konstantinogradskii uezd* (Poltava, 1907), pp. 2-43; Poltavskoe gubernskoe zemstvo, Statisticheskoe biuro, *Obezpechenost' pakhatnoi zemleiu khoziaistv Poltavskoi gubernii. Dopolnenie k "Materialam podvornoi perepisi 1900 goda." Itogi po gubernii.* (Poltava, 1907), pp. 26-31.

Table 5. Errors of Estimation in Tables 7-9
Absolute Values of Error as Percentage of Reported Asset Totals

Asset	Mean	Minimum	Maximum
A. Konstantinograd District			
Own Plowland, Households with 0-50 des.	3.6	0.0	11.6
Own Plowland, All Households	3.0	0.0	8.9
Sown Area, Households Sowing 0-50 des.	4.0	0.3	11.8
Sown Area, All Households	3.6	0.2	11.7
Draft Animals, Households Sowing 0-50 des.	3.4	0.4	9.9
Draft Animals, All Households	5.7	0.6	12.1
B. Poltava Province			
Own Plowland, Households with 0-50 des.	2.2	0.6	4.6
Own Plowland, All Households	1.9	0.6	4.3
Sown Area, Households Sowing 0-50 des.	2.2	0.1	5.6
Sown Area, All Households	2.1	0.0	5.4
Draft Animals, Households Sowing 0-50 des.	1.1	0.0	3.2
Draft Animals, All Households	1.7	0.3	5.7

Sources: Poltavskoe gubernskoe zemstvo, Statisticheskii biuro, *Materialy podvornoi perepisi Poltavskoi gubernii 1900 goda. Konstantinogradskii uezd* (Poltava, 1906), pp. 412-413; and Poltavskoe gubernskoe zemstvo, Statisticheskii biuro, *Materialy podvornoi perepisi Poltavskoi guvernii 1900 goda. Poltavskii uezd* (Poltava, 1906), pp. 270-273, supplemented with data on households sowing 0-50 des. from pp. 2-151. Poltavskoe gubernskoe zemstvo, Statisticheskii biuro, *Materialy podvornoi perepisi Poltavskoi gubernii 1900 goda. Itogi po gubernii* (Poltava, 1907), pp. 74-89.

In effect, then, the estimation procedure leeches assets from the upper intervals to the lower, smoothing out the distribution of assets and depressing the value of the Gini index. Calculation of the Gini index requires that the groupings be arrayed in ascending order of the $Y:P$ ratio and is impossible if a group has a lower $Y:P$ ratio than any of the groups below it. It is, therefore, necessary to determine the estimated mean of the *aggregate* for households in the 15-50 interval and impose that aggregate mean on all cantons (or districts). For example, the district-level estimated mean for the group "households holding 15-50 des." of 19.965 was used to calculate the Gini indexes for own plowland for the cantons of Konstantinograd District in Tables 7 and 8.[18]

This estimation procedure generates errors, the magnitude of which can be determined by subtracting the sum of estimated asset values from the reported total of the asset for the district or canton in question. The range of these errors for the Gini indexes in Tables 7-9 is shown in Table 5. As a rule, the error of estimation is tolerably small, but on occasion it is more than 10% of the reported total. There is no correlation between the magnitude of the error and the value of the Gini index or the pattern of distribution.

The estimation procedures spelled out so far require a source that states the absolute value of the total holdings in the top (here 50+ des.) interval. If this information is lacking, then a cruder estimation procedure is forced upon us. We must subtract the sum of estimated holdings of households with 15 or fewer des. from the reported total of all holdings and take the residue as the estimate of holdings of households with 15 or more des. This procedure has two major shortcomings. The possibility of imposing a ceiling so as to exclude the few nominally "peasant" households with more than 50 des. is precluded, and "15+ des." becomes the top interval. More important, Gini indexes derived by this estimating procedure deviate sharply from those we might derive from absolute reported values.

Table 6 illustrates the effects of estimation.[19] It is based on the data of the sources for Tables 2 and 3. Column 2 shows Gini indexes derived from absolute reported values. In column 3, three intervals are collapsed into one, to correspond to the intervals found in other Poltava census publications, such as those underlying Tables 7-11. In column 5, the preferred estimation procedure outlined above is applied: estimating the holdings of intervals up to 15 des. by taking the midpoint of each interval as the mean, adding to the sum of these estimated values the reported total of holdings of households with 50+ des., and subtracting this sum from the reported total of own plowland to estimate the holdings of households in the 15-50 des. interval. Then, in column 7, we proceed as if the holdings of the 50+ des. interval were not reported: estimating the holdings of intervals up to 15 des. as before and subtracting the sum of these estimates from the reported total of own plowland to estimate the holdings of all households with more than 15 des.

It is clear that the first estimation procedure is satisfactory and that the second is not. On the district level, the estimated Ginis in column 5 are consistently about .035 below the true Ginis, but the range of these shortfalls is small (.008), and the rank order of the Ginis in column 5 is essentially the same as in column 2. In column 7, the rank order is still fairly close to column 2—only two scores are out of place by more than one rank—but the range of the differences between column 2 and column 7 is a substantial .072. On the canton level, where the number of households does not exceed 3,000, the distribution of plowland can be radically skewed by a few rich households, as can be seen from the fact that the range of "true" Ginis (based on reported asset values) is more than three times greater for the cantons of Konstantinograd District than for the districts of Poltava Province. Given this range in the Gini indexes, the range of the shortfalls[20] registered in column 6 is acceptable, and only two of the 20 cantons in column 5 depart from their true rank order. In column 7, however, the range of deviations from column 2 is an intolerable .282 (even excluding the outliers of Ganeboe and Staroverovka, it is .177), and the correspondence of rank orders is even worse."[21]

Table 6. Gini Indexes for Distribution of Own Plowland Using Reported and Estimated Y-Values

Canton or District	Total dvory (1)	Reported Values, All Intervals (2)	Reported Values, Nine Intervals (3)	Column 2 Less Column 3 (4)	Estimated Values, Nine Intervals (5)	Column 2 Less Column 5 (6)	Estimated Values, Eight Intervals (7)	Column 2 Less Column 7 (8)
A. Konstantinograd District, 1900, All Unprivileged Dvory								
Belukhovka	1337	.525 (11)	.512 (11)	.013	.499 (11)	.026	.453 (11)	.072
Berestoven'ka	1274	.379 (17)	.374 (14)	.005	.361 (17)	.019	.424 (14)	-.045
Dar Nadezhda	2615	.695 (4)	.694 (4)	.001	.677 (4)	.018	.581 (5)	.114
Ganeboe	877	.670 (5)	.668 (5)	.002	.649 (5)	.021	.522 (10)	.149
Karlovka	2136	.389 (15)	.374 (15)	.015	.362 (16)	.027	.389 (17)	.000
Kegichevka	1244	.637 (6)	.634 (6)	.002	.608 (6)	.029	.550 (8)	.087
Mashevka	1335	.622 (7)	.617 (7)	.006	.592 (7)	.030	.576 (7)	.046
Natal'ino	1337	.758 (2)	.756 (2)	.002	.746 (2)	.012	.631 (3)	.126
Nekhvoroshcha	2365	.389 (14)	.369 (16)	.020	.377 (14)	.013	.386 (18)	.003
Novo–Tagamlik*	2853	.828 (1)	.827 (1)	.001	.815 (1)	.013	.760 (1)	.067
Paraskoveia	1368	.383 (16)	.368 (17)	.016	.366 (15)	.017	.375 (19)	.008
Peschanka	1315	.366 (18)	.363 (18)	.003	.356 (18)	.010	.417 (15)	-.051
Petrovka	1620	.397 (13)	.379 (13)	.018	.386 (13)	.011	.417 (16)	-.020
Riasskoe	1134	.358 (19)	.337 (19)	.022	.328 (19)	.030	.364 (20)	-.006
Runovshchina	2397	.480 (12)	.473 (12)	.007	.452 (12)	.027	.447 (13)	.033
Staroverovka	1216	.314 (20)	.313 (20)	.001	.328 (20)	-.014	.447 (12)	-.133
Tagamlik	1300	.702 (3)	.699 (3)	.004	.680 (3)	.023	.651 (2)	.052
Velikie Buchki	2401	.614 (8)	.612 (8)	.002	.592 (8)	.022	.580 (6)	.034
Zapechilovka	2613	.578 (10)	.572 (10)	.006	.540 (10)	.039	.539 (9)	.039
Zhirkovka	1626	.592 (9)	.587 (9)	.005	.561 (9)	.031	.585 (4)	.007

B. Poltava Province, 1900, All Unprivileged *Dvory*

Gadiach'	23,351	.587 (13)	.581 (13)	.006	.552 (13)	.036	.567 (12)	.021
Khorol	27,259	.649 (8)	.643 (8)	.006	.610 (8)	.038	.600 (9)	.049
Kobeliaki	35,144	.712 (1)	.709 (1)	.003	.680 (1)	.033	.660 (2)	.052
Konstantinograd	35,364	.614 (12)	.609 (11)	.005	.581 (11)	.034	.521 (15)	.093
Kremenchug	29,593	.700 (4)	.696 (4)	.004	.665 (4)	.035	.659 (4)	.042
Lokhvitsa	26,248	.615 (11)	.609 (12)	.006	.583 (10)	.032	.586 (11)	.029
Lubny	21,424	.667 (5)	.663 (5)	.004	.632 (5)	.036	.624 (6)	.043
Mirgorod	26,300	.653 (6)	.648 (6)	.005	.614 (7)	.039	.625 (5)	.027
Periaslavl'	32,824	.616 (10)	.611 (10)	.005	.579 (12)	.038	.596 (10)	.021
Piriatin	26,960	.561 (14)	.552 (14)	.008	.521 (15)	.040	.525 (14)	.036
Poltava	29,593	.710 (3)	.706 (3)	.004	.678 (3)	.032	.659 (3)	.051
Priluki	32,721	.559 (15)	.550 (15)	.008	.526 (14)	.032	.538 (13)	.021
Romny	29,715	.638 (9)	.632 (9)	.006	.605 (9)	.033	.608 (8)	.030
Zen'kov	25,021	.710 (2)	.707 (2)	.003	.679 (2)	.031	.680 (1)	.030
Zolotonoshna	39,706	.649 (7)	.643 (7)	.006	.619 (6)	.030	.621 (7)	.028

Note: *Malo-Pereshchepina combined with Novo-Tagamlik; data for Konstantinograd in part B. includes district town. The rank of each canton or district is shown in parentheses to the right of the corresponding Gini index.

Sources: Poltavskoe gubernskoe zemstvo, Statisticheskii biuro, *Obezpechennost' pakhatnoi zemleiu khoziaiastv Poltavskoi gubernii: Dopolnenie k "Materialam podvornoi perepisi 1900 goda. "Konstantinogradskii uezd* (Poltava, 1907), pp. 26-31; Poltavskoe gubernskoe zemstvo, Statisticheskoe biuro, *Obezpechennost' pakhatnoi zemleiu khoziaistv Poltavskoi gubernii. Dopolnenie k "Materialam podvornoi perepisi 1900 goda." Itogi po gubernii.* (Poltava, 1907), pp. 26-31.

It follows from these examples that taking interval midpoints as means to estimate Y-values yields results that are adequate for further statistical analysis provided the absolute value of the holdings of the top interval can be incorporated. If that value is not reported, the Gini indexes one can generate by estimation may, provided the sample is large, be of the some value for illustrative purposes but should not be peddled to the public as sound goods.

There is a further question concerning estimation. The numerator of each Y-value is the estimated total of assets for the group. It would seem that the denominator should be the reported total of assets for all groups, just as it is when we have reported absolute assets values for each group. It can be shown, however, that we achieve a more accurate Gini index using the sum of *estimated* asset values as the denominator. Such Ginis correspond more closely to "true Ginis" than do Ginis calculated in the same way using the reported total of asset values. The latter do not correlate so closely to the "true" Ginis and are more likely to deviate further from them. Most important, the mean of the absolute values of the discrepancies between "true" Ginis and Ginis based on the sum of estimated asset values is always smaller than it is for Ginis using the sum of reported values. Hence, throughout this paper, I use the sum of estimated asset values to calculate each Y.

To summarize, estimation generates Gini indexes that deviate from Ginis based on reported values (values which are rarely reported in zemstvo publications) and, because of the "leeching" process previously mentioned, are almost always lower. However, the depressing effect is fairly uniform so long as one can draw on absolute values for the top interval. Estimation depresses the absolute value of the Gini index, but does not much distort the relative position of the territorial units in an array.

DISTRIBUTION OF WHAT?

We can measure the distribution of plowland, of sown area or of cattle. Distribution of "own plowland" (i.e., plowland on allotments and on purchased land) is the asset for which information is most fully available (perhaps also most reliably available, because the primary purpose of the zemstvo census was fiscal). This measure has the disadvantage that peasants' transactions in land were inhibited by statute and by the commune; 60.6% of the households in Konstantinograd District held land on communal tenure.[22] It is a reasonably satisfactory measure of productive capacity for the middle peasants, who constituted a majority, but not for those households at the extremes. Households owning little land responded either by renting out their own land and seeking wage work or by supplementing the little they had with rented land.

Sown area per household is a better measure of productive capacity, particularly within a compact area such as a province, and is sensitive to

Table 7. Gini Indexes, 1900, Unprivileged Households Holding (or Sowing) 0-50 des.—Konstantinograd and Poltava Districts

Canton	Total dvory	Own Plowland	Sown Area	Draft Animals
A. Konstantinograd District				
Belukhovka	1332	.408 (31)	.310 (40)	.342 (39)
Berestoven'ka	1270	.356 (34)	.381 (34)	.403 (31)
Dar Nadezhda	2510	.520 (23)	.551 (26)	.397 (34)
Ganeboe	840	.430 (30)	.386 (33)	.337 (40)
Karlovka	2121	.352 (35)	.350 (39)	.373 (37)
Kegichevka	1220	.451 (28)	.405 (29)	.396 (35)
Mashevka	1320	.490 (27)	.447 (25)	.479 (19)
Natal'ino	1312	.553 (19)	.462 (21)	.471 (22)
Nekhvoroshcha	2342	.329 (38)	.391 (31)	.466 (25)
Novo-Tagamlik*	2776	.718 (3)	.651 (3)	.592 (7)
Paraskoveia	1365	.341 (37)	.395 (30)	.402 (32)
Peschanka	1312	.351 (36)	.359 (38)	.354 (38)
Petrovka	1617	.382 (32)	.381 (35)	.433 (28)
Riasskoe	1131	.326 (39)	.374 (36)	.427 (29)
Runovshchina	2372	.364 (33)	.387 (32)	.401 (33)
Staroverovka	1212	.325 (40)	.359 (37)	.379 (36)
Tagamlik	1274	.576 (17)	.468 (20)	.436 (27)
Velikie Buchki	2335	.496 (26)	.459 (23)	.414 (30)
Zapechilovka	2588	.447 (29)	.420 (28)	.440 (26)
Zhirkovka	1606	.497 (25)	.459 (22)	.466 (24)
B. Poltava District				
Bairak	1537	.648 (7)	.505 (15)	.533 (12)
Baliasnoe	1189	.602 (14)	.513 (12)	.536 (10)
Brateshki	1313	.515 (24)	.423 (27)	.489 (16)
Chutovo	1856	.542 (20)	.474 (18)	.471 (21)
Demidovka	1089	.531 (22)	.454 (24)	.483 (17)
Dikan'ka	1721	.647 (8)	.606 (6)	.603 (6)
Elizavetino	1320	.608 (12)	.490 (17)	.493 (15)
Machekhi	1962	.620 (10)	.592 (7)	.608 (5)
Nikol'skaia	1626	.748 (2)	.702 (2)	.561 (9)
Pervozvanovka	1186	.600 (15)	.468 (19)	.471 (22)
Peschanoe	1258	.533 (21)	.496 (16)	.494 (14)
Plosskoe	883	.558 (18)	.512 (13)	.523 (13)
Poltava	654	.760 (1)	.755 (1)	.695 (1)
Reshetilovka	2670	.603 (13)	.588 (8)	.634 (4)
Runovshchina	1859	.597 (16)	.548 (11)	.534 (11)
Starye Senzhary	1314	.662 (4)	.633 (4)	.588 (8)
Suprunovka	1655	.626 (9)	.566 (9)	.641 (3)
Takhtaulovka	1434	.657 (6)	.615 (5)	.660 (2)
Vasil'evka	1292	.620 (11)	.509 (14)	.479 (18)
Vasil'tsy	1457	.661 (5)	.553 (10)	.478 (20)

Notes: The rank of each canton is shown in parentheses to the right of the corresponding Gini index.
*Malo-Pereshchepina included with Novo-Tagamlik.
Sources: Poltavskoe gubernskoe zemstvo, Statisticheskii biuro, *Materialy podvornoi perepisi Poltavskoi gubernii 1900 goda. Konstantinogradskii uezd* (Poltava, 1906), pp. 412-413; and Poltavskoe gubernskoe zemstvo, Statisticheskii biuro, *Materialy podvornoi perepisi Poltavskoi gubernii 1900 goda. Poltavskii uezd* (Poltava, 1906), pp. 270-273, supplemented with data on households sowing 0-50 des. from pp. 2-151.

Table 8. Gini Indexes, 1900
All Unprivileged Households, Konstantinograd and Poltava Districts

Canton	Total dvory	Own Plowland	Sown Area	Draft Animals
A. Konstantinograd District				
Belukhovka	1336	.498 (31)	.394 (34)	.356 (40)
Berestoven'ka	1271	.359 (36)	.381 (36)	.434 (34)
Dar Nadezhda	2622	.679 (10)	.551 (18)	.441 (30)
Ganeboe	877	.652 (19)	.497 (26)	.382 (38)
Karlovka	2123	.357 (37)	.350 (40)	.380 (39)
Kegichevka	1242	.608 (23)	.522 (21)	.436 (32)
Mashevka	1335	.592 (24)	.499 (25)	.506 (16)
Natal'ino	1337	.746 (5)	.582 (12)	.500 (19)
Nekhvoroshcha	2353	.387 (33)	.406 (32)	.475 (25)
Novo-Tagamlik*	2841	.814 (1)	.714 (3)	.619 (6)
Paraskoveia	1366	.365 (35)	.402 (33)	.426 (36)
Peschanka	1313	.355 (38)	.362 (38)	.384 (37)
Petrovka	1618	.385 (34)	.384 (35)	.447 (29)
Riasskoe	1131	.326 (39)	.374 (37)	.438 (31)
Runovshchina	2395	.452 (32)	.422 (31)	.434 (33)
Staroverovka	1212	.325 (40)	.359 (39)	.429 (35)
Tagamlik	1300	.682 (8)	.556 (15)	.462 (27)
Velikie Buchki	2399	.591 (25)	.513 (22)	.456 (28)
Zapechilovka	2612	.539 (29)	.468 (28)	.470 (26)
Zhirkovka	1619	.547 (28)	.491 (27)	.492 (23)
B. Poltava District				
Bairak	1550	.735 (6)	.555 (16)	.553 (12)
Baliasnoe	1196	.653 (18)	.539 (19)	.555 (11)
Brateshki	1319	.536 (30)	.427 (30)	.504 (17)
Chutovo	1865	.665 (14)	.565 (14)	.485 (24)
Demidovka	1092	.549 (27)	.468 (29)	.493 (21)
Dikan'ka	1726	.679 (9)	.632 (5)	.607 (7)
Elizavetino	1333	.675 (11)	.533 (20)	.512 (14)
Machekhi	1978	.663 (16)	.601 (8)	.621 (5)
Nikol'skaia	1652	.808 (2)	.740 (2)	.583 (9)
Pervozvanovka	1194	.670 (13)	.506 (23)	.492 (22)
Peschanoe	1261	.554 (26)	.505 (24)	.507 (15)
Plosskoe	896	.643 (20)	.579 (13)	.543 (13)
Poltava	655	.767 (4)	.755 (1)	.706 (1)
Reshetilovka	2681	.622 (22)	.591 (9)	.644 (4)
Runovshchina	1879	.665 (15)	.588 (10)	.560 (10)
Starye Senzhary	1319	.690 (7)	.643 (4)	.597 (8)
Suprunovka	1656	.629 (21)	.583 (11)	.648 (3)
Takhtaulovka	1435	.663 (17)	.621 (7)	.670 (2)
Vasil'evka	1311	.773 (3)	.631 (6)	.502 (18)
Vasil'tsy	1461	.672 (12)	.553 (17)	.498 (20)

Notes: The rank of each canton is shown in parentheses to the right of the corresponding Gini index.
*Malo-Pereshchepina is included with Novo-Tagamlik.

Sources: Poltavskoe gubernskoe zemstvo, Statisticheskii biuro, *Materialy podvornoi perepisi Poltavskoi gubernii 1900 goda. Konstantinogradskii uezd* (Poltava, 1906), pp. 412-413; and Poltavskoe gubernskoe zemstvo, Statisticheskii biuro, *Materialy podvornoi perepsi Poltavskoi gubernii 1900 goda. Poltavskii uezd* (Poltava, 1906), pp. 270-273, supplemented with data on households sowing 0-50 des. from pp. 2-151.

Table 9. Gini Indexes, Poltava Province, 1900

A. Unprivileged Households Sowing 0-50 des.

District	Total dvory	Own Plowland	Sown Area	Draft Animals
Gadiach'	23334	.527 (12)	.539 (11)	.538 (6)
Khorol	27182	.559 (9)	.499 (13)	.523 (11)
Kobeliaki	35026	.621 (4)	.550 (10)	.576 (2)
Konstantinograd	35119	.472 (15)	.439 (15)	.454 (14)
Kremenchug	29581	.623 (2)	.556 (7)	.571 (3)
Lokhvitsa	26213	.549 (11)	.580 (3)	.526 (10)
Lubny	21366	.583 (7)	.570 (5)	.534 (8)
Mirgorod	26256	.586 (6)	.556 (8)	.567 (5)
Periaslavl'	32759	.555 (10)	.581 (2)	.496 (12)
Piriatin	26929	.487 (14)	.453 (14)	.447 (15)
Poltava	29504	.621 (3)	.558 (6)	.568 (4)
Priluki	32695	.504 (13)	.509 (12)	.464 (13)
Romny	29686	.572 (8)	.579 (4)	.535 (7)
Zen'kov	24975	.645 (1)	.647 (1)	.610 (1)
Zolotonoshna	39646	.588 (5)	.551 (9)	.534 (9)

B. All Unprivileged Households

District	Total dvory	Own Plowland	Sown Area	Draft Animals	Allotments (1905)
Gadiach'	23351	.552 (13)	.547 (11)	.546 (6)	.132 (14)
Khorol	27259	.612 (8)	.532 (12)	.534 (10)	.246 (10)
Kobeliaki	35144	.680 (1)	.571 (8)	.584 (2)	.241 (11)
Konstantinograd	35371	.581 (11)	.499 (14)	.471 (13)	.332 (4)
Kremenchug	29645	.666 (4)	.571 (7)	.580 (3)	.286 (8)
Lokhvitsa	26248	.583 (10)	.595 (2)	.533 (11)	.130 (15)
Lubny	21424	.632 (5)	.589 (5)	.546 (7)	.287 (7)
Mirgorod	26300	.614 (7)	.570 (9)	.576 (5)	256 (9)
Periaslavl'	32783	.579 (12)	.592 (3)	.506 (12)	.425 (1)
Piriatin	26961	.521 (15)	.470 (15)	.456 (15)	.311 (6)
Poltava	29593	.678 (3)	.590 (4)	.578 (4)	.374 (3)
Priluki	32721	.526 (14)	.519 (13)	.470 (14)	.201 (13)
Romny	29717	.605 (9)	.588 (6)	.540 (9)	.222 (12)
Zen'kov	25021	.679 (2)	.661 (1)	.618 (1)	.386 (2)
Zolotonoshna	39706	.619 (6)	.567 (10)	.544 (8)	.330 (5)

Note: The rank of each district is shown in parentheses to the right of the corresponding Gini index.
Sources: Poltavskoe gubernskoe zemstvo, Statisticheskii biuro, *Materialy podvornoi perepisi Poltavskoi gubernii 1900 goda. Itogi po gubernii* (Poltava, 1907), pp. 74-89. Data on allotments in 1905 from Tsentral'nyi statisticheskii komitet, *Statistika zemlevladenia 1905 g.,* fasc. 48: *Poltavskaia guberniia* (St. Petersburg, 1907), p. 56.

economic conjuncture, but it does not register the terms of trade of nonallotment land—for example, *golodnaia arenda* ("hunger rental"), whereby, in order to meet subsistence needs through the exploitation of allotment and rented land a household would pay more in rent for additional land than the value of the product it could expect to obtain from that land. In Konstantinograd and Poltava districts, particularly onerous labor-rental (*otrabotka*) arrangements were common, whereby a household would cultivate as much as three des. of demense land, using its own tools and animals, in return for each des. for its own cultivation.[23] Finally, draft animals have the advantage of being a relatively liquid asset, compared to plowland; indeed, poor peasants would often sell their horse after the harvest and buy a new one in the spring.[24] The beasts have the disadvantage of being gross units; if a horse dies just before the census-taker calls, the household is thrown into another category.

The distribution of each kind of asset is a reflection of rassloenie, and each asset has something to recommend it. Hence, Tables 7, 8 and 9 show the Gini index for plowland, sown area and draft animals in 1900.[25] We may recall at this point, however, that we turned to the Gini index for order and for efficiency of analysis. If we must, reckoning only with "unpriviledged households," compute the Gini index for two categories of household (those with 0-50 des. and all households), and three kinds of asset, we wind up with six measures of rassloenie and have to ask if we are better off than those who never heard of Sig. Gini. And our problems are compounded, as we shall see, when we attempt to compare the results of two or more censuses, as we must do to establish the extent to which rassloenie increased over time.

THE PROBLEM OF COMPARABILITY

Within the limits of a single census, comparisons among the Ginis for particular districts or cantons may be vitiated by differences in the composition of the peasantry and hence by differences in asset-distribution that date back to the era of serfdom. For example, Table 8 shows a Gini index for the distribution of own plowland in Staroverovka Canton of .325 and of .591 in Velikie Buchki Canton. The former canton consisted almost entirely of former state peasants, whereas cossacks comprised 16% of the households in the latter. The cossacks may have been better prepared to participate in capitalist agriculture than their neighbors were, but their capacity did not derive primarily from the initiative of cossacks alive in 1900.

It is comparisons over time for a particular canton, district, or province that will be most telling. Here problems of comparability obtrude themselves painfully. We know from Table 6 that the Gini index for distribution of own plowland among all peasant households of Konstantinongrad District in 1900 is .614. Using estimated asset values, as we must for other assets and other years and hence for making comparisons, the Gini becomes .581, as in Table 9. How does this Gini compare with those for 1888-1889 and 1910? For our convenience, the Poltava statisticians produced comparative tables for the censuses of the 1880s and 1900 and for those of 1900 and 1910. Turning to the former,[26] we obtain a Gini index for own plowland in Konstantinograd District in 1888-1889 of .484. Calculating from the data in *that* comparative table, however, and using the same estimating procedures as in our Table 6, we derive a Gini for 1900 of .576. Turning to the comparative table for 1900 and 1910, and using the grouping the arrangement of the data imposes on us (as in column 7 of Table 6)[27] we derive a Gini for Konstantinograd District of .566 for 1900 and .585 for 1910.[28]

We can say, then, that the Gini indexes for plowland reveal the increase in rassloenie that we would expect—more of an increase that we would expect for the period 1888/1889-1900 and less for the period 1900-1910. We cannot say much more than that because of the vagaries of our middle term, the index for 1900, and the peculiarities of the census materials for 1910. These vagaries and peculiarities create problems of comparability, which multiply when we turn from plowland to sown area and draft animals. Bear in mind that the Poltava zemstvo statisticians were punctillious; I have never found an arithmetical error in the tables they published. Bear also in mind that Poltava is the optimal case, because it is the only province in which the zemstvo conducted three censuses for all districts.

The basic problem is this: minor differences of classification and categorization from census to census, and even within a single census, impair our capacity to ascertain changes in the distribution of assets among peasant households. One problem is variation in the number of intervals. Table 6 shows that a mere alteration of the number of intervals, without any changes in the values computed, can change the value of a Gini index by as much as .022. Another problem is a failure to report the absolute value of the holdings of the top group (always 50+ des.). In that case, we cannot calculate the Gini index for holders or sowers of 0-50 des., and must simply assign the residue (reported total for all households less the estimated total for households with 0-15 des.) to all households holding 15 or more des.[29] This manipulation, as we have seen, tends to depress the value of the Gini index.

Further, the definition of "household" was subject to change. The term used by statisticans, *khoziaistvo,* denotes a free-standing economic unit, with the implication that servants and others might not be separately counted even if they maintained living quarters apart from their employers.[30] Finally, there are minor and usually unstated differences of categorization. For example, Jews were manifestly (and formally) "unprivileged," but they were not peasants, and might be included or excluded according to taste.[31]

Table 10. Canton-level Gini Indexes, 1880s-1910

	1880s		1900		1910	
	Total dvory	Gini Index	Total dvory	Gini Index	Total dvory	Gini Index
Konstantinograd District, Households with 0-50 des.						
Own Plowland	28,931	.434	33,855	.471	37,966	.515
Sown Area	29,334	.444	34,050	.441	37,966	.465
Draft Animals	N.D.	N.D.	34,050	.432	37,966	.478
Konstantinograd District, All Unprivileged Households						
Own Plowland	29,414	.484	34,302	.576	37,897	.606
Sown Area	29,414	N.D.	34,302	.499	37,897	.503
Draft Animals	29,414	.434	34,302	.467	37,897	.390
Poltava District, Households with 0-50 des.						
Own Plowland	24,902	.604	29,275	.624	34,478	.634
Sown Area	N.D.	N.D.	29,415	.559	34,478	.557
Draft Animals	N.D.	N.D.	29,415	.556	34,478	.628
Poltava District, All Unprivileged Households						
Own Plowland	25,070	.646	29,459	.679	34,402	.676
Sown Area	25,070	N.D.	29,503	.590	34,402	.543
Draft Animals	25,070	.542	29,503	.571	34,402	.469

Note: 1880s = 1883 for Poltava District, 1888/89 for Konstantinograd District.
Sources: Values for 1880s and 1900 as Table 7. Values for households with 0-50 des. in 1910 calculated like their canton-level counterparts in Table 11; values for all unprivileged households in 1910 calculated from Poltavskoe gubernskoe zemstvo, Statisticheskoe biuro, *Tret'ia podvorno-khoziaistvennaia perepis' v Poltavskoi gubernii 1910 g. Svod po gubernii* (Poltava, 1914), pp. 89-99, 232-239.

So it is that the reported total of unprivileged households in Konstantinograd District in 1900 (to return to that example) varies from one zemstvo publication to another. The source for Tables 7 and 8 states that in 1900 the number of unprivileged households (excluding the district town) was 34,302; elsewhere in the same volume, $N = 34,370$; the supplementary volume used as the source for my Tables 3 and 6 offers $N = 34,364$; the table just cited comparing the censuses of 1900 and 1910 states that $N = 34,370$ (again), but it is appended to a text that insists that $N = 34,899$. And the source for Table 9 has $N = 35,371$. One can say that the maximum discrepancy of 1069 households (3% of the smallest possible N) is nothing between friends and still lament the lack of fully comparable data for the three censuses.

Worse still, for the 1880s and for 1900, cows are included in the data for cattle per household; this was sensible because the cows, poor creatures, were frequently used as draft animals by peasants of this area. The corresponding data for 1910 covers only oxen and horses per household; there is no way one can factor the cows in for 1910 or factor them out for the earlier censuses. Worst of all is the problem of sown area in Poltava District. There is no data at all for the 1880s for this and five other districts. Further, the canton-level data for 1910 register only "households present" (*nalichnye khoziaiastva*). For most districts, the difference between "households present" and total households is not significant; for Poltava District, it is large, and the reliablity of the Gini index for sown area in 1910 is correspondingly small. Finally, for 1910, canton-level data (such as is used in Table 10) are available only for petty proprietors without regard to status, so that a small number of nobles, clergy and such, carefully excluded from our calculations for the 1880s and 1900 must be included in the indexes for 1910 in Tables 10 and 11.

What light do my data shed on the question with which I began this paper? It is Tables 10, 11, and 12 that are relevant here. In general, these tables show a development of rassloenie—and hence of capitalism in the peasant village— that is discernible, but sluggish. It is especially sluggish for the period 1900-1910, when we would expect a sharper rise, but we must recall that problems of comparability and estimation reach a crescendo with the census of 1910. This sluggishness finds expresion not only in the slow increase of the Gini indexes from census to census, but in this consideration: the intercensus correlations for the same kind of asset (for example, cattle) are stronger than the intracensus correlations among various assets. That is to say, the distribution of plowland in 1900 is a better predictor, for a given canton, of the distribution of plowland in 1910 than is the distribution of any other asset in the latter year. Hence there was no significant intensification of the concentration of all kinds of assets in the richer households. Further, the relatively high correlations between the Ginis for cattle and for sown area may derive from the persistence of labor rental, which was an adaptation of precapitalist, servile forms to postreform agriculture.

The pattern that emerges, it must be emphasized, is, to an extent we cannot determine, a product of the intractable characteristics of the data—the problems of estimation and comparability. The asset for which the rise in the Gini indexes is strongest and clearest is that for own plowland, which rises smoothly and shows an increase, among holders of 0-50 des., in 32 of 40 cantons between the 1880s and 1900 and in 27 of 40 between 1900 and 1910; for all unprivileged households, 35 cantons show an increase between the 1880s and 1900. Plowland is the asset for which the distribution would be least sensitive to economic and social conjuncture, but the asset for which our data are most reliable. The Gini index for sown area actually decreases between 1889 and 1900 in Konstantinograd District, probably for the reasons discussed above with regard to ceiling, and increases very modestly between 1900 and 1910. It does, however, increase in 18 of 20 cantons of that district between the latter two years. Intercensus comparisons of the distribution of sown area in the

Table 11. Gini Indexes, 1883-1910, Two Districts Holders or Sowers of 0-50 des.

A. Konstantinograd District (1880s = 1888/89)

Canton	1880s		1900			1910[a]		
	Own Plowland	Sown Area	Own Plowland	Sown Area	Draft Animals	Own Plowland	Sown Area[b]	Draft Animals[c]
Belukhofvka	.351 (34)	.332 (20)	.408 (31)	.310 (40)	.342 (39)	.491 (31)	.362 (40)	.391 (38)
Berestoven'ka	.329 (36)	.383 (17)	.356 (34)	.381 (34)	.403 (31)	.432 (36)	.409 (35)	.442 (34)
Dar Nadezhda	.469 (22)	.444 (7)	.520 (23)	.436 (26)	.397 (34)	.534 (21)	.460 (24)	.466 (31)
Ganeboe	.382 (30)	.388 (15)	.430 (30)	.386 (33)	.337 (40)	.440 (34)	.387 (38)	.384 (39)
Karlovka	.246 (39)	.347 (18)	.352 (35)	.350 (39)	.373 (37)	.517 (25)	.454 (25)	.475 (29)
Kegichevka	.407 (28)	.403 (13)	.451 (28)	.405 (29)	.396 (35)	.516 (26)	.475 (20)	.475 (30)
Mashevka	.448 (25)	.472 (3)	.490 (27)	.447 (25)	.479 (19)	.496 (29)	.460 (23)	.494 (25)
Natal'ino	.488 (20)	.438 (10)	.553 (19)	.462 (21)	.471 (22)	.559 (18)	.486 (16)	.510 (22)
Nekhvoroshcha	.339 (35)	.450 (6)	.329 (38)	.391 (31)	.466 (25)	.405 (38)	.417 (31)	.495 (24)
Novo-Tagamlik[d]	.703 (3)	.617 (1)	.718 (3)	.651 (3)	.592 (7)	.707 (3)	.644 (3)	.607 (11)
Paraskoveia	.370 (31)	.414 (11)	.341 (37)	.395 (30)	.402 (32)	.434 (35)	.409 (34)	.478 (27)
Peschanka	.296 (37)	.334 (19)	.351 (36)	.359 (38)	.354 (38)	.441 (33)	.384 (39)	.372 (40)
Petrovka	.363 (33)	.441 (9)	.382 (32)	.381 (35)	.433 (28)	.422 (37)	.387 (37)	.430 (35)
Riasskoe	.294 (38)	.497 (2)	.326 (39)	.374 (36)	.427 (29)	.373 (39)	.410 (33)	.478 (28)
Runovshchina	.366 (32)	.407 (12)	.364 (33)	.387 (32)	.401 (33)	.452 (32)	.412 (32)	.421 (36)
Staroverovka	.238 (40)	.388 (16)	.325 (40)	.359 (37)	.379 (36)	.294 (40)	.388 (36)	.404 (37)
Tagamlik	.522 (17)	.451 (5)	.576 (17)	.468 (20)	.436 (27)	.593 (15)	.483 (17)	.490 (26)
Velikie Buchki	.452 (24)	.462 (4)	.496 (26)	.459 (23)	.414 (30)	.515 (27)	.440 (27)	.446 (33)
Zapechilovka	.399 (29)	.398 (14)	.447 (29)	.420 (28)	.440 (26)	.492 (30)	.436 (28)	.448 (32)
Zhirkovka	.442 (27)	.441 (8)	.497 (25)	.459 (22)	.466 (24)	.526 (24)	.477 (19)	.501 (23)

The Polarization of Peasant Households in Prerevolutionary Russia 499

B. Poltava District (1880s = 1883)

Bairak	.641 (8)	.648 (7)	.505 (15)	.533 (12)	.633 (8)	.508 (13)	.585 (12)
Baliasnoe	.571 (14)	.602 (14)	.513 (12)	.536 (10)	.621 (11)	.493 (15)	.567 (14)
Brateshki	.475 (23)	.515 (24)	.423 (27)	.489 (16)	.512 (28)	.433 (29)	.568 (13)
Chutovo	.480 (21)	.542 (20)	.474 (18)	.471 (22)	.606 (12)	.518 (12)	.629 (10)
Demidovka	.493 (19)	.531 (22)	.454 (24)	.483 (17)	.529 (23)	.422 (30)	.518 (21)
Dikan'ka	.644 (5)	.647 (8)	.606 (6)	.603 (6)	.651 (6)	.522 (11)	.644 (8)
Elisavetino	.618 (10)	.608 (12)	.490 (17)	.493 (15)	.530 (22)	.444 (26)	.528 (20)
Machekhi	.634 (9)	.620 (10)	.592 (7)	.608 (5)	.645 (7)	.571 (6)	.649 (6)
Nikol'skaia	.724 (2)	.748 (2)	.702 (2)	.561 (9)	.737 (2)	.695 (2)	.671 (3)
Pervozvanovka	.588 (13)	.600 (15)	.468 (19)	.471 (22)	.577 (16)	.501 (14)	.550 (15)
Peschanoe	.448 (26)	.533 (21)	.496 (16)	.494 (14)	.566 (17)	.472 (21)	.544 (18)
Plosskoe	.506 (18)	.558 (18)	.512 (13)	.523 (13)	.547 (20)	.471 (22)	.547 (17)
Poltava	.757 (1)	.760 (1)	.755 (1)	.695 (1)	.817 (1)	.835 (1)	.826 (1)
Reshetilovka	.550 (16)	.603 (13)	.588 (8)	.634 (4)	.603 (13)	.547 (8)	.662 (5)
Runovshchina	.557 (15)	.597 (16)	.548 (11)	.534 (11)	.594 (14)	.556 (7)	.647 (7)
Starye Senzhary	.681 (4)	.662 (4)	.663 (4)	.588 (8)	.671 (5)	.574 (5)	.663 (4)
Suprunovka	.593 (12)	.626 (9)	.566 (9)	.641 (3)	.628 (10)	.528 (10)	.641 (9)
Takhtaulovka	.662 (6)	.657 (6)	.615 (5)	.660 (2)	.688 (4)	.580 (4)	.702 (2)
Vasil'evka	.611 (11)	.620 (11)	.509 (14)	.479 (18)	.553 (19)	.482 (18)	.530 (19)
Vasil'tsy	.642 (7)	.661 (5)	.553 (10)	.478 (20)	.631 (9)	.533 (9)	.550 (16)

Notes: The rank of each canton is shown in parentheses to the right of the corresponding Gini index.
[a] Data for 1910, Konstantinograd District only, refer to all small-holding (*melkie*) households, including a small number of nobles and clergy.
[b] Data for sown area in 1910 refer to "households present" (*nalichnye khoziaistva*), which for Poltava District means that almost 20% of total area sown by smallholders is excluded; the difference for Konstantinograd District is significant.
[c] Data for draft animals in 1910 cover horses and oxen only.
[d] Malo-Pereshchepina is included with Novo-Tagamlik.

Sources: Data for 1880s and 1900 as Table 7; data for 1910 from *Tret'ia podvorno-khoziaistvennaia perepis'... Svod po guberniii*, pp. 82-99, 222-239, except data on smallholders' total horses and oxen from Poltavskoe gubernskoe zemstvo, Statisticheskii biuro, *Tret'ia podvorno-khoziaistvennaia perepis' v Poltavskoi guberniii, 1910 g. Itogi po volostiam i uezdam (po pervomu podshchetu)* (Poltava, 1911).

Table 12. Correlation Coefficients of Gini Indexes, 1883-1910
Cantons of Konstantinograd and Poltava Districts
Corelation Coefficients (prob > |R| under H0:RHO = 0)

A. Households Holding or Sowing 0-50 des.

	GINV8	GINP8	GINV00	GINP00	GINSK00	GINV10	GINP10	GINSK10
GINV8 Plowland, 1880s	1.00000 0.0000	0.74520 0.0002	0.97690 0.0001	0.92325 0.0001	0.82794 0.0001	0.91149 0.0001	0.81684 0.0001	0.83165 0.0001
GINP8 Sown area, 1888/89	0.74520 0.0002	1.00000 0.0000	0.64838 0.0020	0.85405 0.0001	0.87633 0.0001	0.48316 0.0309	0.775592 0.0001	0.80934 0.0001
GINV00 Plowland, 1900	0.97690 0.0001	0.64838 0.0020	1.00000 0.0000	0.91666 0.0001	0.80742 0.0001	0.93327 0.0001	0.82914 0.0001	0.82615 0.0001
GINP00 Sown area, 1900	0.92325 0.0001	0.85405 0.0001	0.91666 0.0001	1.00000 0.0000	0.90557 0.0001	0.90739 0.0001	0.92856 0.0001	0.91223 0.0001
GINSK00 Draft animals, 1900	0.82794 0.0001	0.87633 0.0001	0.80742 0.0001	0.90557 0.0001	1.00000 0.0000	0.80363 0.0001	0.80735 0.0001	0.93692 0.0001
GINV10 Plowland, 1910	0.91149 0.0001	0.48316 0.0309	0.93327 0.0001	0.90739 0.0001	0.80363 0.0001	1.00000 0.0000	0.89727 0.0001	0.86514 0.0001
GINP10 Sown area, 1910	0.81684 0.0001	0.75592 0.0001	0.82914 0.0001	0.92856 0.0001	0.80735 0.0001	0.89727 0.0001	1.00000 0.0000	0.89190 0.0001
GINSK10 Draft animals, 1910	0.83165 0.0001	0.80934 0.0001	0.82615 0.0001	0.91223 0.0001	0.93692 0.0001	0.86514 0.0001	0.89190 0.0001	1.00000 0.0000

B. All Households

	GINPAX8	GINCAT8	GINPAX0	GINSOW0	GINCAT0
GINPAX8	1.00000	0.72973	0.91572	0.91883	0.79847
Own plowland, 1880s	0.0000	0.0001	0.0001	0.0001	0.0001
GINCAT8	0.72973	1.00000	0.60986	0.77711	0.92969
Draft animals, 1880s	0.0001	0.0000	0.0001	0.0001	0.0001
GINPAX0	0.91572	0.60986	1.00000	0.92047	0.63188
Own plowland, 1900	0.0001	0.0001	0.0000	0.0001	0.0001
GINSOW0	0.91883	0.77711	0.92047	1.00000	0.80730
Sown area, 1900	0.0001	0.0001	0.0001	0.0000	0.0001
GINCAT0	0.79847	0.92969	0.63188	0.80730	1.00000
Draft animals, 1900	0.0001	0.0001	0.0001	0.0001	0.0000

Note: Number of observations = 20 for GINP8, 40 for all others.

Sources: Data for 1880s and 1900 as Table 7; data for 1910 from *Tret'ia podvorno-khoziaistvennaia perepis'... Svod po gubernii*, pp. 82–99, 222–239, except data on smallholders' total horses and oxen from Poltavskoe gubernskoe zemstvo, Statisticheskii biuro, *Tret'ia podvorno-khoziaistvennaia perepis' v Poltavskoi gubernii, 1910 g. Itogi po volostiam i uezdam (po pervomu podshchetu)* (Poltava, 1911).

cantons of Poltava District is essentially impossible, for the reasons indicated above. And in both districts, because of the vagrant cows, changes between 1900 and 1910 in the Gini indexes for the distribution of cattle are of uncertain significance.

There is an additional consideration about which one can only frame hypotheses: significant but undetectable changes in the population at risk. The first years of the Stolypin reforms fell between the second and third censuses in Poltava Province. These reforms enabled households to disappear through migration to Siberia or simply through liquidation. Some of these vanished households may have been replaced on the census rolls by households formed by separation (*vydel*). Processes associated with the development of capitalism might not, by virtue of the legislation of 1906-1911, have produced a corresponding increase in rassloenie as reflected in the zemstvo census. It is not possible to integrate data on migration and liquidation with census data in such a way as to test this hypothesis, but it remains attractive. For the three Poltava censuses do register dramatic changes in sowing structure between the 1880s and 1900 and between 1900 and 1910. These changes indicate an accelerating increase in production for the market and, by extension, suggest an accelerating development of capitalism in the villages of Poltava Province.

In short, Gini indexes drawn from zemstvo census are of considerable value in making comparisons between territorial units for a given year. They are of much lower value in making comparisons over time because it is difficult to maintain a uniform population at risk and a tolerable level of comparability. Insofar as the latter kind of comparisons are valid here, they provide some ammunition for those historians who emphasize the weight of the dead hand of the past on the prerevolutionary Russian village and give little encouragement to those who emphasize the burgeoning of capitalism.

ACKNOWLEDGMENTS

I would like to express my gratitude to those who gave me advice on the substantive and statistical aspects of this work: John Agnew, Zack Deal, Martha Wegner, Victor Hoffman, B.N. Mironov, L.I. Borodkin, L.V. Milov, and other colleagues at Moscow, Columbia, and Syracuse Universities who commented oral presentations of earlier versions.

Few zemstvo statistical materials are available in any library in the United States, and they have not been easy to obtain by exchange from Soviet Libraries (of which the Library of the Academy of Sciences in Leningrad has the best collection). I brought some back on microfilm from the Lenin and INION libraries in Moscow, and I want to thank Professor David Macey of Middlebury College and Professor Carol Leonard of SUNY-Plattsburgh for providing me with others.

NOTES AND REFERENCES

1. See A. V. Chaianov, *The Theory of the Peasant Economy* (Homewood, Il, 1966); and T. Shanin, *The Awkward Class* (Oxford, 1972).
2. Historians sometimes refer to the process portentously as *razlozhenie,* or "disintegration"— what was once a coherent whole becomes disconnected elements—but I will use rassloenie here.
3. For recent examples see A.N. Anfimov and P.N. Zyrianov, "Elements of the Evolution of the Russian Peasant Commune in the Post-Reform Period, 1861-1914," *Soviet Studies in History* 21, 3 (1982-1983): 82; and I.D. Koval'chenko, "O burzhuaznom kharaktere krestian'skogo khoziaistva Evropeiskoi Rossii v kontse XIX-nachale XX veka (po biudzhetnym damnym srednechernozemnykh gubernii)," *Istoriia SSSR* 5 (1983): 50-51.
4. For an introductory discussion of the Gini index, see Charles Dollar and Robert Jensen, *A Historian's Guide to Statistics* (New York, 1971), pp. 121-124.
5. Compare K.V. Litvak, "Komp'iuter obrabatyvaet zemskuiu statistiku," in *Chislo i mysl',* fasc. 9, ed. by L.I. Borodkin (Moscow, 1986), pp. 66-85.
6. The Gini index, it will be recalled, is compounded of an ascending sequence of Y:P ratios, where Y is a group's percentage of assets held and P its percentage of the population, and is twice the area between the line of equality and the Lorenz curve.
7. When I gave a paper on the subject at Moscow University, critics responded that the Gini index does not measure rassloenie, but "concentration." Because the concentration of productive assets in the upper groupings is the primary quantitative expression of rassloenie, this does not seem to be a potent objection.
8. As central-government statisticians were quick to concede; see *Materialy Vysochaishe uchrezhdennoi 16 noiabria 1901 g. Kommissii po issledovaniiu voprosa o dvizhenii s 1861 g. po 1900 g. blagosostoianiia sel'skogo naseleniia...* (St. Petersburg, 1903), part 3, pp. 75, 115.
9. Zemstvo statistical publications are listed and characterized in V.N. Grigor'ev, *Predmetnyi ukazatel' materizlov v zemsko-statistichekikh trudakh s 1860-kh po 1917 g.,* 2 vols. (Moscow, 1926-1927). See also N.A. Svavitskii, *Zemskie podvornye perepisi (Obzor metologii)* (Moscow, 1961); and I.D. Koval'chenko et al., *Massovie istochniki po sotsial'no-ekonomicheskoi istorii Rossii perioda kapitalizma* (Moscow, 1979), pp. 279-287.
10. For the census of 1900, the published results descend to the level of the survey tract (*mezhevaia dacha*), usually consisting of one or two villages and some outlying settlements.
11. The Statistical Bureau employed 37 regular and 594 temporary census-takers; the highest totals employed in any other province hitherto were 25 and 71, respectively. V.V. Bedin, "Krestiianstvo i krest'ianskoe dvizhenie v Poltavskoi gubernii na rubezhe XIX-XX vv.," Kandidatskaia dissertatsiia (Leningrad, 1961), p. 188.
12. Compare Polltavskoe gubernskoe zemstvo, *Spisok naselennykh mest Poltavskoi gubernii (po obshchestvam i na zemliakh sel'skikh soslovii) za 1900 g.* (Poltava, 1904), pp. 1410-1411, 1424-1425; and two volumes of Poltavskoe gubernskoe zemstvo, Statisticheskii biuro, *Materialy podvornoi perepisi Poltavskoi gubernii 1900 goda:* (1.) *Poltavskii uezd* (Poltava, 1906), pp. 270-273; (2.) *Konstantinogradskii uezd* (Poltava, 1906), pp. 412-413.
13. A desiatina was equivilant to 2.7 acres, or about a hectare.
14. For a study of one such in Konstantinograd District, see A.M. Anfimov, "Karlovskoe imenie Meklenburg-Strelitskikh v kontse XIX—nachale XX v." *Materialy po istorii sel'skogo khoziaistva i krest'ianstva SSSR, sb. VI* (Moscow, 1962), pp. 348-376.
15. For all unprivileged households in the 40 cantons of Konstantinograd and Poltava Districts in 1900, the correlation coefficients between the proportion of cossack households and the Gini indexes for distribution of own plowland and sown area are respectively .611 and .660; for the 15 districts of Poltava Province they are .709 and .883. Data from the sources cited in note 10 above and Poltavskoe gubernskoe zemstvo, Statisticheskii biuro, *Materialy podvornoi perepisi Poltavskoi gubernii 1900 goda. Itogi po gubernii* (Poltava, 1907).

16. On the 50-desiatina ceiling see A. Anfimov, *Krest'ianskoe khoziaistvo Evropeiskoi Rossii, 1861-1904* (Moscow, 1980), p. 65.

17. Herbert M. Blalock, Jr., *Social Statistics,* 2nd ed. (New York, 1979) p. 62; V. I. Lenin, *Razvitie kapitalizma v Rossii* (*Polnoe sobranie sochienii,* 5th ed., vol. 3), pp. 116-117.

18. The procedure for calculating Gini indexes for distribution of draft animals is essentially the same. The aggregate reported total of head less the estimated holdings of all but the top interval is divided by the total of households in the top interval, and this mean is used for all cantons (or districts) in the array.

19. The Gini indexes in column 5 do not exactly match the corresponding indexes, also based on estimated asset values, in Tables 7-10; the latter are based on different Poltava census publications with slight variations in the reported subtotals and totals for unprivileged households. Columns 3-8 of Table 6 are intended to isolate the problems of estimation.

20. For Staroverovka Canton, where no household held more than 50 des. of plowland, the Gini based on estimation is higher than the "true" Gini.

21. The coefficient of determination for the canton-level Ginis is columns 2 and 7 is only .874—very low since the two columns are supposed to register the same distribution.

22. Tsentral'nyi statisticheskii komitet, *Statistika zemlevladeniia 1905 g.,* fasc. 48: Poltavskaia guberniia (St. Petersburg, 1907), p. 33.

23. On labor-rented in general, see my introductory remarks to I.D. Koval'chenko and N.B. Selunskaia, "Labor Rental in the Manorial Economy of European Russia at the End of the 19th Century and the Beginning of the 20th," *Explorations in Economic History,* 18, no. 1 (1981): 3-4. For examples of the onerous terms that prevailed in Konstantinograd District see B.B. Veselovskii and I.F. Tsyzyrev, eds., *Krest'ianskie dvizheniia 1902 g.* (Moscow-Leningrad, 1923), p. 76, passim.

24. The census of 1900, which was conducted in the fall, attempted to register holdings of cattle as of August 6. Poltavskoe gubernskoe zemstvo, Statisticheskii biuro, *Sel'skokhoziaistvennoe skotovodstvo v Poltavskoi gubernii po damnym podvornoi perepisi 1900 g.* (Poltava, 1906), p. 2.

25. Table 9 (B) also registers the Gini for the distribution of allotment land in 1905. The comparatively low values for this index derive in part from the relatively even distribution of allotments and in part from the failure of the source to register households with no allotment land separately from those with allotments of 0-1 des.

26. Poltavskoe gubernskoe zemstvo, Statisticheskii biuro, *Materialy podvornoi perepisi Poltavskoi gubernii 1900 goda. Konstantinogradskii uezd* (Poltava, 1906), pp. 412-413.

27. That is, with a single grouping for all households holding more than 15 des. See Poltavskoe gubernskoe zemstvo, Statisticheskoe biuro, *Izmeneniia v khoziaistvennoi zhizni naseleniia Poltavskoi gubernii po damnym perepeisei 1900 i 1910 gg.* (Poltava, 1915), appendix, pp. 2-3.

28. The same table generates Ginis for Poltava District of .672 in 1900 and .674 in 1910.

29. For the census of 1900, one can establish the holdings of households sowing 50+ des. for each canton by laboriously summing the data of each census tract, but this is not possible for the first and third Poltava censuses.

30. As the sedulous Svavitskiis point out. They compound confusion, however, by reproducing a table comparing the censuses of the 1880s and 1900 together with another comparing the censuses of 1900 and 1910; they do note that the former covers rural-dwelling unprivileged households and is completely incomparable with the latter, which includes city-dwellers and all status groups, being based on a preliminary computation of the census findings of 1910. See Z.M. Svavitskaia, N.A. Svavitskii, *Zemskie podvoryne perepisi, 1880-1913: Pouezdnye itogi* (Moscow, 1926) pp. 198-311; and compare Poltavskoe gubernskoe zemstvo, Statisticheskii biuro, *Tret'ia podvornokhoziaistvennaia perepis' v Poltavskoi gubernii, 1910 g. Itogi po volostiam i uezdam* (*po pervomu podschetu*) (Poltava, 1911).

31. As they were from the sources for my Tables 7, 8, and 9 derive. In Poltava Province as a whole, there were 4391 rural-dwelling Jewish households in 1910, of which 48 held two des. or more of arable. Poltavskoe gubernskoe zemstvo, Statisticheskii biuro, *Tret'ia podvornno-khoziaistveennaia perepis' v Poltavskoi gubernii 1910 g. Svod po gubernii* (Poltava, 1914), p. 316.

POSTSCRIPT

Carol S. Leonard

A body of theory explains economic transformation in terms of work and production, the influence of the market and of new technology, and changes in peasant behavior under pressure of population growth. In some ways Soviet scholars find this framework compatible; Soviet history is a field organized around understanding evolutionary patterns. The tendency of Soviet history, however, is to focus less on the causes than the consequences of sustained growth. For the history of Ruissia, for example, Lenin's description of the development of capitalism in Russia, emphasizing the formation of a rural class structure, retains a central place. Soviet historians measure the impact of economic opportunity on the frequency and intensity of conflict between social groups and classes. They look at the nineteenth-century economy from the vantage point of the Revolution of 1917, seeking to explain peasant involvement in the social upheaval that ended the old regime.

They see rural protest as a self-replicating process, reflecting the maturation of historical consciousness during industrialization; they trace regional differentiation and specialization of labor as a condition for the formation of class; they calibrate movements of the internal market and the rise of hired labor in order to explain the polarization (*rassloenie*) of the peasantry, leading to the revolutions of 1905 and 1917.

The centrality of the theme of revolution is perhaps best understood in the context of national experience. Soviet history draws on distant but distinct memories of the decades following 1917, when the agrarian society was left behind and a shock course of industrialization demonstrated the potential results of empowerment by revolution. Soviet historians see in the capitalist economic environment an unfolding antagonism between capitalism and socialism, and their national history has led them to make categorical distinctions in stages of growth.

In their writing on capitalist development, Soviet scholars have devoted considerable attention to agriculture. This was made possible by the groundwork laid by the nineteenth-century populist historians and ethnographers, whose concern was to record, somehow keep, peasant society as it was. Government officials also compiled statistics on work and production, because the relative backwardness of Russian agriculture was a heated question within the late imperial regime. The rich ethnographic sources and profusion of statistical surveys attest to the search for explanations and solutions to the agrarian question. Volumes of political literature sympathetic to peasants attempted to identify the constraints of local conditions—political institutions, climate, and class. Soviet scholarship builds on a tradition of solid and inventive scholarship by V. I. Semevskii, I. I. Ignatovich, Iu. V. Got'e, A. V. Chayanov, among the most prominent. V. I. Buganov, N. M. Druzhinin, L. M. Goriushkin, Ia. V. Iatsunskii, I. D. Koval'chenko, B. G. Litvak, L. V. Milov, B. N. Mironov, N. L. Rubinshtein, and P. G. Ryndziunskii, are authors of some of the pathbreaking works of the Soviet period.[1]

Relatively few of these monographs have been translated into English. We have the classic works by Western scholars: works by Alexander Gerschenkron and Jerome Blum, the superb analytic studies of serfdom by Michael Confino; the excellent set of essays on serfdom and industrialization by Olga Crisp and Evsey Domar's theoretical explorations of the origins of serfdom and the profitability of serf estates; a textbook on the tsarist economy by Peter Gatrell, another by Arkadius Kahan, and a few somewhat less ambitious surveys published several decades ago; a recent attempt to reassess national income in the late nineteenth-early twentieth century by Paul Gregory; and the study of peasant society in the early twentieth century by Teodor Shanin. These works add new materials to the study of agrarian history. But they do not supplant the rich methodological and microregional studies that have appeared in the Soviet Union the past two decades. The section of papers on Russian history made no effort to provide a survey of the literature or an outline history of the nineteenth century. We included only a few papers, representing recent contributions to the field.

I. D. Koval'chenko's books and articles have helped found the Soviet school of quantitative methods. The laboratory he created in quantitative source study at Moscow University has brought together historians with little formal training in statistics and mathematicians with little training in history for a combined effort to overcome the problems presented by statistical sources. He and his colleagues have succeeded in improving the tools of research and in refining the questions asked about the nineteenth century.

Some findings are undeniably controversial. For example, the numbers thus far produced do not convince all historians that Lenin was right about the development of capitalism in the countryside before the revolution. Despite statistical findings, the fundamental issues are still a matter of considerable debate. Part of the reason is that in the Soviet Union, as elsewhere, the gathering of more reliable data on Russian agrarian history is an ongoing task, and the empirical foundation is incomplete.

CAPITALISM IN RUSSIA

According to Lenin's *Development of Capitalism in Russia,* feudalism[2] came to an end with the abolition of serfdom in 1861, and capitalism was well advanced by the 1880s and 1890s. To be sure, forms of serfdom survived after 1861 in legislation which did not improve the mobility of the former serfs. There were other survivals. Until 1914 much of the land in Russia was still held by large landlords who rented it out to sharecroppers or for labor services, *otrabotka*.[3] However, Lenin argued, the new rhythm of capitalist production could distinctly be felt in the spread of machine-operated factories, the industrial revolution, and, he argued, in agriculture, where wealthy and poor peasants were increasingly polarized.

The Soviet historians who sometimes have taken issue with the emphasis of Lenin's thesis, including A. M. Anfimov and L. P. Minarik, argue that although capitalism was evident in industry, the sway of landlord-peasant relations and precapitalist practices was the main feature of agriculture. Labor-rental on landlords' estates was serfdom in all but name; and wealthy or entrepreneurial peasants, not independent small farmers, dominated other forms of private agriculture. Against this point of view, Koval'chenko and Ryndziunskii argue that the external form of obligation is not the only indicator of capitalist relations in agriculture, and that the penetration of market forces, which was very deep, places Russian rural development within the sphere of capitalism.[4]

How can one judge? Is the development of capitalism a matter of definition rather than measurement? That is, because capitalism was a precondition for socialism, according to Marxist theory, is the evidence for capitalism stretched, therefore, to fit definition and theory? Daniel Field's research on polarization of the peasantry sheds light on this issue without stilling the controversy.

POLARIZATION OF THE PEASANTRY

Although social stratification was observed by serf villages before 1861, repartition of land most often inhibited the extremes of wealth. By contrast, after emancipation, differentiation became marked, and, as a consequence of intense growth of trade, by the end of the nineteenth century in some regions wealthy peasants had purchased much property. The new economic environment in some places encouraged the acquisition of entrepreneurial skills and investment of capital in agriculture; elsewhere, agriculture was abandoned. In some areas the development of crafts and industry in villages competed with urban factories for rural labor and preserved the traditional village structure; in others, the division of land and unfavorable population-resource balance led to increased differentiation and to the migration of some of the poor to urban areas.[5] Almost all Soviet scholarship touches in some way on the issue of differentiation, or polarization of the peasantry, confirming its bourgeois nature and its result in the hostility among social classes at the end of the nineteenth century.

Soviet historians look at polarization not so much to determine allocation of resources and savings as to illustrate the advent of capitalism in the economic decline of the many and the simultaneous rise of the fortunate few, the agrarian bourgeoisie, or *kulaks*. Field drew attention to possible exaggeration of polarization by his findings on average assets, the results of applying the Gini index to regional data. He used census and other survey data for one province of Russia in which, because of the diversity of the population, differentiation measured by land and draught animals was likely to be great. Field's results, however, show slim support for the rise of a rural bourgeoisie, although he emphasized the limitation of using data from just one region.

In spite of the rapid growth of population, there were powerful constraints on the formation of a rural elite. The importance of technological change and rural credit in the shaping of new power and property relations makes it apparent that, for Russia as a whole, the ingredients for new rural order were slow to develop and in some regions, such as Poltava province in the early twentieth century as Field showed, almost entirely missing. Many of the preemancipation institutional arrangements, therefore, survived into the twentieth century. Life in Great Russia was profoundly influenced by institutions such as the commune, or *obshchina,* which inhibited the release to labor to industry, and, more important, by a centuries-old tradition of periodic redistribution of the arable, which spread risk and equalized the burden of work and dues on members of the peasant community. These traditions were reinforced by law, giving the commune the right and the power to determine the limits of households' autonomy. And the commune was only one such legal and financial constraint on family fortunes in rural Russia. Steven Hoch described others for an earlier era, before the emancipation of the serfs, when the bridewealth, or kladka, also showed the adjustment of the community to problems of the shortage of labor. Hoch's conclusion (drawn from a region near the frontier) is that traditional equalizing mechanisms of communal life prevented the polarization of the peasantry in the early nineteenth century.

The idea of polarization, therefore, has been challenged. Can it be dismissed? Were Hoch's and Field's data too limited? For central Russia, there is plentiful research on the proletarianization of the poorest peasants and the rise of a wealthy stratum within the commune.[6]

There can be no doubt of sharp distinctions between conditions on blackearth and non-blackearth soils, between areas of light and heavy rainfall, between the urbanized and densely settled areas around the industrial districts of Moscow and Vladimir, and between local institutional arrangements. Koval'chenko's paper provided a close look for one region at variation in investment and income of groups of peasants, distinguished by amount of land belonging to single households. Although he acknowledged that some provinces in the blackearth region were generally characterized by poverty, the poor households nevertheless had a strikingly different portfolio from those that were relatively prosperous. Taken together, Soviet and Western regional studies show the continuing problem of generalizing from any distinctive unit of study to the level of the whole country.

REGIONALIZATION

The Soviet Union, a multinational state, has attracted collective scholarship designed to embrace the history of the separate republics as well as regions. The enormous size of the country subjects the history of agrarian change in the nineteenth century to a staggering variety of influences: differences in inheritance and property disposition customs, seigneurial rights, crop rotation systems, agricultural practices, and industrial development. Taking regions as a whole—Great Russia, the Ukraine, and Siberia, where some historical traditions are similar—one still finds vast divergences in economic characteristics and social conditions. The main differences in Russia were produced by soil and climatic conditions, which ranged from the rich black earth of the south, where fertilizer was unnecessary and the climate was favorable, and where wheat was grown for export, to the far north, where only hemp and flax and small amounts of rye could be produced due to long winters and poor soils. There was a mid-range in the north-central region of Russia, where the non-blackearth soil, fluctuating climate, and inefficiencies of the three-field system prevented the successful transfer from rye to wheat and necessitated considerable seasonal nonagricultural work for year-round subsistence. In each of these areas, the seigneurial prerogatives varied from a situation of close control and labor services in the south to a situation of relative freedom from labor services and lax supervision in the north.

Soviet scholars would like to pull this history together, and their partitioning of economic history into regional studies has the assumption of guiding patterns. Yet, routines of land cultivation and other traditions change slowly, as Goriushkin pointed out, and, therefore, as regional studies accumulate, distinctive patterns emerge—not one or two, but dozens. Scholars immersed in the history of their own regions with separate social institutions and political organizations, changing by the decade, provide rigorous source study and extensive detail about forms of agriculture in the major regions of the former empire. And for this kind of intensive research, they are most comfortable with two or three decades. The task of Soviet quantifiers will be to overcome problems in both research and theory in the selection of regions and periods; too limited an application fails in the same way as excessive aggregation in generating persuasive results.

PRODUCTION FOR THE MARKET

The development of commercial agriculture began to have effect on institutions of rural life beginning in the mid-eighteenth century, with the shift in form of serfs' dues from labor services to money rent (by the end of the century inflation had reversed the effect). The most important early studies of production for the market were by P. Struve, A. V. Shestakova, S. N. Smirnov, A. N. Nasonov, and B. D. Grekov, who concentrated on large landholdings as the main source of marketed grain. Their research confirmed the impression of contemporaries (and Western scholars) that the landlords dominated the market as well as the land up until 1917.[7] These scholars accepted the powerful influence of the grain trade on economic growth and the manorial economy as the mainspring of progress, with its access to market information.[8] Grekov emphasized the force of the market already in the early nineteenth century in the stratification of the peasantry.[9]

Historians now consider this picture misleading. Output also responded to reduction of transportation costs and to the rise of the internal demand that accompanied population growth and urbanization, factors affecting all kinds of farming. Searching for more refined distinctions and exact measurement of the market's effect, in a landmark of scholarship, N. L. Rubinshtein in the 1920s directed Soviet historians toward the difficult taks of separating landlords' and serfs' economic operations in the sources and discovering the extent of the serfs' production for the market.[10] Koval'chenko emphasized the reality as well as the potential of small peasant farming in late imperial Russia, showing by differences in income and expenditure, how the market gave advantages to larger producers among the peasants. On the whole, his recent work has been devoted to showing the significant contribution of peasant producers to farm output in Russia. He has shown elsewhere that the volume of marketed grain produced by peasants on their own lands rather than landlords' arable may possibly have been as high as 45% already in the mid-nineteenth century.[11] Koval'chenko's point was that capitalism in Russia did not entirely conform to a Prussian form of evolution, where conservative landholding interests dominated production and the market; it also gave evidence of the presence of family farming, the American path in agrarian evolution. Koval'chenko's opponents, however, insist that the American path was only a potential in Russia at the time of the revolution.[12] L. M. Goriushkin constructed a contrasting picture based on evidence from Siberia.

RUSSIA'S UNIQUENESS

Among the questions Western historians will not find in Soviet work are those raised by Gerschenkron about substitutions and institutional arrangements that made Russia's economic development seem to follow a course unique to itself. Gerschenkron's view of the exceptional nature of Russian economic development has also been challenged outside the Soviet Union. Russia's course of growth has familiar features. The persistance of kustarnye occupations (in which peasants marketed their own cottage output) retarded factory development in the late nineteenth century, and it showed the striking effect of urban disamenities, the rural roots of urban labor, and morcelization of land holdings accompanied by intensification of nonagricultural labor within the household.

There are aspects of Russia's agricultural history that can best be understood by reference to peculiar institutional arrangements and governmental policy. The failure of government intervention to eliminate the land commune or to ease restrictions on the supply of credit for industry is evidence of the influence of institutions, in this case, the restrictive effect of the emancipation statutes.

But there are new leads from unexpected quarters, such as the history of urbanization and markets, where Russian history may more fully be integrated into comparative frameworks. B. Mironov's examination of literacy rates, for example, brings Russia closer to the level of Western European in regard to one of the key indicators of standard of living. His and other Soviet research in the 1980s is headed in new directions, and the continuing exchange of ideas between Western and Soviet economic historians should bring some common pursuits more clearly into focus.

NOTES AND REFERENCES

1. Among the achievements of collective work, see the multivolume *Materials on the History of Agriculture and the Peasantry of the USSR,* published by the Soviet Commission (founded by B. D. Grekov in the Academy of Sciences of the Institute of History) on the History of Agriculture and the Peasantry in the USSR.
2. Soviet historians have preserved the terminology of liberal historiography and Marxist writing in describing the preemancipation economy, the manorial regime, as feudal; see J. Banaiji, "The Peasantry in the Feudal Mode of Production: Towards an Economic Model," *Journal of Peasant Studies* 3, 3 (April 1976): 299.
3. L. P. Minarik, *Ekonomicheskaia kharakteristika krupneishikh zemel'nykh sobstvennikov Rossii kontsa XII—nachale XX v.* [*Economic Characteristics of Large Landowners in Russia From the End of the 12th Through the Beginning of the 20th Century*] (Moscow, 1971).
4. I. D. Koval'chenko and L. V. Milov, *Vserossiiskii agrarnii rynok XVIII—nachala XX v.* (opyt kolichestvennogo analyza) [*The All-Russian Agrarian Market From the 18th Through the Beginning of the 20th Century (A Quantitatiave Analysis)*] (Moscow, 1974); P. G. Ryndziunskii, "Ekonomicheskii stroi krest'ianskogo nadel'nogo khoziastva Rossii v poreformennoe vremia," *Voprosy istorii* ["Economic Structure of Peasant Allotments in Post-Reform Russia," *Problems of History*], No. 11 (1971).
5. J. de Vries, *The Dutch Rural Economy in the Golden Age, 1500-1700* (New Haven, 1974).
6. See A. M. Anfimov and A.M. Solov'eva, "Izuchenie sotsial'no-ekonomicheskoi istorii poreformennoi Rossii," in *Izuchenie otechestvennoi istorii v SSSR mezhdu XXIV i XXV s'ezdami KPSS, dooktiabr'skii period* [*Accomplishments in Social-Economic History of Post-Reform Russia, Accomplishments in Soviet Historical Writing About the Fatherland Between the 24th and 25th Congresses of the Communist Party, the Pre-October Period*] (Moscow, 1978), pp. 44-45.
7. J. Blum, *Lord and Peasant in Russia from the Ninth to the Nineteenth Century* (Princeton, 1961), p. 471.
8. P. G. Ryndziunskii, "Sotsial'no-economicheskaia istoriia Rossii XIX v. v rabotakh sovetskikh istorikov," in *Ocherki istorii istoricheskoi nauki v SSSR* ["The Socio-Economic History of Russia in the 19th Century in Works by Soviet Historians," in *Essays in the History of Historical Science in the USSR*], Vol. 4 (Moscow, 1966), pp. 308-334.
9. B. D. Grekov, "Khoziastvennoe sostoianie Rossii nakanune vystupleniia dekabristov," in *Bunt dekabristov* ["The Economic Condition of Russia On the Eve of the Decembrist Uprising," in *The Decembrist Revolt*] (Leningrad, 1926), pp. 12 ff.
10. N. L. Rubinshtein, "Ekonomicheskoe razvitie Rossii v nachale XIX veka kak osnova dvizheniia dekabristov," in *100-letie vosstanie dekabristov, Sbornik statei i dokumentov* ["The Economic Development of Russia at the Beginning of the 19th Century As the Basis for the Decembrist Movement," in *100-year Anniversary of the Decembrist Uprising, Collection of Articles and Documents*] (Moscow, 1927).
11. See Gatrell's discussion in *The Tsarist Economy, 1850-1917* (New York, 1986), pp. 128-129.
12. S. M. Dubrovskii, *Sel'skoe khozaistvo i krest'ianstvo Rossii v period imperializma* [*Agriculture and the Russian Peasantry in the Period of Imperialism*] (Moscow, 1975).

INDEX

Abel, Wilhelm, 20
Abramova family, 396
   Karneia, Praskov'ia
Abthorpe, 105
Addington, Rev. Stanley, 120
Afanas'ev, A., 393, 408, 409, 410
age, 265, 270, 281, 294, 341
Aglovin family, 396
   Arkhip, Elena
agrarian capitalism, 58, 64, 415
agricultural development, 337
agricultural elite, 385
agricultural organization, 3
   ladder, 332
agricultural revolution, 31, 52
   in France, 125, 129
   second, 192
Agricultural Society, 131-132, 135, 178
Akademiia nauk SSR, 408
Alabama, 263, 272
Albert, Marcellin, 175
Aleksandrov, V.A., 409
Alexander II, 439

Alexander II (Emperor of Russia), 426
alfalfa, 128
Allen, George, 273
Allen, Robert C., 8, 28, 56, 65, 87, 88
Alston, L.J., 344
Altai, 415, 444
Alter, George, 23
American agriculture, 415, 451
Anderson, Barbara A., 387
Andrews, Robert, 41
Anfimov, A.M., 412, 427, 503, 504, 509, 514
animals, draft, 11, 143, 256, 259, 294, 389, 403, 461-462, 464, 468, 486, 491-496, 500-501, 510
Ankli, Robert E., 158, 294, 310
Annals of Agriculture, 41, 43, 47
Anscomb, J.W., 117
Anstey, R., 65
Antonov, Terentei, 374
Antonovich, Ivan IV, 416
apples, 370

Applewhite, Marjorie Mendenhall, 276
aramon rootstock, 169-170
Arburthnot, J., 47
aristocrats, 230, 243-244
  vs. non-aristocratic landowners, 236, 246
  (*See also* nóbels)
Aristov, N., 393, 408, 409
Arkangel' guberniia, 392-393
Armstrong, W.A., 215
arson, 421
artisans, 262
Ashbury, M.K., 119
Association of Winegrowers of Natural Wine of the Midi and Algeria, 180
Astier, F., 186
Astrakhan', 435
Atack, Jeremy, 10, 22, 253, 269, 273, 274, 275, 276, 277, 309, 310, 311
atamans, 416
Atherton, Lewis, 274
Atlanta (U.S.), 262-263
Atlas, "Economic Notes" to (1820s-1830s), 356
Aube, A.D., 148, 155
Aubries (England), 41
auction, 446-447
Aude, 167
Auffret, M., 185
Augé-Laribé, M., 185, 186
Austin, M.R., 66
Australia, 297
Austria, 220
Austro-Hungarian Monarchy, 220
Avril, Jean-Baptiste, 131-133, 136
Aydelotte, William O., 282, 309

bail à cheptel, 145
Baker, Alan R.H., 88
Bakshirs, 415

Baldoc, 41
Baltimore (MD), 297
Banaiji, J., 514
Bank of England, 41, 42
Bank of France, 164, 175-176, 180-181, 183-184
banking mechanisms, 183
barin, 416
barley, 53-54, 71-72, 74-76, 77, 81, 318, 325, 360, 370, 372
  yields, 32, 53, 75
barschina, 354-355, 362-364, 378, 380-381, 383, 386
barter, 256
Bartissol, E., 186
Batchelor, T., 87
Bateman, Fred, 10, 153, 159, 253, 269, 273, 274, 275, 276, 277, 309, 310, 311
Baulant, Micheline, 21
beans, 51, 71-72, 74-76, 77, 81, 83, 267
  yields, 75
Beauce, 21, 140-142, 148
Béaur, Gérard, 155
Bedford, 70
Bedford, Duke of, 43
Bedfordshire, 37, 41, 52, 86, 200, 202
Bedin, V.V., 503
bedniaks, 402
Beenham, 207
Behrman, Jere R., 410
Bell, C., 345
Bellerby, J.R., 216
Belovod'e Anapa, 416
Ben-Porath, Yoram, 21
benefits, 302
Berg, Maxine, 215
Berkshire, 37, 85, 207, 212
  Record Office, 119
Berkshire Downs, 206
Bernstein, Michael, 272
Beveridge, William, 213, 216

Bezdna, 423
Bézier, 174, 180-181, 183
Béziers, 167, 182, 184
Bidwell, Percy, 273
Billingsley, J., 63, 67
birth rates, 215, 283
  (*See also* nativity)
birth spacing, 288
black soil belt, 423, 430
  (*See also* blackearth region)
Black, Cyril E., 409
blackearth region, 350, 353, 355, 357, 430-432, 434-435, 438, 457, 466, 470, 472-473, 511
blacks, 295
Blalock, Herbert M., Jr., 484, 504
Bledlow, 59
Blum, Jerome, 20, 29, 248, 387, 508, 514
Board of Agriculture (Britain), 37, 40, 42, 47
Bogue, Allan G., 24, 273, 274, 275, 309
Bohac, Rodney, 6, 13, 349, 386, 387
Boisseau, Pierre, 133, 136
bol'shak, 405-407
bol'shitsa, 405
Bolsheviks, 478
Bondarenko, 410
bonds, 306
Bories, P., 186
Borisogleb, 391
Borodavkin, A.P., 453
Borodkin, L.I., 503
borrowing, 40-41, 112
Boserup, E., 397, 402, 409
Bouches-du-Rhone, 170
Bourne, George, 117, 120
Bournemouth, 197
Bowden, Witt, 248
Boyer, George R., 22, 120
Boys, John, 41
Brenner, Robert, 386

brideprice
  (*See* bridewealth, kladka)
bridewealth, 389, 391, 394-397, 402, 511
  (*See also* groomwealth, kladka)
Bridges, John, 115
Bristol, 35
Broad, John, 46
Bruce Waterloo, 336
Brundage, Anthony, 120
Brunet, Pierre, 156
Brzheskii, 408
Buchanan, B.J., 66
Buckinghamshire, 55,57, 59, 60, 62, 63, 85-86, 89, 92-93, 106
buckwheat, 319, 326, 370, 372
Buganov, Viktor I., 350, 427, 428, 508
Bugbrooke, 91, 96, 104, 108-109
Burn, Richard, 118
Burtniak, J., 344
Burton, Orville Vernon, 274
Butlin, Robin A., 88

cadastral hold, 220
cadastral key, 222-223
cadastre, 134
Caird, James, 210, 216
Caird, Sir James, 42, 47
Caisse du Midi, 178-180
Caldwell, J.C., 410
Cambridge, 70
Cambridgeshire, 75, 85-86, 115
Canada, 314, 333, 341
  East, 329
  Lower, 314
  Pre-Confederation, 313
  Upper, 313-314
Canada West, 298, 313-315, 318-324, 329
  Farm Sample, 1861, 315-317, 324, 327-328
  (*See also* Ontario, Canada [Upper])

capital, 39, 151, 191-193, 198, 260, 281, 382, 385, 444, 448, 456, 462-463, 468, 471, 473
  accumulation, 390-391
  agricultural, 139, 145, 464
  costs of enclosure, 60
  expenditures, 460, 462, 474
  gains, 308
  human, 287
  improvements, 55
  industrial, 57
  investment, 451, 464
  to labor ratio, 205
  productive, 461, 464, 466
  requirements of production, 138
  (*See also* financial resources)
capitalism, 413, 443, 445, 451, 453, 455-456, 477, 483, 497, 508
  agrarian market, 460
  capitalist structure, 442
  development of, 474, 502, 509
  market, 466-467, 473-474
  production, 509
  relations, 456
  rent, 450
  in Russia, 507, 513
  and socialism, 508
  transition to, 411, 426
capitalist farms, 3, 7, 12, 17
  (*See also* agrarian capitalism)
Cardwell (Canada), 336
carrots, 38
Catholicism, 288, 439
cattle
  (*See* livestock)
census (manuscript), 263
  of 1860, 261, 264-265, 275, 276, 277
Census (U.S.)
  1840, 287
  1860, 291, 294, 298
Census of Canada (1871), 333, 336, 344

Census Office, U.S., 309, 310
Census, 1911 (England), 195
census, zemstvo, 479-480, 490, 495
cereal, 3, 8, 144, 149, 353-354, 390, 402
  -based farming, 12
  -based husbandry, 148
  cultivation, 398
  prices, 111
  winter, 138
Chambers, J.D., 87, 106-107, 109-110, 115, 118, 119
Chambray, Le Marquis de, 135
Champagne, 139, 141-142, 148
Chapman, J., 66
Chartist land colonies, 195
Chayanov, A.V., 475, 478, 503, 508
cheese, 35, 319, 325
Chelveston, 97
Chernyi peredel, 424
Cheshire, 36-37, 45
Cheung, Steven, 339-340, 344, 345
Cheverry, Victor de, 136
chickens, 256
child-woman ratio, 287, 289
Chinese labor, 14
Cholvy, 185
Chorley, P., 88
Chubinskii, P., 408
church, 62
  priests, 392
  as property owner, 225, 231
  seminary students, 392
Church of England, 45
Civil War (U.S.), 18, 253, 255, 279, 308
Clare (England), 41
Clare (poet)
  "The Parish," 56
Clark, Christopher, 274, 275
clergy, 497
Clifford, Francis, 210, 216
climate, 370, 511

Index 519

cloth, 319
 clothing, 391-392
clover, 34, 71-72, 75-77, 81, 128
Clutterbuck, J.C., 216
Coale, 407
Coale, Ansley, 23
Cobb-Douglas production function, 148-149
Coke, 43
coleseed, 71, 76
Collins, E.J.T., 7, 10, 124, 216
Collison, William, 59
colonization, 447, 451-452
colons
 (*See* sharecropping)
Comices Agricoles, 148
commenda contract, 145
Commerce, U.S. Department of, 309
commercial farming, 194, 263
common resources
 rights to, 8
common rights of access, 28, 98, 113, 258, 260
 owners, 63
 and pasture, 111
commons, 79, 97
 availability of, 28
 disappearance of, 38
 enclosure of, 37, 59
 selling of, 28
 size of, 83
 wastes, 113
communal lands, 402-403
 management, 424
 redistribution of, 371
 selling of, 59
communal rights, 34
commune, 349-350, 510-511
 management, 424
 repartitional land, 391-392, 394, 398, 402-403
 (*See also* obschina)
competition, 15, 473-474

Condran, Gretchen A., 23, 273
Confino, Michael, 409, 508
Connecticut, 286, 296-297, 300
Conrad, Alfred H., 312
conscription, 416
Constable, Sir Marmaduke, 35
 estates of, 35
Constant, J.-M., 21, 155
Constituent Assembly, 130
contracts, 2
 rental, 331
copyhold tenement, 140
corn, 73, 83, 208, 266-267
 harvest, 211
 Indian, 314, 318, 323, 326
 yields, 78, 80-81
Corn Law, 192
corps de ferme, 142-144
 size constrains, 143
corvee obligations, 390
Cossacks, 415-416, 452, 481, 483
 Don Cossacks, 416
 Zaporozh cossacks, 416
Costin District (MD), 297
costs of farming, 39-40, 191, 461
 enforcement, 332
 supervisory, 332
 transaction, 332, 337
 (*See also* capital)
cottage industry, 6, 398
 output, 513
cottages, 10
cotton, 14, 267-268
 economy, 263
 growers, 306
 industry, 414
Cotton Belt (U.S.), 256
Counter-Reformation, 220
counter-revisionism, 58
courts, township, 391
 (*See also* volostyne sudy)
Coverley, Sir Roger de, 45
Craigie, P.G., 47

credit, 171, 253, 259
  emergency, 175, 177-181
  immobilization of, 178
  land-, 424
  nonlocal, 166
  short-term, 168, 174, 178
  long-term, 17
Credit Agricole, 176-181, 183
  Board of Directors, 178
Credit Foncier, 162, 165-166, 168-174, 176, 184-185
Crimean War, 419
criminals, exile of, 444-445
Crisp, Olga, 367, 387, 407, 508
Croatia-Slavonia, 223, 225
croit, 153
Crop Returns (1801), 51
crop rotation, 32, 34, 46, 143, 149, 151-152, 354, 364, 370, 511
  biennial, 126, 128, 138
  changing, 83
  Norfolk, 70, 75, 77, 82
  three-course, 139
  three-field farming, 77
crops, 298
  vs. animals, 50
  cash, 268, 306
  choice of, 50
  as a commodity, 268
  cultivation, 459-460, 466-467, 469, 471
  distribution, 53
  failure, 357, 371, 374, 376, 381
  fertility, 357
  fodder, 334
  geographical influence on, 361
  of the Middle Ages, 81
  mix, 340
  production, 268, 281
  truck, 306
  yields, 72, 451
  (*See also* root crops)
Crowther, J.E., 67

cultivation, 70, 442
  cultivators, 301
  shifting, 11
  soil-exhausting, 11
cultural heritage, 285, 288
Cunynghame, A., 310
Curti, Merle, 274, 275, 309
Czap, P., 407, 409

D.I., 407
dairy farming, 32, 36, 152, 266-267, 298, 306, 319, 324-325, 446, 450
  cows, 256
  milk production, 153, 257
Dal', V., 408
Dallas, Gregor, 21
Danhof, Clarence, 273, 274, 275, 291, 294, 310, 311
Danube, 225-227, 231-233, 237-238, 240-241, 244
Darby, H.C., 87
Davenport, William, 55
David, Paul A., 158, 273, 311
Davies, E., 118
Davies, W., 87, 106, 109
Davis, James E., 274
Davis, Lance E., 23
Davis, R., 65
de Vries, J., 514
death, 390-391, 398
debt, 126, 161, 447
  debt-slavery, 474
  debtors, 447
  size of, 164, 171
De Canio, S.J., 345
dedushka-domovoi (the grandfather house-spirit), 406
Defoe, Daniel, 35, 46
DeKalb County, Georgia, 256, 261-272
Delaware, 285, 302
Demeny, 407

demesne, 378, 405
  obligations, 398
demesne farms, 140, 354, 362, 364
demographics, 315-316
Department of Agriculture (U.S.), 301
deportation, 378
depression, 162
Derbyshire, 109-110
Deslandes, 154, 155
Devon, 36-37
Diderot, 154
diet, 38, 306
  meat, 51
discount rate, 148
discrimination, 295
disease, 34
  "cattle plague" (rinderpest), 34
distribution, 195-197
diversification, 376
Dobrozrakov, M., 410
Dollar, Charles, 503
domaines (compact farms), 126
Domar, Evsey, 19, 24, 350, 365, 367, 435, 438, 508
Dombasle swing plow, 151
  vs. wooden plow, 151
Dombasle, Mathhieu de, 158, 159
Domrachev, A., 453
Don, 419, 435
Dorset, 37, 38, 196-197, 200, 202
dowries, 163, 389, 391, 395-397
  direct, 392
  as measure of economy, 134
  (*See also* pridanoe)
drainage, 8, 34, 60, 70, 74-75, 80, 83, 130, 371
  hollow drains, 74, 81-82
  open vs. enclosed, 74
  tile drains, 70
drought, 211
drovers, 256
Druzhinin, N.M., 412-413, 426, 427, 428, 508

Dubrovskii, S.M., 514
Duby, Georges, 21
dues, 362
  mixed, 362-364
  mixed vs. barschina, 363
Dugrand, R., 184, 185, 186
Dunfries, 196, 200, 202
Dunn, Richard S., 19
Dupâquier, Jacques, 23
Durham (Canada), 336
dvor, 391, 395, 398, 401-402, 404, 406-407, 479
dvorianstvo, 436
Dymond, 67

E-iu, Pr V., 408, 409
East Coast (U.S.), 287, 291, 297
East Riding, 91
Easterlin, Richard A., 23, 273, 310
Eatwell, J., 340, 345
economics
  decisions, 404
  differentiation, 398, 403
  equilibrium, 397
  inflexible, 50
  security, 446
  stratification, 371, 403
Economics Surveys, 359
economies of scale, 28, 151, 187
  landowner, 451
  peasant, 451
Eddie, Scott, 124, 248, 249
Edelstein, Michael, 272
Editorial Commission List, 359, 367
education, 32, 270
  (*See also* training)
efficiency, 331, 359
Efimenko, Aleksandra, 392, 394, 408, 409
Efimenko, P., 408, 409
Egrovo, Pavel, 385
election, 479

Eletsk, 416
　Livensk District, 416
Eltis, David, 19
Emancipation (1861), 350, 353, 403, 429-430, 436-437, 451
Emancipation Statues, 359
emigration, 313
employment, 376
　nonagricultural, 370, 377, 383
enclosure, 32, 35, 37, 46, 52, 58, 63, 82, 85
　Acts, 55, 60, 71, 98
　diversification due to, 52, 75, 78
　economic gains due to, 54
　efficiency gains of, 49-50, 53, 64
　financing of, 62
　improvements, 69
　and landholding, ,92, 99, 103, 105, 107-109
　preparliamentary, 70, 105
　and productivity, 81
　and rates of sale, 94-97, 102
　and rents, 33, 54, 56, 60
　repair, 63
　yields, 74
　(*See also* commons, Enclosure Movement, open-field farming, parliamentary enclosure)
Enclosure Movement, 27-28, 49, 104
Engels, F., 188, 475
Engerman, Stanley L., 19, 20, 23, 312, 366
English Midlands
　(*See* Midlands counties)
English speakers, 286
Enquête Agricole, 150
　of 1852, 141
　of 1862, 147
epizootic outbreaks, 145
Eriksson, Ingrid, 23
Essex, 35, 40, 75
estate formation, 144
estate surveys, 78, 412

ethnicity, 288
Eure-et-Loir, 148
Europe, western, 389-390, 397, 513
Evans, E.J., 87
Evans, Robert J., 312
Eversden, 82
Evershed, H., 216
expenses, 59
experimental farms, 43
exports, 188
extraction industry, 444
Eye, 105

Falconer, John, 273
fallow land, 71, 76, 77
family
　farm, 4, 302
　labor, 257
　nuclear, 2
　size, 383
　status, 401
family farms, 3, 4, 17, 42, 112, 138, 253, 281, 290, 298, 301, 314, 325, 513
　labor, 285, 288
　size of, 9
　(*See also* farm families)
famine, 419
Faragher, John Mack, 273, 274
Farcy, Jean-Claude, 22, 140, 155, 158
Farey, J., 47
fermage
　(*See* leases [long-term])
Farmer's Guide in Hiring and Stocking Farms, 40
farms
　allocation, 356
　diversification of, 324
　expansion, 41-42
　field surpluses, 299
　North American vs. European, 253

Index 523

size of, 32, 36, 261, 265, 284, 300, 306-307, 316-322, 324, 326, 338, 357, 362
  value, 322, 324, 326
  "yeoman," 266, 272
farmsteads, 11
Fedorov, V.A., 367, 387, 412, 420, 426, 427, 428
Felvidék, 236
fences, 60, 259, 291
Ferleger, Louis, 272
fertility, 287-288, 405, 442
  behavior, 290
  decisions, 404
  differences, 290
  high, 406
  and household size, 401
  rate, 288
fertilizer, 17, 18, 34, 193-195, 301, 361, 363, 371, 378, 511
  application of, 32
  cost of, 34
  liming, 130
  manure, 143, 146, 150
feudalism, 398, 411, 413, 443-444, 448, 452-453, 474, 509, 514
  evolution of, 426
Field, Daniel, 5, 20, 24, 350, 509-511
Field, E., 366
financial efficiency, 56
financial resources, 315, 385
financing, 139, 144-145
Fishlow, Albert, 275
Fitzwilliam estates, 56
flax, 32, 370, 373, 511
Fleet Street Farmers, 43
Fleisig, Heywood, 19
Floyd County, Georgia, 256, 261-272
Fogel, Robert W., 20, 281-282, 309, 312, 366
food consumption, 465
Ford, Lacy K., 20, 276
foreclosure, 176-177, 184, 446

foreigners, 288, 290
forest, 231
Forster, C., 310
Forster, R., 135
Foust, James, 309
Fox-Genovese, Elizabeth, 273
France, 137
fraud, 436
French Revolution, 140
French Treasury, 168
French Wars, 61
  (*See also* Napoleonic Wars)
Friedmann, Harriet, 19, 273, 274, 275
Fringford, 57
Frontenac, 334
feudal, 27
Fussell, G.E., 88, 216

Gegarin family, 370-371, 376-378, 380
  Land Survey Books, 386
  Papers, 386
Gainsborough, 41
Galentorn, N., 409
Gallman, Robert, 20, 297, 311
Galloway, 196, 200, 202
Galloway, Lowell, 312
Gambus and de Martin, 164
Ganeboe, 487
gardens, 256-257, 341, 390, 405
Gates, Paul W., 275, 306, 310, 312
Gatrell, Peter, 351, 508, 514
Gavrilova, Varvara, 386
Gayer, A.D., 213, 216
General Land Survey, 356
Genovese, Eugene D., 23
George, Dorothy, 111, 120
Georgia, 253, 262-263, 272
  antebellum, 256, 262-263
  Railroad, 262
  Upcountry, 256, 261-264, 267-268, 272

Germans, 236, 290
Gerschenkron, Alexander, 407, 409, 430, 433, 437, 438, 508
Gervais, Charles, 169-170, 185, 186
Gini coefficients, 5, 297
Gini Index, 291, 297, 479-484, 486-503, 510
glaciation, 287
Gladstone, 195
glebe terriers, 84
Gloucestershire, 36
golodnaia arenda (hunger rental), 494
golytba, 483
Goodman, David, 386
Goody, J., 397, 402, 408, 409
Goriushkin, Leonid M., 350, 453, 454, 508, 511, 513
Got'e, Iu. V., 508
grains, 15, 38, 53, 71, 80, 141, 258, 268, 298, 306, 334, 371, 385, 434, 447
  acreage, 54
  marketed, 512-513
  reserves, 370-372, 365
  sale of, 403
  surplusses, 140, 382
  threshing, 399
  yields, 128
  (*See also* individual varieties of grain [e.g., wheat, corn, barley, etc.])
grange farms, 140
Grantham, George, 17, 21, 22, 24, 29, 123, 155, 158, 159, 272
grass leys, 32, 34
Gray, Lewis C., 258, 274
Great Depression (1875-), 207, 210-211
Great Plains (U.S.), 339
Greek-Orthodox, 439
Greens North, 97, 104
Gregory, Paul, 351, 508

Grekov, B.D., 409, 512, 514
Grey District (Canada), 336
Grigor'ev, V.N., 503
groomwealth, 395
Grover, Richard, 116, 118
Gueslin, A., 186
Guiet, E.L., 156, 157
Guillanumin, Emile, 19, 24, 135

Habsbawm, Eric J., 275
Haddenham, 60
Haeger, John Denis, 275
Hahn, Steven, 274, 275
Hair, P.E.H., 65
Hamilton, 334
Hammond, B., 65
Hammond, J.L., 65
Hammonds, the, 57-58
  pro-, 65
  (*See also* B. Hammond and J.L. Hammond)
Hampshire, 37
hand tools, 206
handicraft industries, 382-383, 385, 398
  development of, 510
  (*See also* cottage industry)
Hannington, 104
Hannon, Joan Underhill, 22
Hareven, Tamara K., 23, 273, 310
Hargrave, 104
Harkness, J.G., 344
Harman, H., 66
Harris, A., 65
harvest, 389
  technology, 15, 17
Hatwley, V.A., 119
Hau, M., 185
Havinden, M.A., 65, 88
hay, 319, 325-326
Hay, Douglas, 114
Heady, E.O., 345
Hébert-Barrat, Susanne, 155

Heim, Carol, 275
Helpston, 56
Helpstone, 104
hemp, 32, 370, 373, 383, 385, 390, 511
  processing, 381
Henretta, James, 273, 274
Hérault, 167-172, 174, 176, 180
herbicides, 18
Hereford, 196
Herefordshire, 75, 200, 202
Hertfordshire, 207
Hibbard, Benjamin H., 310
Higgins, J.P.P., 66
Higgs, Robert, 331, 340, 344, 345
highways, 448
Hobsbawm, Eric, 216, 386
Hoch, Steven L., 6, 22, 350, 367, 510-511
Holderness, B.A., 47, 60, 66
Holkham, 43
Holstein, 416
Home Counties, 208
Homer, H., 66
Hoover, Edgar M., 23
hops, 32
horses, 32, 191, 294, 320, 360, 383, 385, 394, 399, 401, 406, 447, 497
  distribution of, 402-403, 479
  draft, 467
  as measure of wealth, 375, 385, 398
  thoroughbred, 450
Hoskins, W.G., 88, 115, 116, 120
House of Commons, 109, 111
household registers, 370-371, 380
household size, 398-400, 403, 405
  division, 402
  extinction, 402
Hubscher, Ronald H., 14, 22, 23, 151, 154, 155, 158, 159
Humphries, E.F.M., 88

Hungary, 124, 220-221, 230, 236-237, 245, 247
  proper, 223
Hunt, E.H., 216
Hunt, H.G., 65, 116, 118
Huntingdon, 70
Huntingdonshire, 196, 200, 202
husbandry, 50-51, 75, 91, 130, 141
Hutchinson, William K., 273
hybrid seeds, 301

Iaik, 416
Iakovlev, Anisem, 385
Iana River, 362, 364
Iaroslav Province (guberniia), 350, 356-359, 365, 393
Iatsunskii, Ia. V., 508
Ignatovich, I.I., 412-413, 427, 508
Ile-de-France, 141-142, 148
Illinois, 285-286, 292-293, 296, 298, 300, 302, 304, 334
  Agricultural Experiment Station, 310
Imazon, I., 453
immigration, 283, 313
  immigrant-headed households, 290
immiserization, 187
Imperial Russian Geographic Society, 392
imports, 188-189
  prohibitions on, 192
incentive systems, 355
income, 11, 61, 258, 383, 459-460, 462-474, 512
  cadastral net, 221
  cash, 256
  gross, 390
  master's, 434
  national, 281, 283, 508
  nonagricultural, 381-382, 384
  redistribution of, 56
  rental, 283

saving of, 385
supplemental, 385
(*See also* profits)
Indian, 295
  labor, 14
Indiana, 285-287, 292-293, 296, 300, 304
indigo, 3
Industrial Orders, 195-196, 200-201
Industrial Revolution, 219, 279
Industrial Revolution (British), 188, 203
industrialization, 8, 16, 60, 187, 290, 455, 507-508, 510-511
  and labor, 204
  preindustrial America, 255
  in Russia, 349
information
  dissemination of, 129
inheritance, 40, 42, 257, 270, 371, 391, 401
  heirs, 302
Inland Revenue, 192
intensification, 16
inventory reform, 419
investors, 308
Iowa, 285-286, 292-294, 296, 300
Irish, 288, 290-291
  labor, 214
Irkutsk, 443
irrigation, 301
Iskra, 362
Islip, 104
Isoré, J., 154, 157, 158
Iusupov family, 403

Jacquart, Jean, 21
Jaynes, Gerald, 14, 20, 23
Jefferson, Thomas, 253, 280, 297-298, 309
  Jeffersonian democracy, 280, 294
Jeffries, Richard, 208, 216
Jensen, Joan, 273
Jensen, M.C., 438

Jensen, Robert, 503
Johnson, D.G., 339, 345
Johnson, L.A., 344
Johnston, C.M., 344
Johnston, H.J.M., 344
Johnston, W.S., 344
Jones, David J.V., 117
Jones, E.L., 21, 66, 155, 216
Jones, R.L., 333, 344
Joppé, André, 158
Journal d'agriculture pratique, 153
Junker estates, 6

kabala, 423, 474
  (*See also* debt-slavery)
Kabuzan, V.M., 365
Kafengauz, B.B., 366
Kagarov, E.G., 409
Kahan, Arkadiu, 367, 508
Kain, R.J.P., 87
Kakwani, N.C., 311
Kalachov, N., 394, 407, 408
Kalmyks, 415
Kaluga gubernaii, 393
Kandeevka, 423
Kanin, Maksim, 416
  (*See also* Peter III)
Kansas, 281, 285-286, 292-293, 296, 300, 304
Kaplan, Steven L., 21
Karlovka Canton, 484
Karpovich, Michael, 248
Kaufman, A.A., 453
Kavelin, K.D., 415, 427
Kazan, 416, 423
Kazan' gubernaii, 393
Kent, 35, 41, 208
Kent (Canada), 336
Kent, J.H., 117
Kentucky, 285
Kerridge, E., 65
Kettering, 91
Keyder, Caglar, 158

Keynes, 146
Kharkov, 424, 470-471
khutor, 483
King, J. Crawford, Jr., 274
Kingston (Canada), 336
Kingston, Duke of, 36
kinship, 2
Kishkin, M.N., 407
kladka, 391-397, 402-403, 511
Klein, Judith L.V., 158, 302, 311
Klingaman, David C., 273, 310, 312
Kolchin, P., 365
Kolossa, Tibor, 237, 248, 249
Komlos, John H., 231, 249
Konstantinograd District, 480-482, 484-496, 498-500
Kornievskaia, N.N., 475
Korovka, Anton, 416
Kostrov, N., 408
Koval'chenko, I.D., 12, 20, 350, 355, 365, 366, 386, 387, 398, 409, 412, 414, 420, 426, 427, 428, 454, 475, 503, 504, 508-509, 511-513, 514
Krutikov, V.I., 367
kulaks, 402, 444, 446, 448-450, 453, 478, 510
Kunreuther, Howard, 274
Kursk, 423
Kursk guberniia, 393
Kussmaul, A., 47
kustarnye, 513

labor, 37, 89, 203, 206, 209-210, 259, 262, 264-266, 287, 328, 332, 340, 385, 405, 407, 448, 457, 472-474
  absorption, 205
  adult, 483
  agricultural, 189, 205, 389
  balance of, 403
  as capital stock, 39
  cheap, 444
  child, 288
  cost of, 193, 469
  curve, 283
  day, 37-38, 272
  decline in labor force, 194
  demand for, 207, 272
  as determinant of output, 389
  differentiation of, 390
  distribution of, 282, 405
  diversion of, 327
  division of, 139
  employers of, 280
  and enclosure, 57-58
  estimates, 153
  expenditures, 462-464
  hired, 443-446, 456-459, 468
  hired vs. unfree, 414
  indentured, 447-448
  in industry, 459
  intensity of, 465
  involuntary, 380
  landless, 195, 264, 266, 314, 404
  mobility of, 5, 204, 280, 283, 370
  nonagricultural, 350
  obligations, 390
  productivity of, 32, 301-302, 462-463, 468, 471, 474
  rights of, 207
  rural, 510
  seasonal, 150, 272, 294
  service, 414, 509, 512
  sexual division of, 257
  shortages of, 385, 511
  social division of, 258
  specialization of, 507
  strikes, 424-425
  supply of, 4, 146, 150, 213, 280
  surpluses, 204, 280
  unskilled, 262
  urban, 513
  wage, 261, 302, 320, 323, 326
  (*See also* barshchina, otrabotka)
labour
  (*See* labor)

Labrousse, C.E., 22, 135
Lake Erie, 336-337
Lake Huron, 336
Lake Ontario, 334, 336
Lake Region (Russia), 438
Lánc, Margit, 248
Lancashire, 36
land, 402-403
  allocation, 483
  arable, 436
  balance of, 403
  cultivated, 466
  distribution of, 400, 405, 449
  federal land policy, 282-283, 291
  market prices of, 436
  redistribution of, 404, 510
  reserve arable, 398
  surplus, 371
  title to, 281
land allotment, 390, 399
Land Tax, 89, 91, 95, 97-98, 103, 106, 116
  collectors, 91
  returns, 91-96, 106, 111, 114
  records, 115
  (*See also* landlords, tenants)
land-credit, 424
landholders, 110
  disappearance of, 92-93
  small, 404
landlord-tenant, 44, 190, 199
landlords, 35, 39, 56-57, 100, 193, 195, 356, 362, 365, 392, 403, 418, 513
  absentee, 89
  attempted murder of, 420-421
  Land Tax returns, 94
  landlord-peasant relations, 509
  vs. landowners, 94
  nobel, 404
  vs. owner-occupiers, 94
  sovereignty of, 5
  wills of, 421

Languedoc, 14, 123, 162-163, 168, 172, 175-176
latifundia, 24, 247, 451, 483
  latifundistas, 246-247
Laurence, E., 47
Lavoisier, Antoine, 144, 156
Lavrovsky, V.M., 66, 98, 116, 117
Law V (1909), 221, 248
Lawrence, Sarah, 272
lease, 10, 35, 39, 56, 83, 146
  emphyteutic, 140
  long-term, 132, 134
  short-term, 130
  in Siberia, 450
Lebedev, N., 408, 409
Leclerc-Thouin, O., 154
Lee, C.H., 200-202
Lee, Ronald D., 329
Leet, D., 310
Lefebvre, Georges, 135
legumes, 37
Leicester, 84-85
Leichestershire, 36, 79
Lenin, V.I.
  (*See* Ulianov, V.I.)
Lennox, 334
Leonard, Carol, 11, 13, 349-350, 367, 368
Levant trade, 55
Levenson-Gower estates, 36
Levine, Daniel P., 275
Levy, S., 216
Levy-Leboyer, M., 158, 159, 185
Lewis, W. Arthur, 23
Liashchenko, N.N., 413
Liashchenko, P.I., 437
life cycle (biological), 401-403, 406
Liger, Louis, 146, 154, 156, 158
Limanton, 134
Lime
  (*See* fertilizer)
Lincolnshire, 91, 109, 200, 202
  estates, 56

Lindert, Peter H., 247
Linkov, I.I., 412, 427
Lisle, 42
literacy, 269, 271, 281, 294-295, 385
Little Russia, 392
Little, H.J., 216
Litvak, B.G., 412-413, 420, 423, 426, 427, 428, 508
Litvak, K.V., 503
Litvakov, B.M., 366, 454
Liverpool, 55
livestock, 81, 144, 256-259, 266, 291, 298, 301, 306, 316, 320, 323-324, 326, 334, 360, 363, 370-371, 385, 398, 401, 405-407, 442, 450, 459-462, 466-467, 469-471
  balance of, 403
  breeding, 16, 36, 50
  distribution of, 405, 490
  epidemics, 374
  fairs, 131
  feed, 316, 324
  management, 16
  marketing, 131
  production, 32, 325
  products, 319
  sale of, 403
  shortages of, 385
  as status symbol, 402
  stocking practices, 8, 448
  surpluses, 382
  value of, 281, 294
loans, 161, 434
  nonsecured, 148
Loire, 126
London, 212
London (Canada), 334
Lorraine, 141-142
Lositskii, A., 430, 432-434, 436, 437, 438
losses to animals, 45

lucerne, 128
Lutton, 105

Macaulay, Frederick R., 312
Macdonald, Stuart, 47
Macé, George, 155
Machina, Mark J., 24, 365, 435, 437, 438
machinery, 151, 195, 291, 446
  depreciation, 151
  disadvantages of, 210
Machinery Question, 203
Madingley, 82
Maine, 285
Maison rustique, 156
  du xix siecle, 157
Malcolmson, Robert W., 114
Maloga District, 356-364
Maloga River, 362
Maloga Uzed
  (*See* Emancipation [1861])
Malone, Anne Patton, 20
Malykhin, 410
management structure, 362
  estate, 374, 376, 378, 405
Manchester, 207
manorial organization, 5, 27, 365
manorial rights, 62
manufacturing industry, 188, 258, 266, 304, 308
  home, 268
  urban, 369
Manuilovskoe estate, 370-371, 374, 376, 378, 381-382, 385
Marczewski, J., 159
Maria Theresa (Empress of Hungary), 222, 236
markets, 138, 257, 259, 291, 314, 356, 369, 374, 399, 456, 512-513
  capaicty, 460
  commodities, 456
  formation, 445

free, 437
integration, 260
involvement, 472
job, 445
participation, 478
system, 414
(*See also* capitalism)
Marpas, M. Pinet de, 136
Marr, William L., 10, 253, 328, 329, 333, 336, 344, 345
marriage, 288, 390-391, 395, 397-398, 402-403, 405
    age of, 287
    contract, 140, 392
    early, 403-404
    inspection of households, 395
    marital agreement, 395
    permission to marry, 396
    rituals, 395
    seasonal pattern of, 396
    wedding expenses, 392, 394
Marshall, W., 43, 47, 205, 216
Martin, J.M., 65, 66, 67, 89-90, 103, 110, 114, 115, 118, 120
Marx, Karl, 28, 204, 215, 260, 275, 475
Marxism, 105, 478, 509
Maryland, 281, 286, 296-297, 300, 304
Mashkin, 393, 407
Massachusetts, 279, 285, 287, 302
Mastin, J., 88
mate selection, 395
Mathias, P., 66, 216
Matthaei, Julie A., 273
Mavrodin, V.V., 412, 427
Maxey, 104
Maynell, Hugo, 44
Mazur, A.G., 437
McCloskey, D.N., 21, 50, 62, 64, 66, 87, 189-190
    method, 190
    -prices formula, 190

McDonald, Forrest, 273
McInnis, Marvin, 10, 253, 298, 311, 329
McMath, Robert C., 274
McWhiney, Grady, 273
meat, 152, 324
mechanical technology, 302
    development of, 138
mechanization, 147, 193, 197, 203-205, 207-208, 213, 215, 301-302, 329, 445
    autonomous, 214
    induced, 213-214
    opposition to, 207
    social costs of, 214
Mel'gunov, Governor General Aleksei, 367
Mellor, J.W., 410
Mende Collection, 356
Mennonites, 336
merchandising, 260
merchants, 259-260, 263
Merrill, Michael, 272, 274
metayage
    (*See* sharecropping)
Metelkin, 421
Meuvret, Jean, 20, 155
Meyer, John R., 312
Michigan, 285-286, 292-294, 296-298, 300, 304, 306, 314
mid-chernozem region
    (*See* blackearth region)
Middle Atlantic, 287, 300-301
Middlesex, 59
Midlands counties, 62, 63, 69-70, 73, 80, 90-91, 111, 212
Midwest (U.S.), 284-285, 287, 289-293, 296-298, 304, 306
migrant workers, 379, 383, 450
migration, 287, 313, 376, 381, 398, 442-443, 445, 447, 510
    assigned, 376
    forced, 19

Index 531

in-migrant decisions, 285
organized, 380
resistance to, 376, 378
rural, 212, 215
substitutes, 385
(*See also* emigration, immigration, peasant movements)
Mikheev, M.E., 408, 409
Mills, Denis, 116
Milov, L.V., 366, 475, 508, 514
Minarik, L.P., 509, 514
Mingay, George E., 8, 21, 28, 46, 47, 49, 56, 64, 65, 66, 87, 94, 106, 110, 115, 116, 118, 119
minifundia, 9
mining, 414
Ministère d'Agriculture (France), 21, 176
Ministry of Agriculture (England), 192-193
Ministry of Finance (France), 168, 180
Ministry of Internal Affairs (Russian), 412
Minnesota, 285-286, 291-294, 296-298, 300, 304, 306
  Commissioner of Statistics, 310
mir, 411
Mironov, B.N., 365, 508, 513
Mississippi Delta, 20
Missouri, 281, 286, 292-293, 296-298, 300, 304, 306
Moeller, Robert G., 14, 20, 23
Mokyr, J., 367
Molinier, Alain, 157
Monks Risborough, 59
Montpellier, 165, 178, 183
Moore, John Hebron, 20
Mordovtsev, D.L., 415
Morgan, Edmund S., 19
Morineau, Michel, 22
Morokhovets, E.A., 426, 427
mortality rates, 405
  child, 89

mortgages, 55, 62, 112, 140, 148, 161, 163-164, 168, 173-174
withdrawal of, 181
(*See also* foreclosure)
Morton, J.C., 216
Moscow, 357, 370, 374, 376, 380, 396, 407, 416, 511
Mosley, John, 42
Mourgues, F., 186
Muhkin, V.P., 392, 394, 408
Musin-Pushkins, 354, 364, 366, 368
  Ivan Iakovlevich Musin Pushkin, 364
Mutch, Robert, 275
Myiant, H., 410
Myl'nikova, K., 408, 409

N.R.-v, 409
Napoleonic Wars, 35, 42, 55, 60, 191, 210
(*See also* post-Napoleonic depression)
Naseby, 105
Nasonov, A.M., 403, 407, 409, 410, 512
Nassau Senior, 205-206, 216
nativity, 294
(*See also* birth rates)
Neeson, J.M., 8, 66, 67, 115, 116, 118, ,119, 120
Nelson, Richard R., 19
Nene valley, 91, 96
Nevers, 127, 132
New Brunswick, 334
New England, 287-288, 290, 300-301
New Hampshire, 281, 286-287, 296-297, 300, 302, 304, 306
New Jersey, 286, 296, 298, 300
New York, 286, 296, 298, 300, 304
Newbery, D.M.G., 345
Newbury, David S., 22
Newhall, J.B., 310

Newton Bromswold, 104
Niemi, Albert W., Jr., 275
Nièvre, 126, 135, 136
Nikolaev, A., 409
Nivernais, 123, 126, 129, 132, 134
  Canal, 128
Nizhegorod guberniia, 393, 395
Nizhnyi Novgorod, 357, 415
nobles, 356
  as landowners, 444, 474
non-blackearth region, 355, 357, 370, 430-432, 434-435, 438, 511
nonagricultural sector, 376, 380
  (*See also* employment [nonagricultural])
Norfolk, 35, 37, 42, 75, 212
Norfolk rotation
  (*See* crop rotation)
Norris, Roberty, 55
North (U.S.), 262, 297-298, 308
  rural, 295-296
North Carolina, 272
Northampton, 91
Northamptonshire, 51-53, 56, 63, 79, 84-86, 90-91, 93, 95, 98, 103, 106, 109-111, 115
  Record Office, 117
Northeast (U.S.), 283-284, 287, 289-293, 296, 298, 300, 304, 306, 308
Northumberland, 336
Northwest Ordinance, 283
Northwest, Old, 287, 300-301
notarial insolvency, 164, 166
Nottinghamshire, 36, 55
Nouvelle maison rustique, 145, 157, 158
Nova Scotia, 334
Novgorod guberniia, 393, 416
  Porkhovskii District, 416
nuclear families
  (*See* families [nuclear])

O'Brien, Patrick, 158
oats, 53-54, 71-72, 74-76, 77, 81, 267, 318, 323, 360, 370, 372, 390
  yields, 32, 75, 371
obrok, 6, 354-355, 362-364, 370, 421, 449
  estates, 355
  (*See also* rent from wages)
obshchina, 350, 449, 510
occupations, 261-262, 270, 281, 294-295, 380, 383
  nonagricultural, 370
occupiers, 90
Ohio, 283, 286, 291-293, 296, 300, 314
Ojala, E.M., 216
Old Poor Law, 206
Olmstead, Alan L., 158, 274, 311
Ontario, 253, 313, 331, 333-334, 337, 343
  (*See also* Canada West)
open-field farming, 27, 50, 54, 69, 71, 77, 80, 82-83, 86, 112-113
  vs. enclosure, 52, 54, 78-80, 91, 99-103, 108, 110, 112
  incentives of, 81
  sale of land, 61
  yields, 74
orchards, 256-257, 321, 341
Orel, 479
Orlov, 354, 416, 423
Orwin, C.S., 120
otrabotka (labor-rental), 494, 509
Ottawa, 334, 336
Otto, John Solomon, 273, 274
Otto, N., 408, 409
output, 152
  costs of, 193
  field crop, 315
  different rates of, 210
Ovchinnikov, 416
overseers, 264-265

owner-occupiers, 100, 103, 107, 109, 140-141, 259, 265, 328, 332, 337, 343
  vs. tenant-run farms, 333, 338, 344
ownership categories, 230, 232, 243
Owsley, Frank Lawrence, 273
Oxfordshire, 57, 85-86, 115, 206, 214

Pach, Zs. P., 248
Paina, E.S., 426
Pakhman, S.V., 408
Paris, 21, 128, 141-145
Parker, William N., 20, 21, 22, 23, 66, 155, 158, 272, 273, 274, 275, 302, 311
Parkinson, R., 77, 87
  A General View of the Agriculture of the County of Huntingdon, 71-72, 75-76
  A General View of the Agriculture of the County of Rutland, 71-72, 75-76
Parliament, 55, 58
  Members of, 45
parliamentary enclosure, 32, 49, 70, 78, 83, 89-91, 105-106, 109-111, 113
  and disappearance of the English peasantry, 114
  (*See also* enclosure)
Pasquet, 186
passports, 374, 376, 396
pasture
  conversion of arable to, 82
patriarchal authority, 405, 407, 448
peas, 51, 71, 76, 81, 267, 318, 323, 325, 373
peasant dues, 413, 421
peasant economy, 386
peasant farms, 17, 401

peasant movements, 378, 380, 411-413, 415, 417-421, 425
  armed, 416
  manorial, 420
Peasant War, 416
peasants, 419, 480
  allotments, 398
  bourgeoisie, 443
  mobility, 394
  proletariat, 443
  rural, 443
Pech, R., 185, 186
Peel (Canada), 336
Pennsylvania, 286, 296, 298, 300
Penza guberniia, 393, 423, 457-463, 465-466, 468, 470
Perche, 148
Perm guberniia, 393
Perpignan banks, 164
Peter III, 416
Peterborough, 336
petitions, 411, 419-420
Petrine Russia, 349
Petrovich, Paul, 416
Petrovskoe, 389-391, 394, 396-406
  serfs, 395, 397, 399, 407
petty production, 256, 260
  vs. commercial production, 256
  producers, 261
Phillips, A.D.M., 66, 115
phylloxera, 162-172
  Commission Superieure du, 168
  post-phylloxera recovery, 177
  resistant stocks, 168
physiocracy, 140
Physiocrats, 144
Picard, 151
piecework, 209
Pinchemel, Phillippe, 154
Pitt, William, 88, 120
plant varieties, 17, 18
plantations, 3, 4, 12, 314
  needs of, 4

transport systems, 14
  (*See also* slave plantations)
ploughs, 190, 445
  plow cutlivation, 397
plowland, 484, 491-493, 496, 498-501
  distribution, 482, 488-490, 497
  holdings of, 481, 485
Podder, N., 311
podvornye opisi, 370
Pokrovskii, M.N., 437
Pokrovskii, V.I., 386, 387
Polanyi, K., 410
politics, 405
  political literature, 508
Pollack, Robert A., 21
Pollard, S., 66, 216
Poltava Province, 425, 480-482, 484-487, 489, 491-497, 499-502, 510
Provincial Zemstvo, 480
Poltavskoe gubernskoe zemstvo, 503, 504, 505
pomeshchiki, 436
Pomfret, Richard, 158
Poole, 197
poor rate, 205, 209
poor relief, 46
Popkin, Samuel L., 386
population, 482
  density, 397
  distribution of, 281-282
  diversity of, 510
  growth, 8, 283, 371, 442-443, 510, 512
  mobility of, 451
  shifts, 370
  village, 398
post-Napoleonic depression, 56
  (*See also* Napolenoic Wars)
Postan, M.M., 20, 216
Postel-Vinay, 14, 123
Potanin, G.N., 441, 453
potash, 314
potatoes, 38, 267, 319, 341, 360-361

poverty, 290
Precambrian Shield, 334
Preobrazhenskii, A.A., 393, 407, 421, 427
Preobrazhenskii, V.A., 386, 387
Preradovich, Nikolaus von, 220, 248
prices
  movements of, 33, 35, 38
  index, 190
  collapse of, 42
  free market, 430
  movements of, 33, 35, 38
pridanoe, 391
Prince Ivan, 416
Princes Risborough, 55, 59
private property, 27
production, 461
  development of, 442, 445-446, 448
  expenditures, 457
  productive capacity, 490
  work and, 508
productivity, 33, 50, 57, 80, 189, 282, 447
  assessing gains in, 34, 190
  changes in, 198
  growth of, 69, 83
  influences on, 139
  of labor, 204
  of land, 53
  land/labor ratio, 361
  maximization of, 407
  yield/seed ratio, 364
profits, 40-41, 54, 81, 112, 140, 184, 280, 304, 471, 473
  farming vs. manufacturing, 304
  farming vs. transportation, 304
  landlord vs. sharecropper, 131
  margins, 55
  profitability, 302-303, 306, 462
  rates of return, 148, 151, 304-308
  sharing of, 130
proletariat, 457-458, 465, 474, 478
  class struggle, 424
  proletarianization, 511

property, transmission of, 391
Prude, Jonathon, 274
Pruitt, Bettye Hobbs, 21, 22
Prussia, 220-221, 415, 451, 513
Pugachev, 415-416, 418, 421-422
Pugachev's rebellion (1773-1775), 415-416
pulses, 53
Purdum, J.L., 54-55, 65
Pushman, 362
Puskás, Julia, 237, 248, 249
Pusy, P., 87
Pyotr Khripunov, 415
Pyrénées-Orientales, 163

Quarn country, the, 44
Quebec, 334, 337
Quesnay, 153
quit-rent, 414, 421, 449
 (*See also* obrok)

race, 294-295
railroads, 142, 434, 444, 448
 Trans-Siberian, 443, 445-446, 448, 450
 Western and Atlantic, 263
 (*See also* Georgia)
Rajczonek, Joseph, 119
Ransel, David L., 407
Ransom, Roger L., 21, 275, 331, 339, 344, 345
Rao, C.H., 345
rape (crop), 71, 76
rassloenie, 478, 497, 503, 508
Raunds, 97, 104, 108-109
Razin, 422
Read, C.S., 206, 216
real estate, 288
Reaman, G.E., 344
recruitment levies, 398
Redclift, Michawel, 386
redemption payments, 449
Redford A., 216

Reed, M., 117
Regan, John, 310
regional differentiation, 507
Register of Landowners, 220-223, 231-237, 246
 legal persons, 221
 natural persons, 221
regulation of agriculture, 113
Reid, Joseph D., Jr., 331, 344, 345
reinvestment, 133, 140
religion, 45, 288
 (*See also* Catholicism, Greek-Orthodox)
rent, 7, 34, 35, 44, 45, 62, 80-82, 113, 127, 132-133, 143, 150, 190, 193, 302, 304, 370, 374, 378, 382, 398, 450
 abatements, 56
 arrears, 381
 Cossack troops' rent fund, 450
 commercial, 199
 and crop rotations, 70
 division of, 191
 and enclosure, 33, 110
 fixed, 146
 incomes and, 192
 land, 447, 474
 low, 140
 movements of, 33, 57
 payments, 139
 rental relations, 451
 renters, 265, 451
 Ricardian, 56
 rolls, 56
 from wages, 376
 (*See also* capitalist rent)
Rent Assessment Register, 386
rental plow teams, 9
repartitions, 398
reproduction, 257-258
resorts, 197
resources, 188
responsivity, 7

retirement, 391, 398
  mean age of, 407
revenues, 403, 415, 469
  per laborer, 470
Revision Act (1829), 285
revisionism, 58
  (*See also* counter-revisionism)
Revolution of 1917, 507-508
Reynolds, L.G., 345
Rhode Island, 279, 285, 302
Riazan guberniia, 393, 416, 423
Ricardo, 190
Richardson, David, 55, 65
right of seizure, 450-451
Rikhter, D.A., 433, 438
risk, 333, 337
  distribution of, 332
risk-avoidance, 404
Roade, 105
roads, 35
  Royal Highway (in France), 127
Robin, Tourin-Theodore, 135, 136
Robinson, G.T., 437
Robinson, J., 340-345
Rockingham Forest, 91, 115
Roebuck, Peter, 46
Rogers, John, 23
Romania, 225
Romanov, Egor, 387
root crops, 34, 37, 51
Rose, W., 66
Rose, Walter, 208, 216
Rosovsky, H., 158
Rostov, 357
Rostow, W.W., 213, 216
Rothenberg, Winifred, 273
Rothkegel, Walter, 248
Rothstein, Morton, 19, 275
Roudier, L., 181
Rouen, 139
Roumasset, J., 345
Rozhestveno, 368
Ruback, R.S., 438

Rubinek, Gyula, 248
Rubinshtein, N.L., 367, 412, 426, 508, 512, 514
Rude, G., 216
Rudnev, 408
Rudolph, Richard, 20
Ruggles, Mr., 41
rukobit'e, 395
Rushden, 91, 96, 98, 104, 108-109
Russia, European, 392, 441-442, 445, 450, 452, 457, 473
  vs. Siberia, 444, 447
Russia, Great, 391, 393, 396-397, 406, 510-511
Russia, Imperial, 389, 441, 512
Russia, White, 438
Russian Emancipation (1861), 18
Russian repartitional commune, 6
Russian Revolution (first), 425
Russo-Siberian nation, 441
Rutland, 36, 79, 84-86, 196, 200, 202
Rutner, Jack, 281-282, 309
Rybinsk, 364
rye, 81, 139, 267, 318, 359-361, 364, 370-372, 390, 511
Ryndziunskii, P.G., 427, 508-509, 514
Rzhev, 370-371, 380-382

sabotage, 207
sainfoin, 34, 81
Saint-Jacob, Pierre de, 155
Saint-Phalle, M. le Marquis de, 136
Salcey, 115
Saloutos, Theodore, 308, 312
Sándor, P., 248
Sandwich, 41
Saratov guberniia, 392, 479
Saville, J., 65, 215
savings, 133
Saxonhouse, Gary, 24, 311
Scarborough, Lord, 56
scattered holdings, 27

Schaeffer, Donald F., 20
Schissler, Hanna, 20, 21
Schlotterbeck, John T., 274
Schmitz, Mark D., 20
Schwartz, A.J., 213, 216
Scotland, 196
　the Highlands, 196-197, 200-202
Scott, James C., 386, 410
Seaman, Ezra, 287, 310
seasonal work, 383
Second Empire, 162
Secret Senate Expedition (1774-1793), 415
Sedrup, 62
seigniorial estates, 3
　seigneural rights, 511
Seine-et-Oise, 148
self-sufficiency, 9, 194, 255, 257, 259, 298
Selunskaia, N.B., 366, 454, 504
Semenova, 408
Semevskii, V.I., 393, 408, 410, 412, 427, 508
serfdom, 6, 18, 349, 397, 413, 415-416, 421-422, 430, 443, 449, 451, 475, 478, 508-509
　abolition of, 421, 426, 442, 509
　distribution of power among serfs, 404
　ex-serfs, 483
　and industrializaiton, 508
　influence on industry, 414
　origins of, 508
　permission of serfs to leave village, 364, 374, 376
　proprietary serfs, 370
　reforms of, 421
　rights of serfs, 6, 398
　serfs, 5, 280, 354-355, 358, 362, 369-371, 390, 399, 402-403, 509, 511-512
　serfs due, 356, 365
　serf estates, 389, 433, 508

serf villages, 510
serfowners, 436
　in Siberia, 442
　value of serfs, 433
service charges, 172
service workers, 197, 262
Severn, 35
sex, 294-295
Shaffer, John W., 123, 135, 136
Shanin, Teodor, 112, 120, 386, 409, 478, 503, 508
share contracts, 146
sharecropping, 10, 14, 125-132, 145, 166, 331, 448, 509
Shcherbina, A.F., 466
sheep, 36, 320, 325, 450
　Dishley, 34
　New Leicester, 34
　husbandry, 75
Sheksna, 362
Shenley Brook, 59
Shepukova, N.M., 367
Sheremetev family, 385
Shestakova, A.V., 512
Shiskov, A.N., 409
Shlomowitz, Ralph, 23
Shropshire, 36, 57
Shternberg, N., 409
Siberia, 350, 416, 441-442, 445-446, 448, 450-453, 511, 513
Siberian highway, 443
Simbirsk guberniia, 393, 468-470
Simcoe (Canada), 336
Sivkov, K.V., 366
Skazkin, S.M., 386
skills, 382, 385, 395
　(*See* training)
slash/burn agriculture, 364, 397
slavery, 2, 4, 18, 261, 280, 300, 304, 423
　slave owners, 261, 265-266, 270-271
　slave plantations, 3, 7
　slave trade, 12

Slicher van Bath, B.H., 367
Slovakia, 225, 236
smallholders, 104
Smetanin family (Savelii, Fedot, Ivan), 396
Smirnov, A., 407, 408, 409
Smirnov, S.N., 512
Smith, J. Harvey, 186
Smolensk, 355, 479
smuggling, 35
Snell, K.D.M., 65
Snow, R., 442
social status, 436
 mobility, 113
social stratification, 375, 397-398, 402, 404, 414-415, 425, 444-445, 478
 Europe vs. Russia and Siberia, 443
socialist revolution, 455
socioeconomic differentiation, 389, 396-398, 401-404
 layers, 478
soil, 287
 alluvial, 362
 fertility, 73, 128, 133
 heavy, 8, 75
 light, 8
 heavy vs. light, 149
 Oxford clay, 70
 quality, 52
 variation, 361
Sokolov, Ivan, 415
Solov'eva, A.M., 514
Soltow, Lee, 274
Somerset, 59
sosloviia, 483
 soslovie, 483
South (U.S.), 308
South Carolina, 272
South Wales, 212
Spain, 164
specialization, 14, 16, 383

speculation, 281
sport, 44
squatter's rights, 448
St. Christol, 165
St. John Priest, 72, 76, 88
St. Lawrence River, 334, 336, 337
St. Petersburg, 357, 374, 378-380, 382-383, 385, 416, 430
 migration, 381
St.-Jacob, Pierre de, 20
Staffordshire, 36-37, 57
Stakanovo, 416
Stanwick, 105
Starista, 382
Starobel'skii District, 470-471
Staroverovka, 487, 494
steam-power, 14
Steckel, Richard, 23, 310
Steppe, 355
Stevenson, Ian, 185
stock "laws," 259
Stockdale, David, 312
Stolypin reforms, 481, 502
stradnaia pora, 389, 394
Studendkii, G., 475
subsistence, 127, 138, 371
 ethic, 404
subsistence farms, 13, 199
Sudbury, 41
Suffolk, 35, 36-37, 40, 41, 75
sugar, 3
Suma, 416
Sumtsov, N.F., 409, 410
Sundstrom, William A., 273
support workers, 197-198
Surrey, 208
Sutch, Richard, 22, 277, 331, 339, 344, 345
Sutton Bassett, 97, 104
Svavitskaia, Z.M., 479, 504
Svavitskii, N.A., 479, 503, 504
swede, 34, 38
Swierenga, Robert P., 275

Index   539

Swing Riots (1830), 204-205, 208
Szuhay, Miklos, 248

Taeuber, C., 310
Taeuber, I., 310
Tambov guberniia, 376, 391, 393, 423
Tarleton, John, 55
Tatars, 415
  slavery, 423
Tate, W.E., 66, 72, 76, 91, 115
taxes, 27, 56, 133, 220-222, 374, 382, 395, 398, 446-449
  base, 403
  financial, 58
  forms of taxation, 260
  income, 191
  land, 126
  nonpayment of, 443
  payments, 139
  property, 39
  rates, 106, 449
  and social repercussions, 58
  soul, 424
  systems of taxation, 444
  Yasak, 449
Taylor, Arthur J., 247
tenancy, 64, 328-329, 332, 334, 337
  and farm size, 338-339, 343
  rate, 334-336
  share, 339
tenants, 35, 56-57, 83, 101, 107, 112, 127, 133, 195, 260-261, 264-267, 404
  defined, 95
  foreign-born, 341-343
  income of, 82, 134-135
  Land Tax returns, 94, 96
  obligations of, 45
  owner-occupier, 95, 101
  resistance, 130
  reasons for becoming, 332
  rights of, 259-260
  as substitute for wage labor, 332

Tennessee, 272, 285
tenure, 46, 129, 131, 263-265, 269-270, 331, 469, 472
  agricultural ladder, 272, 337
  insecurity of, 340
  and race, 340
  shortcomings of, 34
terrain, 287
terres volantes, 141, 143
theft, 421, 425
Third Department of His Imperial Majesty's Privy Chancellery, 412, 421
Third Republic, 178
Thirsk, J., 88
Thomas, J.J., 312
Thompson, E.P., 58, 65, 114, 124
Thompson, F.M.L., 216, 219, 248
Thompson, Flora, 206, 216
Thompson, W., 310
threshing machine, 32
Thuillier, Guy, 135, 157
tiaglo, 390-391, 394, 398-400, 403
Tikhonov, Yu. A., 427
timber, 314
Time of Troubles, 422
Tisza, 225, 227-228, 231, 233-234, 237-239, 241-242, 244-245
Tisza-Marcos Angle, 225, 228, 235, 237, 239, 242, 244, 246
Tithe Commutation Act of 1836, 77, 85
tithes, 39, 45-46, 56
  appeasement of, 62
  commutation, 107
  compensation, 98
  (*See also* Tithe Commutation Act of 1836)
Tiumen', 415
tobacco, 3
Tobolsk, 443, 447
Tofts, 42
Tomsk, 443-445, 447
Topchii, A.T., 453
Toronto, 334

Torzhok, 382
tourism, 197
Toutain, 159
trade, 188, 262, 382, 385
  centers, 283
  cycle, 211-213
  reciprocal, 260
  retail, 259
  traders, 362
  (*See also* imports, exports)
trade/craft, 12, 261, 370, 381
  skilled, 263
tradesmen, 90
  distributive, 195
training, 32, 43, 259
Transdanubia, 236-237, 245
transportation, 12, 14, 34, 35, 126, 262, 300, 304, 357, 371, 381, 385, 390, 399
  cost of, 137, 314, 339, 512
  improvements, 13, 15
  network, 260
  railroads, 128, 301
  sleighing, 314
  trans-Atlantic, 314
  wagon, 301
  water, 301
  workers, 197
  (*See also* railroads)
Transylvania, 225, 229-231, 235, 237, 239, 242, 244-245
travel, 142, 374
Treadgold, D.W., 442, 453
Tribe, K., 65
Troitskii, 408, 410
trousseau, 392
  (*See also* pridanoe)
Trudy kommissi po preobrazovaniiu vbolostnykh sudov, 408
Tsar Paul, 418-419
Tsarism, 413, 436
  tsarist economy, 508
  Tsarist Russia, 248

TsGADA, 394, 399, 400, 407, 409
Tsintsius, V., 408
Tsyzyrev, I.F., 504
Tucker, G.S.L., 310
Tuila, 423
Tuitriumov, I., 407, 408, 409
Tula Province, 472-473
Tull, 46
  seed drill, 32
Turbai, 416
Turchaninov, N.A., 453
Turner, Michael E., 8, 28, 46, 65, 66, 67, 72-73, 76, 87, 89-90, 92-93, 115, 116, 120
turnips, 34, 38, 51-53, 71, 75-78, 85, 191
Turton, B.J., 66, 115
Tver', 349, 369, 371, 374, 382, 416
  Provincial Committee on the Betterment of the Condition of the Peasantry, 386, 387
Twywell, 111
Tyron, Rolla M., 273, 274

U.S. Census Office, 276
U.S. Congress, 311
U.S. Patent Office, 276, 311
udobnaia zemlia
  (*See* land [arable])
uezdy, 391
Ufa, 435
Ukraine, 350, 355, 415-416, 423, 483, 511
  Sub-Carpathian, 236
Ulianov, V.I. [pseud. V.I. Lenin], 204, 413, 422, 428, 448, 452, 453, 454, 475, 479, 484, 504, 507, 509
unemployment, 213, 215
  technological, 214-215
Union Chargeability Act (1864), 206
Union Générale, 164

Ural Mountains, 355, 414-416, 422, 443
urbanization, 187, 279, 414, 510-513
  and labor, 204
  and markets, 195, 306
  and tenancy, 337
Uselding, Paul, 21, 311
Usher, Abbot Payson, 248

V.B., 393
V.P., 409
Vale of Aylesbury, 57
Vancouver, C., 75, 87, 88
  General View of the Agriculture in the County of Cambridge, 71-74
  General View of the Agriculture in the County of Essex, 71-72
Varga, J., 248
Vedder, Richard K., 273, 310, 312
Velikie Buchki Canton, 494
Vermont, 286, 295-296, 300, 302
Veselovskii, B.B., 504
Viatka, 416
Viatka guberniia, 393
Victoria (Canada), 336
Vil'son, I., 367
Vinogradov, N., 408, 409
Vinovskis, Maris, 23, 273, 310
Virginia, 285
victicultural slump, 174-175
Vladimir guberniia, 393, 479, 511
Volga River, 353, 355, 362, 364, 370, 382, 416, 421, 423
  merchants, 357
Vologda, 415, 419
volostnye pravleniia, 480
volostnye sudy, 391
  (*See also* courts [townships])
von-Thunen ring mechanism, 13
Voronezh, 423, 479
Voronezh guberniia, 393, 466-468, 470
vote, 45

Wadenhoe, 104
wages, 38, 40, 138, 205, 259, 283, 302, 376, 378, 381, 383, 385, 445
  agricultural, 204, 337
Wages Fund, 209
Wales, 35, 36
Wallace, Sir Donald Mackenzie, 403, 409
Walton, J.R., 66, 115, 118
Warburton, Sir Peter, 45
Ward, W.R., 188
Warriner, D., 23
Warwick, 84
Warwickshire, 62, 63, 89-90, 106
water, 259
  meadows, 32
Watkins, Susan Cotts, 23
Weald, 97
wealth, 256-259, 263, 265, 270, 294, 296-298, 401-402, 404, 466, 510
  accumulation, 260-261, 268-270, 288, 290
  disputes over, 405
  egalitarian distribution of, 404
  equalizing, 394
  intergenerational transfers, 270
  per capita, 399
  private, 261
  redistribution of, 391, 396, 403-404
Weber, Eugene, 154
Weiman, David F., 11, 20, 21, 253, 273, 275, 276
Weir, David, 23
Western (U.S.), 306, 308
Westmorland, 38, 196, 200, 202
Weston by Welland, 97, 104
Weymouth, 197
Wharton, C.R., Jr., 410
Whatley, Warren C., 22
wheat, 53-54, 71-72, 74-76, 77, 81, 267, 306, 314, 318, 323-324, 326, 370, 372, 390, 511

acreage, 302
  market for, 142, 328
  yields, 32, 53, 75, 80
Whellan, William, 116
Whelpton, 310
Whichello, Amy, 119
White, E.P., 45, 216
Whitfield, 97, 104
Whittlebury, 97, 104
Whittlewood, 97
  Forest, 115
Williamson, Jeffrey G., 60, 66, 247
Williamson, Samuel H., 273
Williamson, Thomas, 216
Wiltshire, 36-37, 59, 208
wine, 14
  production, 162
Winter, Donald L., 274, 275, 276, 344
Winter, Sidney G., 19
Wisconsin, 285-286, 292-294, 296, 300, 302, 304, 334
Wolf, Eric, 120
Wollaston, 96, 98, 104, 109
wood, 298
wool, 189, 197, 319, 325
Worcester County (MD), 297
Worcestershire, 195
Worchestershire, East, 52
Wordie, J.R., 47, 57, 65

work force, 280
worker-farmers, 10
World War I, 124, 192, 195, 205, 450
World War II, 211, 297
Wray, Trevory, 67
Wright, Carroll D., 309
Wright, Gavin, 19, 24, 272, 273, 274, 311, 345

Yasuba, Y., 310
Yelling, J.A., 65, 87
Yenisei, 443, 445
York County (Canada), 331, 333, 336-338, 340, 342-343
Yorkshire, 36, 91
  East, 52, 63
Young, Arthur, 39-41, 43-46, 47, 57, 65, 87, 119, 126-127, 135
Yugoslavia, 225

Zaionchkovskii, P.A., 409, 430, 432, 437, 438
Zaloskin, A., 408
Zaprometov, I.P., 421
Zelenin, D.K., 393, 408
zemstvo, 412
Zlatoustov, 415
Zubtsov, 382
Zvonkov, 408, 410
Zyrianov, P.N., 503